The Open
University

A206
The
Enlightenment

Studies, II

*Edited by Michael Bartholomew, Denise Hall
and Antony Lentin*

First published in 1992 by

The Open University
Walton Hall
Milton Keynes
United Kingdom
MK7 6AA

ISBN 0 7492 1111 3

Edited, designed and typeset by The Open University.

This book forms part of an Open University course A206 *The Enlightenment.*

Printed and bound in Great Britain by The Bath Press, Bath
1.7
16500C/A206studiesIIi1.7

Contents

Part D
Religion and Humanity

Contents

Study Timetable

Hume's Dialogues Concerning Natural Religion *(Study Weeks 18–19)*

Studies/Texts	Radio	TV	AC	Set books
Studies, II	–	TV10	–	–
Texts, II	–	–	–	–

Lessing and a religion for humanity: Nathan the Wise *(Study Weeks 20–21)*

Studies/Texts	Radio	TV	AC	Set books
Studies, II	–	TV11	AC1623 (yellow)	*Nathan the Wise*
–	–	–	AC1624 (yellow)	–
–	–	–	AC1625 (yellow)	–

Mozart's The Magic Flute *(Study Weeks 22-23)*

Studies/Texts	Radio	TV	AC	Set books
Studies, II	–	TV12	AC1629 (grey)	–
Texts, II	–	–	AC1630 (grey)	–
–	–	–	AC1631 (grey)	–

Introduction

Prepared for the Course Team by Robert Wilkinson

Contents

Introduction

In the countries directly affected by the European Enlightenment, religious belief and practice were the subject of constant debate. This is because religion was an important fact of everyday life at the time: to use Keats's admirable phrase, it was 'felt on the pulse'. This means more than that, with few exceptions, almost every inhabitant of every country would have professed to be a Christian, either Catholic (the majority in France, and far more so in Italy, Spain and Portugal and Ireland) or some type of Protestant (England, Wales, Scotland and the Netherlands) or Russian Orthodox. (Of the German states, you will recall, some were Protestant, some Catholic.) More important than such professions of faith is the fact that religious belief and debate about it were matters of urgent concern to those at the forefront of intellectual life, to which they devoted time, energy, and a good deal of print, sometimes at some risk to themselves. We have already seen, for example, how matters of religious belief were of concern to the Encyclopedists in general and to Voltaire in particular, and how they affect Gibbon's attitude to Christianity. In this Part of the course are gathered three further works in which religious concerns are, in different ways in each case, of great importance. (This is not to say that the religious aspect of these works exhausts their significance: far from it. It is to say only that, as for so many of the works produced in this period, they are not fully intelligible unless their religious dimension is understood.)

Much of the debate about religious matters in our period centres around movements which, in one way or another, constitute a departure from the religious orthodoxy of the countries in which they occur, Catholic or Protestant as the case may be; and it is worthwhile spelling out those major features of orthodox Christian belief which were at the centre of the main controversies. The God of orthodox Christianity (Catholic or Protestant) is transcendent and personal: he exists apart from his creation, and is in some sense held to be like a person or to have a personality, that is he is not just an impersonal first cause or prime mover, needed to get the universe going. He is benevolent and just, and intends only the well-being of his creatures. Moreover, God has intervened in human history, since the creation, in a number of ways. Thus, he is held to have communicated directly with Jewish prophets (e.g. Moses); to have informed them directly of his law (the Ten Commandments) and to have inspired the prophets to make predictions which have been demonstrably fulfilled by subsequent events. Again, he is held to have sent his son, Jesus Christ, into this world to save mankind. Both Jesus and some of his immediate followers, the Apostles, are held to have performed miracles at the start of the Christian epoch. All this is known because it is related in the Bible, which was held to be the revealed Word of God, that is God directly inspired the writers of the scriptures, and from this it follows that the scriptures are unalloyed truth. Most truths thus revealed were held to be undiscoverable by the use of human reason unaided, though they might be corroborated by it.

The intellectually most significant challenge to orthodoxy in the Enlightenment, both in Great Britain and continental Europe, came from those thinkers now collectively referred to as deists. It was the members of this group who focused attention on the idea of natural (as opposed to revealed) religion, and who in many ways set the agenda for religious debate. To appreciate the nature and appeal of deism, it is necessary to say something of the background from which it arose.

1 Background to deism

One of the chief roots of deism lies in a reaction to the long, bitter and sometimes bloody history of religious schism, which had characterized Europe since the Reformation. Not only had Catholics and Protestants persecuted one another regularly in the name of God, but disagreed amongst themselves about which set of dogmas were God's truth. As Montesquieu wrote a little later: ... 'no kingdom has ever had as many civil wars as the kingdom of Christ' (Montesquieu, 1721, p.64). Factionalism was especially rife in the case of Protestantism, the history of which must have appeared, by the end of the seventeenth century, to be a history almost solely of sectarian conflict: Lutherans, Calvinists, Zwinglians, Anglicans and more besides, all claimed to be the sole custodians of the true Christian revelation. These endless quarrels provided ready material for satire by the deists, who rarely missed the chance to emphasize them. For example, Anthony Collins (1676–1729), one of the leading English deists, here commenting on a very basic area of theological disagreement, concerning the attributes of God:

> The whole difference between the Arminians and Calvinists is founded on different Notions of the Attributes of God; and this Dispute is kept up in most Christian Churches on the face of the earth. It is carry'd on in the Romish Church under the names of Jansenists and Jesuits, Thomists and Molinists etc. It has been for near a Century last past debated among the Divines of the Church ... Indeed the Differences among the Priests in every Church about the attributes of God, are as numerous as the Priests who treat the Divine Attributes; not one agreeing with another in his Notions of them all. (Collins, 1713, pp.87–8)

The Christian faith was supposed to bring peace (*pax fidei*) to its adherents; instead it appeared to bring dogmatic disagreement linked not infrequently with aggressive zeal which the people of this period called 'enthusiasm'. If a way could be found, the deists argued, to discern a common core of religious belief which relied on no special revelation and so could be agreed on by all by the use of reason alone, this had to be an advance on what they saw around them and in their recent past. By the time deism became an important feature of intellectual life in Great Britain (roughly 1695–1740), it appeared that such a set of universally acceptable beliefs could be worked out. The deists took their lead from what might seem to a modern reader an unexpected quarter, namely physical science, and especially its greatest exemplification, Newtonian mechanics.

2   *The impact of Newtonian science*

It is difficult to overestimate the impact of Newton's science, both with
regard to its method and its findings, on the thought of the Enlightenment. His laws of motion and associated theory of gravitation extended
regularity and predictability (in principle, at any rate) to the entire universe: where before there had been baffling mystery there was now an
intelligible order. The universe was organized according to laws, and
these laws had been discovered by human reason, following the empirical
method of observation and experiment. Pope's well-known couplet,
intended as an epitaph for Newton, sums up, with very little hyperbole,
the attitude of the time to the great scientist:

> Nature, and Nature's Laws lay hid in Night:
> God said, *Let Newton* be! and All was *Light*.

It is hard now to imagine the impact these discoveries had on those alive
at the time: the revolutionary change in outlook that followed Newton's
work is as profound as any in the history of Western thought. The reach
of science was now effectively co-extensive with the universe. He had
found the key to the universal mechanism itself, a key unavailable to
every previous generation.

Note that Pope wrote '*God* said, Let Newton be!': he, like nearly all
his contemporaries, saw no incompatibility in accepting both Newton's
discoveries and a belief in God. Indeed, Newtonian mechanics seemed to
many to furnish the strongest of reasons for belief in God, and of this
view Newton himself was a leading advocate. The universe is everywhere
orderly; and its components are so well suited to certain purposes that
neither blind chance nor necessity alone can account for them. Where
there is order and design, there must be an intelligent creator who is the
source of this order and purposiveness. This is an outline of what is
termed the 'argument from design'. It was the most important argument
for God's existence during the Enlightenment, popular with both the
orthodox and deists alike, and it was so because of Newton's discoveries.
He himself had recourse to it repeatedly: the following version is from
the series of questions Newton added to the second edition of the *Opticks*
(1717); question 28:

> Whence is it that nature does nothing in vain, and whence arises all
> the order and beauty which we see in the world? To what end are
> comets, and whence is it that planets move all one and the same way
> in orbs very eccentric, and what hinders the fixed stars from falling
> upon one another? How came the bodies of animals to be contrived
> with so much art, and for what ends were their several parts? Was
> the eye contrived without skill in optics and the ear without knowl-
> edge of sounds? How do the motions of the body follow from the
> will, and whence is the instinct in animals? ... And these things
> being rightly dispatched, does it not appear from phenomena that
> there is a Being, incorporeal, living, intelligent, omnipresent ... ?
> (Newton, 1717, pp.155–6)

It is this argument which is the central subject of Hume's *Dialogues Concerning Natural Religion*, where it is given an analysis as shrewd and penetrating as any it has ever received.

3 Deism or 'natural religion'

I said above that the deists in our period sought religious beliefs which could be agreed on by everyone in virtue of being founded on the use of reason alone, it being presupposed that human nature is constant everywhere and at all times, and therefore that human reason is equally invariant. It seemed to these thinkers that the Newtonian world-picture furnished an indisputable fixed point on which their arguments could be based. (Before going on, however, it must be stressed that Newton himself would not have accepted any of what follows below: despite his own difficulty in accepting the doctrine of the Trinity, he was in nearly every respect, as he liked to proclaim himself, an orthodox Anglican.)

As has been indicated, the argument from design was accepted by the orthodox and deists alike; but beyond that acceptance their agreement ceased. For the orthodox, this argument merely confirmed by rational means what revelation had told them already, whereas for the deists, using reason alone, the consequences appeared very different. Newton had proved that the universe is governed by immutable laws, and these laws must have been furnished by a law-giver; but, if one takes seriously the notion that these laws *are* immutable (and it is easy to argue that mutable laws could not be framed by an omnipotent God) then it follows that, once the universe has been created, its creator need never and will never intervene in its running again. This is a key belief in deism, and its consequences are far-reaching. It entails firstly that all orthodox beliefs which presuppose that God has intervened in the universe since its creation are false: it cannot be true that God communicated with prophets, or directly inspired the writers of the Bible, or sent his Son Jesus Christ into the World. Secondly, it entails that there can never have been miracles, since miracles necessitate the suspension of laws of nature. Thirdly, it entails that all churches and priesthoods basing their authority on divinely inspired scripture, prophecies or miracles are either mistaken or practising an imposture. Fourthly, it follows that if we wish to discern God's will and purpose, which is the same as to establish his true religion, then we must seek it in the fabric of nature. There have been no revelations, and the only reliable sacred book is the book of nature. This book we must seek to construe, both in the universe at large and as it is manifested in our own human nature. The true religion is, as the deists term it, the religion of nature or natural religion; and the evidences of this religion, being part of the order of nature, are as old as the creation itself. The point of view is summed up in the last major work of English deism, *Christianity as Old as the Creation* (1730), written by Matthew Tindal (1657–1733):

> By *Natural Religion*, I understand the Belief of the Existence of a God, and the Sense and Practice of those Duties which result from the Knowledge we, by our Reason, have of him and his Perfections; and of ourselves, and our own Imperfections; and of the relation we stand in to him and our Fellow-Creatures; so that the *Religion of Nature* takes in everything that is founded on the Reason and Nature of things ... If God is unchangeable, our Duty to him must be so too ... And consequently our duty both to God and Man must, from the Beginning of the World to the End, remain unalterable; be always alike plain and perspicuous ... which demonstrates that

no Person, if he comes from God, can teach us any other Religion,
or give us any Precepts, but what are founded on those Relations.
(Tindal, 1730, pp.102–3, 107)

The essence of deism, then, is belief in a divine creator, beneficent and
just no doubt, but, by comparison to the God of the orthodox, a remote
being, who has never communicated and will never communicate directly
with his creatures. In advocating this, and denying miracles, prophecies
and the divinity of Christ, and so striking at the foundations of the
Church, the English deists set the main agenda for religious debate in
our period. In England, that debate had been exhausted by the mid-century; in Europe, to which deism spread from England after a delay of one
generation or so, the debate continued for several decades more.

     This was due not only to the later start (so to speak) of Continental
deism, but also to the fact that European deists included in their number
some figures of first-rate importance, whereas none of the formulators of
English deism could lay claim to such stature. Frederick, Voltaire, Rousseau, Lessing (in his way) and many others accepted some form of deism.
Moreover, they gave special weight to one of its important consequences,
namely a belief in religious toleration. If it is the case that all revealed
religions are equally false, or equally true, then adherence to any one
cannot rationally be made the ground for persecution of adherents of all
the rest. This point of view underlies and inspires Lessing's play *Nathan
the Wise*, one of the most eloquent and sincere pleas for religious toleration ever written.

4   *The rise of freemasonry*

Deism is one form of departure from religious orthodoxy, and one which
coheres well with descriptions of the Enlightenment as the 'age of reason'; but there were other departures, equally important, of a very different kind. Recent scholarship has rightly stressed that Enlightenment
Europe supported a rich selection of secret societies, many of a religious
or quasi-religious character, some becoming important enough to be
regarded as a threat by various states and churches. We have space here
to look briefly only at the most important of these societies, the Freemasons.

     Like deism, the masonic movement in the Enlightenment began in
England, with the founding of the Grand Lodge in London in June 1717.
The movement, which spread throughout Great Britain, was deeply
influenced by the deism of the time and, with the adoption of the *Book of
Constitutions* of 1723, dropped the requirement that its members should
be Christians. English-style deistic lodges continued to flourish throughout the eighteenth century, spreading rapidly from Great Britain to continental Europe. They employed the usual three degrees of initiation
(Entered Apprentice, Fellow Craft and Master Mason). Members were
pledged to seek to bring about the brotherhood of humankind and simultaneously to enhance their own capacity for moral insight by study of
the symbolic rituals of the society.

     Again like deism, freemasonry spread to Europe where, from the
1730s onwards, it split into many different branches: by the 1780s, there
were at least seventeen different types of masonic rite, each with its own
associated lodges, throughout Europe (including Russia). The differences

between the various rites were manifold, but the most important distinction was that between the deistic English-style lodges and those which employed what are termed the higher degrees of masonry.

Credit for the introduction of the notion of higher degrees into masonry is usually given to a Scotsman associated with the Jacobite cause and exiled in France, Andrew Michael Ramsay (1686–1743). In the late 1730s, Ramsay introduced degrees of initiation beyond that of the Master in the English lodges; and those who penetrated to the levels of insight involved were deemed to have achieved 'spiritual knighthood'. Ramsay sought to legitimate this change by attempting to extend the history of masonry backward to the Middle Ages, linking it with the notions of chivalry and knighthood. (He chose to link masonry with the Knights of St John.) Higher degree masonry found a ready home in the German-speaking states, in which the Knights Templar or Teutonic Knights took over as favoured medieval forebears of the movement. The higher degree lodges became a focus for those who could find neither peace nor a sense of communion within the rigid dogmatism of the various Protestant sects (chiefly Lutheran) or who were of a mystical disposition and were again unwelcome in such a church.

Many of the leading figures of the period were masons – Frederick II, Lessing, Goethe, Haydn, Gibbon, Voltaire and Burns, for example – and in late 1784 Mozart was initiated into one of the eight lodges in Vienna. By no means all these figures were equally impressed by freemasonry after initiation – Lessing soon became disenchanted – but masonic teachings impressed Mozart deeply. The final work in this part of the course, *The Magic Flute*, is throughout informed by masonic symbolism and feeling. The masonic elements, however, are only the starting point for this extraordinary opera. A fairy-tale plot is turned into a work which is not only beautiful but profound. How can this be done? Add the music of Mozart.

5 *References*

Collins, A. (1713) *A Discourse of Free-thinking* in Gay (1968).

Gay, P. (ed.) (1968) *Deism: An Anthology*, Van Nostrand, New York.

Montesquieu (1721) No. 29 in J. Roger (ed.) (1964) *Lettres Persanes*, Paris.

Newton, I. (1717) *Opticks* in H.S. Thayer (ed.) (1953) *Newton's Philosophy of Nature*, Hafner Press, New York.

Tindal, M. (1730) *Christianity as Old as the Creation* in Gay (1968).

Hume's Dialogues Concerning Natural Religion

Prepared for the Course Team by Rosalind Hursthouse

Contents

Hume's Dialogues Concerning Natural Religion *(Study weeks 18–19)*

Studies/Texts	Radio	TV	AC	Set books
Studies, II	–	TV10	–	–
Texts, II	–	–	–	–

For your work on Hume's *Dialogues*, you will need this volume of *Studies* and *Texts*, II. Unlike any of the previous studies, this one consists mostly of questions (and answers); after you have read the introductory sections you will need a large workbook in which to write down your own answers. TV10, 'Dialogue in the Dark (A Conversation with David Hume)', though intended to give you a sense of eighteenth-century philosophical conversation, also functions as an exercise on the importance of texts and calls for some preliminary reading, specified in the broadcast notes. You will also find helpful the general background in Angus Calder's 'historical survey of Scotland in the eighteenth-century' at the end of *Studies*, I, which touches upon Hume's position in the Scottish Enlightenment.

Hume's Dialogues Concerning Natural Religion

1 Introduction

1.1 Relevant biographical background

David Hume was born in Edinburgh in 1711, went to Edinburgh University just before he was twelve (the usual age in Scotland at the time) for three or four years, and only a few years later ('before I was one and twenty', he says in a letter) had planned his first major philosophical work – the three-volume *Treatise of Human Nature*. This was largely written during 1734–7, when Hume 'retreated' to peaceful surroundings in France; the first two books were published in 1739, when Hume was 28; the third a year later. Between 1741 and 1742 he published *Essays, Moral and Political*, and then his recastings of the first and third books of the *Treatise*, as what came to be called the *Inquiry Concerning Human Understanding* (1748) and *Inquiry Concerning the Principles of Morals* (1751) respectively. A flood of further publications followed, including *Political Discourses* (1752), and in 1757 *Four Dissertations* (including *Of the Standard of Taste*, and *The Natural History of Religion*), as well as *A History of England* (1754–62). *Dialogues Concerning Natural Religion* was first published in 1779, three years after Hume's death in 1776, but it is clear from letters that he was well on with its composition in 1751, and that it was finished, and circulating in manuscript, by 1763.

The *Treatise* was largely ignored when it first appeared, but the two *Inquiries* fared much better. According to Mossner, Hume's definitive biographer, Hume's fame 'burst out spontaneously on both sides of the Channel in 1752, ... the fires were fed by the later publications, 1754–62, and by the increasing tempo of the several controversies' (Mossner, 1954, p.225). From 1752 onwards, the increasing flow of publications responding to Hume's arguments shows how seriously they were being taken, and how widely and thoroughly read. By 1758, the young Edward Gibbon was telling his father 'I am ... to meet ... the great David Hume'; by 1762 the young Boswell confidently describes Hume as 'the greatest Writer in Britain', and when Hume returned to France in 1763, he was greeted with almost universal adulation. The *philosophes*, in particular, welcomed him with open arms and he was, for the two years that he was in Paris, a highly esteemed member of their circle. (He did not meet Voltaire, who had long since retired to the Swiss frontier, but they exchanged letters of mutual admiration; Voltaire is reported to have been in the habit of referring to Hume as 'my St David'.)

What had Hume become so famous for? In part for his style of writing, whose wit, elegance, 'spirit', and clarity were constantly remarked upon, even by his most hostile critics. In part for the (not entirely separable) style of his thought – its clarity and precision, its ingenuity and subtlety, the power of his arguments – which was also mentioned again and again. But two further features of his thought were commonly identified, the two which brought him notoriety rather than fame in some circles. These were his scepticism and (according to many of his readers) his atheism.[1] The first book of the *Treatise* (*Of the Understanding*), having cast much sceptical doubt on our (putative) knowledge of the world around us, of the past, the future, and of cause and effect, had originally contained at least one further chapter on religion. This was *Of Miracles*. Hume was persuaded not to publish it as part of the *Treatise,* but insisted (against the advice of several friends) on including it, as Section X, in the *Inquiry* of 1748, where it was followed by an essay which came to be called *Of a Particular Providence and a Future State.*[2] In *Of Miracles* he may be taken as arguing that there cannot be any justification for a belief in miracles; in *Of a Particular Providence* he may be taken as attacking the argument from design, that is the view that the order in the universe provides good evidence for the existence of God, its Designer and Architect.[3]

These sections, particularly *Of Miracles,* did cause deep offence in theological circles when they appeared and were the source of two of the 'several controversies' which Mossner mentions. They were also, of course, the sections that particularly delighted the atheists amongst the *philosophes.* Whether Hume was himself an atheist (rather than a deist) is disputable – it is indeed one of the things you must decide for yourself when you have read the *Dialogues* – but it is beyond dispute that the first *Inquiry* convinced many people he was one. This made him enemies, and it seems that Hume was readily persuaded that it would be far too dangerous for him to attempt to publish the *Dialogues* – a greatly extended attack on the argument from design – during his lifetime. Instead, he devoted much of the little energy remaining to him on his death bed (he died of a 'Disorder of the Bowels', perhaps cancer, perhaps, according to Mossner, 'chronic ulcerative colitis') to trying to ensure that the work would be published posthumously.

Fortunately it was, and stands to this day among the classics, not only of the Enlightenment, but of any philosophy of religion. No modern text on the subject is complete without at least a mention of it, and no modern text has replaced it as *the* textbook in any philosophy of religion course. A variety of further texts might indeed be set; but Hume's *Dialogues* is always there. Its popularity testifies not only to the originality and thoroughness of Hume's arguments, but also to that clarity of style and thought which his contemporaries praised. Across the gap of over two

---

[1]   Samuel Johnson, notably, held Hume 'in abhorrence'. When Boswell, describing Hume's courage on his death bed, said that Hume seemed to be 'quite easy at the thought of Annihilation', Johnson had an explanation. 'He lied,' Johnson said. 'He had a vanity in being thought easy. It is more probable that he lied than that so very improbable a thing should be as a Man not afraid of death; of going into an unknown state and not being uneasy in leaving all that he knew. And,' Johnson continued, with little regard for logic, 'you are to consider that upon his own principle of Annihilation he had not motive to lie' (Boswell, quoted in Mossner, p.606).

[2]   It is not known whether this, which formed Section XI of the *Inquiry,* was written with the original *Of Miracles* or (more probably) later.

[3]   I say 'he may be taken as' since, inevitably, there is much scholarly controversy about the subtle details of Hume's argument in these two essays. But, notwithstanding such controversy, these are the obvious ways to take Hume's arguments, and certainly the ways in which they were taken by most of his outraged contemporaries.

hundred years, Hume speaks to us with a directness that students just beginning philosophy find readily comprehensible. The odd detail may escape one, some bits may be obscure, but much of the argument leaps off the page, and many of its readers have been amazed to discover how exhilarating philosophy can be.

1.2 Approaching the text

Let us begin our consideration of this classic by noting its title – *Dialogues Concerning Natural Religion*. As all of Hume's contemporary readers would have realized, the word 'natural' contrasts, in this context, with 'revealed'. As the Part D Introduction has explained (pp.4–7 above), the distinction between *natural* and *revealed* religion had an especial significance for the deists, who largely rejected knowledge by revelation and concentrated on 'natural' knowledge of God.

The simplest way to grasp the distinction is to think of what, if anything, anyone could know about God if they had never come across, or heard anything about, the Bible. Clearly, they could not know (unless they were alive when Christ or the disciples were, and heard about it) that there was a God who 'so loved the world, that he gave his only begotten Son, that whosoever believeth in him should not perish, but have everlasting life' (John 2: 16). But it seems initially possible that someone who had never come across the Bible, for example, someone who lived before Christ, might nevertheless conclude that there is a God who is the supreme creator, infinitely wise, powerful and benevolent. Indeed, this was just what Aquinas thought of Aristotle, who, despite living in the fourth century BC, produced a number of arguments for the existence of a sort of God which, it seemed to Aquinas, was recognizably the God of Christianity.

One of Aristotle's arguments was an early version of what came to be known as the argument from design. According to Aristotle, all of nature is orderly and purposive, and the existence of such order and purpose presupposes a rational design, and hence, in a sense, a rational designer, or, as Christians might say, God. The argument did not originate with Aristotle; other ancient Greeks had thought of it and it has appeared convincing to many people ever since. A version of it appears in the Koran, it was frequently appealed to by medieval Christian theologians, and it became particularly popular in Europe in the two centuries following the rise of science in the seventeenth century.

Many people nowadays think of the scientific and religious perspectives on the world as being opposed to each other, but, as we have just seen (p.6 above), in our period, the development of science had *increased* conviction in the existence of God, rather than weakened it. Although Newton's discoveries were undoubtedly the pinnacle of seventeenth-century scientific achievement, other important advances were being made. Much that Aristotle had known of zoology and botany, lost to Western Europe during the Dark Ages, was rediscovered by groups of proto-scientists who collected a mass of detailed information which demonstrated order in the animate world; and new, further, confirmation came with the invention of the microscope (about 1590) which revealed the hitherto unsuspected order in the minute creatures invisible to the naked eye. Chemistry as we know it became distinguished from alchemy, and the first principles of chemical change were laid down – principles that

described an order in what had previously seemed magical and unpredictable. Bertrand Russell describes the change in outlook these discoveries wrought as follows:

> The result of the scientific work we have been considering was that
> the outlook of educated men was completely transformed. At the
> beginning of the century, Sir Thomas Browne took part in trials for
> witchcraft; at the end, such a thing would have been impossible. In
> Shakespeare's time, comets were still portents; after the publication
> of Newton's *Principia* in 1687, it was known that he and Halley had
> calculated the orbits of certain comets, and that they were as obedi-
> ent as the planets to the law of gravitation. The reign of law had
> established its hold on men's imaginations, making such things as
> magic and sorcery incredible. In 1700 the mental outlook of edu-
> cated men was completely modern; in 1600, except among a very
> few, it was still largely mediaeval. (Russell, 1961, p.522)

I would qualify what Russell says only to reiterate that nearly all the 'educated men' in question saw their discoveries as overwhelmingly convincing evidence for the existence of God, the infinitely powerful, wise and
benevolent Designer.

To sum up the points in the above paragraphs: (1) The argument
from design is an argument within *natural* religion or theology (as
opposed to *revealed* religion or theology). (2) Such an argument is supposed to lead us to knowledge of the existence and nature of God without any aid from revelation: '... does it not appear from phenomena',
asks Newton (quoted in the Introduction, p.6), 'that there is a Being,
incorporeal, living? ...' (3) Although very ancient, the argument gained
new impetus with the rise of science; far from being inclined towards
atheism or agnosticism, the scientists of the seventeenth and eighteenth
centuries regarded their discoveries as proving, in a way hitherto impossible, the existence of a Designer of the universe.

The argument from design was particularly popular in Protestant
England. Several other arguments for the existence of God existed within
natural theology but they were all associated with the Roman Catholic
saint, Thomas Aquinas. Moreover, they were all arguments '*a priori*', that
is arguments based on premises that were known by pure reason, *prior to*
experience (whence the name). The prevailing British philosophy was
empiricist, claiming that all knowledge was derived from experience, that
is, *a posteriori*. Many thinkers were therefore uneasy about relying on *a priori* arguments as a sound basis for natural religion. The argument from
design is explicitly *a posteriori*, since it is our experience of the order in
the world or universe which provides its basis.

Let us return to our title, and consider what is involved in Hume's
work being written in the form of 'Dialogues'. (You might at this point,
like to look quickly at the first three or four pages of your text; it would
probably make the following more intelligible.) The work basically consists of an extended argument between *Cleanthes*, who supports the argument from design, and *Philo*, who attacks it; there is a third character,
Demea, who is present throughout (or almost) and quite often joins in.
The whole conversation is supposedly recorded by a fourth character,
Pamphilus, who introduces and concludes it, supposedly in a letter to a
fifth person, Hermippus. Hermippus is irrelevant; Pamphilus, as we shall
see, is not quite.

The presentation of an extended philosophical argument in dialogue form was common amongst classical writers (notably Plato and Cicero) and hence amongst seventeenth- and eighteenth-century writers deliberately modelling themselves on their admired ancient predecessors. In this case, the allusion to ancient sources is immediately acknowledged in the choice of Greek names for the characters, and Hume has undoubtedly taken Cicero's dialogues *On the Nature of the Gods*, which also has three speakers, as his model.

A philosophical writer who employs the dialogue form *may* thereby make our task as readers easier; he makes one of his characters his mouthpiece, and the other characters serve as vehicles for objections to his views that either have been made by his opponents, or which he thinks it likely his readers might make – objections which, of course, are always shown to be mistaken. We know which character represents the author, because he is the character who is made out as the winner of the argument. Any reader of the Platonic dialogues quickly identifies 'Socrates', as Plato, as the other characters are reduced to saying 'It seems it must be so Socrates'; in Berkeley's *Three Dialogues Between Hylas and Philonous* (1713), though Hylas, arguing for the materialist philosophy, is less docile than Socrates' usual opponents, it is no less obvious that Philonous is Berkeley. (And in case his readers might suffer from a lingering doubt, Berkeley has chosen the names of his characters advisedly. In ancient Greek, as all Berkeley's readers would have known 'hyle' means 'matter', appropriately enough, while 'philonous' means 'lover of mind'. So we know which character the author approves of.)

But which character, Philo or Cleanthes, in *Dialogues Concerning Natural Religion* represents Hume? Indeed, whether either of them does so fully has been the topic of much scholarly dispute. As noted above, Cleanthes supports the argument from design and Philo attacks it. Given that Hume attacks the argument from design in Section XI of the first *Inquiry* (in the essay *Of a Particular Providence* mentioned above), it may seem obvious that Philo must represent Hume, and Cleanthes Hume's opponents. But the difficulty with this view is, as you will discover, that Philo is not indisputably represented as the winner of the argument. And if he is not presented as the winner, how can he be Hume?

Hume's dialogues do not contain the clear clues given by Plato and Berkeley. Neither Philo nor Cleanthes is reduced to saying to the other 'Yes, it seems it must be so ... Yes ... Yes ... I agree ... I see I was wrong', as Socrates' hapless opponents are. Nor do the names of the characters tell us anything definitive as Berkeley's do.[4] Lacking such simple clues, we are forced to fall back on more complicated ones. And these generate the dispute about whether Philo, or Cleanthes, or indeed neither of them, is

---

[4] 'Philo' was indeed the name of a sceptic with whom Cicero studied, as Hume, a great admirer of Cicero, would have known. And Hume was certainly a sceptic. But Cicero drew a distinction between different sorts of sceptics (as Hume also knew) and it is not perfectly obvious that Hume was the same sort as Cicero's Philo. 'Cleanthes' is the name of a Stoic philosopher (who appears in Cicero); as an early Stoic he would have believed in a god of sorts, namely a pantheistic god manifest in Nature. So his name is appropriate to his views, as Philo's and Hylas's are to theirs. But 'Cleanthes' does not mean anything significant (such as 'credulous' or 'wise'), which would give us a clear clue like Berkeley's choice of 'Philonous'.

represented as the winner of the argument. The reason why the character Pamphilus is not entirely irrelevant is that it is given to him to suggest that Cleanthes is the winner. But the question is whether this should be taken at face value as Hume's statement, or whether Hume is being ironic.

When you come to read the *Dialogues*, this is one of the questions you should bear in mind – not in order to form firm convictions about it, but in order to understand why it has been, and still is, such a disputed question. The *Dialogues* is a highly contrived literary work. It was written at a time when overt attacks on the Christian religion could not find a publisher; it was, moreover, written for an audience accustomed to the sophistications of irony. We should not be surprised if we find the interpretation of it a subtle and delicate matter.

1.3   The structure of the arguments

1.3.1   The argument from design

It is important to understand the logical structure of the version of the argument from design that Hume is considering. What he does early on is bring out the fact that many statements of it, for example Newton's, which we read earlier (p.6 above), contain a couple of unstated premises. A brief, crude statement of the argument would be as follows:

Premise: the universe, and all the things within it, are orderly, as if designed.

Conclusion: so it must have had a designer.

Suppose someone were to ask, 'But why *must* it have had a designer?' The obvious answer brings us close to the first unstated premise of the argument. The obvious answer is 'Think of lots of the things you have come across that are orderly, as if designed – watches and clocks, buildings, formal gardens, books, musical instruments – anything we would call an artefact. They *are* all designed and they all have designers, namely human beings. Well, the things in the universe that we have not designed and made – all the natural things, and indeed the universe itself – they are all like (i.e. analogous to) our artefacts, in their order and design. And since they are so like (analogous to) our artefacts, they must have been caused, or brought about, in a similar (analogous) way, namely by a designer'.

This answer reveals that the argument from design is an *argument by analogy*. One of its unstated premises is the appeal to what we know, by experience, about many of the things in the world which exhibit order and design (artefacts), namely that they are caused by designers (human beings). So a fuller statement of the argument from design is as follows:

Premise 1.   Artefacts are caused by designers (human beings).

Premise 2.   The universe, and all the natural things within it are *like* artefacts.

Conclusion.   So they must be caused by something *like* us – a Designer.

An argument by analogy does not claim to be logically valid; it is a form of reasoning we use to reach *probable* conclusions, not absolutely guaranteed ones. But why, if not logically valid, is it a decent form of reasoning at all? Why is it ever worth using? The answer to this question brings us to the second unstated premise. Argument by analogy is worth using because of the truth of the following principle – 'similar effects have similar causes'.

We rely on this principle constantly in everyday life when we are trying to work out what (probably) caused some effect that we have experience of. For example, in cooking. The stew tastes odd – what might have caused that? Well, last week I made gravy using a rather old stock cube, and it tasted odd in a *similar* way. Similar effects have similar causes. So, I infer, maybe the odd taste of the stew has a *similar* cause – I didn't use a stock cube, but I did use stock; it's probably time I threw it away. Gardeners use it: my roses are all leaf and few flowers – what can be causing that? Other plants similarly affected last year had too much nitrogenous fertilizer; similar effects have similar causes, so maybe that is the problem with the roses. People without much mechanical knowledge (and even people with quite a lot) use it on their cars – what can be causing that strange noise? A similar noise was caused by a loose exhaust pipe, so perhaps this is caused by something similar – a hole in the exhaust? Again, to cite an example used in Part III of the *Dialogues*: the sounds of deep male voices are usually caused, as I can observe, by men speaking; when I hear a sound in the dark which sounds like a man speaking, I infer the presence of a man as its cause. 'Who's there?' I say.

So, laid out fully, the argument from design is as follows:

Premise 1.   Artefacts are caused by designers (human beings).

Premise 2.   The universe, and all the natural things within it are *like* artefacts.

Premise 3.   Like effects have like causes.

Conclusion.   So the universe must be caused by something *like* us – a Designer.

1.3.2   Arguments against the argument from design

It is only when the logical structure of the argument from design is laid out fully that one can understand the corresponding structure of arguments attacking it. Any argument can be attacked in two (and only two) ways.

A We can argue that one or more of the premises is false.

B We can argue that the conclusion is not adequately supported by the premises, even allowing that they are true.

Are the effects in question similar?

Which of the premises might be attacked? Premise 1 is unquestionable – an artefact *is* something made by design. One might attack Premise 3 – perhaps you noticed in the humdrum examples to do with cooking or gardening that it is a rather shaky principle. (Sometimes *very* similar effects have utterly different causes, and sometimes one might be wrong about the immediate cause – perhaps the voice I hear is caused by the radio). But Hume does not do this; he treats Premise 3 as being as unquestionable as Premise 1. That leaves Premise 2 – the premise which claims that the effects in question (artefacts on the one hand, and the universe and all its natural parts on the other) really are similar or 'like'. Clearly, if Premise 2 is false – if artefacts on the one hand, and the world and its natural parts on the other are *not* really similar, then we cannot use the 'like effects have like causes' principle to draw the conclusion.

Or rather, we *can* but our 'conclusion' will be much more akin to a speculation, or mere guesswork, than something supported by evidence. We will have jumped to the conclusion because we already believe it is true (through revelation perhaps), rather than having *reasoned* to it. Another example should help to make this clear. Hume's own example, (from Section XI of the *Inquiry*, not from the *Dialogues*), perhaps inspired by

Robinson Crusoe, is finding a (human-looking) footprint on the sand and inferring that it was made by the foot of a passing human. In this case, the inference is reasonable, because the footprint Crusoe finds is very similar – indeed just like – a human footprint (which it subsequently turns out to be). But suppose Crusoe had found, not a footprint, but some marks that looked only somewhat like human footprints. Being lonely, he might be eager to detect in these marks signs of the presence of a fellow human being. But given that the marks are not very like human footprints, he cannot believe on reasoned grounds that they were caused by a human foot. Perhaps they also look quite like chimpanzee footprints, or like marks caused by the accidents of wind and water. He might, in his eagerness, jump to the conclusion, that they were caused by a fellow human; and of course *he might be right.* But, even if he turned out to be right, he would still have jumped to his conclusion, not reasoned to it.

This example should be constantly borne in mind while reading Hume, particularly, the last point – that it is possible to *jump* to a right conclusion. The conclusion of the argument from design is that the world was created by God, the Designer, assumed throughout the *Dialogues* to be the God of Christianity. Hume is careful to deny in the *Dialogues* that the existence of God is in question. The *Dialogues* are not about *revealed* religion, and no character in them denies that we know from revelation that the world was created by God the Designer – it says so in the Bible – so it is not denied that we can get to this conclusion in *revealed* religion. What is at issue is whether we can reach the same conclusion within *natural* religion, by reason and experience, using the argument from design, and not relying at all on what, it is assumed, we already know from revelation.

I shall stress this point several times later, because it is one that even philosophically sophisticated readers forget. Students familiar with any religious tradition other than the Judaeo-Christian one may find it easier to bear it in mind, but we are all prone to allow our convictions about religion to distort our grasp of logical argument. Theists are prone to take Philo as arguing that God does not exist, and hence feel compelled to come up with lots of objections to him. But Philo is not arguing that at all, so many of their objections are irrelevant. Atheists likewise are prone to take Philo as arguing that God does not exist, and to think he proves it. But Philo is not arguing that, and hence does not prove it.

Philo does not argue against 'the world was created by God, the Designer' that is the *conclusion* of the argument from design. He argues against the argument itself.

As I said above, there are just two ways to do this:

A by arguing that at least one of the premises is false;

B by arguing that the conclusion is not adequately supported by the premises, even supposing they are true.

We have noted which of the premises is attacked in the *Dialogues*; it is Premise 2, which claims that *the effects in question are similar.* Now let us consider the second way, *B*, of attacking the argument. How might one argue that the conclusion is not adequately supported by the premises?

Are the causes in question similar?

The conclusion, remember, is supposed to be about a *similar* cause. If we used the 'like effects have like causes' principle to infer a dissimilar cause, we obviously would not be using it properly. (Suppose, seeing a very human-like footprint, and utterly convinced he was alone on his island, Crusoe inferred a dissimilar cause – a chimpanzee. Once again, he might be right, but the dissimilarity of the cause makes it less probable; his conclusion is not well supported by his premises). If the conclusion of the argument from design is to be well supported by its premises (supposing them all to be true) then *the causes in question must be similar.* So to argue that the conclusion is not adequately supported by the premises, even supposing they are true, one argues that the causes in question are not similar.

The causes in question are, on the one hand, human beings (as causes of the artefacts), and God, the Designer, on the other (as the cause of the universe). But at this stage, perhaps we should say more cautiously that the cause on the other hand is not 'God, the Designer' with a capital 'G' and capital 'D', but 'some sort of designer(s)'. For in this attack on the argument from design, the attack that consists of *B* above, Cleanthes is confronted with a dilemma.

Suppose he, Cleanthes, insists that the conclusion is about God, the God of Christianity – infinite, omnipotent, omniscient, perfectly good, eternal, supernatural, immaterial, etc. Then the cause in question is totally unlike us, and hence the conclusion is not supported by the premises.

Suppose on the other hand that Cleanthes insists that he is inferring a genuinely similar cause. Then 'the' cause must be very like us, and hence very unlike the God of Christianity – more like, if anything, the pagan gods.

To sum up the above points: (1) What is being debated by Philo and Cleanthes is *not* the truth of 'The world was created by an infinitely wise, benevolent and powerful Being'. (2) What is being debated is the truth of *'We can infer* (or 'draw the conclusion') that the world was created by an infinitely wise, benevolent and powerful Being, from the nature of the world, that is from its similarity to our artefacts'. (3) Philo's attack is not on revealed religion, but on the claims of science-inspired natural religion. It is an attack on the argument from design itself, and (4) there are only two ways to attack an argument. One (*A* above) is to argue against at least one of its premises – in this case the premise that the world really is similar to an artefact. The other (*B* above) is to argue that the (purported) conclusion is not adequately supported by the premises of the argument; either the conclusion is about a cause which is very dissimilar, or it is about a cause which is very similar but is not what it purports to be, namely the God of Christianity.

But even as I sum up thus, remember the point from the preceding sub-section. The *Dialogues* is not a straightforward philosophical argument cast in dialogue form, but a highly contrived literary work. Though the above is an accurate description of what Philo and Cleanthes are up to, you might note that, cautiously, I say nothing about what *Hume* is doing. You may find that things are not quite as straightforward as I have just made them out to be.

You might like to know that non-philosophical members of the course team found it helpful to refer back to this section several times while they were reading Hume; I suggest below occasions when it is particularly relevant.

2   *Reading the* Dialogues

In the preceding Introduction, I hope to have given you an adequate background to reading the *Dialogues* with understanding and enjoyment. There is much I have not mentioned, concerning for instance Hume's ironic use of the character Demea, and the many subsidiary arguments that Philo, in particular, puts forward. But, with respect to Demea, I do not want to spoil the fun; and with respect to the subsidiary arguments, we do not have time to consider them all. You will see, from the questions that follow, that I am not asking you to read all parts of the *Dialogues* with equal care; we want to be able to see the wood despite the trees. Moreover, I make some of the questions optional, indicating that they are more difficult than others, and that one could still have understood a lot of Hume without being able to answer them.

I now give questions and answers for each part of the text. Most, but not all, of the questions include hints about where to look for the answers in the text. Unless otherwise stated, you may assume that a single sentence (sometimes no more than 'Yes' or 'No') is sufficient to answer the question. My 'answers' will frequently be longer, since I add further comments where I think it would be helpful, but their greater length should not be taken to reflect any implicit criticism of your answers.

You will find that, although the questions follow the order of the text, they cannot always be answered comfortably until one has read on for a few more pages. I would think that by far the best method to approach the text would be to read the questions for each part, then read the part, and then attempt its questions, which in many cases would necessitate re-reading it, before going on to the next part.

But you may prefer to follow some other method. If you are going to begin by reading the whole text through, before reading any of the questions or their answers, note that parts VIII and IX are *optional.* You might also note that I ask very few questions about some of the parts, indicating that they can be read less attentively than others.

Do number your answers and note down page numbers for the text as you refer to it. You might also, according to your preferred method of working, find it useful to underline, or copy out, those bits of the text that are most relevant to answering the questions. Remember that we constantly ask you in the TMAs to 'support your answer with references to the text'. If you do this, your notes will be most useful to you in revision. (At the end of this study, I suggest a way for you to use your notes to make a summary of your work.) All page references to Hume are to *Texts,* II – the letter *a* and *b* after the page number indicates whether the relevant passage is found in the left (a) or right (b) column.

2.1   *Pamphilus to Hermippus*

This sets the stage.

QUESTION   Q.1. What judgements about the philosophies of Cleanthes, Philo, and Demea are ascribed to Hermippus (p.8a–8b)?

Answer and comment   A.1. Hermippus, so it appears, had thought that Cleanthes was of an 'accurate philosophical turn', Philo a 'careless sceptic', and Demea committed to a 'rigid inflexible orthodoxy'.

So the three protagonists are immediately introduced – not by Hume, but by one of Hume's created characters – ranked in a certain order. Cleanthes is the accurate one; Philo, though at least he is flexible enough to be open to argument, unlike Demea, is a careless sceptic. But is this how *Hume* ranks them? We have yet to see.

2.2   Part I

There is much of interest in this part about different forms of scepticism – you may recall the *Encylopédie* extract on Pyrrhonian scepticism (*Texts*, I, pp.28–32) – but we shall concentrate on just one question.

QUESTION   Q.2. Does Demea appear to think that *natural* theology is a good way to teach religious knowledge (pp.8b–9a)? Does Cleanthes (p.12b and p.13a)?

Answer and comment   A.2. Demea: no. Cleanthes: yes.

Demea, as Hermippus' judgement on him implies, relies on *revealed* theology. He thinks that our religious knowledge should be soundly instilled 'by continual precept and instruction', and that the study of *natural* theology should be 'postponed'. He smiles with 'unreserved satisfaction' at Philo's description of the 'frail faculty of reason' and its utter incapacity to give us any knowledge, let alone religious knowledge.

But Cleanthes rejects this scepticism about the faculty of reason, maintaining that it has brought us much knowledge (through Copernicus, Galileo and Newton, for example (pp.11b–12a)). Moreover, he is sure it can bring us religious knowledge, since 'the religious hypothesis' is 'founded on the simplest and most obvious arguments' and has 'such easy access and admission to the mind of man' (p.13a).

2.3   Part II

In this part, Cleanthes introduces the argument from design for the first time and Philo makes two objections to it. It is a densely argued part. You may need to spend some time on it, as well as to refer back to section 1.3 above on 'The structure of the argument'.

QUESTIONS   Q.3. Does Demea appear to think that God is mysterious and incomprehensible (pp.14b–15a)? Does Cleanthes (p.16a)? Does Philo (p.15b)?

Q.4. Where does the first statement of the argument from design occur? (p.15b–16a)

Q.5. Why is it important that 'the cases' should be 'exactly similar' (p.16b)? (Cf. section 1.3.2 above, 'Are the effects in question similar?')

Q.6. What is Philo's first objection to the argument from design (p.16b)? (Can you, referring back to pp.18–21 above, identify in which of the two possible ways Philo is attacking the argument from design here?

Is he *A* objecting to Premise 2 or *B*, is he denying that the conclusion is adequately supported by its premises, even supposing they are true?)

Q.7. What is Cleanthes' reply (pp.16b–17a)?

Q.8. What is Philo's next objection (pp.18b–19)? (Once again, is he objecting to Premise 2, or denying that the conclusion is adequately supported? A succinct sentence would do, to sum up quite an extended discussion, but you might find it easier to say more.)

Answers and comments   A.3. Demea: yes. Cleanthes: no. Philo: perhaps.

According to Demea, we ought not to imagine 'that the spirit of God has human ideas or bears *any* resemblance to our spirit' (p.15a). According to Cleanthes, the argument from design proves the existence of a God *similar* 'to human mind and intelligence'. Philo certainly *says* he agrees with Demea. But is he, this 'careless sceptic', sincere when he claims to have established 'the adorably mysterious and incomprehensible nature of the supreme being'? One may suspect irony here. And if Philo has his tongue in his cheek when he agrees with Demea here, we may be suspicious of any continued support he appears to give Demea.

A.4. The first statement of the argument from design occurs in Cleanthes' speech on p.15b, beginning 'Look round the world'. It is well worth comparing this statement of it with the text of Haydn's *Creation*. The latter emphasizes the majesty and beauty of God's creation; one might say that what is praised is God the Great Artist. By contrast, Cleanthes' speech praises God the Designer or Engineer; he compares the world to a machine; what ravishes us is not its beauty but the 'accuracy' with which its parts are adapted to each other. The text of *The Creation* says nothing, not even (as far as I can see) implicitly, about the adaptation of means to ends, but this is the most significant feature of the observable world according to the argument from design.

Note that an 'argument *a posteriori*' is an argument from premises established by observation and *experience* (see above, p.16).

A.5. Any of the three following one-sentence answers would be equally good.

As soon as you make the cases even slightly dissimilar, you 'diminish proportionably' or weaken the argument and become 'liable to error and uncertainty' (p.16b).

Unless the effects really are 'like', the known causes of the first ones will not be very strong evidence for the 'like' nature of the unknown cause of the second ones.

If we are employing an argument by analogy, the cases must really be analogous; the less analogous they are, the weaker the argument.

A.6. The universe is not really like, 'similar' or analogous to a house. (Of course, you might have it the other way round; a house is not really like the universe.) Philo is here objecting to a particular version of Premise 2. (Notice that he does not produce any argument; his objection consists of a flat denial of the claimed similarity – 'The dissimilitude is so striking ...'.) So we cannot *reason* to the conclusion that, like houses, the universe had an architect, though we might 'guess', 'conjecture', or jump to the conclusion that it has.

A.7. The universe *is* like, 'similar' or analogous to a house. (Or the other way round.)

Cleanthes not only asserts this, but goes on to give a reason or argument for it. They are alike in this all important respect – that they both contain many parts which are adjusted and contrived to serve, and serve neatly ('economically'), certain purposes. ('Final ends', a term from Aristotelian philosophy, may here be understood as meaning 'purposes'.) We make stairs to serve the end or purpose of mounting to higher floors; we could dangle ropes through holes between floors, but this would not be as 'economical' or convenient. Similarly, human legs serve the purpose of walking and mounting very neatly.

A.8. The universe is not really like a house (or a ship, or furniture or machines or any artefact of ours) because (here is his argument) the latter are all *parts* of the universe, of whose nature and origins we have experience, and thus very different sorts of thing (dissimilar, unlike, not analogous) to the *whole* universe. Here Philo again objects to Premise 2, this time in general terms, *and* gives an argument.

You may have picked up the point that Philo is objecting to Cleanthes' transferring a conclusion from parts to the whole without your having quite seen how this relates to the debate about the supposed *similarity* between artefacts and the universe. Such an answer would be a good one – there is much in the text to support it – but it does leave unexplained why there is also so much in the text about resemblance, analogy and similarity. You might also have considered the related point that it sometimes *is* all right to transfer conclusions from parts to wholes. Copernicus and Galileo, after all, start with observations about the behaviour and nature of *parts* of this planet – bits of clockwork, say – and get to conclusions about not only the *whole* planet, but the *whole* solar system of which our planet is a part (cf. Cleanthes on p.20a). But their conclusions, according to Philo, are justified, because they are based on analogies, resemblances and similarities which we can observe to hold between the various parts and wholes (pp.20a–20b). But the whole universe, and its origin, is not the kind of thing we can possibly observe. ('Have worlds ever been formed under your eye?' asks Philo (p.20b).)

2.4   Part III

In this part, Cleanthes responds to Philo's objection. He maintains that the universe, and all the natural things within it are sufficiently analogous for us to use the 'like effects have like causes' principle (i.e. he reiterates Premise 2). Once again, while you are 'getting the hang' of the structure of the argument, you might like to refer back to section 1.3 above, especially the summary on p.21.

This is one of the parts where the question of interpretation becomes particularly acute. For this reason, Q.9. is optional (but please think about it) and I do not answer Q.11.

QUESTIONS   Q.9 *optional.* What is Cleanthes' reply to the objection in Q.8 (pp.20b–22a)?

Q.10. Where does Cleanthes state the argument from design again (p.22a)?

Q.11. In your opinion, has Philo any reason to be 'embarrassed and confounded' (p.22b)?

Q.12. What objection does Demea make to the argument from design? (p.22b–23a) Is he objecting to Premise 2? (Just answer 'Yes' or 'No', referring back to section 1.3 if necessary.)

Answers and comments   A.9. Cleanthes' response to Philo in the first six paragraphs of this part has occasioned much debate.

On one reading of these pages, Cleanthes makes no adequate reply at all; he simply asserts that Premise 2, the similarity of the works of nature to those of 'art' (i.e. skill or craft) is 'self-evident and undeniable' and then goes on to consider a number of fantastic imaginary cases which accord ill with his claim that his argument is based on *experience,* (is *a posteriori*); (see above A.4.) and that its conclusion is founded on 'the simplest and most obvious arguments' (see above A.2.).

On a second way of reading him, Cleanthes is much more subtle. He concedes, implicitly, that the whole universe is, as such, different from those few parts of it of which we have experience. It is *vast.* But we are, after all, inferring the existence of a cause of it which is different from us in being in a sense, vast, namely God. Since what we are after is a conclusion about a cause which is *essentially* similar to us (rational, intelligent, ingenious in designing things, having the power to create things) but different in being on a vastly greater scale, the premise that we need is that the universe and our artefacts are *essentially* similar, but that the universe is on a vastly grander scale. It is certainly the latter. Is it 'essentially similar'? Yes, if what we take as essential are the adaptations of means to ends or purposes. That these exist in nature as well as our artefacts is self-evident and undeniable. So the universe, and our artefacts are (a) made out of the same matter and (b) similar or 'like' in essence. (This is what is meant, on this reading by 'The same matter, a like form' (p.21a), 'form' being a term in scholastic philosophy for 'essence'.) And that is all we need to 'show an analogy between their causes' (p.21a).

Then, in order to show that this indeed is all we need, Cleanthes produces his fantastic cases; cases in which, faced with something on a vast, grand, scale, we would infer a suitably grand cause. Of course, they have to be imaginary, because there is nothing in this planet anything like as vastly grand as the universe. But why should there not be 'irregular' arguments which, like good poetry, 'animate the imagination' (p.22a)?

On a third reading, Cleanthes' argument is indeed as outlined in the second way of reading him given above, but *Hume* reduces the argument to absurdity by putting in Cleanthes' mouth these ridiculous imaginings. *If* everyone all over the world, no matter what their native language, had the experience of suddenly hearing a voice saying 'I am God, and I created the world'; *if* a book or tablet suddenly grew spontaneously from the earth on which were written the words 'I created this; and I am God and created the world'; *then* indeed, natural religion would have all it needed. Everyone would know from experience, unaided by the special revelation provided (it is assumed) by the Bible, that a supremely powerful Designer existed. But nothing like this is to be found in experience. All we have are our artefacts, and the vast universe.

A.10. He restates the argument from design on p.22a beginning 'Consider, anatomize the eye'.

A.11. This is a question about what your opinion is, so I do not give an answer. Your answer should depend on what you thought of Cleanthes' reply (in A.9) and on whether you think you can detect any significant advance in the re-statement of the argument from design.

A.12. Demea's objection is that the conclusion of the argument from design represents God as 'intelligible' and 'similar' to man (p.23a). (Remember, that Demea thinks that we ought not to imagine that there is any resemblance between God and us; God is utterly mysterious and incomprehensible (cf. A.3).) This is not an objection to Premise 2 (it is not about the universe and artefacts). It is, implicitly, an objection of the *B* sort (cf. p.21 above, the three paragraphs beginning 'The causes in question ...'), which Philo will develop later.

2.5   *Part IV*

In this part, Cleanthes responds to Demea's objection, and is then confronted with a new objection from Philo. It is a tricky section, and my discussion of it is quite long.

QUESTIONS   Q.13. What is Cleanthes' reply to Demea's objection? (It can be found in the first paragraph.)

Q.14 *optional.* What 'inconveniences' does Philo find for Cleanthes in the latter's anthropomorphism (pp.24b–25b)? Is Philo attacking Premise 2, or arguing that the conclusion of the argument is not well supported by its premises? (At least two sentences, and probably more.)

Answers and comments   A.13. Cleanthes' reply is that maintaining that God is absolutely incomprehensible and 'has no ... resemblance' to us, is no different from scepticism or atheism.

This is an important point which many people find hard to grasp. What *is* the difference between theism and atheism? It is surely 'worth insisting on', but what *is* it? 'Obviously,' you reply, 'the theist believes that God exists and the atheist believes that God does not exist'. But is it the *name*, 'God', which is 'of such mighty importance', if it is 'without any meaning' or if it, the name, does not *mean* God?

Suppose, as a Christian missionary, I came across some people hitherto unknown to European culture (something that was, of course, happening in Hume's day). I master enough of their language to begin a question about their religious beliefs – 'Do your people believe in ...?' But how shall I go on? If I knew the right name, in their language, I would know the answer to my question already. But I do not know. So I have to find out. What questions shall I ask? 'Do your people believe that the world had a unique first cause?' 'Yes' the answer comes. 'What do you call it?' I ask. 'Boom' they say. 'So you believe in Boom,' I say. 'Of course,' they say, 'the world had to come from something.'

Now should I conclude that 'Boom' is their word for 'God'; as 'Dieu' is the French word for it, and 'Deus' the Latin? Well, that would be very reckless of me, as further questions might reveal.

'Is Boom good and intelligent/rational?' I ask. They look puzzled. 'Do you thank Boom for the sunshine and the success of your crops?' I ask. They look even more puzzled. 'How do you praise him?' I ask. They now clearly think I am mad. After a bit more conversation (all in their language remember), it becomes clear why. According to them, the world was created by a Big Bang, Boom! Boom! This is, naturally, mysterious and incomprehensible, but they accept it. But they think it is sheer lunacy to ascribe to this Big Bang attributes that apply to us, such as being good or rational, or doing things for us that one might be thankful for, or being praiseworthy. (And as for *its* being a *him*!)

It seems reasonably clear that these people are not theists, do not (as we say in English) believe in God, but are 'sceptics or atheists', like some scientists today who believe in the Big Bang theory of the origin of the universe, but do not believe in any God.

Do not be distracted by the well-known fact that all peoples appear to be theists of some sort. This *imaginary* example is intended to help you to understand Cleanthes' claim that Demea's 'mystical' position is no different from atheism. Demea *says* 'I believe that God exists'. But at the same time, in saying that 'God' is incomprehensible, and should not be imagined to bear *any* resemblance to human beings (in goodness, rationality, designing things for our benefit, and so on), he reveals himself to have just the same beliefs as the atheist who says 'The universe began with an incomprehensible Big Bang, but God does not exist'. He is an atheist 'without knowing it'.[5]

Of course, Demea is not consistent. Although he has said that the nature of God is '*altogether* incomprehensible and unknown to us' (p.14b, my italics) he claims to know that His nature is 'immutable and simple' (p.24a) – the point Cleanthes takes him up on (p.24a–b). He wants to maintain that God's attributes are 'perfect, *but* incomprehensible' (p.23a, my italics). But our concept of perfection is based on human attributes. Demea obviously does not believe that God is perfectly evil, perfectly stupid, perfectly incompetent – that He has *those* attributes to perfection. If he believed that, he would perhaps be a theist of sorts, but hardly a believer in the God of Christianity.

A.14 *optional*. This is a rather complicated bit of Philo's argument. The question, and the discussion of it, are 'optional', because of the time involved in working through its complications. Philo's argument, briefly, is as follows.

Suppose that the effects (the universe and our artefacts) are similar. (That is, suppose that Premise 2 is true.) Infer that the causes are similar (the universe is created by a mind like ours). What do we notice about *our* minds when we are designing artefacts? That we set about it in different ways, and that the ordering of our ideas, which causes the different

---

[5] Cleanthes' attack on Demea has a modern counterpart. In the late 1960s, the philosopher, Anthony Kenny, interviewed the Anglican Bishop Robinson about the views the latter had expressed in his book *Honest to God*. Robinson said, sincerely, that he was a Christian and believed in God; but he also, in his book, denied that God had created the world, denied that He 'has intervened in human history' (p.4 above) as described in the Bible, denied that Jesus was literally His son ... And at the end of the interview, Kenny said he thought Bishop Robinson was the most convinced atheist he had ever come across!

ways in which we do it, *is itself something that we think has causes* – our age (and hence experience), the books we have read, the weather, our emotions (passions) and so on (p.25a). (Think of the variety of buildings we have designed, in different places and at different times.) The order in our artefacts is caused by the order in our minds – but that itself, we are certain, is caused by something else. So if the Designer's mind is *like* ours, then its order must likewise be caused by something else. But we would then have to ask about the causes of that something else, and the argument would proceed to infinity.

Why not suppose (Philo says, not even allowing Cleanthes a chance to voice the objection) that the order of the Designer's mind, unlike the order of ours, just *happens*, without any further cause? The Designer is the supremely rational God, after all. But to say that is to move outside *natural* religion and appeal to revelation. It may be said that we know from revelation that God is supremely rational. But within natural religion, we are advancing hypotheses on the basis of evidence. If we allow that something, for example an ideal mind, can be orderly with no cause of its orderliness, why hypothesize so far? Why not just allow that something, that is the universe, can be orderly with no cause, that is, 'stop at the material world' (p.25a)? (It seems likely that the mention of the 'Indian philosopher and his elephant' (p.25b) is intended as a reminder that followers of religions which do not regard the Bible as a source of revealed truth may not regard the existence of a supremely rational God as the obvious explanation of the order in the universe. In the Hindu myth, the world is supported by an elephant, which in turn is supported by a tortoise, which swims in an endless sea. Though this has nothing to do with the *order* in the universe, it illustrates the point that different religions have different ideas about where explanation stops. In revealed Christianity, the orderliness of God's supreme rationality explains the order in the universe. But someone brought up in a different religion might ask 'But what causes the order in God's mind?')

This is one of Philo's arguments which involves *B* above, namely arguing that the purported conclusion is not adequately supported by the premises. The argument just stops at the existence of the Designer, but the premises do not support its stopping there.

2.6   Part V

In this Part, Philo makes another objection to the argument, and draws out its consequences. (You may find it helpful to refer back to section 1.3, p.21 above, especially the paragraph beginning 'Suppose on the other hand ... ')

QUESTIONS   Q.15. What objection does Philo now make to the argument from design (pp.26a–27b)? Is his objection the same as the one made by Demea (cf. Q.12)? Is it an attack on Premise 2?

Q.16. What consequences does Philo draw about the nature of the deity (or deities), which is (or are) required, by the 'like effects like causes' principle, to be *like* us? (You should be able to list at least four, and could list as many as six or even nine, beginning on p.27b.)

Q.17. Is Cleanthes' response adequate, in your opinion? (Last paragraph.)

Answers and comments   A.15. Philo's objection is that the argument from design must conclude that God, or 'the designer' is similar to us. It is not an attack on Premise 2; it is the same objection as Demea's. It is however used in a very different way, as the consequences that Philo draws from it make clear.

A.16. If 'God' or 'the designer' is like us (as required by the 'like effects, like causes' principle) then (1) 'God' is not infinite (*'first'* ... p.27b); (2) 'God' is not perfect (*'secondly'* p.27b); (3) 'God' is not necessarily unique but may be one amongst several gods, who 'combined' as designers (p.28a–28b); (4) this god, or gods, is/are mortal; (5) is/are gendered; (6) is/are corporeal with eyes, nose, mouth, ears, etc. ('But farther, ... ' p.28b); (7) This god may have been an infant; (8) incompetent; (9) not only incompetent but by now long dead (p.29a).

If you are at all offended by Philo's suppositions, please recall the point I emphasized in the Introduction above (p.20). Philo is *not* saying that God is imperfect, or but one amongst many, or incompetent, or dead. He is saying that, though we may know from revelation that God is perfect, the one and only living God, omniscient and omnipotent, we cannot come to this knowledge by the argument from design.

And if you are an atheist, and particularly delighted by this passage, you should recall the same point. Philo has not proved here, and is not represented as aiming to prove, that God is incompetent or dead. He is represented here only as aiming to prove that the argument from design will not yield a well-supported conclusion about the existence of the God of Christianity, (so it is an attack of the *B* sort). Instead, according to Philo, the argument (granted its premises) would yield a well-supported conclusion about the existence (or past existence) of (a) very different sort(s) of god(s). Such a god or gods is/are much more analogous to us than the God of Christianity – and it is analogy that the argument from design depends on.

A.17. This is a question about your personal opinion, so I do not answer it.

2.7   *Part VI*

In this part, Philo produces another objection and Cleanthes responds to it.

QUESTIONS   Q.18. What is Philo's next objection to the argument from design? (p.30a. You may find it useful to look at how Cleanthes interprets the objection, on p.30b, in the sentence beginning 'Why then, ... '). Is it an objection to Premise 2, or to the argument's conclusion being adequately supported by its premises?

Q.19. What is Cleanthes' reply? (*Either:* a limited response, taken from the first paragraph of Cleanthes' reply ('Why then, ...) and ignoring all the rest, *or* (optional, if you have time) a succinct sentence briefly summing up a complicated discussion whose details we must leave to one side.)

Answers and comments   A.18. Philo's next objection is that the world does not resemble an artefact so much as an animal actuated by a soul. It is another version of an attack on Premise 2, for, if this is so then, once again, the premise of the argument from design that 'the universe is like an *artefact*' is shown to be very weak.

Philo's opening remarks ('But there is another principle ... ' p.29b) may lead one to think that he is going to go outside the argument from design in the form that we have been relying on and begin some wider criticisms. But Cleanthes' interpretation of the objection makes it clear that we have returned to the question of whether the universe resembles artefacts.

A.19. A short-term answer, taken from the first paragraph of Cleanthes' response and ignoring all the rest, would be: 'Cleanthes' reply is that the world is not particularly like an animal, but if anything more like a plant (this is what is meant by 'vegetable'), because it has no sense organs, no capacity to think or reason (which he implies, most animals have to at least a minimal extent), and does not move itself and act (as animals do, but plants do not)'.

An answer that took account of the rest of his response must be crude if it is to be brief. Briefly and crudely, his reply is: 'We can't suppose that the world is like an animal actuated by a soul unless we suppose the eternity of the world. (Note that he just assumes this.) But we cannot suppose the world to be eternal'. We do not have time here to consider his argument fully, nor Philo's response.

2.8 Part VII

In this Part, Philo produces another objection and responds to Demea's criticisms of it; Cleanthes dismisses Philo's objection.

QUESTIONS   Q.20. What is Philo's next objection to the argument from design (p.30a–b)? (Two or three sentences, laying out moves in the argument.) Can you see why it is difficult to classify this objection as simply *either A*, an attack on Premise 2 *or B*, as arguing that the conclusion is not adequately supported by its premises, even supposing they are true?

Q.21. What two objections does Demea raise to Philo's objection (p.33a)?

Q.22. What single response, in effect, does Philo make to both (p.33a and 33a–34b)? (Two short sentences.)

Q.23. Should Cleanthes (the supporter of *natural* religion) worry about being unable to solve the difficulties presented by Philo's 'whimsies'?

Answers and comments   A.20. The universe 'bears a greater likeness' (p.32a) to animals and to plants than it does to artefacts. So, according to the 'like effects like causes' principle, its cause is more probably like the causes of animals or plants (i.e. generation or vegetation) than like the causes of artefacts (i.e. us, rational designers). For instance, perhaps this world grew from a comet (p.32b).

The objection begins in just the same way as Part VI (cf. A.18 above) as a denial of Premise 2. But this time Philo uses his rival premise to infer, by analogy, to a cause very unlike God (as the incompetent or dead gods are unlike God). So one could see his objection here as a double-barrelled one. Not only is Premise 2 of the argument from design very weak, and hence the conclusion about the existence of God 'lame and defective', but there is a much stronger premise in an argument by analogy, which yields a different, rival, conclusion.

A.21. Demea objects (a) that we have no data to support such 'wild suppositions', and (b) that we cannot 'anatomize' (analyse or explain) how such generation or vegetation of worlds would work.

A.22. To both Demea's 'objections' Philo's brief reply is, in effect, – '*of course* we do not and cannot. And Cleanthes' religious "conjecture" (kept strictly within natural theology) is no better off.' (Can he explain or anatomize God's reason? Cf. p.34a.) Indeed, it is worse off – Cleanthes' analogy is 'less striking'; Philo's is supported by 'at least some faint shadow of experience' (p.34b).

A.23. It seems to me that he should, but note that this is controversial. The 'whimsies' (p.35a) about the comet seed and the spider etc. are not essential; Philo has presented a very straightforward, unwhimsical, objection to the argument from design (given in A.20) and Cleanthes has not come up with any response to it at all.

We could take Cleanthes, in the last words of this Part, as responding by saying that Philo's premise (the universe is more like an animal or a plant than it is like an artefact) is simply implausible and 'never can convince us' (p.35a). But Philo has, in fact, implicitly already dealt with this point. It would not be surprising if his premise was implausible to his hearers (and Hume's readers) since 'we' have received the benefits of revelation. 'We' know (it is assumed) that the world was created by a Designer, and hence incline towards seeing it as similar to an artefact. But what about people who have not acquired this assumed knowledge of revealed Christian religion – the ancients and the Brahmins (p.34b)? They incline towards seeing the universe as like an animal. But *natural* religion is supposed to produce premises and arguments which not only convince those acquainted with the Bible, but other people too.

2.9 *Parts VIII and IX* (optional)

No questions. In Part VIII, Philo offers another 'hypothesis' about the origin of universe and all its parts. In Part IX, he and Cleanthes depart momentarily from natural religion and discuss an *a priori* (see p.16 above) argument for the existence of God.

There are still three major parts of the text to come, and if you are getting behind, you are advised to leave Parts VIII and IX for study at a later time. It would be a pity not to approach Part X with some enthusiasm in hand, for it is there that Hume introduces the problem of evil and the text covers ground familiar to you from your study of *Candide*.

2.10   Part X

In this Part Philo introduces the problem of evil and develops it as an attack on the argument from design.

QUESTIONS

Q.24. What (in one very short sentence) are Demea and Philo claiming in the first three and a half pages of this part (pp.40a–43a)?

Q.25. What is Philo's next objection to Cleanthes (pp.43a–43b)? (Optionally, if you have time to attempt a deeper answer to Q.25, try to recast Philo's objection for him as, explicitly, an attack on the argument from design, considering, as always, whether it is an attack on Premise 2 or on the conclusion's being well supported by the premises.)

Q.26. Does Cleanthes appear to think it is a serious objection (pp.43b and 44a)?

Q.27. Does Demea (pp.43b–44a)?

Q.28. Why do they disagree about this (p.44a)? (One very succinct, or two longish sentences.)

Q.29. What reply does Cleanthes make to Philo's objection referred to in Q.25 (p.44a)?

Q.30. What objections does Philo make to Cleanthes' reply (pp.44a–45a)? (There are four, each of which needs at least one sentence; the fourth probably needs two sentences. Note how each advances on the one before.)

Answers and comments

A.24. The world is full of evil. We could imagine here that Demea and Philo, instead of making the general claims they do make, cited a number of particular examples similar to those described in *Candide*.[6]

A.25. A perfectly good answer would set up Philo's objection as a statement of the problem of evil, familiar to you from 'Voltaire and Optimism', the *Candide* study in *Studies*, I, pp.338–46. If God is both all-powerful and benevolent (and, indeed, just), how does it come to be that the world is full of evil?

The answer to the second *optional* question might go something like this:

Like effects have like causes. The sort of people who cause evil are either unable to prevent it (are impotent) or malevolent. So the cause of this world, which is full of evil, is similar. So the Designer must be either impotent or malevolent. He cannot be impotent if he is the Designer and cause of the whole vast world. So he must be malevolent.

Spelt out in this way, the objection is an attack of the *B* sort. Premise 2, that the universe is like an artefact, is not in question. Philo is now arguing that the premises of the argument from design provide adequate support not for the God of Christianity, who in his 'benevolence and mercy' resembles good people, but, on the contrary, for a malevolent one, who resembles evil people.

---

[6]   You might note that both Demea and Philo make the standard mistake of attributing to Leibniz the simple brand of optimism according to which there is no evil in the world. (Cf. 'Voltaire and Optimism' in *Studies*, I.) It is quite possible that this is Hume's mistake.

A.26. Yes. (' ... you have now fallen upon a subject worthy of your noble spirit of opposition and controversy') (p.43b).

Note that this is the point at which Hume's ironic use of the character of Demea is avowed. Demea has served as a screen behind which Philo has been erecting his 'concealed battery'. Had you suspected this long since?

That Philo's agreement with Demea has, throughout, been ironic is indisputable. But this brief speech of Cleanthes' brings up an aspect of the text about which there is much debate.

Note that Cleanthes *appears* to regard the problem of evil as potentially destructive not simply of the argument from design but 'of *all* religion' (p.43b), natural or revealed. However, this is not certain. For, given the context of the *Dialogues,* we may be entitled to read 'of all religion' as meaning 'of all *natural* religion' and this reading can be supported by the way Cleanthes continues in his next speech, (beginning '"No!" replied Cleanthes' (p.44a)). This speech, with all its references to the 'phenomena', 'suppositions', 'hypotheses' etc. is clearly set within the terms of *natural* religion.

But then again, as we have noted, Cleanthes tends to regard revealed religion, at least as represented by Demea, as indistinguishable from atheism (cf. Part IV above). And, with reference to the argument from design, Cleanthes had said early on 'By this argument *a posteriori,* and (my italics) *by this argument alone,* we do prove at once the existence of a Deity, and his similarity to human mind and intelligence' (p.16a). Cleanthes has also allowed Philo to ascribe this view to him: 'This (the argument from design) is the experimental argument; and this, you say too, is *the sole* theological argument' (p.26b, my italics). So if the argument from design fails, we have nothing to go on; so 'all natural religion' *is* 'all religion' according to him.

But one could object that the sentence from p.16a I have just quoted need not, and perhaps should not, be interpreted in this way. (Can you see the other ways of interpreting it?) And so the debate about how to interpret this further bit of the text continues.

A.27. No, because he thinks there is an easy answer to it. His answer is (ironically) the simple optimism earlier attributed to Leibniz and rejected. It is, in fact, Pope's. (Compare the three sentences beginning 'this life but a moment ...' with Robert Wilkinson's discussion of Pope in 'Voltaire and Optimism', the *Candide* study, *Studies,* I, pp.338–41.)

A.28. Briefly: because Demea is content with revealed knowledge, but Cleanthes wants natural knowledge. At greater length: for Demea, the existence of a benevolent all-mighty God (and the assurance of an eternal life after death) is not a hypothesis, a conjecture, but a certainty, derived from revelation. But for Cleanthes, causes cannot be known except from their known effects. (Here, as was just noted, it is uncertain whether we are to take Cleanthes as implicitly attacking revelation as no source of religious knowledge at all, or whether we should read him as saying '*Within natural religion,* causes cannot be known except from their known effects'.)

A.29. Cleanthes' reply is *not*, as initially appears, 'to deny absolutely the misery and wickedness of man' (the very existence of natural and moral evil). That would make him agree with Demea. His reply, as Philo's response makes clear, consists in claiming that the amount of evil in the world has been exaggerated: there is *more* good than evil.

A.30. Philo's four objections are as follows – note how each goes beyond the one before:

1 There is more evil than good. (The paragraph beginning 'Admitting your position ...' p.44a.)

2 Even if (1) were not true, i.e. even if there is more good than evil, 'no decisive proofs' could ever be produced for this; so it would always remain uncertain. (The next paragraph; 'But not to insist ...' p.44b.)

3 Even if it were certain that there is more good than evil, the existence of *any* evil ('Why is there any misery at all in the world?') is sufficient to generate the problem of evil ('Is it from the intention of the Deity? but ...') and hence show that the existence of evil is incompatible with the existence of a powerful and benevolent God. (The next paragraph; 'But allowing ...' (p.44b).)

4 Even if the problem of evil does not show this (i.e. even if, in some mysterious Demean way, the existence of evil *is* 'compatible' with the existence of a powerful and benevolent God), this 'mere possible compatibility' is no use to Cleanthes, the natural theologian, as he has himself admitted (p.44a). For Cleanthes is committed to proving the actual existence of this God (or cause) from the known effects – the 'phenomena'. (Aided by revelation, he might *jump* to the conclusion that there is a powerful and benevolent God, but this is not enough for natural religion.) (The next paragraph; 'But I will be contented ...' (p.45a).)

2.11 Part XI

Cleanthes makes a concession to Philo, who continues to press objections based on the evil in the world.

QUESTIONS

Q.31. What concession does Cleanthes make to Philo (first paragraph)? Do you think it is a major concession, or only a minor one?

Q.32. What objection does Philo make (pp.45b–46b)? (Two or three sentences.)

Q.33. Why does Philo emphasize that 'the consistency is not absolutely denied, only the inference' (p.46b). (Compare this with what he says in the penultimate paragraph in the preceding Part – 'A mere possible compatibility is not sufficient. You must *prove* ...' (p.45a).)

Q.34. Is he making the same point when he says 'And though the mere supposition, that such reasons exist, may be sufficient to *save* the conclusion concerning the divine attributes, yet surely it can never be sufficient to *establish* that conclusion '(p.47b)?

Q.35. Does he make the same point later? Where (p.49b)?

Q.36. What hypothesis about the first causes of the universe does Philo say is most probable, and why (p.50a)? (Two or three sentences.)

Q.37. Has Cleanthes made any reply to Philo's objection in Q.32 in the course of this Part?

Answers and comments

A.31. Cleanthes concedes that we cannot infer the existence of an *infinitely* perfect (infinitely powerful and infinitely benevolent) deity from 'the known effects' i.e. this universe, with its evil. (My own opinion is that, at this stage, the concession is fairly minor. It does not immediately return us to the possibility of the all-too-human deities described by Philo in Part V, for Cleanthes still insists that the author of nature, though finite, *far* excedes mankind in his perfections. This is what Philo goes on to attack.)

A.32. Philo claims that the 'known effects', i.e. our world full of 'vice and misery and disorder' do not support Cleanthes' conclusion – the existence of a designer whose perfection *far* exceeds ours. Quite the contrary. The world does not, to the innocent and unprejudiced eye (which is not 'antecedently convinced' (p.46a) of the existence of God), resemble a house designed by a vastly superior architect, but, on the contrary, a house designed by an incompetent one.

Note that this is, still, an attack of the *B* sort, maintaining that the premises of the argument from design provide inadequate support for a conclusion about a Designer like the God of Christianity; on the contrary, they support the conclusion that there is an incompetent Designer.

A.33. Philo is once again insisting on what is required from *natural* religion (cf. (4) under A.30, p.35 above).

Of course it is *possible* that the world was designed by a deity with perfections that far exceed ours: the world's imperfections may be consistent or compatible with that hypothesis. (And revelation may tell us that this is not only possible, but actual fact.) But, within natural theology, that the designer has such perfections is just a conjecture, a speculation. One cannot *infer* the existence of such a designer from the known effects.

A.34. Yes.

A.35. Yes, in the passage beginning, on p.49b, 'Let us allow ...' Here he is making the same point (as in A. 30, 33 and 34) about what is required from natural religion. (A minor difference is that natural theology is here contrasted not with revelation, but with proofs *a priori*.) The goodness of God may be 'compatible' with the phenomena; the goodness of God might indeed be established *a priori* (without relying on any premises about the phenomena), but none of this is of any help to *natural* theology. It requires that the goodness of God be well supported or proved by the phenomena; so that we can infer the goodness of God from them.

'The phenomena' in question are the same as the 'known effects' mentioned in A.33, i.e. this universe, with its 'many ills ... (which) might so easily have been remedied' (p.49b).

A.36. The most probable cause has neither goodness nor malice, because the other hypotheses are not supported by the phenomena.

Logically, there are just four different ways in which the attributes of goodness and/or malice can be present, according to Philo. The two 'unmixed' cases (perfect goodness and perfect malice) could not be inferred from mixed phenomena (the world contains a mixture of good and evil). But neither is the mixture of goodness and malice in the *cause* (the Manichean system mentioned on p.50a) supported by the phenomena, because, although the phenomena are mixed, they are also 'steady and uniform', whereas if they were caused by a mixture of goodness and malice, they would be full of strife, conflict, and disorder.

Philo undoubtedly deals too hastily with the mixture of goodness and malice. If he grants the mixture of good and evil in the world, and its steadiness and uniformity, *and* the occasional breakdown of that uniformity, should he not infer that a fairly probable cause of the universe would be a mixture of goodness and malice, but much more good than malicious? (The general goodness explains the steadiness; the occasional flashes of 'malice' or evil, the breakdowns.)

Is this a mistake on *Hume's* part, or could this be a gap in Philo's argument which Hume has left in on purpose? Is the reader being invited to consider, yet again, the possibility that the Designer is all too like us, that is basically decent (for Hume was undoubtedly optimistic rather than pessimistic about human nature) but still essentially prone to the occasional lapse into viciousness?

Similarly, one might object to Philo that the universe contains a mixture of good and evil in which evil rather than good predominates. Pursuing this line, and taking a pessimistic view of human nature, we would say that Philo should infer the existence of a Designer who is all too like us in being basically cruel, vain, self-indulgent and (or) stupid.

Such a conclusion will obviously not be welcome to supporters of the argument from design; indeed, it strengthens Philo's attack on it. So again the question presents itself; has *Hume* simply overlooked this possibility, is it a mistake on his part? Or is he fully aware of the possibility and expecting his discerning reader to spot it and realize that Philo could say even more?

A.37. No.

2.12 *Part XII*

In this concluding Part of the *Dialogues*, Demea has left, and there is at least a suggestion that Cleanthes and Philo, free at last of the oppressive presence of an adherent of 'rigid orthodoxy', now settle down to say what they 'really think', philosopher to philosopher. ('I should rather wish to reason with *either* of you apart' (p.51a) says Cleanthes (my italics) but, given Demea's earlier contributions, we may suspect irony here; it is with Philo alone that the deist Cleanthes wants to argue.) However, when we bear in mind that the *Dialogues* are not the transcript, by Pamphilus, of a real conversation, but have been contrived from beginning to end by Hume, the interpretation of this Part becomes noticeably difficult. We have already encountered particular passages concerning the interpretation of which there is clearly room for much debate. But the *whole* of this Part, apart from its opening paragraph, constitutes such a 'passage'.

QUESTIONS

Q.38. Does Cleanthes make any reply to Philo's objection (in Q.32) in the first few pages of this part?

The four questions which follow, given that they all involve matters of difficult interpretation, are to think about and puzzle over rather than to give definite answers to. They are discussed (but not answered) in the next section 'Concluding thoughts'.

Q.39. Do you think that Philo, in his first long speech (pp.51b–52b), is now saying that he accepts the argument from design, despite all that has gone before? Or do you think something else is going on?

Q.40. What do you think Philo is saying in his next long speech (from p.52b 'So little, replied Philo' to p.54a 'These, Cleanthes, are my unfeigned sentiments')? Is he, again, accepting the argument from design, and admitting he is a theist ('Here then the existence of a Deity is plainly ascertained by reason ...' (p.53a))? Is he saying there is no difference between theism and atheism ('Where then, cry I to both these antagonists, ... ' (p.53b))? Does this imply that he is admitting that he is an atheist?

Q.41. What do you think Philo's conclusion is regarding 'the whole of natural theology' (p.58b)? How does it differ from Cleanthes' view of natural theology/religion?

Q.42. Do you think Pamphilus is justified in saying that Cleanthes' principles 'approach still nearer to the truth' than those of Philo?

Answers and comments   A.38. No.

Questions 39–42 are discussed (but not answered) in the next section.

3   Concluding thoughts

How then, having read it, shall we describe *Dialogues Concerning Natural Religion* as an expression of *Hume's* views? Is Philo the winner, and Hume's representative? Or is Cleanthes? Or neither of them? Was I right even to say that the work is concerned only with natural religion, as the title promises, or does it contain a covert attack on revealed religion as well?

Hume scholars have come to different conclusions about these questions, formed not solely on the basis of the *Dialogues* but on their readings of Hume's other works, the two volumes of his letters (Grieg, 1932), and Mossner's comprehensive biography. Anyone who has not read these other writings should hesitate before coming to any firm conclusions, but one may gain much without coming to conclusions.

What you have just read is a single text, astonishingly rich in arguments and dialectical complexity. Our major concern has been to understand and appreciate those arguments. Questions concerning their overall success take us well beyond the text to the higher reaches of the philosophy of religion and its assessment of the argument from design. At this stage one may, of course, have convictions about the adequacy of the arguments, and they may, quite properly, *incline* one to this interpretation rather than that; but it would be presumptuous, given the amount of debate that has gone on, and is still going on, about it, to think that one had 'got it right'.

Our concluding concern is to understand and appreciate which features of the work support different interpretations. I shall now lay out the three main lines of interpretation, referring back to some of the crucial answers concerning earlier Parts. This may be a good moment, as a sort of quick, preliminary revision, to read through your numbered answers and notes.

3.1 Hume as Philo

We have seen that Philo is given not only the most to say, but a most impressive collection of arguments against the argument from design, arguments which, many readers believe ('believe', not 'know') prove conclusively that the argument from design is of no use to the Christian religion at all, that it cannot be used, as an argument of natural theology, to provide any reason whatsoever for believing in the God of Christianity.

In order to support this interpretation, one must produce explanations of the following three significant points:

1   that Cleanthes is never presented as conceding any major failure of the argument to Philo (note A.31 above);

2   that in his final speeches, (those referred to in Q.39 and 40) Philo (apparently) concedes everything to Cleanthes;

3   that in the concluding sentence of the work, Cleanthes is declared the winner of the argument.

Before reading on, try to think of ways in which adherents of the view that Philo is the winner and represents Hume might attempt to explain these three points. (You may have done this already while thinking about Qs 39–42.)

The explanations all rely on the entirely plausible premise that, even aiming for no more than posthumous publication, Hume would have found it necessary to conceal his radically anti-theistic views from all but the most discerning and sympathetic reader. So the response goes:

1   Cleanthes never *says* 'I am refuted', but time and again (to the discerning reader) he obviously is. Philo constantly makes objections to which Cleanthes has no adequate reply. Sometimes Cleanthes' replies are manifestly inadequate (see A.9 on the first and third reading of Cleanthes' response to Philo, p.26 above). Sometimes he just laughs off Philo's objections as something that need not be taken seriously (see Q.17, which I did not answer, and A.23, which I said was controversial) when they do need to be taken seriously. Sometimes he does not even attempt a reply (though no character draws attention to this fact, allowing the undiscerning reader to overlook it) (see A.37 and A.38).

You will notice that this line of interpretation depends heavily on judgements about the adequacy of arguments (note again particularly A.9, Q.17 and A.23). That is why I said above that opting for one line of interpretation rather than the other takes one beyond the text into the higher reaches of philosophy of religion, and why I emphasized that adherents of this line *believe*, rather than *know*, that Philo is given arguments which prove conclusively that the argument from design is no use at all to the Christian religion. The response continues:

2   Philo's final speeches apparently agreeing with Cleanthes are ironic (and Hume was famous for his irony).

3   Pamphilus's concluding sentence is mere lip-service, intended to disarm charges of blasphemy. (And a similar claim may be made about his description of Philo as 'embarrassed and confounded' – see Q.11.)

3.2   Hume as Cleanthes

The support for this second line of interpretation basically consists of rejecting the preceding explanation of the three significant points. So, inevitably, it too, concerning the first point, depends heavily on judgements about the adequacy of arguments. But here the judgements go the other way.

1   None of Cleanthes' replies is manifestly inadequate; quite the contrary (see A.9. on the second reading of Cleanthes' response). He is entirely justified in dismissing Philo's wilder imaginings and 'whimsies'. (This interpretation answers Q.17, and Q.23 with 'Yes' and 'No' respectively.) And Philo's deployment of the argument from the problem of evil calls for no reply, being reduced to its own absurdity by his claim that the most probable cause of this universe is neither good nor evil.

2   These judgements are supported by Philo's concluding speeches, which are not ironic, but which explicitly admit the force of the argument from design. (This had been hinted at earlier, at the end of Part X, where Philo says 'In many views of the universe, and of its parts, particularly the latter, the beauty and fitness of final causes strike us with such irresistible force that all objections appear (*what I believe they really are*) mere cavils and sophisms' (p.45a). (My italics, on behalf of this response.)

3   There is no reason to regard Pamphilus's concluding sentence as mere lip-service.[7]

3.3   Hume as neither

(This line of interpretation might also be labelled 'Hume as the-Philo-in-Part-XII', but the label is not important.) It interprets the *Dialogues* as being without a winner, and, interestingly, finds this suggested right at the beginning, where Pamphilus says 'Any question of philosophy ... which is so obscure and uncertain, that human reason can reach no fixed determination with regard to it; if it should be treated at all, seems to lead us naturally into the style of dialogue and conversation' (pp.7b–8a). The interpretation continues:

'Suppose *Hume* is saying this. Then he is telling us that he has chosen the dialogue form because *he* thinks that 'human reason can reach no fixed determination with regard to' the argument from design.

'On the one hand there are all Philo's objections to it which Cleanthes cannot rebut.' (On this point, the third line of interpretation relies on *some* of the judgements of the first. But note that its adherents need not agree with adherents of the first that Cleanthes never has adequate replies. As long as Philo has some objections that Cleanthes cannot rebut, the point stands.)

'On the other hand, as Philo acknowledges in Part XII, the argument from design won't go away; even to someone who can see all the objections to it, it has an irresistible attraction.'

---

[7]   And we might attach significance to the fact that the name 'Cleanthes' is the one Hume gives to his exemplar of virtue in the *Inquiry Concerning the Principles of Morals*. I owe this point to Jean Spendlove.

This interpretation finds a significant addition to Cleanthes' second statement of the argument from design in Part III, an addition that Cleanthes is not making advisedly (because he never takes it up) but which *Hume* is making advisedly. 'Consider, anatomize the eye', says Cleanthes 'and tell me, *from your own feeling*, if the idea of a contriver does not *immediately* flow in upon you with a force *like that of sensation*' (p.22a; my italics throughout). According to this interpretation, Hume's point here is that our belief in a Designer is, as an *immediate* response to the world, a natural, instinctive belief, unreasoned, and in that sense akin to *feeling* and *sensation*.

If one is not acquainted with Hume's other works, this may seem to be reading a great deal into just one passage. But (it may plausibly be said that) the most striking feature of Hume's other philosophy is precisely the fact that in it he claims that *most* of the beliefs we think we hold on reasonable grounds are in fact no better than natural instincts. Our belief in the external world, our belief in causality, our belief that the future will resemble the past – in the first book of the *Treatise*, and in the first *Inquiry*, these beliefs have all been subjected to the most searching scepticism, and Hume has concluded that we have no *reason* to believe any of them. These beliefs, he thinks, are not 'mediated' by reason but are *immediate*, natural, responses to the world.

And (it may plausibly be said), he does not move to the further conclusion (of Pyrrhonian scepticism) that we should deny these beliefs, or be agnostic about them. On the contrary, he is certain that we are quite incapable of doing so, so there is no point in trying. Any 'attempt' or claim to success in doing so could only be pretence; anyone who denies he believes in the external world must be insincere. (Compare the remarks on scepticism and suspense of judgement in Part I pp.10b–12b and in Part XII, pp.52b and 58b–59a.)

'So,' the interpretation goes, 'we find Hume coming to a precisely parallel position on our belief in a Designer. It is not rationally based (i.e. 'mediated' by reason) – so Cleanthes, as the supporter of natural religion, is wrong. But Philo, the sceptic, cannot argue us out of it, and it is a mistake on his part to try. So Hume's conclusion is not in agreement with the approach of either Cleanthes, nor Philo; he is neither of them.'

3.4 'Conclusion'

The above, as I said, are the three *main* lines of interpretation; of course there are others, and subtle differences between the adherents of any of these three. Please do not fall into the error of assuming that the third is the only one that takes account of Hume's other philosophy; the other two do too, but I did not need to describe how in order to make them intelligible. The third, as I said, looks ill-supported if one does not know about Hume's other philosophy; the other two did not. But obviously, if their adherents did *not* take account of Hume's other philosophy, they would not be plausible interpretations for Hume scholars to produce. But there are disputes about Hume's other philosophy too (hence my cautious use of 'it may plausibly be said' above – not everyone agrees with what adherents of the third interpretation say about Hume's scepticism).

I hope you have not reached any firm conclusion about which interpretation is the right one. For if you have, you will have jumped to it precipitately, rather than proceeding with 'the slow and deliberate steps of philosophers' (p.18a). But I hope too that you have enjoyed taking these 'deliberate steps' through Hume's arguments. Inevitably, you will have had to take them quickly rather than slowly, so I append some notes which may aid you with revisions and further study.

3.5 Revision and further study

You should have a series of numbered answers and notes to (most of) the questions you were asked to tackle in the exercises. A good way to summarize and revise your work on the *Dialogues* would be to arrange those answers and notes (suitably amended or corrected if necessary!) under the following three headings. I cite the answers below as the shortest way of directing you to the relevant parts of the text, but of course the text is what you should concentrate on.

1   Objections to the argument from design which consist of attacking its Premise 2, 'The universe is (very) like an artefact'. (Cf. Answers 6, 8, 18, 20.)

2   Objections to the argument from design (excluding those based on the existence of evil) which leave its Premises unquestioned but argue that its conclusion is not adequately supported by them. (Cf. Answers 12, 14, 15, 16, 20.)

3   Objections to the argument from design based on the existence of evil. (Cf. Answers 25, 30, 32, 33, 34, 35.)

Exams: When you are revising in preparation for the exams, make note of any connections with other parts of the course, both those you remarked when you studied the *Dialogues* and any that occurred to you later. Here are a few suggestions to start you off:

1   Deism, natural religion, the rise of science: section 1.2 and 1.3 of the Introduction, pp.15–16, and p.20 above. Answers 2, 14, 23, 30, 33, 35.

2   Scepticism: Part I of the text, pp.10a–13a, Part III, p.22a; Part XI, p.49b and 51a, Part XII, pp.52b and 58b–59a.

3   Reason and feeling: section 3.3 above, 'Hume as neither', p.41.

4   Irony: Philo's apparent agreement with Demea until the last stages of the *Dialogues* (e.g. Answer 3 (and much of Part II), Answer 15, Answer 26), and (2) in the interpretation of 'Hume as Philo' (section 3.1 above, p.39).

4   References

Grieg, J.Y.T. (ed.) (1932) *The Letters of David Hume*, 2 vols, Clarendon Press, Oxford.

Mossner, E.C. (1954) *The Life of David Hume*, Clarendon Press, Oxford.

Russell, B. (1961) *History of Western Philosophy*, Allen and Unwin Ltd, London.

Lessing and a religion for humanity: Nathan the Wise

Prepared for the Course Team by Stephanie Clennell, with a contribution by Robert Wilkinson

Contents

Lessing and a religion for humanity: Nathan the Wise (Study weeks 20–21)

Studies/Texts	Radio	TV	AC	Set books
Studies, II	–	TV11	AC1623 (yellow)	*Nathan the Wise*
–	–	–	AC1624 (yellow)	–
–	–	–	AC1625 (yellow)	–

In this study you will meet a great work of the German Enlightenment, Lessing's play *Nathan the Wise*. Your study materials are the set text, an English translation of *Nathan the Wise* with an introduction and notes; an audio-cassette recording of a complete performance of the play (AC1623–5, yellow); TV11 'Nathan der Weise', showing an extract from a performance of the original German text; and this study, which discusses Lessing's ideas and gives a guide to the play. The aim of these is to help you enjoy the play, to understand Lessing's views, and to study both in the context of the Enlightenment.

You are strongly recommended to use the study materials in the following order:

1   Read section 1 of this study on the German enlightenment.

2   Read the Introduction in the set text on Lessing's life and work.

3   Read sections 2–5 of this study.

4   Listen to the performance of *Nathan* on cassette in conjunction with the set text.

5   Read the study guide, section 6.

6   Watch TV11.

7   Read sections 7–8 in this study.

8   Listen again to the performance of *Nathan* on the audio-cassettes with the set text.

Lessing and a religion for humanity:
Nathan the Wise

1 The German Enlightenment

In the eighteenth century 'German' and 'Germany' did not mean what they mean today, as you will recall from your study of Frederick the Great (see *Studies,* I, pp.55–6). In letters to Voltaire Frederick expressed some pessimism about the state of German literature (see documents 47–8 in *Texts,* I, pp. 63–4). He also wrote an essay on the subject in the same pessimistic vein: *De la littérature allemande (On German Literature).* The official German translation (Berlin, 1780) used the term *Deutschland* (for *l'Allemagne*), but 'Deutschland' was not at that time a political entity as France and Britain were. Frederick was referring to all those German states, including his own Prussia, where German (of a sort, according to Frederick) was spoken. There was a motley collection of over 300 such states, varying in size and power. Northern and central states were mainly Protestant. Southern states bordering on the Habsburg dominions were Catholic, as were some Rhineland territories. Prussia, as you have seen, became larger and increasingly powerful over the course of the century.

Almost all these states had some kind of autocratic rule and often, with the notable exception of Prussia, chaotic finances and stagnant economies. The growth of a middle class was limited, but not entirely retarded, by the hold of traditional hierarchies and old-style methods of production. Political stability of sorts had been achieved after the divisive and devastating Thirty Years' War (1618–48) of the previous century; there was at least coexistence of Catholic and Protestant states. But this stability was precarious, being heavily dependent on the balance of power between Austria and Frederick's Prussia.

What, then, was the German Enlightenment? There was a German word for it, *Aufklärung,* as you learned at the beginning of the course. The word suggests a clearing up of the weather and increasing light, but what did this mean when applied to culture? *Aufklärung* was still being defined and re-defined in the 1780s when Immanuel Kant and Moses Mendelssohn gave their answers to the question: What is Enlightenment? in the *Berlinische Monatschrift* in 1783 (see *Texts,* II, p.305). Kant wrote: 'Enlightenment is man's emergence from his self-incurred immaturity' ('Aufklärung ist der Ausgang des Menschen aus seiner selbstverschuldeten Unmündigkeit').

This view that being unenlightened is a sign of immaturity applies very well to German culture in the early part of the century. Then a revival took place, became strong in the second part of the century, and the last decades were a golden age for German (and European) culture – the age of Lessing, Goethe and Schiller.

There were some rays of light at the end of the seventeenth century. Leibniz after all was one of the leading philosophers and mathematicians in Europe. Christian Thomasius (1655–1728), often seen as 'the father of the German Enlightenment' was the first to lecture in German instead of Latin at the University of Leipzig in 1687. His views, especially his advocacy of the use of reason, did not find favour with the Dresden court and he moved to the new University of Halle (1694) where the Elector of Brandenburg was ready to accept him. Already we see two aspects of the German Enlightenment which are different from what we find in France and Britain. Firstly, the German language itself had to develop into a modern cultural language. Secondly, there was no one great cultural centre such as Paris, or London, or Edinburgh, but a number of centres such as Leipzig, Berlin, Göttingen, Halle, Hamburg, Jena, which became important, culturally speaking, not least because of the outstanding people who were working and writing in them. These academics and writers could move about; they were not totally silenced by the legal power of one ruler, nor the hostility of the cultural or religious establishment, since they could move to another German state which promised to be more liberal. It was not only Frederick the Great who professed enlightened ideas (despite his denigration of German culture), but rulers or nobility in some of the lesser German states; for example, Voltaire's friends and correspondents, the Elector of the Palatinate and the Duchess of Saxe-Gotha, and also the aristocratic subscribers to Grimm's *Correspondance Littéraire* (see the *Encyclopédie* study in *Studies*, I, p.21). Although the intellectuals were scattered, mobile, and without one focal point, they knew each other, or about each other, met, corresponded, argued in print, and so were able to communicate very much as the French *philosophes* did.

In France, as we have seen, the *philosophes* had to contend with a powerful Roman Catholic Church. The situation in the German states was more complicated. The main growth of Enlightenment was in the Protestant states, such as Brandenburg-Prussia, Saxony, Hanover. Philosophical and theological questions and disputes played a large part in intellectual life. Questions about reason and faith, revelation or natural religion, were discussed from a wide range of standpoints. One of the most influential thinkers of the early part of the century was Christian Wolff (1679–1754). He had been expelled from Prussia by Frederick William I, but invited back by Frederick the Great who, as a young man, was much influenced by his writings. Also, as you will recall from Madame du Châtelet's interest in him (see the *Candide* section in *Studies*, I, pp.343–4), he made some impact in France too. It was very difficult for intellectuals not to get involved to some degree in religious debate. Lessing, as we shall see, became very heavily involved.

In the long run it was the development of German culture that was the most important feature of the Enlightenment in the German states. Britain, despite its seventeenth-century civil war, had a solid cultural heritage; France looked back to the brilliant age of Louis XIV; but the Thirty Years' War and its aftermath had left German culture at a low ebb; the achievements of medieval times and the Renaissance seemed far away.

There were two main tendencies in this revival of German culture. One was to look to foreign models, particularly for court entertainment in opera, ballet, drama and fine arts. In literature the main interest was in French literature – notably in the case of Frederick the Great. A firm move in this direction was made by Johann Christoph Gottsched (1700–66). Gottsched had left Königsberg to avoid military service, and settled in Leipzig. He wished to gain prestige for German culture, particularly in the theatre, and so took French classical plays as his models; he succeeded in getting them performed and wrote plays of this kind himself. He was later criticized by Lessing for his rigid and academic approach, but he had some success in his initial aim of raising standards.

The other trend was to develop an independent German culture which absorbed ideas from other cultures, particularly French and British, but did not merely copy them. Two Swiss academics, Bodmer and Breitinger, also had an early influence on literature in stressing sensibility rather than classical perfection. By the middle of the century there was a revival of German poetry. Klopstock's long epic poem *The Messiah* (1748–73) is often cited as an important landmark.

Though patronage inevitably played a considerable part in these absolutist states, the spread of middle-class culture was helped by the slow, but steady development of publishing and the growing number of periodicals. The hope of a real German culture was realized by the end of the century, not without difficulty, and in the face of much hostility or indifference to the watchwords of humanity, tolerance, and freedom. The hope had to be realized by independent writers, and the movement toward Enlightenment needed a leading architect. It was Lessing who played this vital role. From his life and work we get a good idea of the conditions and progress of Enlightenment in the German states. How did the son of a poor Protestant pastor come to be the leading figure of the German Enlightenment and the first great modern German writer? I suggest you now read the short account of Lessing's life and work which you will find in the Introduction to your text.

2 Gotthold Ephraim Lessing (1729–81)

Figure 1
Portrait of Lessing.
(Mansell Collection, London)

In his lifetime Lessing was admired by his friends and supporters, and reviled, yet often respected, by his opponents, as much for being the kind of man he was, as for what he wrote. 'We needed a man like Lessing', Goethe said later (in 1825; Eckermann, 1984).

By the time he wrote his last great work, *Nathan the Wise,* in 1778–9, Lessing was regarded as the foremost, and the most controversial, writer of the Enlightenment in Germany; he was one of its leading spokesmen and indisputably its greatest dramatist. His views were contested, but his integrity was unquestioned. Like Voltaire and Diderot he was never dull; like them he stirred things up. He attacked mercilessly and wittily views and attitudes which he thought were wrong-headed, but in his stubborn search for truth he was also looking for positive answers.

Lessing's polemical writings were often dramatic and written in a debating style – a kind of dialogue. His comedies put forward serious moral issues for debate. When, in 1778, he was prevented by censorship from publishing further writing on religious matters, he linked the two approaches by presenting his ideas on religious and ethical matters in the form of a play: *Nathan the Wise.*

I think you will find that the questions raised in *Nathan* are still live issues today, but we understand the play better if we study it in the context of the Enlightenment. The next two sections will explain Lessing's views on religion and his place in eighteenth-century drama.

3 Lessing and religion

ROBERT WILKINSON

Figure 2
Portrait of Eva Lessing.
(Archive für Kunst und
Geschichte)

The primary aim of this section is to set out the religious outlook at which Lessing had arrived when he wrote *Nathan the Wise*. In so doing, we will also examine, however briefly, some of his works not considered in the Introduction to the set text. A knowledge of Lessing's religious out-look is essential for a full understanding of the play which, as we shall see, takes its rise directly from his religious concerns. However, to determine precisely what the religious beliefs of the mature Lessing were is by no means a straightforward task. This subject has been the occasion for a debate which has continued unbroken since Lessing's death.

The reasons for the difficulty are not far to seek. A born controver-sialist who enjoyed combative debate, Lessing often championed a view simply because it had been attacked without good reason, and his doing so did not always imply that he himself adhered to it. Again, Lessing often had to be extremely circumspect in stating views to which he did incline, because in general they were unacceptable to the prevailing orthodox Lutheran institutions whose power he could not afford to ignore. As a result, his published remarks on religion are often deliber-ately ambiguous or imprecise, with the further consequence that his own positive convictions must be worked out by extrapolation from his various writings. Faced with this problem, even so formidable a commentator as the Danish philosopher Søren Kierkegaard (1813–55) had to admit to a degree of puzzlement:

> Has Lessing accepted Christianity or has he rejected it ... no-one could carry himself more circumspectly than Lessing, while achiev-ing the still more difficult task of keeping silent through speaking ... So difficult is it to approach Lessing on the religious side. (Kier-kegaard, 1941, pp.61, 66)

However, with the benefit of the work of Lessing scholars, it is possible to discern in his later works a particular point of view on religion, and this is set out below.

Before approaching this subject, however, two further general points concerning the character of Lessing's thought are appropriate. The first is that it is a mistake to seek in his writings a fully worked-out and finalized point of view. Partly, this is because he died before he might have achieved such a goal; but I would argue further that the production of a complete system is not a goal that interested him. The activity Less-ing valued most was inquiry or the pursuit of truth, quite as much as any truth thus gained. He wrote accurately of himself as follows:

> If God held in His right hand the whole of truth and in His left only the ever-living desire to seek the truth, but connected for me with the certainty of being permanently mistaken, and He said to me: choose! I would throw myself humbly on the left hand and say: Father, give! Pure truth is for You alone! (*Eine Duplik* (*A Rejoinder*, 1778) in Lachmann and Muncker, 1886–, vol.13, pp.23–4).

This attitude is closely related to the second general feature of Lessing's thought, its eclecticism. Lessing's key ideas are gathered from a number of sources: he took what he needed whence he found it, and in conse-quence cannot be summed up as a disciple of any particular school of thought. He pursued the line of inquiry wherever it led, and concluded that no one thinker or school had a monopoly of the truth. His friend, the philosopher and critic Johann Gottfried Herder (1744–1803), summed the matter up: 'He was not made to be an "-ist"' (from *Gott* (*God*, 1787); quoted in Bell, 1984, p.85). With these points in mind, we can now investigate Lessing's religious outlook and the way in which it informs *Nathan the Wise.*

Nathan the Wise is often described as the first 'drama of ideas' ('Ideendrama') in German literature. This description is meant to draw our attention to two major features of the play: firstly, that the way in which the characters behave, which generates the dramatic situations, is as much a result of the beliefs they hold as the emotions they feel; and secondly, that the play as a whole is designed to advocate a moral belief. As is the case with *Candide*, the main impulse to write *Nathan* arose from the impact on the author of a certain set of ideas; but whereas the main thrust of Voltaire's philosophical tale is the satirical destruction of a particular point of view (that of philosophical optimism), the main thrust of *Nathan* is constructive: Lessing is seeking to advocate a point of view in which he believed with passionate sincerity and which he wants us to accept.

The central belief advocated in *Nathan*, and which permeates every aspect of the play, is that of religious toleration. Like Recha, Lessing had a dream

> Where Christian, Jew and Muslim can unite
> As one – a dream that is so sweet (ll. 152–3)

Such a belief was not unusual amongst leading figures of the Enlightenment: for example, as we have seen (*Studies*, I, pp.71–2), Frederick the Great practised toleration within Prussia; and the Savoyard Priest in Rousseau's *Émile* (considered at more length in Part E)[1] speaks for the majority of the deists of the period when he inveighs against the cruelty of intolerance (Rousseau, 1966, p.382).

However, whilst all these figures agreed that religious toleration was wholly to be desired, the sets of reasons they had for holding this belief were somewhat different. In Frederick's case, the *chief* reason was undoubtedly that, by practising toleration, he thereby benefited the state, that is because he could make use of the skills of members of religious groups exiled from other European countries. Again, the atheists of the time advocated toleration: since for them, all theistic religious beliefs were false, these beliefs could not constitute a rational ground for persecution. The position of the deists, again summed up by the Savoyard Priest, is that, whilst most of the apparatus of dogma of the major religions is false, each contains a common core of religious truth and so each is, in its way, of value to humanity and so should be tolerated (cf., for example, Rousseau, 1966, p.381.)

In the remainder of this section, I will set out the reasons which Lessing had for his belief in religious toleration. To a limited degree, his views are like those of the deists, but the similarity, as we shall see, does not go very deep. Lessing had meditated on matters of religious belief all his life and, once he had obtained the post of Librarian at Wolfenbüttel, which freed him from the necessity of writing just to earn a living, this area of thought came to occupy his attention almost exclusively. His views about the nature of God and religious belief were centrally important to him, and a constant presence in his life. By the time he came to write

---

[1]   There is a substantial selection from Roussseau's *Émile* in *Texts*, II, pp.169–237; selections from *The Profession of Faith of a Savoyard Priest* appear on pp.205–10.

Nathan, he had arrived at a point of view on these matters which, whilst not unprecedented in the history of religious thought, is of a kind unusual in the West, and one which diverges from orthodox Christianity on a number of basic issues. Some of the following ideas are hinted at in the text of *Nathan*; others, by contrast, were carefully concealed by Lessing during his lifetime; but they all inform and illuminate the play, since they add up to the point of view from which it was written.

Lessing disagreed not only with orthodox Christian belief but also with deism at the most profound level, that is with regard to the nature of God. Though the deists rejected a good deal of orthodox theology, they did retain one central tenet of orthodoxy, namely that God is transcendent, that is God exists in some sense apart from and not subject to the limitations of his creation. On this view, God and his creation can meaningfully be said to be distinct. The Savoyard Priest takes the trouble to stress this point as he unfolds his deist credo: '... the supreme Intelligence which rules the world is no longer the world itself ... ' (Rousseau, 1966, p.346; my translation). Lessing, who in earlier years had accepted this form of deism, came to regard it as untenable. The God of the deists may have made the world in the beginning, but he had not intervened since and would not do so again. Such a God, Lessing thought, had no real role to play in any theology: there was no work left for the concept of a transcendent deist God to do. Convinced of the existence of God, Lessing's meditations on the complex problem of the nature of God's relation to the world led him to a form of the view that this relation is one of *immanence*. On this view, God and his creation cannot meaningfully be said to be distinct; rather, in most versions, God is conceived of as identical with the universe, this being the view called pantheism. (The logical difficulties involved in the articulation of this view are formidable, but it would not add greatly to our understanding of *Nathan* to go into them here.) This area of thought occupied Lessing intermittently for some years. Thus, in a fragment written in 1763, *Über die Wirklichkeit der Dinge ausser Gott* (*On the Reality of Things outside God*), Lessing can find no reason to deny that the ideas of real things which exist in the mind of God are identical with those things themselves. Much later, in one of the remarks made in conversation with the philosopher F.H. Jacobi (1743–1819) which can be taken to indicate one of Lessing's own convictions, he states:

> The orthodox concepts of the divinity are not for me; I cannot stand them. *Hen kai Pan*! [=One and All] I know naught else. (See below, *Note 1*)

'*Hen kai Pan*' is a Greek phrase reminiscent of the Neoplatonic philosophy of Plotinus or Porphyry (both roughly third century CE (AD)). It epitomizes the thesis that, underlying the apparent division of the universe into discrete phenomena is a divisionless oneness which is the only and ultimate reality. Applied, as in the case of Lessing, to theistic religious belief, this becomes a form of immanentism, since it entails that God and the creation are one and the same. That Lessing had moved some distance from both orthodoxy and the most widely accepted form of deism in this period is clear: to go beyond this and to try to find in his fragmentary remarks a more precise doctrine is to enter the realm of conjecture.

A second major point on which Lessing disagreed with both orthodox and deists concerns the doctrine of the freedom of the will. In orthodox theology, it is asserted that God has given human beings freedom of choice: we can do other than we do, and the future is open. This is taken to be a condition of moral responsibility, and is often offered as part of the answer to the problem of evil. Lessing, by contrast, accepted the view called determinism, that is that human beings have no freedom of choice, and that their belief that they do is an illusion. (This thought is, I think, behind Nathan's words at the end of Act V, Sc.4 (l. 3333), where he speaks of 'our deeds, which rarely are our deeds, oh God'.) Further, Lessing stated that he took pleasure in the notion that he had no freedom of choice: since God is benevolent, and so must order all things for the best, whatever we do, we do for the best. He makes this clear in some annotations he made to an edition of the *Philosophical Essays* of K.W. Jerusalem (the young man whose suicide gave Goethe the idea for the conclusion of *Werther*) which Lessing published in 1776. In his notes on Jerusalem's third essay, *On Freedom*, Lessing remarks:

> Compulsion and necessity, in accordance with which the idea of the best operates, are much more welcome to me than the bare ability to act in different ways under the same circumstances! I thank the Creator that I *must*: must do the *best*. (Lachmann and Muncker, 1886–, vol.12, p.298; quoted in Bell, 1984, p.87. This is a view that Lessing reiterated in conversation with Jacobi, see Vallée, 1988, p.89)

Hardly less startling is the way in which Lessing construes the process of historical change, which includes change in religious belief. Before he had become convinced of the truth of immanentism, he had been greatly influenced by the philosophical optimism of Leibniz, and his theory of history is a blend of the two philosophies personal to him. From Leibniz, Lessing retained the belief that, since God is benevolent and omnipotent, all must be for the best. From his own immanentism, Lessing took the belief that God and his creation are not distinct. From this latter view, it follows that all historical change is in some way an activity of God because God and the world are not separate; and from the Leibnizian premise, it follows that this change must always be for the best, that is it must be a *progress*, not just a process of change now progressive, now retrogressive. This view of history as the progressive activity of God is a further central belief in Lessing's mature religious outlook. It allows him to evaluate the major religions with which he was most concerned (Judaism, Christianity, and Islam); to give a new meaning to the idea of revelation; to separate what was inessential from what was essential in the major religions and to provide the grounding for his belief in religious toleration.

All three of the religions represented in *Nathan* (i.e. those mentioned above), involve the concept of a revelation superior to reason. In orthodox theology, a revelation is a direct communication between a transcendent God and a chosen person or group of persons, usually prophets. The content of the revelation is generally a truth or truths which, as has been indicated, human reason unaided could never discover and each revealed religion claims that its revelation is the only true one. Since Lessing denied the existence of a transcendent God, he had to reject this orthodox view, and, if he was to use the term 'revelation' at all, had to construe it in a quite unorthodox way. His view of revelation is one of the main themes of the only major work he published after *Nathan* (although at least half of it had been written earlier): this was *Die Erziehung des Menschengeschlechts* (*The Education of the Human Race*, 1780), the nearest we have to a complete statement of his religious credo.

As we have seen, Lessing construes historical change as a progress: the change is always, appearances notwithstanding, for the better. It must therefore follow that each major religion, as it arises, represents a change for the better, and it is this view which Lessing advances in *The Education of the Human Race*. He argues that revelation, which is to the human race what education is to the individual (Chadwick, 1956, p.82), has occurred in stages. The first major revelation God made He made to a particular race, the Jews, and to them He revealed the truth of monotheism (Chadwick, 1956, p.83ff.). When He judged it appropriate, He revealed to humankind, via Jesus and the writings of the New Testament, the doctrine of the immortality of the soul (Chadwick, 1956, p.85ff.). Thus both Judaism and Christianity embody valuable religious truths. To this view Lessing added two qualifications, both entirely unacceptable to the orthodox: (a) that what was revealed would in time have been discovered by unaided human reason: by revelation God simply speeded up the pace of progress (Chadwick, 1956, p.83; see below, *Note 2*, p.58); and (b) there is no reason to assume that there will not be further revelations, which will advance human understanding beyond the position embodied in Christianity (Chadwick, 1956, p.94). Indeed, it follows from the beliefs Lessing sets out in this work that Islam must be a more advanced form of religion than Christianity, since it came later (Muhammad lived from *c*.570 to *c*.632), though Lessing chooses not to make this implication explicit, for reasons of political prudence. The same prudence dictated that in *Nathan*, the three major religions are represented as vessels of truth of equivalent value, a view in tension with the progressive view of religious history in *The Education of the Human Race*.

The text of *The Education of the Human Race* also makes explicit a further major divergence from orthodoxy and deism on Lessing's part, in relation to the doctrine of the immortality of the soul. The orthodox view is that there will be an eternal afterlife of either reward or punishment in which the individual soul will remain recognizably individual. Lessing's views concerning the nature of God and historical change pushed him away from this view towards the ancient doctrine of metempsychosis, that is reincarnation or the transmigration of souls. As we have seen, and probably influenced in this respect by Leibniz, Lessing believed that history is a progress, and the goal of progress is perfection. Now one lifetime is manifestly too brief a period for each individual to proceed from ignorance to perfection, and therefore if, as Lessing believed, each individual is to attain perfection, more than one lifetime is necessary. Hence he remarks:

> ... But why should not every individual man have been present more than once in this world? ... Why should I not come back as often as I am capable of acquiring new skills? Do I bring away so much from one visit that it is perhaps not worth the trouble of coming again? (Chadwick, 1956, pp.97–8. See below, *Note 3*, p.58.)

As to whether we are reincarnated as humans or other creatures or on other worlds, Lessing is silent. However, the distance he has travelled from orthodoxy is clear.

A further consequence flows from Lessing's interpretation of the history of religion. Each revealed religion claims to be the true religion, and each has evolved, around the revelations and teachings of its founder(s) an elaborate theology, an organized 'church' and set forms of religious observance. From Lessing's premises, it follows that all claims to be *the* true and final religion, and any dogmas and practices founded on such claims, must be either false or inessential. This view provided Lessing with a principle by means of which he could discriminate between those core aspects of religion which were true and important, and those which constituted merely an inessential husk conditioned by local custom. There are indications that Lessing had begun to move towards a view of this kind in the early 1760s, though the essay in which he first recorded it, *Über die Entstehung der geoffenbarten Religion (On the Origin of Revealed Religion*, 1784), was not published until after his death:

> ... all positive and revealed religions are equally true and equally false ...
>
> ... The best revealed or positive religion is that which contains the fewest conventional additions to natural religion, and least hinders the good effects of natural religion ... (Chadwick, 1956, pp.104–5)

This view invites two comments in the present context. Firstly, the view that all revealed religions are equally valuable looks very like the standard deist position. Rousseau's Savoyard Priest arrives at an apparently quite similar conclusion (Rousseau, 1966, p.381). But it should be clear that the similarities are only verbal. What Lessing came to regard as natural religion (a form of immanentism) is very different from the transcendent deism Rousseau had in mind. Secondly, the thesis of the equivalent truth, and so value, of Christianity, Judaism and Islam, is an idea taken for granted in the parable of the rings at the heart of *Nathan the Wise* (III.7).

As we shall see presently, Lessing applied this distinction between the essential and inessential in religion at great length to Christianity. Before examining how he did so, we should note that he applied exactly the same test to the beliefs and practices of freemasonry. Indeed, so important was the subject to Lessing that he devoted an entire book to it: *Ernst und Falk: Gespräche für Freimaurer (Ernst and Falk: Dialogues for Freemasons*, 1778 and 1780). That Lessing should have been attracted to freemasonry is not surprising. Its avowed ideal of human brotherhood, and professed indifference (among its members) to race, religion or class, were deeply congenial to him, and these are the chief features of the picture of freemasonry built up in the first three Dialogues. These were researched before Lessing's initiation as a freemason in 1771, in Hamburg; the two final dialogues, published perhaps without his consent, from illicitly made copies of his manuscript, record his bitter disillusionment with the reality of the lodges. Instead of a membership drawn from all classes, he found only the well-heeled and upper class; instead of activity designed to bring about universal brotherhood, he found charlatans and mystagogues pursuing alchemical fantasies: the philosopher's stone and the elixir of life. Falk, the defender of freemasonry, replies by distinguishing the trappings and ceremonies of the lodge from the valuable core of masonic belief:

> ... a lodge bears the same relationship to Freemasonry that a Church does to the Faith. From the external prosperity of the Church there is nothing, absolutely nothing, to be deduced as regards the Faith of the members. Rather, there is a certain external prosperity in connection therewith, of which it would be a miracle if

> it could exist together with the true Faith. The two have never got
> on well together ... ('Fourth Conversation'; Cohen, 1896, p. 79)

Again, just as Lessing had suggested that Christianity might in time be
replaced by a more advanced religion, Falk speculates that the current
forms and trappings of freemasonry will be swept aside as history unfolds,
and the masonic spirit invested with a new form (Cohen, 1896, pp.79–
80).

Holding that all historical change, and in consequence all change
in religions, is progress (i.e. change for the better), it is not surprising
that Lessing should have felt it his duty to help the historical process
along as best he could, especially as it applied to the vitally important
matter of religion. There were two elements in the religious outlook of
his time which in Lessing's view were particularly outmoded or retrogressive and so needed to be cleared away by means of open, rational
debate. The first of these was the type of liberal theology advocated by a
group of thinkers referred to as neologians, for example J.A. Eberhard
(1738–1809) and J.S. Semler (1725–91). Their views were called 'neology'
because they were supposed to constitute a new, advanced theology. The
approach of these thinkers was to try to reason away the more extreme
orthodox doctrines, so making the remaining beliefs seem more attractive. Thus, for example, Eberhard in his *Neue Apologie des Sokrates* (*New
Apology for Socrates*, 1772) attacked the belief that the heathen, including
those who lived before Christ and so could not have become Christians,
would burn in hellfire everlasting. Lessing, who was a thorough-going
rationalist, regarded this approach as not only half-baked but also pernicious, since it made the aspects of orthodoxy left untouched seem
defensible, which in Lessing's view they were not. This leads directly to
Lessing's second major area of concern.

As we have seen, it follows from Lessing's general outlook that a
great deal of what was regarded by the orthodox as true and essential
Christianity was, to Lessing, mistaken sanctification of local custom and
accident. A huge edifice of dogma, he believed, much of it unnecessary
and impenetrably obscure, had been erected by the Church around the
true and very lucid teachings of Christ himself. (This idea lies behind the
Lay Brother's confession that he does not know the meaning of the theological concept of a sin against the Holy Ghost (*Nathan* IV.7, ll. 2965–
6ff.).) If religion was to progress, this mass of inessential dogma and
practice had to be swept aside. In order to demonstrate its inutility, Lessing considered, a public debate with the neologians and the representatives of Lutheran orthodoxy was needed, and this he set out, very
deliberately, to provoke.

Lessing had to hand an ideal text with which to initiate the hoped-
for debate. Just before his move to Wolfenbüttel, he had obtained (from
the family of the lately deceased author) the manuscript of *Apologie oder
Schutzschrift für die Vernünftigen Verehrer Gottes* (*An Apologia or Plea for the
Rational Worshippers of God*), an enormous work by Hermann Samuel Reimarus (1694–1768). Reimarus, a respected Biblical scholar, had worked
on this book in secret, from 1743 until his death. The secrecy is not surprising: the book contains an interpretation of the Bible from so extreme
a rationalist position that its power to shock survives to this day. Jesus is
portrayed, not as the son of God, but as an imprudent Jewish agitator
whose messianic dreams came to nothing; the Apostles are supposed to

have faked the Resurrection for political purposes, and so on. Granted the sheer size of the manuscript and the provocative nature of its contents, Lessing could not publish all of it, nor could he reveal the author's name since Reimarus' children, living in Hamburg, would have suffered obloquy and probably ostracism as a result. He therefore chose to publish anonymous fragments, claiming to have found them in the Wolfenbüttel library. The first extract was issued in 1774, to be followed by five more in 1777 and a final, much longer, piece in 1778. They are collectively referred to as the *Fragmente eines Ungenannten* (*Fragments of an Anonymous Author*). There can be no doubt that Lessing entered on this debate with a serious and high-minded purpose. As he says in one of the essays he wrote in the course of the argument, *Eine Duplik* (*A Rejoinder*, 1778), his aim is to serve God's purposes by 'clearing mud from Thy path' ('Schlamm Dir aus dem Wege räumen'): the 'mud' is the (to him) inessential and damaging part of Christianity.

The aspect of Lutheran orthodoxy which Lessing chose as his chief target was the doctrine of theopneusty (from *theos* = God, plus *pneuma* = breath), namely that every part of the Bible is the inspired Word of God, from which it follows that every Biblical statement is both true and essential to Christianity. Lessing thought that to be obliged to defend every word of the Bible opened Christianity to serious objections. For several generations, Biblical scholars had been amassing evidence of internal inconsistencies in the Bible, and Lessing's contrary view that only parts of the Bible are divinely inspired, the rest being straightforward history, would neutralize these objections, that is because they would be objections only against fallible, human historians.

The publication of the first, fairly innocuous, Reimarus fragment, *Von der Duldung der Deisten* (*On the Toleration of Deists*, 1774) produced no reaction from the orthodox party, and so in 1777 Lessing published five more, rather more contentious in content. For example, in the fifth of this set, *Die Auferstehungsgeschichte Jesu Christi* (*On the Resurrection Narrative*), Reimarus argues that the accounts of the Resurrection given by the Evangelists are inconsistent, and he concludes that, since they disagree over the details, this indicates their being disingenuous as to the central fact. These fragments did provoke a response. Two orthodox Lutherans, J.D. Schumann and J.H. Ress, wrote replies to Lessing, who in turn replied to them. (*A Rejoinder*, mentioned above, is addressed to Ress.) At this point, the man who was to be Lessing's chief opponent entered the controversy. He was Johann Melchior Goeze (1717–86), a Chief Lutheran Pastor in Hamburg. In 1777, Goeze published two newspaper articles attacking Lessing (Schumann and Ress had tried to answer the author of the fragments, but Goeze decided that Lessing himself was the appropriate target) and followed them with a series of pamphlets, with the general title, *Etwas Vorläufiges gegen des Herrn Hofraths Lessings mittelbare und unmittelbare feindselige Angriffe auf unsere allerheiligste Religion* (*Something Provisional against the Direct and Indirect Attacks of Hofrat Lessing on our most Holy Religion*, 1778).

Lessing's first reply to Goeze, couched in very moderate language, was *Eine Parabel* (*A Parable*, 1778). The parable tells of a King (God) who has a wonderful palace (his True Church), with many doors (i.e. it can be entered by means of many faiths). In the palace live Architects (priests of the major religions), each of whom believes he has the correct plan (the

Figure 3
*Engraving of Johann
Melchior Goeze (Herzog
August Bibliothek,
Wolfenbüttel)*

relevant scriptures) of the palace. So blinded are the Architects by their pride in seemingly knowing of the true plan that they think more of the plans than of the palace itself. When there is a (false) alarm that the palace is on fire, all they can think of is to save their own plans, and they flee with them. They have lost sight of the most important truth of all, that 'the most benign Wisdom fills the whole Palace, and that Beauty, Order and Blessedness alone spread themselves thence over the whole land' (Bernard, 1862, p.4). The message of this parable is much the same as that of the rings, that is each major faith, properly understood, is a valuable route to God. The parable also shows the continuing influence on Lessing of Leibniz: the image of God as the architect of a wonderful palace is taken from the latter's *Theodicy*, i, 78 (1710). (This image is also consonant with the masonic view of God as the Divine Architect.)

Before Lessing could publish *A Parable*, Goeze had issued a further attack in which Lessing is accused, in his notes on one of the Reimarus fragments, of announcing as if they were axioms (by which Goeze meant 'self-evident truths') certain highly contentious beliefs. Lessing's reply to this attack, *Axiomata* (1778), is a systematic defence of ten propositions which lie at the heart of the controversy. The main thrust of Lessing's argument is that there is a distinction to be drawn between the Bible on the one hand and true Christianity on the other. Lessing does not deny that the central truths of Christianity are expounded in the Bible, but asserts that the Bible contains much more which is neither the inspired Word of God nor essential to Christianity (*Axiomata*, I; Bernard, 1862, pp.23–5). Analogously, he draws a distinction between the letter and the spirit of the Bible, arguing that the letter is not the spirit, nor is the Bible identical with Christianity (*Axiomata*, III; Bernard, 1862, pp.29–30). It follows further that criticisms of the Bible are not necessarily criticisms of religion (*Axiomata* IV; Bernard, 1862, pp.30–2). Moreover, Christianity existed before any of its truths were written down; the truths existed before the Bible, and therefore they are not to be regarded as true because the Apostles wrote them down: the Apostles wrote them down because they are true (*Axiomata* V–IX; Bernard, 1862, pp.32–46). (Sittah upbraids Christians like the Patriarch for not believing this, *Nathan* II.1, ll. 869ff.)

This distinction between letter and spirit entailed more than Goeze could concede, and from this point on the controversy became increasingly acrimonious. Goeze was utterly sincere in his concern for the spiritual well-being of his congregation, and Lessing was adamant that his views were a force for progress. Neither side would budge, and as is often the case in such circumstances, positions became entrenched and tempers frayed. To say that the polemics which resulted are robust hardly conveys the unrestrained intensity of the debate. During the course of 1778, Lessing published eleven diatribes, collectively known as the *Anti-Goeze*. The Chief Pastor is accused of lying, barbarity, hypocrisy, intolerance and the like. The lofty aims with which Lessing initiated the controversy are gradually lost sight of in the heat of debate. With hindsight, it appears no bad thing that the orthodox party, unable to silence Lessing by argument, approached the Duke of Brunswick. The Duke ordered that all Lessing's future works be submitted to the censor – a regulation from which Lessing had secured exemption in February 1772 – and this brought the *Anti-Goeze* series to a halt at once. Lessing was furious.

He was not a man, however, to admit defeat easily, and it occurred to him that he could still write something which might advance the debate about religion in the direction he hoped for. The views put forward in *A Parable* and the *Axiomata* furnish rational grounds for religious toleration. The central thesis of these works is that each of the major revealed religions contains a kernel of truth of the greatest value and importance, and we should not be deflected from an appreciation of this by over-zealous adherence to the less important local forms of worship and 'church' organization. To persecute other human beings simply because they do not share our beliefs concerning the non-essential components of religion makes no sense, precisely because these *are* beliefs about what is non-essential. On the essential matters, the major revealed religions agree. Now a belief in toleration involves a recommendation as to behaviour, and behaviour is the substance of drama. Hence Lessing decided that he could cast the ethical viewpoint to which his theology tended in dramatic form, and the play which resulted was *Nathan the Wise*. It is not surprising that many have regarded this play as the twelfth *Anti-Goeze* polemic.

Nathan appeared in its completed form in 1779, and *The Education of the Human Race* in 1780. Lessing was by then exhausted and very ill. He died in Brunswick on 15th February 1781. With him was a young Jewish businessman, Alexander Daveson, whom he had rescued from prison and befriended. Daveson said that Lessing was resolute, calm and fully conscious until the last moment.

3.1 Notes to 'Lessing and religion'

Note 1

From Jacobi: *Über die Lehre des Spinoza in Briefen an den Herrn Moses Mendelssohn (On the Doctrine of Spinoza in Letters to Moses Mendelssohn*, 1785) translated in Vallée (1988, p.85). I must point out that, in arguing that Lessing had accepted a form of immanentism but that his remarks are too imprecise to allow one to say exactly which, I am putting forward one of many possible interpretations. The precise nature of Lessing's beliefs on this matter, and in particular the extent to which he had been influenced by the form of pantheism put forward by the great philosopher Baruch Spinoza (1632–77) is one of the most discussed issues in Lessing studies, and has been so since Jacobi and Mendelssohn disputed about it in the mid-1780s. Lessing has been variously interpreted as everything from a thoroughgoing Spinozist to someone who had only a passing interest in Spinoza. For a summary of views, see Vallée (1988, p.1). Vallée is following a much more detailed synopsis in J. Schneider (1952, pp. 7–15). Cf. also Georges Pons (1964, pp.428 ff.) and David Bell (1984, pp.85–93). The main documents in the Jacobi–Mendelssohn debate (from which Vallée translates key passages) are collected in H. Scholz (1916). The subject is too extensive for detailed consideration in the present context, important though it is. Lessing certainly studied Spinoza in some detail; but I would argue that his works give no real evidence for any view other than that, as is the case with his study of Leibniz, Lessing used Spinoza's philosophy chiefly as a stimulus to the formation of his own ideas.

Note 2

The difficulty of sorting out what Lessing believed is well illustrated by this point. The early sections of *The Education of the Human Race* do state the view that revealed truths merely speed up progress, rather than supplying truths in principle inaccessible to reason. Many scholars have rightly noted, however, that he appears to contradict himself in section 77 of this same work, where he writes: 'And why should not we too, by means of a religion whose historical truth, if you will, looks dubious, be led in a similar way to closer and better conceptions of the divine Being, of our own nature, of our relation to God, which human reason would never have reached on its own?' (Chadwick, 1956, p.95). Bell (1984, p.92) suggests that the apparent contradiction can be resolved if this latter proposition is regarded as a pragmatic recognition of the value of revelation in certain historical epochs when reason is comparatively undeveloped, rather than a theoretical remark on the relation of reason and revelation. A move of this kind is certainly needed if Lessing's consistency is to be saved.

Note 3

The doctrine of metempsychosis is also found or presupposed in one or two fragmentary writings by Lessing unpublished during his lifetime. The most interesting of these is *Dass mehr als fünf Sinne für den Menschen sein können* (*Whether Man might come to have more than Five Senses*, ?1780). In it, Lessing considers the idea that human perfection might be increased as a result of our coming to have more than five senses. The only way in which an individual might achieve this is on the presupposition of metempsychosis. It is worth noting that speculation about the possibility of senses other than the human ones is not confined to Lessing in our period. The idea is canvassed, for example, by Fontenelle in the *Entretiens sur la pluralité des mondes* (*Dialogues concerning the Plurality of Worlds*), 'Third Evening', and by Diderot in *Le Rêve de d'Alembert* (*D'Alembert's Dream*). (I owe this second point to my colleague Linda Walsh.)

4 Lessing and the theatre

By the time Lessing wrote *Nathan the Wise*, he had thirty years experience of the theatre, as playwright, theorist and critic, and considerable knowledge of actors and stage production.

His attack on the state of the German theatre was biting:

> Nobody, say the literary authorities, will deny that the German stage owes a great deal of its early improvements to Professor Gottsched. I am this Nobody. I deny it categorically. It would have been better, if Mr. Gottsched had never meddled with the theatre. His supposed improvements are either concerned with unimportant details or else make things much worse. (Lessing, 1759, No. 17)
>
> We have no theatre. We have no actors. We have no audience.
>
> What a gulf between the French and the Germans ... The French stage at least provides pleasure for a whole great capital; while in the German capitals the makeshift stages are ridiculed by the mob.
>
> But let us be honest about it ... If they look at our actors, what can these people offer them? People without education, without manners, without talent ... (Lessing, 1759, No. 81)

Figure 4
Wolfenbüttel. (Herzog August Bibliothek, Wolfenbüttel)

Lessing, as ever, makes his point forcibly. But there were changes in the course of the century. A number of companies, run by better educated actor-managers, did raise standards, perform good plays (notably Lessing's own) and were invited to perform at court theatres. By the 1770s, projects for prestigious court theatres, 'national theatres', were no longer so unrealistic.

Lessing had two aims. It was useless to demand improved standards of performance, if there were no good German plays to perform; hence his concern for so much of his life with the theory and practice of drama. Lessing said that Gottsched wanted to be:

> ... the creator of a new theatre. And what kind of new one? A Frenchified one, without considering whether this Frenchified theatre suited the German way of thinking or not. (Lessing, 1759, No. 17)

Gottsched's models were the great seventeenth-century French dramas of Corneille and Racine, and their eighteenth-century successors, above all Voltaire. In the French classical theatre, modelled on ancient Greek and Roman works, there were strict rules and conventions to follow: tragedy and comedy were separate *genres* and different rules applied to each; they should not be mixed. (Voltaire, for example, was particularly outraged by the gravedigger scene in *Hamlet.*) Tragedies had to be in verse, their subject matter had to come from history, mythology or the Bible, and the main characters had to be of noble rank; and for the sake of verisimilitude, the three 'unities' should be observed.[2] Comedies could be in verse or prose and could have a contemporary setting and characters from bourgeois or low life, as in Molière's plays. Voltaire was the most famous and successful of contemporary dramatists who wrote classical plays, but with a difference: though the form was strictly classical, the ideas were very much Enlightenment ideas of tolerance, religious scepticism and hostility to tyranny.

What was more suited to the Germans, according to Lessing?

> He [Gottsched] might have picked up from the old dramatic pieces of our own, which he banished, that we incline more to the taste of the English than to the French ... If the masterpieces of

---

[2] The 'unities' were: unity of time, the action on the stage should not represent more than twenty-four hours; unity of place, the stage set should represent one location only; unity of action, there should be no sub-plots.

Shakespeare had been translated for us Germans, I am absolutely
certain that the results would have been better than making us so
familiar with Corneille and Racine. (Lessing, 1759, No. 17)

Shakespeare was one model. Spanish drama was another, as Lessing was
particularly interested in Calderón. He was even more interested in ideas
on contemporary drama which were coming from England, but most of
all from France, in the work of Diderot. In the preface to his translation
of Diderot's plays and essays he said: '... since Aristotle, there is no more
truly philosophical spirit, who has been concerned with the theatre than
he' *Das Theater des Herrn Diderot* (*The Theatre of Mr. Diderot*, 1760).

Diderot believed that drama should be faithful to nature and truth.
It followed that there cannot be a rigid separation of tragedy and comedy, which are not separate in real life. If the audience is to believe in the
characters, they must be ordinary people in families, and shown in what
Diderot called their 'condition' – their occupation and status in society.
He made a case for a mixed *genre*, serious comedy. Like Lessing, Diderot
thought that drama has a moral purpose.

What this moral purpose is, and how it can be achieved, Lessing discussed in his essays in his *Hamburgische Dramaturgie* (*Hamburg Dramaturgy*,
1767). He goes back to Aristotle's *Poetics* and discusses Aristotle's idea that
the action of a tragedy arouses pity and fear in the spectator, and leads to
a purification of the emotions; but, according to Lessing, the fear is the
fear that the misfortunes we see may happen to ourselves: '... in a word
this fear is pity transferred to ourselves' (*Hamburg Dramaturgy*, 75). What
Aristotle described as catharsis Lessing saw as the capacity to learn from
the emotions which we experience in the theatre, the capacity, as he put
it, to '... transform our passions into virtuous qualities' (*Hamburg Dramaturgy*, 75). You will see how he puts this idea in *Nathan the Wise*.

Serious comedy was the kind of play which Lessing thought would
best achieve some of the moral aims which he had in mind.

There was one other aspect of eighteenth-century theatre which is
relevant to our study of *Nathan the Wise*. In classical plays and in opera there
was a taste for exotic settings (and indeed in literature too, as you might
judge from the section on *Candide* in *Studies*, I, pp.358–60). Voltaire had set
three plays in the Muslim world: *Zaïre* (first performed in 1732, on the
tragedy caused by religious differences), *Mahomet* (first performed in 1742,
a study of fanaticism and tyranny) and *The Ghebers* (1769, on tolerance).

In the 1760s and 1770s 'Turkish' operas, as they were called, were
popular (Wilson, 1984). These too were set in the Muslim world and in
many the story included the abduction of a Christian girl. Mozart's *Il Seraglio* is the best known of these and the later *Magic Flute* has an exotic setting too.

Lessing took some features of these different kinds of dramatic
work and re-combined them to make a new kind of play in his *Nathan the
Wise*. It is like a French classical tragedy in that it is in verse and has five
acts, but the plot is that of a traditional comedy; it has an exotic Eastern
setting, but with realistic characters; it is a family drama with a moral
message of the kind advocated by Diderot; and it is a play of ideas in
which the tone is light and there is some comedy.

5 *How* Nathan the Wise *came to be written*

In July 1778 the Duke of Brunswick imposed censorship on Lessing. He was forbidden to publish any more writings on religion. His reaction, expressed in a letter to Elise Reimarus (6 September 1778), was: 'I shall try and see whether I shall at least be able to preach freely from my old pulpit, the theatre'.

Nathan was to be the twelfth Anti-Goeze. In August 1778 he wrote to his brother Karl: 'Last night I had a rather crazy idea. Many years ago I sketched out a play, whose theme has some kind of analogy with the battle in which I am involved now. If you and Moses [Mendelssohn] think it is a good idea I shall have the thing printed on subscription and you can have the enclosed announcement printed ... In fact I should prefer the actual content of this play of mine, which is to be advertized, not to be known too soon; but if you or Moses want to know, look up in Boccaccio's *Decamerone*, Day I Novella III, the story of the Jew Melchisedech – I think I have found a very interesting episode there, which should make very good reading, and with it I certainly want to play a sharper trick on the theologians than I could with ten more "fragments"'.

Boccaccio's story is about the Jew Melchisedech, from whom the Sultan wants to get money by asking a trick question about whether the Christian, Muslim, or Jewish religion was the true one. Melchisedech tells the story of a costly ring which was handed down from father to son, until eventually one father had exact copies made, because he could not decide which of his three sons was his favourite. The Sultan takes the point and comes to a friendly agreement with the Jew.

Lessing's friends were expecting the play to be a bitterly satirical comedy, but Lessing wrote to his brother in October: 'It will be very far from being a satirical play, in which I leave the field of battle with scornful laughter. It will be as moving a play as I have ever written'.

The next surprise was that the play was to be in verse. In December he wrote to Karl: '... I haven't yet written to tell you that the play is in verse. You will probably be surprised to find that it is. But at least you needn't worry that it will take me longer to finish because of that. My prose has always taken me longer than verse. Yes, you will say, such verse! But let me say, I think it would be much worse, if it were much better'. Lessing meant that if he concentrated on a more strict verse form he could not include realistic conversation, word-play, and other dramatic effects.

The same month he wrote to his friend Ramler: '... I really didn't choose verse because it would sound more harmonious; but because I thought that the oriental tone which I have to introduce from time to time might have too striking an effect in prose'.

Lessing had drafted the play in prose and then put it into verse but preserving much of the style of language used in the prose version, and again surprised his friends by choosing to use blank verse, Shakespeare's verse form, which had only rarely been used in German up to that time. When Karl and Ramler read the manuscript they criticized the verse as often being 'incorrect'. Lessing did make some changes, but they began to appreciate that he was manipulating the verse freely to suit his dramatic purpose. This decision to use blank verse had a lasting effect on German drama: it became the verse form most often used in poetic dramas in German.

In May 1779 copies of the play were in circulation. Lessing was pessimistic about the chances of its being performed. Writing to Karl Lessing, 18 April 1779, he said: '... it will probably never happen. It is enough if it is read with interest and if, among a thousand readers, just one learns from it to doubt the evidence and the universality of his religion'.

The first readers, mainly Lessing's friends, thought that it was the best thing that he had ever done. In fact the play was first performed in 1783, two years after Lessing's death by the Döbbelin company in Berlin; and except during the Nazi period (1933–44), *Nathan* has been in the repertoire of the German theatre ever since.

6 Nathan the Wise

6.1 *What kind of a play is* Nathan the Wise*?*

A dramatic poem, a modern morality play, a serious comedy? It is all of these, but defies strict categorization. Lessing himself called it a dramatic poem and did not intend it to fit in with any one of the established forms of drama, though it has elements of most of them. It is a play of ideas, but not a philosophical dialogue in which A and B debate theoretical questions. The questions are certainly there, but we are invited to think about them in terms of real life. Lessing as a dramatist presents issues through clashes of personalities and situations. He chose as his setting Jerusalem in 1192, at the time of an armistice in the Crusades, when Jews, Christians and Muslims were all present in the city; this highlights issues which are also all too comprehensible to readers in the second half of the twentieth century. Lessing, as you will recall, intended to use this play as his pulpit; but remember too that he had been a debater all his life. Do not expect a straightforward homily.

6.2 *Reading the play*

How do we *read* a play? In an age when performances on the stage were infrequent, Lessing's contemporaries were used to doing this – and sometimes did so aloud. Now we have the advantage of being able to hear a recorded performance, whether on radio or cassette or television. *Nathan the Wise* follows accepted conventions in the way in which it is set out in print. The play is divided into five acts. Each act is divided into scenes which begin and end when any character enters or leaves the stage. The location of the scene is given, and there are a few stage directions. The action of the play takes place on a single day, there are no sub-plots, but there are a number of changes of scene, which defies one of the orthodox classical 'unities' (see footnote 2 above, p.59). The play is written in blank verse, unrhymed iambic pentameters. Lessing thought this form (explained more fully in the Part E poetry study, below) more suited to the German language than the French twelve-syllable rhymed alexandrine, more commonly used at the time. Each line is of comparable length (with five 'feet' and, normally, ten syllables); but in dialogue, where different parts of a line are spoken by different characters these are printed on separate lines. So much is obvious when you look at the text.

As in most classical plays, and in most plays of ideas, whether classical or not, (such as plays by Ibsen, Bernard Shaw and many plays by

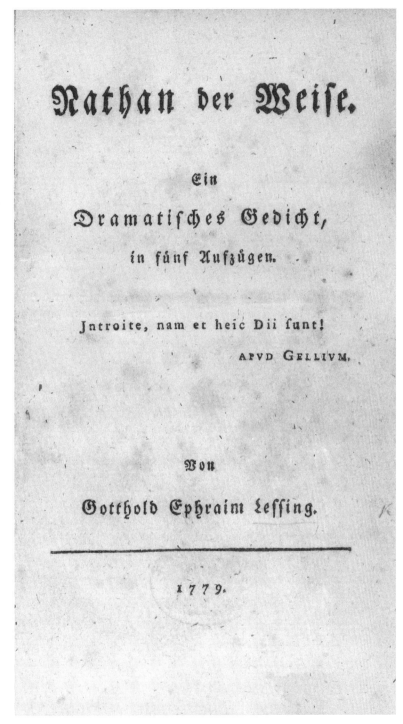

Figure 5
Title page of Nathan der Weise. *(British Library Board)*

Brecht) there is very little physical action on the stage in *Nathan*. The action is in what the characters say, and how they react to each other, and events which affect them are described or mentioned. As you follow their conversation you begin to build up a picture of the characters, their situation, their feelings, ideas and motives. If the dramatist is successful you are not aware immediately how this comes about, particularly if you are watching the play or listening to it. But when you are reading a play, it helps if you study the techniques which are being used. In a novel we may have descriptions, explanations and comments by the author which fill in the background for us. In a play the dramatist uses 'exposition', that is, uses the dialogue to tell us who the characters are, their circumstances and the setting of the action. So Nathan returns from a journey and has to be told what has happened in his absence; the political and religious situation in Jerusalem emerges from conversations between the Templar and the Lay Brother, Saladin and his sister, and so on. Almost as important is what we are *not* told; we are given only hints of something yet to be explained. You will find that this is carefully worked out in *Nathan* – the hints are 'planted' at strategic intervals.

The craft of the dramatist involves the creation of tensions, between people or between ideas, and the timing of these to create points of high tension or interest, in other words – drama. As *Nathan* is both a human drama and a play of ideas Lessing's timing of dramatic moments is adjusted to both. The core of the play, with the expression of its main ideas, is the parable of the three rings. This comes in the middle, vital to the drama, but in a scene which resolves rather than creates tensions. And at this point Lessing's exposition is still incomplete.

In *reading* the play, what is perhaps of most absorbing interest is not only the overt message of the parable, but all the other ideas and differing points of view which are put forward. We have to reflect about these and be alert to the fact that Lessing is presenting us with many questions as well as with some answers.

EXERCISE   I suggest that you listen to the performance of the play on cassette and follow the printed text at the same time. You may find that it helps to pause at the end of an act and make brief notes. As you do so, keep the following questions in mind.

1   What has *happened* by the end of each act?

2   What do we know about the characters and their situation?

3   What hints have we had that there are things which we do not yet know?

4   What *issues* have been raised (e.g. toleration, religious beliefs, moral behaviour, or other issues)?

5   Is there anything which you do not understand or think is not very clear?

The first three questions are about the 'exposition'. Some of your answers to 4 and 5 may come as you study the play in more detail.

DISCUSSION   The exposition. The play is constructed around the ring parable scenes (III.5–7). By the end of Act I we have met all the main characters (except Sittah), either on the stage or by hearing about them. Links have been made between them: Nathan, Recha and Daja with the Templar, the Templar with Saladin, and with the Patriarch through the Lay Brother, and

Nathan with Saladin through Al-Hafi. We have hints that there is a mystery concerning the origins of Recha and the Templar. We are made aware of the importance of religious affiliations and attitudes. We see various aspects of Christianity in Act I and Jewish-Christian-Muslim tensions in Act II. Yet we do not have all the background until Act IV, for it is only then that we fully understand Nathan's position, when he tells his tragic story to the Lay Brother. What Nathan learns then leads to the clearing up of the mysteries and to the ending of the play. In the last scene Lessing uses a traditional comic ending. Comedies through the ages (Greek, Roman, Shakespearian, seventeenth- and eighteenth-century French) often ended with a scene in which revelations about the character's true identity and situation resolve the problems. In *Nathan* the actual ending is a symbolic tableau. You will be able to see this at the end of TV11.

6.3   The parable of the three rings

EXERCISE   You should now re-read III.5–7 (Nathan and Saladin). How would you express in your own words the message of the story of the three rings?

DISCUSSION   The three brothers in the parable represent the three main religions of the Western world – Judaism, Christianity and Islam. Each believes that his own religion is the true one, because he has his father's assurance of it, that is, the truth has been *revealed* to him. Each ring *is* valuable, that is, each religion contains truth. There is no way of proving which religion is ultimately true. Disputes about this cannot settle the matter. The three can best demonstrate what they believe to be the truth of their own faith by behaving in such a way as to deserve love, and by keeping their belief in God. But the truth may emerge only in a very remote future.

What follows from this is that human beings should accept that they do not yet have full religious truth, and that they must continue their search for it. If there is no reliable proof of the truth of any faith, it follows too that toleration of other faiths is the only rational and humane course; and that human beings can best affirm their own belief by striving for the highest moral standards in their own behaviour.

Lessing made a significant addition to Boccaccio's version of the story of the three rings. In Boccaccio's story the ring was 'beautiful and costly'. In Nathan's version the ring 'had secret power to gain favour in the sight of God and humankind for anyone who wore it and who trusted in its power' (ll. 1915–18) What is important is not *possession* of the ring, but *trust*, belief, in its power and also, as the judge says, the way in which the possessor acts 'with gentleness, sincere good nature, charity and deepest devotion to God' (ll. 2046–7).

The relationship which Nathan establishes with Saladin is important to both the ideas and plot of the play.

EXERCISE   How does Lessing present Nathan and Saladin in III.5–7?

DISCUSSION   From the television and cassette performances you will be aware of the change of tone in these three scenes. Scene 5 shows a confrontation in which each man is assessing the other. Scene 6 prepares us for what follows. In Scene 7 we are taken out of the present into an oriental fairy tale which changes into a poetic parable; and the last part of the scene returns to the present and shows Nathan and Saladin becoming friends and returning to their immediate concerns. When Saladin and Nathan first meet, their respective roles are emphasized: Saladin is the powerful Sultan, Nathan the Jewish merchant. Saladin first calls Nathan 'Jew' (almost insultingly?), then 'the wise Nathan'. Nathan plays his merchant part, though his response to Saladin is not the expected one; he is neither fawning nor servile, not 'anxious, miserly and fearful' (ll. 1752–3), but composed and ironic, unintimidated by Saladin. Saladin changes his ground to put his trick question about the three religions. (We now understand that this is the 'snare', devised by Sittah, which she and Saladin talked about in Scene 4.) Saladin's tone, initially perhaps only partly sincere, makes the assumption that both are enlightened men in search of truth; and throughout the scene, when they debate, neither speaks from the point of view of a particular religion, Jewish or Muslim. Nathan's parable wins over Saladin completely. We have by now learned enough about Saladin to make this plausible, and the two end the scene as friends in mutual trust and confidence.

Lessing makes considerable demands on us in these scenes. The basic message is wonderfully simple, but there remains a lot to interpret and think about. It is worth looking at how Lessing sometimes concentrates quite complex ideas into a few words or images.

EXERCISE   What do you find either in Nathan's story of the three rings, or elsewhere in Scenes 5–7, which seem to you particularly relevant to what you have read in the preceding section about Lessing's own views on religion – especially in what Nathan says about truth, history and deception?

DISCUSSION   Truth. Following Saladin's question Nathan is cautious, even suspicious, as his monologue (Scene 6) shows, 'Is he truly searching for the truth at all' (l. 1877). And what is truth? Nathan is not easy to understand here. He seems to suggest that truth has many facets, when he uses his merchant's metaphor about coinage.

Ancient coinage may stand for traditional, perhaps fundamental, truth and 'new kinds of coin, valued by their stamp', might stand for the dogmas of organized religion with the suggestion that these may be superficial. Different interpretations are possible, and indeed have been made (for example, Demetz, 1966), and you may have made your own interpretation.

In the parable the precious stone in the ring is an opal, which can suggest light (enlightenment), but a changing light 'shot through with a hundred lovely colours' (l. 1914). Is this another hint that truth has many facets? You will recall that Lessing said in *The Education of the Human Race* that there is *some* truth in the different religions; and this is expressed, in another way, in the parable itself.

History. When Nathan has told his story, but before he gives the judge's verdict, Saladin challenges the fact that the three rings (religions) are indistinguishable. If you look at Nathan's reply he seems to concede that there are superficial differences, but wants to point out what they have in common: 'all are based on history, handed down or written' which we 'take on trust, on faith' (ll. 1975–7). For Nathan, history here seems to refer to traditional lore, rather than to what we should consider historical records or evidence, and the stress is on trust and faith. Lessing himself was sceptical about historical evidence, especially about the Bible as reliable evidence: some of it might be valid, some not; and as a foundation for religion, belief was more important than attempts at historical proof. Do you think that Nathan here leaves himself, Saladin and others, some justification for not abandoning their own beliefs?

Deception. Nathan says our people 'never have deceived us ...' (l. 1982) The word 'deceit' recurs. Were the brothers 'deceived deceivers'? Were they deceived by the originators of their religions and in their turn deceived others? The answer to potential controversies here, as the judge says, is for each to 'bring to light the power of the stone' in his own ring by the way in which he behaves. Deceit is avoided, if we all acknowledge that we are still at the stage of searching for the truth. 'Father give – pure truth is for You alone' in Lessing's own words (in the passage from *A Rejoinder*, quoted above, p.48). The parable has given a clear message, but it has raised questions too about the role of reason and feeling in religious and moral issues. You could think again here about what you find in Hume's *Dialogues concerning Natural Religion*. Nathan too contributes to the debate about whether reason alone can settle, prove or disprove truths of religion. Like Hume, Lessing leaves much still open to debate.

The parable has given an Enlightenment message in its stress on humanity, tolerance and openness of mind. The rest of the play shows us fallible characters with human problems, and raises many questions about the message in practice. Nathan and Saladin end by coming down to earth. They may talk about millenia, they may be firm about values, but life goes on.

Let us now look more closely at some scenes in the play where the themes of good deeds, toleration and religious belief are presented, in dramatic terms, with 'real' people in 'real' situations.

6.4 I.2, Nathan and Recha

EXERCISE What is Nathan aiming to teach Recha in this scene and how does he do it?

DISCUSSION Did you get a strong impression of the close and affectionate relationship between Nathan and Recha? Nathan's role in this scene is as father and teacher. He understands that in Recha '... heart and head must long have argued ...' (ll. 132–3); Recha's feelings are strong and true, but need to be balanced by reason and practical action. Half-humorously, sometimes directly, sometimes with images, Nathan guides her gently, but firmly, to accept this; first by dismissing what she imagines to be miracles in favour of real-life miracles – 'the greatest miracle is that those miracles which are both real and true can and do become so commonplace to us' (ll. 216–18). He shows first by argument, later by dramatizing the imagined plight of the Templar, how '... rapturous dreaming is much easier than doing good' (ll. 359–60). For Nathan good deeds are done in this world and for human beings.

6.5   II.5, *Nathan and the Templar*

The themes of good deeds, toleration and religious belief are all touched on in this scene.

EXERCISE   How does Lessing present the Templar's attitude at the beginning of the scene. In what way does it change and how is this shown?

DISCUSSION   The most spectacular good action in the play is the Templar's rescue of Recha from a burning house. Yet his own reaction to this is ambivalent. Was he spurred on by his training and his creed as a Templar, as he claims, or by a suicidal impulse, or was it a brave action by a good young man? The young Templar is in a difficult situation and in emotional confusion. (Lessing helps us to understand this best in the monologue in III.8.) He has lost his status as a Templar '... as Templar I am dead'. Being the only prisoner to be spared by Saladin seems a kind of betrayal and he is still at Saladin's mercy. He has some kind of anchor in clinging to a Templar's principles and standards. So he is very much on the defensive with Daja and the Lay Brother in Act I, and initially with Nathan in this scene. In his meeting with Nathan we see prejudice in action. The Templar's anti-semitism is expressed in an arrogant and offensive way – 'A richer Jew is not a better Jew to me'. Nathan does not take offence: he shows understanding of the young man's difficult position and acknowledges the importance to him of the obligations of the Templar's role. In expressing his own genuine emotion – a very quick, but important dramatic touch here – he changes the relationship of Christian versus Jew to that of two human beings. Nathan's initial judgement that the young man has a good heart is sound and he is able to find common ground: 'I know how all good people think' (l. 1273). Then, rather as he has given Recha a lesson about how charitable behaviour is better than dreaming, he gives a short lesson on tolerance and 'live and let live' to Curd, using his image of trees. The Templar asks Nathan as a Jew '... which people was the first to call itself the chosen people...' (ll. 1289–90), but he then acknowledges that Christian and Muslim also make '... this mad and pious claim' that their God alone is the true God. 'Here and now' in Jerusalem, he personally can see this in perspective. Nathan finds the right response. 'Are Jew and Christian, Jew and Christian first and human beings second?' (ll. 1310–11), and at this point Curd says 'We must be friends'. The scene shows a promising beginning to the conversion of the young Templar to enlightened views, but the change is not yet stable, as IV.7 and later scenes show. In fact Nathan has rather little success with the Templar.

6.6   IV.7, Nathan and the Lay Brother

Here we learn about the most important of Nathan's own good deeds.

EXERCISE   How is the scene constructed and what is the effect achieved by putting this scene quite late in the play?

DISCUSSION   The scene begins and ends with Nathan expressing his private thoughts – his wish to keep his daughter. Then comes the Lay Brother's revelation about Recha's origin, which is slightly humorous in tone, as the Brother, like Daja with the Templar, delays his revelation and increases Nathan's impatience with his long preamble. This contrasts with what follows, the totally serious tone of Nathan's own revelation. The last part of the scene returns to the present action and the prospect of the whole mystery at last being solved.

What is the effect of this scene? I think that it makes us change our view of what has gone before. Nathan is not merely a rich merchant in a comparatively safe position who can afford to be tolerant and wise. We realize that the story of the three rings is not based on theoretical wisdom, but is told by a man who has suffered cruelly, and who regained his faith and his capacity to do good only after a bitter struggle. Nathan can tell his story only to the Lay Brother, '... to you and to your simple piety' (ll. 3033–4). The simple, illiterate Lay Brother understands that love is more important than strict adherence to religious doctrine; 'Children at that age need love ... more than they need Christianity' (ll. 3014–16). In Act I we had his view of the Christian church, at least as it was represented by the Patriarch in twelfth-century Jerusalem; and his gentle, sincere faith makes a powerful indictment of it.

When the Lay Brother exclaims 'You are a Christian', Nathan replies: '... what makes me a Christian to you, makes you a Jew to me'; and perhaps we can see Nathan as like Job. He has 'argued bitterly with God' and then his reason is regained and he turns to action. His earlier lesson to Recha is now clear, and that of the ring parable even more so.

Nathan's tolerance and wisdom have developed out of his experience of a pogrom, and his story may be even more shocking to us now, with our knowledge of the Nazi extermination of millions of Jews, than it was in Lessing's day.

In the four scenes we have studied we have seen how Nathan affects other people. The characters in the play are far from being just mouthpieces for ideas or representatives of different religious standpoints. Let us look at them now in the light of the play as a whole and of its main themes.

6.7   *Characters and action*

You have had what I think you will agree is a very good interpretation in the performance which you have heard. In any drama, interpretations of personalities can of course vary, and in reading the text you may think that you find different possibilities.

What did Lessing intend his readers to think?

Is Nathan himself Lessing's mouthpiece? His contemporaries did not think so, although they saw Lessing's experience and ideas in every line of the play. Elise Reimarus, an old friend,[3] wrote in a letter on 3 June 1779: 'My hero is Lessing, it was he whom I read in the Templar, the Lay Brother, the Dervish and the Wise Man'. Later the critic, Friedrich Schlegel (1772–1829) wrote in *Über Lessing* (*Essay on Lessing*, 1797) 'Anyone who really understands *Nathan* knows Lessing', and he was referring to the play as a whole and not just to the character of Nathan himself. But we need to look at the character of Nathan first of all.

EXERCISE   What is your own view of the character of Nathan?

DISCUSSION   Perhaps no two people will entirely agree. It is a part for a great actor, and there can be different interpretations and emphases.

Nathan steps on to the stage as the play begins. This is a bold stroke for any dramatist; there is no build-up, no background, we see him at once in action and see other people's view of him. Nathan is firmly placed in his social position: family man, business man, Jew. He has to face stereotypes and prejudice; in his meetings with the Templar and Saladin we have seen how he starts from their preoccupation with religious affiliation and social position and tries to change it to a relationship in which they meet him as human beings. Yet we get frequent reminders of Nathan's merchant role and see him wishing to express gratitude with material rewards – gifts to Daja, money to the Lay Brother. He meets prejudice at home too. Daja speaks of his kindness, says 'there's none more honest and more generous than you', but he is aware of her reservations because he is a Jew, and because of something else, which he will not let her speak about.

We learn in the first minutes of the play that what Nathan cares most about is his daughter, Recha, and we learn how strong his feeling for her is. He wants her to share his concern for living in a real world, not a world of dreams. Yet he can take a humorous view (see ll. 274–316), and though his tone is light, he clearly enjoys presenting a case with 'all this subtlety', as Daja says, and teaching by argument about miracles and good actions. To Recha, and throughout the play, Nathan expresses a firm belief in God. You might like to consider when and how he does this, in the light of what you read previously about Lessing's view of the immanence of God.

When Al-Hafi bounds in we see Nathan with an old friend and the style changes to quick repartee. These two, who are both chess players, can rapidly take each other up on points which they both understand

---

[3]   And daughter of H.S. Reimarus, author of the 'Fragments', published by Lessing (see above, pp.54–5).

and agree about. Nathan responds to Al-Hafi's vehement exasperation and self-reproach with slightly amused sympathy but, you may think, with not enough concern.

Nathan is not always successful; after the initial rapport which is set up, he cannot influence the Templar's subsequent reactions and actions. Still less does he understand or influence Daja; he seems to take for granted that the kindly, slightly teasing tone which he uses with his worthy but tiresome house-keeper will go on avoiding trouble, but he seriously underestimates Daja's stubbornness.

Consider not only what Nathan says and does himself, but what others – Daja, Sittah, Al-Hafi, Recha, the Lay Brother, the Templar – think about him. He is seen as tolerant, generous, cultivated, shrewd, didactic, devious, irritating ... Nathan is not a saintly figure; in a sense he is a man who must continue to learn to assess his own feelings, and to face loss again, and to come to terms with it. He is not the equivalent of the judge in the ring parable, but undoubtedly and justifiably the most charismatic character, the dominant figure in the play. Lessing, I think, invites us to respect and admire him, but not to accept everything he says and does without question.

EXERCISE   What view have you formed of each of the other characters and how do they stand in relation to the themes of good deeds, toleration and religious belief?

DISCUSSION   The Templar seems the most complex character in the play, and the one who stirs up most of the action. He is in an ambiguous position. He might at least have been sure of his position as a Christian, but, as he says: 'In the promised land ... I've cast off many prejudices' (ll. 2133–4). He had hinted to Nathan that he had doubts, and is further shaken by meeting Nathan and Recha, who do not correspond at all with his own conventional view of Jews. To complicate matters, when he meets and talks to Recha, he at once feels love. So he says 'I don't want to understand what's going on within me' (ll. 2112–13). In modern terms, he is facing an identity crisis. For he is confused about his past too: fairy tales, perhaps childhood memories of his own mixed origins, 'my father's native skies'; so he must have some inkling of his background, though he is defensive and evasive about this to Nathan.

After his good deed in rescuing Recha the Templar gets very close to behaving badly. He is baffled and angry when his wish to marry Recha is greeted, not with joyous acceptance, but with questions about his family; he thinks that Nathan is refusing him Recha and refusing to be a substitute for the father he has lost. After Daja's revelation about Recha's birth, Curd reverts to his Templar role and approaches the Patriarch.

Saladin has more success in making an impression on the Templar, perhaps because both have an obscure sense that there is some bond between them. In IV.4, we have the first meeting of Christian and Muslim in the play. Saladin's calm tolerance – 'As Christian, Muslim – either (l. 2684). I've never wanted the same bark to grow on every tree' (l. 2688) – is opposed by the Templar's resentful return to all his old prejudices in his bitterness about Nathan 'This Jewish wolf in philosophical sheep's clothing' (l. 2781). Saladin, like Nathan, tries to teach the young man. He now uses 'Christian' as a word of reproach: 'Do not be a Christian just to spite a Jew or Muslim' (ll. 2802–3).

Saladin's reproach strikes home and in his next monologue (V.3) the Templar tries to examine himself and his motives.

> Is it that the Christian in me is
> More deeply rooted than the Jew in him? (ll. 3237–8)

> Perhaps I merited
> The scorn with which I was dismissed by Saladin. (ll. 3268–9)

But self-examination is followed by slightly defiant self-justification. He still wants to get his own way. He will act well in the end, after recovering from yet more shock: that Recha is his sister and that they are both of mixed Muslim and Christian descent. His dreams were more than dreams.

Things are really made very difficult for the Templar. In the world of religious and moral codes he is, temporarily at least, a displaced person. You may find him sympathetic or infuriating. In this serious comedy the issues are certainly serious, but there is comedy in the character of the Templar too.

Al-Hafi is a comic character who raises some of the most serious questions concerning good actions, in his case, about capricious autocratic philanthropy. 'Isn't it plain folly, when a hundred thousand people are oppressed, impoverished, despoiled, tortured, slaughtered, to play the philanthropist to individuals? … to simulate the Almighty's mercy' (ll. 480–84). This view of the capriciousness of fortune and power reminds us of the kind of world we see in *Candide*. He is a dervish, committed to following God in poverty, but tempted by the offer of power to do good. Doing good is not so easy in practice, as he so vehemently shows, not even with good intentions, or perhaps especially with good intentions. Nathan says: 'You must go back to your desert' (ll. 496–7). Al-Hafi chooses this as his personal solution to the problem of trying to cope with the troubles of the world, that is to opt out of the struggle (which you may think is the solution which Candide chooses too; and you may be reminded of the dervish in *Candide* and what *his* message was). Can someone like Al-Hafi really opt out?

> 'If he can't instantly decide to live
> Just for himself, he'll always be a slave to others.' (ll. 1506–8)

He does not intend to isolate himself, but to find better human beings: 'On the Ganges, only there are human beings' (l. 1492). It is partly a debate about quietism, and Lessing intended to continue it, for he wrote to his brother Karl on 15 January 1779 that he could add a kind of postscript called 'The Dervish' which '… will take up the threads of one episode of the play and bring it to an end'.

The Lay Brother, you may think, is another character who opts out. He has tried to dissociate himself from a corrupt and warring world, but has been sucked back into it from his life as a hermit. He is clearly a simple, good man, who has his own firm ideas about good and evil and about the sophistry which presents one as the other. Nathan for him is a Christian because Nathan has *acted* in a Christian way. Yet, unlike Nathan, the Lay Brother wants to withdraw again from the world and not make a positive contribution to humanity. Lessing presents the Lay Brother humorously and sympathetically. Do you think we are intended to reject this quietist view entirely?

From Recha on the other hand we get a very clear view of faith and works, reason and feeling. In her we see the results of Nathan's teaching: '... the seed of pure reason which he planted in my soul' (l. 1565); and Recha is tolerant of other views (though she may not approve them), as she has been brought up with no sectarian affiliations. But she speaks to Daja of devotedness to God, and this important phrase appears later in the judge's speech in the ring parable. But we don't, I think, see Recha just as an echo of Nathan. She has been taught to use her reason and she uses it; she can show understanding of other people (of Daja, for example); she shows sensibility, tact, even a little humour, in her first meeting with Curd. She is shown too as a young girl who can be overwhelmed by her feelings, but for whom feeling is a sound guide as well as reason. To Recha, Nathan is her true father; and her feeling for the Templar when they meet is sisterly affection not the romantic love which an audience would expect. The calm and rational tone of her reaction in III.2–3 effectively removes from the play any trace of a possible incest theme. Lessing re-inforces this by the marked contrast between Daja's effusive sentimentality and Recha's balanced common sense.

You will find that Pamina in *The Magic Flute* is another young woman who is equally firm about what is right and good, as is shown in her ringing cry (in the finale of Act I just before Sarastro's entrance) of 'die Wahrheit' (truth) as a response to a threatening situation.

Daja, 'good and evil as she is', has a view of good actions which also come from what she has been taught, but in her case she has a rigid, traditional Christian outlook (even the Templar is irritated by this). Yet this quite good-hearted woman, who is not too bright, finds that she has to use her own judgement. For years she has faced the problem that Nathan is good and kind, although as a Jew she should despise him, and a Jew who has brought up a Christian girl in no specific orthodox faith is in her view sinful. Nevertheless she does hesitate before telling the Templar about Recha's birth. She convinces herself that it is a good action, but is it calculated too to fit in with her own interests? Lessing uses Daja for comic effect, making full use of the comic device of her garrulousness, building up tension by failing to come to the point. Is this portrait of a conventional Christian a sympathetic one, do you think?

Of Sittah Recha says: 'she will be convinced simply by reason ... anyone who pleads a cause with reason always wins her over' (ll. 3564–7). Sittah's view of good actions is clear. She is kind, sympathetic within limits to her brother's effusive humanitarianism, but pragmatic. Are we to conclude that, if it is coupled with sound judgement, this may be no bad thing? Is Sittah tolerant? She makes some biting comments about Christians, and indeed about Jews, but in rather a detached way.

Two important characters, Saladin and the Patriarch, are in some ways unlike the rest.

6.8   The power and the glory

EXERCISE   In what ways do Saladin and the Patriarch differ from the other characters?

DISCUSSION   Both are based on historical personages. Both have power in public life. In the scenes with these two, we get references to the historical situation and a reminder of the machinations and conflicts in it, in contrast to any view we have of a fairy-tale Eastern world. Lessing did not aim to be historically accurate in portraying them. He wrote in his draft of the play: 'I have not attempted to keep to the timing of historical events which form the background to the play. I even changed some of the names if I wanted to. My references to actual events are merely intended to motivate the action of my play' (Lachmann and Muncker, 1886–, vol.3, p.491–2).

In 1751 Lessing had translated Voltaire's version of Saladin's life and character in his *Histoire des Croisades* (*History of the Crusades*). According to the legend, which seems to have had some basis, Saladin was generous, humane and tolerant to his opponents. Voltaire wrote: 'It is said that in his will he ordered equal sums to be given as alms to poor Mohammedans, Jews and Christians and that he wanted to make clear by this order that all men are brothers, and to help them. What must be asked is not what they believe, but what they need. He never persecuted anyone for his religion – he was a ruler, a man, and a philosopher' (Pomeau, 1964. Cf. also Gibbon's appreciative: 'The virtue of Saladin deserves our admiration and love' (Gibbon, 1980, vol.6, p.116).)

Lessing created his own complex character Saladin, and you may agree that it is by no means an idealized portrait. Dramatically, Saladin has the role of *deus ex machina*, as he has the political power to resolve conflicts. As a ruler he seems in the play to be not unlike the head of a small German state, such as Brunswick, manifestly not coping with financial chaos, but generous and impulsive rather than systematic in his patronage. Although an absolute monarch with powers of life and death over his subjects, he is apparently little concerned with politics. He is a man with a sincere belief in God: 'one coat, one sword, one horse, one God! what more do I need if I have as much as this?' (ll. 990–1), and is tolerant of others' beliefs; with a mature view of human nature, but not a realist like his sister; enlightened, but inconsistent, you may think. The historical, or legendary, Saladin's character is crucial to the ring parable scene. Thereafter, he plays the wise man and the fair judge and uses his rank and power to resolve the problems at the end of the play. Saladin's strong feeling (almost an obsession) for his dead brother Assad was invented by Lessing and has some significance in the play. Lessing uses one historical fact, that Saladin died in 1193; Saladin predicts that he will die soon: 'What has come over me so near my death?' (l. 3176). This could suggest that the reconciliation at the end of the play will not last.

If Heraklius, Patriarch of Jerusalem in the twelfth century had any good points, history has not recorded them. As Lessing's source, Marin's *History of Saladin*, shows (see Introduction to the set text, p.14, and Demetz, 1966, pp.176–7), Heraklius secured his position by murder, intrigue, greed and cruelty. Lessing himself said: '… in my play he is not nearly as bad as he appeared in history'. Inevitably the question was asked whether the Patriarch was supposed to portray Lessing's enemy, Chief Pastor Goeze. The Patriarch is the only bad character in the play. He has been set up as such in I.5, but when he appears on the stage he is a comic figure, a caricature unlike the other realistic characters. Lessing's technique changes; he uses comic devices of exaggeration and repetition which could remove the suspicion that a malevolent portrait of Goeze or his like was intended; although the main repetition is of the chilling 'The Jew shall burn'. Yet the Patriarch is a mouthpiece for some of the views of Lessing's opponents: support for revelation and against reason '... who then should care to use his reason to examine the authority of Him who first created reason?' (ll. 2486–9); hostility to the theatre '... it does not merit serious consideration. I would refer you to the theatre with it' (l. 2522); belief in eternal damnation (l. 2548); the danger to society inherent in questioning religion: 'All civil ties are loosened, torn apart, if people are allowed to have no faith at all' (ll. 2580–2). Lessing chose to make his villain a Christian prelate and then to mitigate it by making him a farcical figure, blatantly hypocritical, and also one who has limited power; he retreats hastily when he realizes that the Templar may have some influence with the Sultan. This scene was cut when the play was first presented in Vienna, and this has happened in recent times too in some areas where it was feared that it would give offence – as, perhaps, it was probably meant to do.

These two men of power draw attention, I think, to a question which is implicit in the play: should religion be a public or private matter?

6.9 *The brotherhood of man*

The most important word in the original German text of *Nathan the Wise* is *Mensch*, which means human being without distinction of sex, race or religion. 'Are Jew and Christian, Jew and Christian first and human beings second?' says Nathan and the Templar offers his hand in friendship. Friendship is an important theme in the play. Nathan and Al-Hafi are old friends; Saladin says to Nathan 'Be my friend'; and Saladin and the Templar express their friendship by shaking hands. In these cases friendship acknowledges that what they have in common is more important than their religious or racial differences. The basis for toleration is the friendship of two people who are human beings first.

Equally important is the relationship of brother and sister. It is Saladin's lasting affection for his long dead brother Assad which prompts him to spare the Templar's life. Indeed Assad is almost a character in the play. Saladin and Sittah have an easy, frank relationship. Sittah says to Recha: 'Call me Sittah – your friend – your sister'. Recha and Curd are found to be brother and sister, with a Christian mother and Muslim father, and Sittah and Saladin are their aunt and uncle. Recha in her own person brings together Jew, Christian and Muslim. All this seems comic, absurd, you may think, but comedy can make serious points.

The role of the father is emphasized in the play too: a father is the main character in the ring parable; Nathan is recognized as Recha's true father – 'Blood and blood alone can never make a father' (ll. 3662–3); and Saladin offers himself as Recha's father – 'Accept me as your father

...' (l. 3669); some of the Templar's problems arise from his uncertainty about his own father.

The plot of the play is concerned with family relationships, but in the end their true basis is shown to be in human relations rather than in blood ties, important though these may be. Blood, the blood of the religious wars, is rejected in favour of the brotherhood of man – the sort of human brotherhood which Lessing had hoped to find in freemasonry, and which appears again as an ideal in *The Magic Flute*. Humanity comes first. The comic dénouement of the play is a symbolic representation of this.

6.10   *Happy ending*

'*Nathan the Wise* can be called the twelfth Anti-Goeze. There is no thunder and lightening in it, rather it arches like a rainbow in a pure glow of light after the storm', said Erich Schmidt in his biography *Lessing* (Schmidt, 1899, vol.2, p.321).

In using 'his old pulpit, the theatre', why did Lessing choose to write a play which has many features of a comedy? Perhaps, I think, because a play with the theme of tolerance can *be* tolerant, if it looks with gentle amusement at the failings and idiosyncrasies of people who are basically, or potentially, good. A detached view in a kind of fairy-tale world, which can be relevant in all times and places, should encourage a balanced judgement of the issues. A comic plot meshes together people and ideas in a fine dramatic structure with a hopeful conclusion.

7   *Lessing and the Enlightenment*

You will recall that Diderot said that the *Encyclopédie* should concern itself with human beings: 'why not give man the same place in our work as he has in the universe?' (*Texts*, I, p.8). Lessing's religion of humanity embodies many Englightenment views like this. 'Kein Mensch muss müssen' (No one must must) is one of the best known lines in *Nathan the Wise*, but it is difficult to express succinctly in English. *Mensch*, as we have seen, means human being, man and woman, with human qualities and human dignity. So there must be freedom of thought and expression, and toleration of differences in beliefs and behaviour. To try to force conformity of belief onto free human beings is an infringement of their dignity, at least so far as matters of conscience are concerned; and moreover such forcing of one's beliefs on to others tends to stifle the use of reason, and that is the road to 'benighted superstition'.

Kant's essay *What is Enlightenment?* will be discussed in the conclusion to the course. Lessing, like Kant, saw enlightenment as a process of growing up, ('emergence from man's self-incurred immaturity', in Kant's words), of development of the human capacity for reasoning and moral progress. For Lessing moral progress was closely linked with a continuing search for truth about human beings' relations to God and the universe. He was in agreement with many Enlightenment thinkers in his rejection of orthodox Christian doctrines and of adherence to the letter of the Bible, but differed from other Enlightenment deists in his view of an immanent God.

Like Voltaire he saw drama as a forum for debate; like all those contemporaries who were influenced by classical assumptions about art, and like Diderot in particular, he saw the arts as having a moral aim in contributing to human development (and so used *Nathan* as his pulpit). Like Diderot too, and to some extent like Rousseau, he saw the importance of feeling as well as reason. Lessing's polemical writings are the equivalent of Voltaire's satirical works; and like Voltaire and other *philosophes* he suffered from the risks he took. Lessing in all his works, and not least in *Nathan*, is most representative of the Enlightenment in his way of constantly asking questions, constantly exploring, and refusing to give facile or definitive answers. 'The spirit of enquiry meant everything to him' wrote Moses Mendelssohn in 1785 (quoted in Steinmetz, 1969). *Nathan the Wise* demonstrates Lessing's refusal to give up the fight against the enemies of enlightenment.

8 Nathan *and posterity*

Nathan the Wise has been a disturbing work for over 200 years. The ways in which it has been received and interpreted both by readers and in the theatre tell us a lot about the *mores* and climate of opinion in different epochs. Lessing's friends, his enlightened readers, expressed their admiration and delight. Moses Mendelssohn: 'He could not rise higher without going into realms where our mortal eyes could not follow him'. Elise Reimarus: 'No drink of water swallowed in a desert can ever have given as much refreshment as this play gave us'. A less partisan early review said in a Hamburg newspaper in 1779: 'Nathan as a drama is entirely worthy of Lessing and his reputation'.

Figure 6
Engraving of Moses Mendelssohn (Ullstein Bilderdienst)

Goethe was reported to have called the play in 1780: 'a supreme masterpiece of human art'. But Lessing's friend, the poet Gleim, wrote on 22 July 1779: 'I have heard a large number of stupid and waspish comments: to make the best of men a Jew and the worst a Christian – what a crime!'; and the theological faculty of the University of Leipzig complained to the Elector of Saxony: '... there are some passages offensive to the Christian religion, and although they are spoken by Jewish or Turkish characters, they could have a harmful effect on those who read them, especially young people'. The role of the Patriarch was cut for the first performance in Munich and re-written for a performance in Vienna.

Undoubtedly the play had a great influence on German drama, and the blank verse used by Lessing became the customary form for verse drama in German. The German Romantic writers were ambivalent in their reactions. Friedrich Schlegel wrote in his essay *On Lessing* (1797–1801) 'surely immortality is deserved, or rather has already been earned by a work which is admired and loved by all, but which gets different reactions and interpretations from everyone.' He himself elsewhere called it 'an introduction to the drama of the higher cynicism'. *Nathan* was soon translated into French, and into English in 1790 by William Taylor of Norwich.

From the first, the play tended to arouse hostility and suspicion in orthodox Protestants and Catholics, and in orthodox Jews too. The message of tolerance made less impact later in the nineteenth century in Germany, as *Nathan* was a work which had little appeal to Prussian militarism and latent anti-semitism (though it still appealed to liberal thinkers).

At the beginning of the twentieth century the philosopher, Wilhelm Dilthey, expressed a return to ideas of tolerance and humanity: 'Every positive religion is geographically and culturally based and limited by this fact; this divides as well as unites. So human solidarity, general love of mankind, can develop only on the ground of free humanity' (Dilthey, 1906, p.426).

During the Weimar Republic after the First World War *Nathan* was again appreciated for its worth and its message. During the Nazi regime, with its policy of anti-semitism and of extermination of the Jews, the play was banned as a text in schools and performances were forbidden.

In 1945 *Nathan the Wise* was the first play to be presented when theatres all over Germany re-opened after the war. There were twenty-nine productions in the 1945/6 season. In the light of the Holocaust and the need to create a new and humane German state, *Nathan* was the first choice of play, both in East and West Germany. There were still some areas in West Germany where the Christian churches found the issues sensitive and the character of the Patriarch caused embarrassment. After 1945/6 the play has still been regularly presented – on average about seven major productions a year (Dessau, 1986, p.280–2).

In 1975 a reviewer, Manfred von der Milwe, wrote: 'In the Middle East Jews and Muslims are fighting and in the Western and Eastern blocs prejudices between Christians and Jews are far from having disappeared. In this context *Nathan* has a disconcerting actuality' (quoted in Dessau, 1986, p.236). More than a decade later the play is as relevant as ever.

References

Bell, D. (1984) *Spinoza in Germany from 1670 to the Age of Goethe*, Institute of Germanic Studies, University of London, London.

Bernard, H.H. (trans.) (1862) *Cambridge Free Thoughts and Letters on Bibliography*, Trübner & Co, London.

Chadwick, H. (ed. and trans.) (1956) *Lessing's Theological Writings*, A. & C. Black, London.

Cohen, A. (trans.) (1896) *Lessing's Masonic Dialogues (Ernst and Falk)*, Trübner and Co., London.

Demetz, P. (1966) *Nathan der Weise: Dichtung und Wirklichkeit (Nathan the Wise: Poetry and Reality)*, Ullstein, Frankfurt am Main.

Dessau, B. (1986) *Nathans Rückkehr (Nathan's Return)*, Peter Lang, Frankfurt am Main.

Dilthey, W. (1907) *Das Erlebnis und die Dichtung (Experience and Poetry)*, Leipzig, Leipzig.

Eckermann, J.P. (1984) *Gespräche mit Goethe in den letzten Jahren seines Lebens (Conversations with Goethe in the Last Years of his Life*, 1825), C.H. Beck, München.

Gibbon, E. (1980) *Decline and Fall of the Roman Empire*, vol.6, Everyman, London.

Kierkegaard, S. (1941) *Concluding Unscientific Postscript* (1846), translated by D.F. Swenson and W. Lowrie, Princeton University Press, Princeton N.J.

Lachmann, K. and Muncker, F. (eds) (1886–1924) Lessing: *Sämtliche Schriften (Complete Writings)*, 23 vols, 3rd edn, Göschen, Stuttgart and Leipzig. (Unless otherwise stated, quotations from Lessing's writings and corrspondence have been taken from this edition and translated by the authors of this study.)

Lessing, G.E. (1759) *Briefe, die neueste Litteratur betreffend (Letters about Modern Literature)*, Friedrich Nicolai, Berlin.

Mendelssohn, M. (1785) *Morgenstunden oder Vorlesungen über das Dasein Gottes (Morning Hours or Lectures on the Existence of God)* in Steinmetz (1969).

Pomeau, R. (ed.) (1964) Voltaire's *Essai sur les moeurs* (*Essay on Customs*, 1756), ch.56, Garnier, Paris.

Pons, G. (1964) *Gotthold Ephraim Lessing et le Christianisme* (*Lessing and Christianity*), Marcel Didier, Paris.

Rousseau, J-J. (1966) *Émile*, Classiques Garnier, Paris.

Schmidt, E. (1899) *Lessing*, Weidmannsche Buchhandlung, Berlin.

Schneider, J. (1952) *Lessings Stellung zur Theologie vor der Herausgabe der Wolfenbütteler Fragmente* (*Lessing's Theological Standpoint prior to the Editing of the Wolfenbüttel Fragments*), Gravenhage.

Scholz, H. (1916) *Die Hauptschriften zum Pantheismusstreit zwischen Jacobi und Mendelssohn* (*The Chief Documents relative to the Pantheism Debate between Jacobi and Mendelssohn*), Berlin.

Steinmetz, H. (ed.) (1969) *Lessing – ein unpoetischer Dichter. Dokumente aus drei Jahrhunderten zur Wirkungsgeschichte Lessings in Deutschland* (*Lessing – an unpoetic poet. Documents from three centuries on Lessing's reception in Germany*) Dokument 35, Athenäum, Frankfurt am Main.

Vallée, G. (1988) *The Spinoza Conversations between Lessing and Jacobi*, University Press of America, Lanham.

Wilson, W.D. (1984) *Humanität und Kreuzzugsideologien 1780: die 'Türkenoper' im 18 Jahrhundert und das Rettungsmotiv in Wielands* Oberon, *Lessings* Nathan *und Goethes* Iphigenie (*Humanity and Crusade Ideologies 1780: the 'Turkish Opera' in the Eighteenth Century and the Rescue Theme in Wieland's* Oberon, *Lessing's* Nathan *and Goethe's* Iphigenie), Canadian Studies in German Language and Literature, Peter Lang, Frankfurt am Main.

10 Further reading

Lessing's works

Göpfert, H.G. (ed.) (1971–79) *Gotthold Ephraim Lessing: Werke*, 8 vols, Carl Hanser Verlag, Munich.

Lachmann, K. and Muncker, F. (1886–1924). (See References above for full details.)

English translations of Lessing's works

Little is currently available. Please note that some works below are no longer in print.

Cohen, A. (1896). (See References above for full details.)

Dvoretzky, E. (trans.) (1969) *Emilia Galotti* in *Five German Tragedies*, Allen & Unwin, London.

Lessing, G.E. (1930) *Laocöon, Nathan the Wise and Minna von Barnhelm*, Everyman, London.

Vallée, G. (1988). (See References above for full details.)

Voysey, C. (trans.) (1879) *Fragments from Reimarus*, Williams and Norgate, London and Edinburgh.

Biography

Hildebrandt, D. (1979) *Lessing. Biographie einer Emanizipation* (*Lessing. Biography of an Emancipation*), Carl Hanser Verlag, Munich. (This is a lively modern biography, also available in a paperback edition: (1990) *Lessing. Eine Biographie*, Rowohlt Taschenausgabe, Hamburg.)

Schmidt, E. (1882–92) *Lessing. Geschichte seines Lebens und seiner Schriften*, (*Lessing. A History of his Life and Works*), 2 vols, Weidmannsche Buchhandlung, Berlin. (This is still one of the most comprehensive biographies.)

Studies in English

Altmann, A. (1973) *Moses Mendelssohn. A Biographical Study*, Routledge & Kegan Paul, London.

Bell, D. (1984). (See References above for full details.)

Brown, F.A. (1971) *Gotthold Ephraim Lessing*, Twayne Publishers, New York.

Bruford, W.H. (1935) *Germany in the Eighteenth Century. The Social Background of the Literary Revival*, Cambridge University Press, Cambridge.

Bruford, W.H. (1950) *Theatre, Drama and Audience in Goethe's Germany*, Routledge & Kegan Paul, London.

Garland, H.B. (1962) *Lessing, the Founder of Modern German Literature*, Macmillan, London.

Lamport, F.J. (1981) *Lessing and the Drama*, Clarendon Press, Oxford.

Mozart's The Magic Flute

Prepared for the Course Team by
Robert Philip

Contents

Mozart's **The Magic Flute** *(Study weeks 22-23)*

Studies/Texts	Radio	TV	AC	Set books
Studies, II	–	TV12	AC1629 (grey)	–
Texts, II	–	–	AC1630 (grey)	–
–	–	–	AC1631 (grey)	–

The main purpose of this essay is to introduce *The Magic Flute* to you as a superb piece of music, and as a dramatic work of the Enlightenment. You will not be asked to deal with the technicalities of Mozart's music. Many of the ideas in it can be understood without analysis of the music itself, though this essay is also intended to help you to think about how Mozart uses music to make dramatic points.

Together with this essay, you have a recording of the opera on two audio-cassettes, AC1629 and 1630 (grey), two sections of teaching material and some supplementary pieces of music on part of a third cassette, AC1631 (grey), and the libretto (words) of the opera in your *Texts*, II. You will be asked to turn to these different elements as you read through the study. TV12, '*The Magic Flute*', consists of a section of the opera performed in an eighteenth-century theatre: it is your only opportunity within the teaching material to experience *The Magic Flute* in staged performance.

The opera consists of alternating sections of sung and spoken text, and on the cassettes it is performed in the original German. But you do not need to be able to understand German in order to follow it. The text is printed with the German words on the left and the English translation on the right. Singing generally proceeds more slowly than speech, so you should be able to follow the parallel text without too much difficulty. If you find the spoken sections a problem, you can simply read the English translation, and wait for the next sung section.

Mozart's The Magic Flute

1 Introduction

The Magic Flute (*Die Zauberflöte*) was written in the last year of Mozart's life, 1791, and first performed at the Freihaus Theatre, on the outskirts of Vienna, in September of that year. By November 1792 it was being performed for the hundredth time. Mozart died only nine weeks after the première, at the age of 35, but already at an early performance he was able to report that several numbers were encored as usual, adding, '... what always gives me the most pleasure is the *silent approval*. You can tell that this opera is becoming more and more esteemed' (letter to his wife, 7–8 October 1791, Anderson, 1985, p.967).

Figure 7
Unfinished portrait of Mozart
by Josef Lange 1789–90.
(Internationale Stiftung
Mozarteum, Salzburg)

Although Mozart was still receiving a court salary in 1791, he was not employed as an opera composer, and his music was not in favour at court. His old patron, the Emperor Joseph II, had died the previous year, and the new emperor, Leopold II, did not like Mozart's music and never commissioned an opera from him (though whether the principal court composer, Antonio Salieri, had anything to do with this is the stuff of fiction). No doubt it was partly for this reason that Mozart accepted a commission to write an opera for a temporary theatre which had been erected in a courtyard of the Freihaus, a large complex of dwellings and workshops in a Viennese suburb. The proprietor of the theatre was Emanuel Schikaneder.

Schikaneder himself wrote the libretto of *The Magic Flute*, or at least the major part of it, and played the role of Papageno the bird-catcher. Until recently, it was fashionable to regard his libretto as incoherent nonsense, and Schikaneder himself as a man of no artistic importance. But fashions change, and it is now possible to find writers who regard the libretto as a brilliant piece of work, and its author as something approaching a genius. You will have ample opportunity to reach your own conclusion as you work through the opera. Whatever the merits of his libretto, Schikaneder was certainly a remarkable figure. He was an all-round man of the theatre – actor, singer, author, composer and impresario. He was renowned as an actor of Shakespeare (performed in German, of course); when he appeared as Hamlet at the Munich Court Theatre in 1777, he was required to encore the final scene. At that time Schikaneder was running a touring company, and it was during a season in Salzburg in 1780 that he and Mozart first met.

What brought Mozart and Schikaneder together as collaborators eleven years later was the rise of the *Singspiel*, a type of popular musical play in German (unlike opera, which was generally in Italian). The singspiel had developed out of the English ballad opera, of which the first and most famous was *The Beggar's Opera*. By the 1780s singspiel had attracted imperial patronage with the founding of the German National Singspiel Company by the Emperor Joseph II. Mozart wrote one very successful singspiel for this company, *Die Entführung aus dem Serail* (*The Abduction from the Seraglio*). Schikaneder's company at the Freihaus Theatre in Vienna specialized in singspiels and other popular plays in German, often in Viennese dialect, with magical and exotic themes, and with spectacular transformations which used elaborate stage machinery. You will have an opportunity to see eighteenth-century stage machinery in action in TV12, which shows an extract from a production of *The Magic Flute* at the Drottningholm Court Theatre near Stockholm, built in 1766. *The Magic Flute* made full use of the Freihaus Theatre's capabilities, as the libretto makes clear, as well as incorporating magical and exotic elements. It does not contain Viennese dialect, but one could certainly imagine the character of Papageno being played by Schikaneder at the first performances in a broad Viennese accent. *The Magic Flute* was announced as a 'Grand Opera', then meaning simply big and elaborate – the term took on a more specific meaning in the nineteenth century. Certainly, the scale and seriousness of Mozart's music is far greater than in singspiels of the time (even greater than in *Die Entführung aus dem Serail*, which we also now think of as an opera). It is really a hybrid work, an opera in scale, but preserving the spoken dialogue, the elaborate trappings, and the popular appeal of the singspiel.

There was one other interest which Mozart and Schikaneder had in common, and which is relevant to *The Magic Flute*, and that is freemasonry, which has already been discussed briefly by Robert Wilkinson in the Part D Introduction, and in the section on 'Lessing and Religion' in the Lessing study. Both Mozart and Schikaneder were masons. So too were some of the most exalted members of the Austro-Hungarian aristocracy, including Haydn's patron, Prince Nicolaus Esterhazy. However, freemasonry was under official suspicion in Austria by the early 1790s. Many of the leaders of the French and American Revolutions were masons, and the new emperor, Leopold II, saw freemasonry in Austria as potentially dangerous. Mozart was a dedicated member of a Viennese lodge, and had many friends who were masons. Some of them belonged to a particularly radical order called the Illuminati, which had originated in Bavaria in the 1770s. One member of the Illuminati, Ignaz von Born, a scientist and writer, became famous as the master of a Viennese masonic lodge which attracted many of the leading intellects of the day. Born is widely considered to have been the most likely model for the character of Sarastro in *The Magic Flute*.

The founder of the Illuminati, Adam Weishaupt, was steeped in the writings of the French *philosophes*, and he intended, by attracting men of learning and social influence to his cause, to transform society into a 'masterpiece of reason, and thus, to attain the highest perfection in the art of government' (Nettl, 1957, p.9). The reaction of rulers to the secret circulation of such ideas in the years before and after the French Revolution was predictable. You have already seen evidence of Catherine the Great's increasingly hostile attitude to freemasonry, and her imprisonment of Novikóv in 1792 (*Studies*, I, pp.92–3). Secret societies were banned in Bavaria in 1784; in Austria, where the emperors Joseph II and his successor Leopold II remained tolerant for a time, masonic lodges were finally disbanded in 1795, three years after the first production of *The Magic Flute*. However, despite his friends in the Illuminati, there is no evidence that Mozart's interest in freemasonry was primarily political or revolutionary. Masonic elements in *The Magic Flute*, together with clues in his letters, suggest that he was primarily attracted to its mysticism, and to its emphasis on tolerance and brotherhood. *The Magic Flute* is not directly about freemasonry, but it contains many oblique references to its principles and practices. Writers have disagreed about the importance of these references, and about the reasons why Schikaneder and Mozart decided to include them. H. C. Robbins Landon argues convincingly that the opera was intended as a symbolic defence of freemasonry against the attacks of those who saw it as potentially dangerous (Landon, 1988, pp.127–37). Mozart had already written a number of works for use at masonic ceremonies, one of which is included in your cassette material (AC 1631). Details are given in the cassette notes.

2   *The plot and its sources*

It is not necessary to go into great detail about the sources for *The Magic Flute*. As many writers have observed, the plot is rather a muddle, with a number of unexplained puzzles, and it seems to change direction about a third of the way through. A handsome young prince, Tamino, is saved from a serpent by the ladies of the mysterious Queen of the Night. Her daughter Pamina has been kidnapped by the evil Sarastro. Tamino, inspired by Pamina's portrait, sets off to rescue her, armed with a magic flute, and with the jovial birdcatcher Papageno for company. So far this is a fairy rescue-story in the tradition of Schikaneder's magical singspiels, and most of its elements are taken from a fairy-story which Schikaneder had used before, called 'Lulu or the Magic Flute', published in a collection by Wieland in 1789. But at this point in the story (Act I, No. 8), everything changes. Tamino arrives at Sarastro's castle to find that he is the head of a mysterious Egyptian priesthood in the 'Temple of Wisdom'. He learns that the Queen of the Night is evil, and that Sarastro has saved Pamina from her. As Act I ends, Tamino is ready to undergo the initiation trials of Sarastro's priesthood. The whole of Act II is taken up with the progress of Tamino through the trials, in which he is eventually joined by Pamina. Some of the elements in this latter part of the plot are derived from a French novel, *Séthos*, by Jean Terrasson, first published in 1731, which appeared in German translation in 1777–8. It is a masonic story set in ancient Egypt which, like *The Magic Flute*, includes initiation trials by fire and water, and a trial of resistance to the temptations of women. Mozart had earlier written some incidental music for a play based partly on *Séthos*, called *Thamos, King of Egypt*.

According to some writers, Schikaneder and Mozart must have changed their mind during the planning of the opera, deciding to introduce the masonic dimension only after the first part had already been written. Others argue that the plot is no more bizarre than in many exotic plays and singspiels of the time, and that one therefore need not look for reasons for its sudden change of direction. There are inconsistencies in the plot which perhaps support the theory of a re-write. The Three Boys are first supplied by the Queen of the Night, but later turn up apparently having switched sides to Sarastro. The Queen of the Night's Three Ladies sing about love and brotherhood in Act I (No. 5), but have turned into villains by Act II. Whatever the origin of such inconsistencies, it seems certain that the rites of Sarastro's Egyptian priesthood, and the trials through which Tamino and Pamina pass, were intended to symbolize masonic practice and tradition. The masons believed that their craft had affinities with the religious ceremonies of ancient Egypt, and their rituals alluded to Egyptian mysteries. There are also some specific references to masonic symbolism and practice in the opera. The symbolical confrontation with death refers directly to masonic ritual and teaching. Mozart hints obliquely at this in a letter (4 April, 1787) to his dying father, a fellow mason: '... I thank my God for graciously granting me the opportunity (you know what I mean) of learning that death is the *key* which unlocks the door to our true happiness' (Anderson, 1985, p.907). The progress from darkness to light is a central symbol of Enlightenment thought and, as Patricia Howard has shown in her study on 'Music and the Enlightenment' (*Studies*, I, p.193), the idea occurs frequently in music of the period. However, the darkness–light symbolism does also connect specifically with masonic ritual. The number three, of symbolic significance to masons, is much in evidence in the opera: there are three ladies, three boys, three doors of the temple, three initiation trials; and the opera is in the key of E flat whose key signature contains three flats. Then there are 'The Threefold Chords' which punctuate the ceremonies of Act II (and the overture), representing the three knocks which punctuate masonic ceremonies. More specifically, the short-long-long rhythm of these chords is that of the knocks used to refer to the 'second degree' of masonic initiation. It has also been suggested that the plot has political references, the most plausible of which is that the Queen of the Night is intended to represent the Empress Maria Theresa, whose troops raided a masonic lodge in 1743. More fanciful political interpretations were developed when the obvious masonic elements in the opera became officially embarrassing, and were suppressed. These need not concern us here, and in any case saying that the opera contains masonic and political references is not the same as saying that the audience was necessarily expected to recognize them. Anyone with any knowledge of freemasonry would have spotted many of the references straightaway, and if the opera was intended as a defence of masonic principles, that much would have been essential. But the opera's appeal to the whole audience, and its continued appeal now, depends on the fact that many of its themes have significance beyond the narrow references of the plot. Love, brotherhood, tolerance, the search for wisdom, and the education of rulers, are all topics of universal importance, and of particular importance in the context of the Enlightenment.

3 The first production

Before we turn to the opera itself, it is worth looking briefly at some of the evidence relating to the first production. Four examples are reproduced as Figs 8–11.

The engraving (Fig. 8) shows only a small part of the stage and auditorium, crudely drawn, but it does reveal one important feature of the Freihaus Theatre (where *The Magic Flute* was first staged in 1791): the audience nearest the stage is standing, in the parterre or 'pit'. To the side you can see the start of two rows of boxes. Above them, not shown in the picture, were two galleries. The total capacity of the theatre was about 1000, quite large by the standards of the time. Despite this, the contact between the stage and the audience, or at least those in the pit, must have been a good deal more direct than in most modern theatres.

You do not need to read German to be struck by one feature of the programme bill for the opera's first night (30 September 1791): the absence of Mozart's name in the main announcement at the top. Underneath the title, 'Die Zauberflöte', we read, 'Eine grosse Oper in 2 Acten, von Emanuel Schikaneder' (A grand opera in 2 acts, by Emanuel

Figure 8
*Engraving of part of the
Freihaus Theatre by Ignaz
Alberti (also known as
Albrecht). (Allmanach für
Theaterfreunde, 1791.
Österreichische
Nationalbibliotek)*

Schikaneder). The list of singers follows, and you could easily have missed Mozart's name in small print in the first line under the cast list. The translation of this paragraph is, 'The music is by Herr Wolfgang Amade Mozart, Kapellmeister, and Imperial and Royal Chamber Composer [Mozart's official court title]. Herr Mozard [sic] will, out of respect for a gracious and respected public, and out of friendship for the writer of the piece, himself direct the orchestra today.' (Mozart would not have conducted in the modern way with a baton, but would have directed

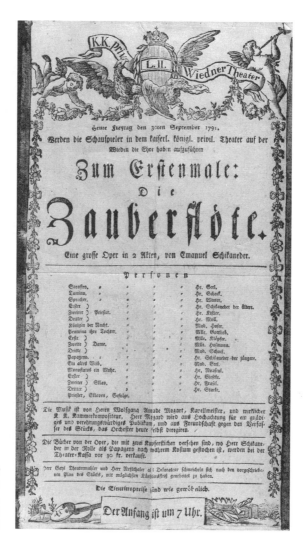

Figure 9
*Programme bill for the first
night of* The Magic Flute,
*30 September 1791. (Mozart
Museum, Salzburg)*

from a piano.) The fact that the work is advertised as Schikaneder's
opera rather than Mozart's can be taken as an indication of his central
role in the project. It was Schikaneder's theatre, by the official licence of
the Emperor, a fact referred to in the elaborate heading of the playbill,
with the imperial eagle and the initials 'K.K.' (Kaiserlich Königlich –
Imperial and Royal) and 'L II' (Leopold II). Schikaneder produced the
opera, wrote the bulk of the libretto, and took one of the leading roles.

Fig. 10 reproduces one of two engravings in the libretto, which was
on sale at the theatre box office. The playbill specifies that 'Herr
Schikaneder has been engraved in the role of Papageno with the actual
costume'. (The playbill also tells us that the libretto costs 30 kreuzer,
nearly twice the cost of a ticket in the pit.) Again, Schikaneder's central
role and efficient self-promotion are emphasized by the fact that this is
the only portrait of a character from the opera to be included in the
libretto. It also shows the elaborateness of his costume. When Tamino
first meets Papageno, he understandably wonders whether he is man or
bird. In many modern productions, which have a less bird-like costume,

Figure 10
*Schikaneder in the role of
Papageno. Engraving by
Ignaz Alberti from the libretto
of* The Magic Flute, *1791.
(Museen der Stadt, Wien)*

the line is an embarrassment and is therefore cut. The enormous bird-cage is also true to the libretto, which describes it as reaching 'high above his head'. In the distance is the 'round temple' specified at the beginning of the opera. Incidentally, one feature of the opera which is lost on modern audiences is that Papageno was the latest incarnation of a traditional comic Viennese character, Hans Wurst (Hans Sausage), whom Schikaneder had often played before in musical plays.

The frontispiece (Fig. 11) was designed by a fellow-member of Mozart's masonic lodge. It is related to the second setting for Act II (transformation after No. 10) in which Tamino begins his trials, and which includes 'the ruins of fallen columns and pyramids' at night. The frontispiece contains many masonic and loosely Egyptian symbols – the base of a pyramid (on the left), with snakes, the head of a bull, and an ibis; in the foreground, a trowel, an hourglass and a pick, with broken masonry; a mysterious light shines from the arch, a five-pointed star hangs from it, and a river flows through it. For masons the references would have been clear, and for members of the audience ignorant of freemasonry, the picture would have conjured up an exotic, mysterious setting in the tradition of the Freihaus productions.

Figure 11
Frontispiece from the libretto of
The Magic Flute. *Engraving*
by Ignaz Alberti, 1791. (Neue
Markt, Graphische
Sammlung, Albertina)

4   The opera

Schikaneder's libretto has come in for a good deal of criticism over the years, starting with a report by one of the directors of the Berlin National Theatre to whom it was sent for consideration by the King of Prussia (Frederick the Great's successor) in March 1792, six months after the première in Vienna. He concluded:

It seems to have been the author's intention to crowd together every conceivable difficulty for the stage designer and machinists, and a work has thus been created whose sole merit is visual splendour. At least, it is impossible for an audience which is ignorant of certain mysteries and incapable of seeing through the dark and heavy veil of allegory [i.e. non-masons], to find the slightest interest in it. I regret moreover that the great composer Mozart has had to squander his talent on such unrewarding, mystical and untheatrical material. (Deutsch, 1966, p.444)

It is important to note that this report is based on a reading of the libretto; the writer earlier makes it clear that he has not seen the opera. If you were to read the libretto without knowing any of the music, you might well get the impression of an absurd jumble of the comic and the serious. If you have not yet played the cassettes of the opera, you might like to try reading some of the libretto without the music, and see what you make of it. It will quickly become apparent, I think, that there is little point in trying to judge an opera libretto by the words alone. A libretto is not a play which is then set to music. The words were conceived from the first as the basis of an opera, and Schikaneder made it clear in the preface to a collection of his works that the effect of the words on the page was not his main concern:

I do not write for the reader, I write for the stage, and that is the place to which I would refer my reviewers. (Schikaneder, 1792, Preface)

Some writers have argued that Schikaneder's absurd libretto has been saved only by Mozart's music. But Schikaneder did not just write a libretto and then hand it over to Mozart for setting to music. Mozart's practice was to work *with* his librettist, and Mozart shares some responsibility for the final form of the libretto, just as Schikaneder is entitled to some credit for the success of the result. For the fact is that *The Magic Flute* does succeed in the theatre, not despite its extraordinary mixture of the comic and the serious, but because of it, and of the way Mozart handles it. One of the aims of this study is to help you to understand how this has been achieved.

Let us now turn to the opera. What you have is, in an important sense, incomplete. There is no real substitute for a staged production, and I hope you may have a chance to see one (it is often staged in Britain). You do, however, have a complete performance on audio-cassette, together with an extract from a staged performance in TV12. You may already have played the cassettes, but now is the time to start giving them concentrated attention.

The total length of the opera is about two hours and twenty minutes. It consists of numbered sections of music, interspersed with passages of spoken dialogue. You should now listen to it right through, following the parallel text. Before you start each side, set the counter of your cassette-player to zero. Then, at the start of each section of the music, identified by a number in the libretto, make a note of the counter reading, so that you can find individual sections again quickly. On the following pages of this essay, you will find brief notes on the music of the opera. They are intended to guide you through, and to start you thinking about the music, and about how Mozart uses it. I suggest that you proceed section by section: first read the note, then play the section, then jot down any thoughts you may have about the characters, their dramatic situation, and about what is happening in the music. Then move on to the next section, including the linking dialogue. Keep your notes brief and simple at this stage. The important thing is to get an overall impression of how the opera goes, not to attempt any detailed analysis. When you have listened right through the opera, at whatever pace suits you, move on to the next part of the essay, 'Musical styles and dramatic effect', which looks more closely at a selection of musical numbers.

5   Notes on the music of the opera

5.1   Overture

The overture consists of a slow introduction followed by a fast section which is interrupted by the masonic Threefold Chords, played three times. The slow introduction also begins with three double chords, with pauses between each.

5.2   Act I
No. 1   Tamino and the Three Ladies

Enter the young prince, pursued by a serpent. Modern substitution of a dragon tends to make this opening comic, but the tone of the music is urgent, predominantly quiet and agitated at first, punctuated by sudden loud chords. (Mozart uses a similar technique in No. 14, which will be discussed in the next section of the essay.) The mood, however, does turn comic as the Three Ladies squabble over who is to guard the beautiful youth while the others report to the Queen of the Night. Notice the pointed offbeat accents in the orchestra as the squabbling begins, at 'So geht und sagt es ihr' (Then go and tell her), and the changes of pace (and, incidentally, key) at 'Ich sollte fort?' (Should I go?), and again at 'Was wollte ich darum nicht geben' (I would give anything). These give the scene a formal structure which makes it seem like a parody of operatic ensemble-writing.

No. 2   Papageno's aria

The first entry of Papageno the bird-catcher (Schikaneder's role), in which he sings a jovial song in three verses. (This aria will be discussed in the next section.)

No. 3   Tamino's aria

Inspired by the portrait of Pamina, Tamino expresses his love for her. (To be discussed in the next section.)

No. 4   The Queen of the Night's aria

The splendour of the Queen's entry, and the transformation of the scene, is enhanced by the gradual crescendo in the introduction. This was a relatively new orchestral effect in Mozart's day, as you will remember from Patricia Howard's discussion of 'Music in the age of Enlightenment' (*Studies*, I, p.188). The aria is in three parts, an opening recitative, a slow section, and a fast conclusion. We do not yet know that the Queen is evil

(some writers have argued that Mozart and Schikaneder had not yet decided to make her evil), and her lament for her lost daughter is genuinely moving. The Queen of the Night's two arias (this and No. 14) were written for Mozart's sister-in-law, Josepha Hofer, who had become a leading singer in Schikaneder's theatre. She specialized in the acrobatic runs and high leaps with which the aria ends, conveying a sense of brilliant power.

No. 5 *Papageno, Tamino and The Three Ladies*

This is a delightful contrast to the high-powered vocal acrobatics of the Queen of the Night. The lying Papageno has had his mouth padlocked, and hums pathetically through it, accompanied wittily by a bassoon. The Ladies remove the padlock, and then all five characters join in a moral homily: 'If only all liars received such a padlock over their mouths, then hate ... would change to love and brotherhood'. Mozart treats this potentially embarrassing moment with such unabashed grace and charm that it becomes one of the high points of the first act. Notice particularly the delightful writing for the oboe as the homily begins, at the words, 'Bekämen doch die Lügner alle' (If only all liars received). The Ladies then present Tamino with the Magic Flute, singing of its worth in another beautiful ensemble, 'O so eine Flöte ... ' (Oh, such a flute ...). Papageno tries to leave, again accompanied by a bassoon, but reluctantly stays and receives the magic bells. Then soft clarinets (which have not played since Tamino's aria, No. 3) announce a sudden change to a quiet, almost processional mood, and the Ladies tell Tamino and Papageno that they will be guided to Sarastro's castle by Three Boys. The men repeat each phrase as if it were a chant or litany, the first hint of a ritualistic element in the opera. It is a remarkable conclusion to a scene which started with Papageno humming through his padlock.

No. 6   Monostatos and Pamina, later Papageno

This is the first scene at Sarastro's castle. Pamina, who had tried to escape, has been recaptured by Monostatos. Monostatos is a tenor (high voice), and is given fast, scurrying music, here and in his later aria (No. 13). The high voice and the liveliness of the music suggest an impish and cunning character; a bass voice would have conveyed a much more substantial type of villain. (Tamino is also a tenor, but his predominantly lyrical music, sung by a high voice, conveys youthful idealism.) Papageno's entrance is signalled, before he sings, by delicate, pointed phrases in the orchestra, suggesting someone on tiptoe. The terrified encounter between Papageno and Monostatos is made to sound comically breathless by the way they can only get two syllables out at a time.

No. 7   Duet of Pamina and Papageno

This charming duet in praise of domestic love is in the tradition of sentimental songs to be found in Viennese singspiels. The first half of its ballad-like tune is within Papageno's (Schikaneder's) capabilities, but the second half, which goes higher, is left to Pamina while Papageno sings the bass line.

No. 8   Act I finale

A staged performance of this finale is shown in TV12. It runs continuously, without spoken dialogue, for more than twenty minutes, and is, in my view, the finest section of the whole opera. The Three Boys (or 'Spirits' in one source of the libretto) lead Tamino to the gates of the temple, where he hopes to find Pamina. Tamino is met by the Speaker (an 'old priest', our first encounter with a quasi-masonic character), and they engage in dialogue. (This first part of the finale will be discussed in the next section of this study.)

     After the Speaker has gone back into the temple, Tamino discovers from a mysterious, unseen chorus that Pamina is still alive. He plays thankfully on his magic flute, singing an easy-going, ballad-like tune, and animals come out to listen to him. From the profound seriousness of the preceding dialogue, we are suddenly back in the world of the singspiel and ballad-opera. This delightful moment of relaxation makes a light-hearted allusion to the ancient Greek legend of Orpheus, who tamed wild beasts with his music, and travelled to the underworld to bring back his wife Eurydice from the dead. This in turn refers not only to Tamino's rescue of Pamina, but also to the masonic symbolism of death and resurrection. The scene switches to Pamina and Tamino attempting to escape. Tip-toeing is again suggested by the delicate, short phrases, 'Schnelle Füsse, rascher Muth' (Swift feet and bold courage). The pace quickens as Monostatos and the slaves intercept them. Papageno bewitches them with his magic bells, a moment of comedy which then dissolves into a simple little duet moralizing about the harmony of friendship, similar to the homily which followed the removal of Papageno's padlock in No. 5. This is interrupted by off-stage trumpets and chorus in march rhythm, announcing the arrival of Sarastro (see Fig. 13 for an early representation of this scene). Papageno's fear is answered by Pamina's ringing declaration that they must tell the truth. This answer comes as a surprise. (Do you agree? If so, what effect does it have on your view of Pamina at this point?) The force of Pamina's

Figure 13
Sarastro's entry (Act I finale).
Engraving by Joseph and
Peter Schaffer, 1793, possibly
based on the first production.
(Museen der Stadt, Wien)

reply is underlined by upward leaps in the melody (compare this with the yearning upward leaps in Tamino's first aria, No. 3). Sarastro is a bass, and the depth of his voice, and the measured pace of all his music, emphasize his position of authority. A tenor Sarastro would be as unthinkable as a bass Monostatos. A triumphal chorus in march rhythm, with full orchestra, brings the act to an end.

5.3   Act II
No. 9   March of the Priests

This is a slow processional march, the first appearance in the opera of masonic ceremonial music, with woodwind and trombones predominant.

No. 10   Sarastro and chorus

A hymn to the Egyptian gods, Isis and Osiris (to be discussed in the following section).

No. 11   Duet of two priests

A brief duet, warning Tamino and Papageno, as they begin their trials, of the treachery of women. That this warning is part of the ritual is conveyed by the music of the last line, where the words 'Tod und Verzweiflung' (death and despair) are set to a snappy march rhythm rather than to music which supports their meaning.

No. 12   The Three Ladies, Tamino and Papageno

The fast pace, and the banter between the different voices, are used to convey the urgent warning of the Three Ladies, the fearful chattering of Papageno, and the irritation of Tamino. All the voices come together for the final moral of the scene, 'Von festem Geiste ist ein Mann' (A man is strong in spirit), before the off-stage chorus of priests banishes the Three Ladies to hell (metaphorically, since they reappear at the end of the opera).

No. 13   Monostatos's aria

This furtive and delicate little aria, marked to be played pianissimo (very softly) throughout, sounds like a distant echo of the fashionable 'Turkish Music' of the time (an example from Mozart's earlier singspiel, *Die Ent-führung aus dem Serail* is given in your cassette material).

No. 14   The Queen of the Night's aria

The second of the Queen's two arias, in which she threatens to disown Pamina if she will not murder Sarastro. It is discussed in more detail in the following section.

No. 15   Sarastro's aria

In this aria Sarastro tells Pamina of the brotherhood's principles of love and forgiveness. It is hymn-like in its solemn pace and even phrase lengths, but the vocal line becomes more elaborate than in a real hymn at the words 'Dann wandelt er an Freundes Hand' (Walking with the hand of friendship). Here the high counterpoint in the violins, echoed in the cellos and basses, adds to the intensity of the melodic line. The words are not only broadly masonic in tone, but refer specifically to the leading in of the blindfolded initiate by the hand.

No. 16   The Three Boys

A brief trio, with a delicately scored accompaniment. (How the Three Boys, who were originally provided by the Queen of the Night, should now appear, sent by Sarastro, is one of the mysteries of the plot.)

No. 17   Pamina's aria

This wonderful aria makes us aware for the first time that Pamina is the one who undergoes the greatest trial. Much of the sorrow of the melody is conveyed by falling phrases, in contrast to the upward leaps of Tamino's first aria (No. 3).

No. 18   Chorus of priests

This is a solemn chorus to Isis and Osiris, but it is more elaborate in structure and expressive in detail than a formal hymn. Note, for example, the contrast between the quiet phrase, 'Die düstre Nacht' (the dark night), and the loud continuation, 'verscheucht der Glanz der Sonne' (the rays of the sun banish). This is an example of the musical characterization of darkness and light which Patricia Howard discussed in her study of *The Creation*.

No. 19   Trio: Pamina, Tamino and Sarastro

With this trio, Tamino and Pamina part as Tamino goes off for the final stage of his trials. The beginning of the trio is accompanied by a constantly repeated motif in the orchestra. There is a strong contrast between Pamina's expressions of fear and the rather formal responses of the men, who often sing together in the first half of the trio. But halfway through, at Sarastro's words, 'Die Stunde schlägt, nun müsst ihr scheiden' (The hour strikes, now you must part), the emphasis shifts subtly. Now Sarastro sings on his own, and Pamina and Tamino sing together, and, after a brief separation, they do so for most of the second half of the trio. At first, therefore, Tamino joins in the formal expression of faith in the gods, but by the end he has joined Pamina in her tender expressions of farewell.

No. 20 *Papageno's aria with glockenspiel*

This was a set-piece for Schikaneder, a folklike tune with three verses and a refrain, in which Papageno expresses his longing for a sweetheart. Viennese singspiels were full of such down-to-earth sentiments, and one can imagine Schikaneder 'working' the audience almost like the modern pantomime actor, directing at them the line, 'Can I not please a single one of all the charming girls?' The glockenspiel accompaniment, to which Papageno mimes, becomes more elaborate at each verse. In a letter to his wife (8–9 October, 1791), Mozart describes how, one night, he went backstage and played the glockenspiel himself. He added extra arpeggios, catching Schikaneder out, 'He then struck the glockenspiel and said "*Shut up.*" Whereupon everyone laughed. I am inclined to think that this joke taught many of the audience for the first time that Papageno does not play the instrument himself' (Anderson 1985, p.969).

No. 21 *Finale*

This long, elaborate finale consists of several scenes and musical numbers played without a break. The divisions in your libretto (a–c) have been added for ease of reference.

(21a)

At the beginning, the Three Boys sing of the coming victory of light over the darkness of superstition. They first sing together, in a formal trio with wind instruments, but as they come upon the despairing Pamina the formal trio breaks up, with the top voice leading in expressing their anxiety. Abruptly, the music moves from the light trio of boys to the full-blown grief of Pamina, with a dagger in her hand. Part of the powerful effect of this transition is the sudden prominence of the strings in the accompaniment. The alternation between the Boys' trio and the highly expressive writing for Pamina continues until the Boys prevent her stabbing herself: 'Ha, Unglückliche! Halt ein!' (Ha! Unhappy girl, stop!). Here the music moves from a minor key to the major key in which the opera began, E flat, and into a flowing three-in-a-bar (like waltz time). A scene which began tragically ends in delightfully relaxed mood, with Pamina and the Boys (who sound almost as if they are dancing) together drawing the moral: the gods themselves protect true lovers.

(21b)

There is a dramatic transformation to the scene of Tamino's final trials, with mountains spitting fire and gushing water. The change in the music is equally dramatic. Two Armed Men intone the melody of an old Lutheran chorale with the orchestra weaving a pattern of counterpoint in the manner of J. S. Bach's church music. The effect is impressively severe, and deliberately archaic. The voice of Pamina is heard approaching, and Tamino and the Armed Men come together to sing (twice) the significant statement, 'Ein Weib, das Nacht und Tod nicht scheut ist würdig und wird eingeweiht' (A woman who does not fear night and death is worthy and will be initiated). Pamina and Tamino greet each other with musical phrases of the utmost tenderness which echo strikingly the opening phrase of Tamino's first aria (No. 3), as if this is to be taken as the moment of fulfilment of the yearning awoken in him then. With calmness and simplicity, Pamina declares that she will lead Tamino through the trials, aided by the power of the magic flute which her father carved. They walk through the fire and the water, to a slow march with muffled kettledrums and Tamino's flute. They emerge to see a doorway open into the brightly lit temple, a sight 'of the utmost splendour', and an off-stage chorus rejoices.

(21c)

Back for the last time to Papageno, in despair because he has lost his Papagena. He returns three times to his tune, before appealing for any other maiden to save him (again one can imagine Schikaneder making a great deal of this). He prepares to hang himself (in the key of Pamina's lament, G minor), but is saved in the nick of time by the Three Boys. Having a noose placed round the neck is another element in masonic initiation, but obviously this scene is also intended as a comic counterpart to Pamina's attempted suicide. The boys remind Papageno of his magic bells, he plays them, and Papagena appears. Mozart's introduction wittily sets the tone of stunned delight, and the two stammer at each other ('Pa – Pa – Pa –'). Their rapid patter duet, and vision of endless numbers of children, must have brought the house down on the first night. The Queen of the Night and her Ladies, now in unholy alliance with Monostatos, appear, intending to break into the temple. The final destruction of the Queen is conveyed by the full power of the orchestra, the first time the full orchestra has been heard since the Three Ladies were vanquished at the end of No. 12, nearly an hour ago. The triumph of light over the darkness is celebrated by the chorus in a majestic hymn of thanksgiving which leads in to a final chorus of rejoicing, as Tamino and Pamina stand, 'both in priestly robes'.

6   Musical styles and dramatic effect

As you listened through *The Magic Flute*, you will have noticed that it contains a great variety of different musical styles – fast, slow, light, heavy, simple, complicated, witty, serious – often juxtaposed in abrupt contrasts. It is one of the most varied pieces of music ever written. What I would like you to do now is to concentrate on five sections of the opera, and think in more detail about how Mozart uses these different styles for dramatic effect.

The five sections are:

Act I

No. 2   Papageno's aria

No. 3   Tamino's aria

No. 8   The beginning of the Act I finale, up to the point at which Tamino plays the magic flute, at the words 'Wie Stark ist nicht dein Zauberton!' (How powerful is your magic tone.)

Act II

No. 10 Sarastro's aria with the chorus of priests.

No. 14 The Queen of the Night's second aria.

EXERCISE   Listen again to each of these five sections. Add to the notes you made during your initial listening any new thoughts you may have about what is happening in the music. The questions I would like you to tackle are the same for each section. They are designed to help focus your attention as you listen. The questions are:

1   How would you describe the general character of the section – is it serious, comic, light, heavy, sad, happy, yearning, angry, urgent?

2   How would you characterize the music itself – is it simple or complicated? Does it have a straightforward tune which you could sing yourself, or is it too elaborate or difficult for that? Does the same music repeat, perhaps several times, or does it proceed without obvious repetition? Does the music change style during the section – indeed, does the section really consist of several contrasted sections – or is it similar throughout?

3   Putting 1 and 2 together, how does the music contribute to our impression of the characters and to the dramatic situation?

You should tackle these sections one at a time. After you have listened enough times and made notes, turn to the 'discussion' of the individual section. You may find it useful, as you read each discussion, to play the relevant section of the music again, stopping to identify the points I have referred to. After you have done the listening, made your notes, and read through the 'discussion', start work on the next section.

EXERCISE   No. 2 Papageno's aria

DISCUSSION   This is Papageno's first entry and he takes a long time to come in; the orchestra plays the complete tune before he starts singing. No other aria in the entire opera has as long an introduction, not even the Queen of the Night's first aria (No. 4), which involves a transformation of the scene. Why does Papageno have so long an introduction? I would guess because he was played by Schikaneder, the star of the show, and that Mozart gave him plenty of time to make his entry, no doubt with comic business on the way, and to receive his usual welcome from the audience.

The tune which Papageno sings is cheerful and straightforward, like a folk-tune, and does not require a wide vocal range or great expertise to sing it. It has three short verses, with identical music.

Of all the music in *The Magic Flute*, this number is the most like songs in earlier singspiels, and in the Ballad Operas from which they were derived. The style of the music suggests Papageno's down-to-earth, cheerful character just as clearly as the words he speaks. But the music also implies something about the singer for whom it was written. Like many of the songs in modern musicals, it can be put over perfectly well by an actor who can sing a bit, as opposed to a trained opera singer. All of the music written for Papageno (Schikaneder) is fairly straightforward compared with the music of the other principal characters. This point is made vividly if you compare Papageno's mock attempted suicide scene (No. 21c) with the scene of Pamina's real attempted suicide (No. 21a). Papageno's phrases are short, and the range of notes is narrow; Pamina's music is much more complicated, with a sustained vocal line and a wide range, including difficult leaps. This is not to say that Schikaneder was not an accomplished singer. He must have been able to hold his part in ensembles (such as No. 5), and his duet with Pamina (No. 7) suggests that he could sing a flowing melody pleasingly. Indeed, a Viennese critic in 1790 described him as 'both a gifted actor and an enthralling singer ... His voice is pure and melodious, and he sings with simplicity and taste' (quoted in Porter, 1980, p.iii). Nevertheless, Schikaneder was an actor first and a singer second, and Mozart's music shows it.

EXERCISE   No. 3 Tamino's aria.

DISCUSSION   In contrast to the canny, rough and ready countryman, 'Ein Natur-mensch' (a child of Nature), as Papageno describes himself, Tamino is the idealistic young prince, suddenly moved to love by the portrait of Pamina. How does the music bring out his character and feelings? The music is slower than Papageno's aria, and the phrases are longer. They demand the fine vocal control of a trained singer to sustain them. (The first Tamino, Benedict Schack, was not only a singer and composer, but also a flautist, and played his own flute solos in the opera.) The melody is very precisely written to suggest a feeling of yearning, as listening closely to the first section of it shows. (You should re-play the beginning of the aria, pausing to identify the following points.) The opening words, 'Dies Bildnis' (This portrait), are set to an upward leap. The same happens at the start of the second phrase, 'wie noch' (such...). But the highest leap is reserved for the fifth phrase of the melody, 'wie dies Götterbild' (...this divine picture). A succession of upward leaps in a melody has often been used by composers to suggest yearning or striving of some kind (a well known modern example is the song *My Way*).

The orchestral accompaniment subtly underpins the character of the melody. For the first five phrases, up to 'wie dies Götterbild', the accompaniment is very cut up, each short phrase separated from the next by a gap. But at the words 'mein Herz mit neuer Regung füllt' (is filling my heart with a new emotion), the character of both melody and accompani-ment changes. Suddenly the melody flows forward, and the accompani-ment adopts an onward tread with a regular rhythm. My impression is that, after feeling its way to begin with, the music at this point has reached the heart of the matter, as the words (and Tamino's emotions) have.

The importance of this phrase is reinforced at the end of the aria. The conventional way to end the aria would have been to return to the beginning of the melody. The point at which this is expected is, I think, after the words 'und ewig wäre sie dann mein' (and she would be mine forever) are sung for the first time. But instead Mozart takes a shortcut straight back to this crucial phrase of the music. It is a most telling effect, pinpointing Tamino's emotional and dramatic situation. The accompaniment has a particularly warm and full sound throughout the aria, partly because of the prominence of clarinets.

(Mozart's use of wind instruments is discussed in a section of AC 1631 (grey), to which you will be referred later in the study.)

EXERCISE   No. 8   Beginning of the Act I finale (to the point where Tamino first plays his flute)

DISCUSSION   The two previous extracts are both self-contained arias. This is the beginning of a long stretch of music which comprises several contrasted sections, and continues, uninterrupted by dialogue, to the end of the act. Here, at the beginning of the finale, Tamino has only just arrived outside the gates of the temple. By the end of the finale, several scenes later, he is ready, with Papageno, to start undergoing his initiation trials. This section, though all contained within a single scene, itself has contrasts of musical style within it. It begins in a rather solemn, processional mood, with wind instruments prominent, and with a suggestion of a slow march in its rhythm. This introduces the Three Boys for the first time. The ceremonial mood of the opening is confirmed by their formal words to Tamino, particularly their repeated threefold instruction to him to be 'standhaft, duldsam und verschwiegen!' (steadfast, patient, and discreet). This is the first suggestion in the opera of some kind of ritual, and the solemn march of the music emphasizes the point.

When the boys leave, the character of the music changes. The rhythm of the march has gone, and no regular rhythm has replaced it. Tamino sings short phrases in something nearer to the rhythm of ordinary speech, accompanied by little more than punctuating chords on the orchestra. You have already encountered this style of writing, called *recitative*, in Haydn's *The Creation*. It was the conventional way of setting passages of dialogue between the formal musical numbers in late eighteenth-century opera and oratorio. In *The Magic Flute*, written in the tradition of the singspiel, there is not very much recitative: most of the dialogue is spoken. Mozart's other operas have a great deal of recitative, sometimes, as here, accompanied by the orchestra, but often accompanied only by a keyboard instrument and cello (*The Creation* has both sorts). This is the first time Mozart has used recitative in *The Magic Flute*, and for a very particular dramatic effect. The sudden loosening into semi-speech rhythm gives a sense of urgency, of disorientation, after the even tread of the music which precedes it. It emphasizes the fact that Tamino, now on his own, does not know quite what to expect.

As in *The Creation*, the recitative varies in pace, and is interspersed with brief passages of more regular rhythm to emphasize particular phrases. The first time this happens is at the words 'Wo Tätigkeit thronet und Müssiggang weicht' (Where action rules and idleness retreats). Here the rhythm of the music suddenly becomes fast and regular; Tamino sings two phrases with upward leaps, reminiscent of the yearning phrases in his earlier aria (No. 3). The pace remains fast, though reverting to the speech rhythm of recitative, until the Speaker comes out, when the pace suddenly drops. He asks Tamino what he seeks in this sanctuary, in a slow recitative. For Tamino's answer, 'Der Lieb und Tugend Eigentum' (The realm of love and virtue), Mozart switches out of speech rhythm, and Tamino sings a sustained phrase like a line of a hymn. This simple device underlines the gravity of his answer. A sort of ritual litany of question and answer follows, which hints at the questioning of candidates in masonic initiation. It ends with one of the most beautiful moments in the whole opera. After a long stretch of recitative in speech rhythm, Tamino asks his final question, 'Wann also wird das Dunkel schwinden?' (When will this darkness fade away?). The Speaker answers, 'As soon as friendship's hand leads you to the sanctuary's eternal bond'. The uncertain progress and short-breathed phrases of the recitative are gone, and the Speaker sings a melody of the utmost solemnity, which consists of just one enormously long phrase, given a grave and ceremonial tread by the rhythm of the accompaniment. The Speaker goes out, and Tamino is left alone in the dark. But the Speaker's melody returns to him out of the darkness, accompanying the unseen voices of the chorus.

Recitative is often thought of as just the padding in opera, a way of setting speech to music so as to get through the action before the next musical number. But in this scene we have reached a dramatic and emotional turning point, as Tamino confronts the unknown. Mozart's use of recitative, subtly varied by brief moments of more formal melody, responds sensitively to every turn of the dramatic situation.

The whole of this finale is performed in TV12.

EXERCISE   No. 10   Sarastro's aria with the chorus of priests

DISCUSSION   There were hints of a religious or ritual element in the words and music of the first act, but this opening scene of Act II brings this element into the open. Sarastro and his fellow priests of Isis and Osiris are meeting to consider whether Tamino is worthy to be initiated into their priesthood. The scene has started with a solemn march as the priests enter in procession, and now Sarastro and the priests sing what the score calls an 'aria with chorus'. That it is a hymn to Isis and Osiris is obvious from the words, but what characteristics of the music make it *sound* like a hymn? Like many real hymns it is slow and quite simple in structure. It is divided into two verses (although the beginning of the second verse is not the same as the beginning of the first), and the chorus repeats the last line of each. The rhythm of the melody is very regular. Every phrase is the same length (four bars), and the stress pattern is also regular:

Ŏ /Isĭs /und Ŏ/Sirĭs /schĕnkĕt
    Dĕr /Weishĕit /Geist dĕm /neuĕn /Paar!

As with most hymns, there is very little characterization in the music of the meaning of individual words. For example, in the first verse, there is no difference in musical emphasis between 'the spirit of wisdom' at the beginning and 'danger' at the end. The only point at which the music responds to particular words is in the second line of the second verse, 'doch sollten sie zu Grabe gehen' (but if they should go to the grave), where the melody at the word 'Grabe' (grave) descends unexpectedly into a minor key.

The accompaniment is the same throughout, a sonorous combination of trombones, woodwind and the lower strings, without any of the higher, bright-toned instruments (oboes, flutes, violins, trumpets). This produces a rather organ-like effect, similar to the ensembles of wind instruments traditionally used during masonic ceremonies (an example of Mozart's masonic music is given on AC 1631).

In sum, this is the least eventful piece of music in the entire opera. The regularity of phrasing and rhythm, the evenness of emphasis, the monochrome accompaniment, all contribute to the impression that this is a hymn, an act of ritual, not music to illustrate particular words or the details of a dramatic situation. At this stage of the opera, the ritual is itself the dramatic point being made.

EXERCISE   No. 14   The Queen of the Night's second aria

DISCUSSION   This is the second of the Queen of the Night's two arias (the other was No. 4 in Act I). Both are completely different from anything else in the opera. They are the only arias which seem designed to show off the singer's capabilities. They stand in a tradition of 'display' arias which originated with the rise of the soprano, and in particular the *castrato*, as the highly-paid star of Italian opera earlier in the eighteenth century. No. 14 is the more spectacular of the Queen's two arias, with a succession of acrobatic leaps to high notes, well beyond the normal range of a soprano. Presumably, Mozart's sister-in-law Josepha Hofer could sing it, otherwise he would not have written it for her. However, a visitor to the Freihaus Theatre who heard her (six months before the première of *The Magic Flute*) in another high role, Wranitzky's *Oberon*, wrote that she was 'a very unpleasant singer, has an insufficiently high voice for this role, and squeaks it out' (Grove, 1980, p.240). Perhaps she had a cold. Ten years earlier, Mozart himself had described her (in a letter to his father, 15 December, 1781) as 'a lazy, gross, perfidious woman, and as cunning as a fox', rather suitable qualifications for the Queen of the Night (Anderson, 1985, p.784).

What distinguishes the Queen's arias from many earlier 'display' arias is the way Mozart uses the acrobatics for dramatic effect. The vocal display develops out of music which is threatening in tone, and this helps the singing itself to sound angry. In the opening bars the vocal line is rhythmically forthright but not particularly acrobatic. It is the orchestra which straightaway establishes the angry mood by the use of sudden accents punctuating a predominantly quiet accompaniment. This technique is both practical, in that it allows the singer to be heard over the orchestra, and highly effective, because it creates an immediate tension, like waiting for the next crash in a thunderstorm. (Mozart uses a similar technique, right at the beginning of the opera, when Tamino enters pursued by the serpent.)

I hope these five examples will have helped you to start thinking in more detail about the range of musical styles which Mozart uses in *The Magic Flute* – in these examples, simple folk-tune, lyrical aria, dramatic recitative, solemn hymn, and vocal display-piece. They should also have shown

that Mozart does what he does for essentially *dramatic* reasons, not for reasons to do purely with music. That realization ought to give you the confidence to discuss what is happening elsewhere in the opera, even if you have no musical training. You may like to go back to the brief notes on the other sections of the opera and use them as a basis for further study and commentary of your own.

Two sections of AC 1631 illustrate and discuss two particular musical topics, namely Mozart's writing for the *orchestra* in *The Magic Flute*, and his use of *keys*. You should listen to these now.

7 *The roles of men and women in* **The Magic Flute**

You have probably been struck already by some of the disparaging references to women in the libretto, and you may well think that the relationship between men and women in the opera relies on many of the traditional clichés. The principal 'baddie' in the opera is a woman, the Queen of the Night, whose helpless daughter has been snatched, supposedly for her own good, by the senior 'goodie', the man Sarastro. The young hero, Tamino, falls instantly in love with Pamina, on the basis of a glance at her portrait. The news that a prince whom she has never met has fallen in love with her fills Pamina's girlish heart with delight, and despite the appalling way in which she is then treated, she follows him faithfully, threatens suicide when he seems to reject her, immediately understands when told that this was merely a test of Tamino's manliness, and the opera ends with them united in bliss. One could be forgiven for finding the whole thing ridiculous or distasteful.

I do not want to make too much of this. After all, the characters of *The Magic Flute* inhabit a fantastic and magical world, in the tradition of the Viennese singspiel. Even though it contains obvious allusions, principally to freemasonry, and even if the tone of its dialogue is sometimes difficult for a late twentieth-century audience to swallow, it would be unwise to treat the work too literally. Perhaps we should therefore accept it as an eighteenth-century period-piece, with its romantic prince and princess, its heroes and its villains, and sit back and enjoy the music. My problem with this is that, in practice, in the opera house, I always find this work delightful, moving and, in the end, uplifting in its view of human nature and human relationships. How can this be? Is it just because of Mozart's music? Or does the opera as a whole justify itself, libretto included, despite its absurdities? Have you formed a view? Spend some time collecting your thoughts on the roles of men and women in the opera before you continue.

Some of the absurdities certainly are embarrassing to a modern audience. There is, for example, the moment near the end of the Act I finale when Sarastro says to Pamina, 'A man must guide your heart, for without that, every woman tends to step out of her rightful place'. Here, and in a number of other places, a shiver runs through a modern British audience, sometimes resulting in a pantomime-style hiss. Papageno's attitude to women is easier for the modern audience to take, because it is earthy and tongue-in-cheek. In his first aria, he sings that he would like to catch and sell women like birds, keeping the best for himself. But when it comes to the point, his intentions are 'honourable'. What he wants is a loving wife and large numbers of children. Papagena (who has been prepared for him, as Pamina has been prepared for Tamino) is happy to oblige. Incidentally, Schikaneder's original libretto contains an instruction to Papagena from the Three Boys:

> Come here, you fair, dear little woman!
> You must dedicate your little heart to your husband.
> He will love you, sweet little woman,
> And be your father, friend, and brother.
> Be this man's property! (Quoted in Porter, 1980, p.vii)

Mozart omitted this (to modern ears) appalling instruction. It is tempting to assume that he did so because he objected to it, but that is a temptation to be resisted except in the imagination.

The other side of this coin is the attitude to men suggested by the opera. Apart from general points about the heroism of Tamino, and the authority of Sarastro (of which more later), there are a number of exhortations to 'manliness' scattered through the libretto, and Tamino is praised for achieving it. But this topic is more complicated than it sometimes appears in translation, because of the existence of two German words which are usually translated as 'man'. The word 'Mann' means, quite simply, a man, without ambiguity, and 'männlich' means manly. But there is also the word 'Mensch', which is often translated as man. It occurs, most famously, in Schiller's *Ode To Joy*, set by Beethoven in his Ninth Symphony: 'Alle Menschen werden Brüder' (All people shall be brothers). In *Nathan the Wise*, you have already met the famous line, 'Kein Mensch muss müssen' (No one must must – that is, no human being must be forced).

When the Speaker raises doubts about Tamino's ability to endure the trials, because he is a prince, Sarastro replies, 'Noch mehr – Er ist Mensch!', often translated, 'Nay, more – he is a *man*!' The trouble is that, particularly in opera, *man* is a very convenient translation for *Mensch*, because they are both one syllable. But, as you have learned in your study of *Nathan the Wise, Mensch* means not just a man, but a human being of either sex, 'man' in the old sense of 'mankind', meaning humanity in general, as in 'The Rights of Man'. Sarastro means, not that Tamino is a man, and can therefore be expected to behave in a manly fashion, like the traditional schoolboy who is expected not to cry, but that he is a human being, and that his human spirit will give him the strength to endure, rather than his mere rank as a prince. Similarly, when Sarastro sings to Pamina about the principles of love and forgiveness in the brotherhood (No. 15), he sings that anyone incapable of learning from these principles is unworthy to be 'ein Mensch', a human being, not just a man. In No. 23 of Haydn's *Creation*, 'And God created *Man*' is rendered in German as 'Menschen', human beings. Even in the aria which follows (No. 24), which is at first specifically about the man, the German is different from the English. 'He stands a man, the Lord and King of all', is in German, 'Steht der Mensch, ein Mann und König der Natur'. He is first a human being, secondly a man, and thirdly the King of Nature. The difference in emphasis is subtle but significant.

The role of Pamina similarly is not as uncomplicated as it may appear. She begins as a helpless victim, and the brotherhood's attitude to her, and to women in general, is summed up by the instruction to Tamino as he enters his trials to guard himself from 'women's treachery' (No. 11). But Pamina achieves an importance, both in the plot and in the music, which goes far beyond the tradition of 'princess gets her prince'.

The first sign that Pamina has unsuspected strengths is her extraordinary outburst as she and Papageno wait to be discovered by Sarastro, near the end of Act I. Fearfully Papageno asks her, 'What will we say?' Pamina replies, 'The truth – even if it were a crime'. Nothing has led us to expect this high moral statement from her, and the point is underlined by the music. Mozart repeats 'Die Wahrheit' (the truth), to a leaping phrase which emphasizes her fearless determination.

During the course of Act II Pamina's role develops further, and, again, it is both the action and the music which make the point. Pamina has, in effect, to undergo trials without knowing that she is doing so. There are two crucial pieces of music for her: the first when she has to endure Tamino's silent rejection without explanation (No. 17); and the second when, trapped between the murderous treachery of her own mother and the apparent betrayal of the man who was sent to redeem her, she sees no way out but suicide (No. 21a). (Her suicide attempt presumably alludes to the masonic trial ritual in which a dagger is held to the candidate's chest.) These two moments – Pamina's rejection, and her attempted suicide – are given music of the greatest poignancy, sounding emotional depths which are not reached anywhere else in the opera.

After the trial by silence, Pamina is brought to Sarastro covered in 'the same kind of sack which the initiates were wearing' (before No. 19). At the end of Act I, Tamino and Papageno were covered with sacks to be led off to the start of their initiation (real freemasons are blindfolded for initiation in the first degree). Pamina was not covered then, but she is now, which suggests that she has in some sense become an initiate herself. This is only hinted at here, but after her suicide attempt, the point is made explicit as she joins Tamino for the trials by fire and water. Tamino and the two Armed Men sing together, 'A woman who does not fear night and death is worthy and will be initiated'. Furthermore, it is Pamina who takes the lead. As she joins Tamino for the trials, she sings, 'I myself will *lead* you, and Love will be my guide'. As they emerge from the trials, the chorus addresses them as 'noble pair!'. Pamina has undergone the trials of the brotherhood, and is initiated together with Tamino. There is no ambiguity about this. At the very end of the opera, as Sarastro and the priests receive them, Tamino and Pamina appear 'both in priestly robes', and the choir hails them as 'Geweihten', people who have been initiated or ordained. Pamina has become the first woman priest of the brotherhood.

Again, I would not wish to overstate the case. There are writers who argue that the general tone of *The Magic Flute* is light-hearted, despite its serious moments, and that, given that it is in the tradition of the singspiel for the prince and princess to be united at the end, Pamina's initiation is no more than a means to this end. Perhaps that is all there is to it. But I must say that it does not *feel* that way to me. The music which Mozart gives to Pamina transcends the convention of the damsel in distress, and makes me take what she does seriously.

It is interesting to speculate what a freemason in eighteenth-century Vienna would have thought of Pamina's initiation. Perhaps he would have taken it all in the spirit of Schikaneder's other fantastical singspiels, and thought nothing of it. But if the opera was seriously intended to convey something about the spirit and principles of freemasonry, and was seen in that light by masonic members of the audience, it must surely have raised some eyebrows. The triumphant admission of man and woman together as priests of the brotherhood strikes at the heart of masonic tradition and rule. As a twentieth-century non-mason, I certainly find that it is Pamina, rather than Sarastro and his brotherhood, who conveys what it is to be 'ein Mensch', and it is this vision of humanity which is seen to triumph, not only over the powers of darkness represented by the Queen of the Night, but also over the dead weight of tradition and authority.

8 Authority

The principal figure of authority, Sarastro, is not an entirely sympathetic character, certainly not to a modern audience. He has captured Pamina, in order to save her from her mother, and has placed her in the care of the evil and lecherous Monostatos. He is certainly holding Pamina against her will, initially at least, and she is delighted to have a chance to escape. When she is recaptured, and tentatively says that her filial duty calls her to her mother, Sarastro abruptly pushes her feelings aside, tells her that she cannot be released, that her mother is an arrogant woman, and that she needs a man to guide her. He sees no need to provide further explanation of his high-handed behaviour. (The contrast in this scene between Pamina's humble petition and Sarastro's brusque rejection of her request is vividly underlined by the contrasts in the music.) In the libretto and the original production, Sarastro is certainly given the style to go with this arrogant behaviour. His first entry is on a triumphal chariot drawn by six lions (see Fig. 13, p.95).

None of this suggests any kind of 'enlightened' ruler, either in a general modern sense, or in the sense of one influenced by the thinking of the Enlightenment. Sarastro is described several times as 'wise', and the chorus sings of their devotion to him as ruler. Sarastro himself sings that the brotherhood lives by the principles of forgiveness and the love of human beings for each other, and he appeals to the gods, Isis and Osiris, to grant wisdom to Tamino. But why does this high-minded ruler place Pamina in the hands of Monostatos? Why, after Pamina has complained of his lecherous threats, is he allowed further access to her? Why does Sarastro employ Monostatos at all? His treatment of Monostatos seems guided by the whim of the moment rather than by notions of justice and appropriate punishment. When Pamina complains about Monostatos at the end of Act I, Sarastro immediately 'rewards' him with seventy-seven strokes on the soles of the feet, without asking any questions. But when Sarastro himself finds Monostatos about to stab Pamina because she refuses to succumb to him, he sends him away unpunished simply because the dagger was forged by the Queen of the Night. Sarastro sings that there is no vengeance to be found within the brotherhood, but this forgiving attitude does not extend to the Queen of the Night, who is 'cast into eternal night' in the closing moments of the opera, together with the Three Ladies and Monostatos.

By contrast, when it comes to Sarastro's central concern, the initiation of the prince Tamino, it is made clear that Sarastro does not have the authority to take decisions alone. The meeting of the priests at the beginning of Act II follows masonic rules, in which candidates have to be voted for by all members of the lodge. Some phrases in the original libretto, which are cut in your recording, tell us something about Sarastro's hopes for Tamino. Sarastro tells the priests that Tamino, a king's son, will fortify their temple against 'base prejudice', and be 'the recompense of virtue, and the scourge of wickedness'. During the trials, Sarastro says to Tamino, 'if you wish to reign as a wise ruler, then may the gods accompany you further'. Much of this is rather vague. Again, it is not clear exactly what is meant by 'wisdom', though 'prejudice' might well refer to the persecution of freemasonry by Catholics. What does seem clear is that the purpose of Tamino's initiation is to enable him to become, in some sense, an enlightened ruler. Some writers and producers, including Ingmar Bergman in his film of *The Magic Flute*, have assumed that he is intended to replace Sarastro as ruler of the brotherhood, though this is not stated in the libretto. The exact nature of Tamino's enlightenment, like so much else, is vague. He is no doubt to be spiritually enlightened, by his exposure to the cult of Isis and Osiris. He will have endured trials of his 'manliness'. He will have learned the rituals of the brotherhood, and its principles of love and forgiveness. To judge by Sarastro's own behaviour, however, he will not necessarily have learned to extend those principles beyond the brotherhood itself, nor have acquired notions of justice or human rights which would make him an Enlightened ruler in the sense we now apply to the eighteenth century. The one way in which his enlightenment is shown to go beyond that of Sarastro is in his relationship with Pamina. Pamina's role in the future is, like everything else, undefined, but it seems clearly implied that, if Tamino is to rule, then Pamina, who has led him through the trials, must surely rule with him. It is impossible to say what, if anything, Schikaneder and Mozart meant by this, and one must avoid twentieth-century wishful thinking. But if Pamina does contribute anything to Tamino's enlightenment, it is despite Sarastro, not because of him.

9 Orientalism

As you have already learned from your study of *Nathan the Wise*, oriental settings are not at all unusual in eighteenth-century writing. There are two important precedents in Mozart's own output: *Die Entführung aus dem Serail (The Abduction from the Seraglio)*, set in a Turkish harem, and, earlier still, incidental music to a play, *Thamos, King of Egypt*. It is significant that neither of these works is a fully fledged opera; one is a singspiel, the other a play. Oriental fantasy was a very popular ingredient in the singspiels staged at Schikaneder's theatre, many of which were written by Schikaneder himself, and it is from this tradition in the popular theatre that the oriental elements in *The Magic Flute* derive, rather than from the conventions of opera.

The fact that oriental fantasy was a popular feature of productions in Schikaneder's theatre is perhaps a warning not to make heavy weather of the oriental ingredients in *The Magic Flute*. Much is left unexplained. We are not even told where we are as the opera opens; the scene is merely 'a rocky landscape', with a 'round temple'. There is nothing particularly oriental-looking about the round temple shown in early illustrations (for example, Figs 10 and 12). It looks like the sort of classical building to be found in eighteenth-century European gardens, as do the gates of the temples in later scenes (Fig. 13). There is only one specifically oriental reference before we reach Sarastro's castle, and that is the description of Tamino's costume as a splendid 'javonischen' hunting costume. This is assumed by most writers to be a misprint for 'japanischen' (Japanese). This does not necessarily mean that Tamino is himself supposed to be Japanese, but Chinese and Japanese cultures were certainly respected by a number of Enlightenment writers, including Voltaire and d'Holbach. Giving Tamino a Japanese flavour was a hint that he was foreign but civilized (like some of the figures in the Chinese Tea-House at Sans-Souci (TV2)), a suitably exotic seeker after truth.

By contrast, Monostatos represents barbarism and lechery which had long been associated in the European literary imagination with the Islamic 'orient'. The character is something of an embarrassment in the modern theatre, but I would guess that he was intended as a stock comic villain rather than anything seriously threatening. He is described in the cast list as a 'moor'; he calls himself 'black and ugly'; and, in a scene omitted in this recording (before No. 6), even the slaves refer to him as 'black Monostatos'. The word 'moor' had been used, often loosely, since medieval times to refer to any Muslim. Certainly the Ottoman Empire remained a very real threat to Europe throughout the eighteenth century. There was war between Habsburg Austria and Turkey from 1787 to 1791, shortly before the first performance of *The Magic Flute*. As I mentioned earlier, there is a hint of the Turkish in Mozart's music for Monostatos. The little aria in which Monostatos expresses his desire for the sleeping Pamina (No. 13) is the only point in the whole score at which there is any suggestion in the music of an explicitly oriental flavour. But Monostatos can hardly be literally a Turk any more than the 'Egyptians' who describe him as 'black' are literally Egyptians.

The most important oriental element is, of course, the Egyptian setting for Sarastro's brotherhood. Freemasonry uses symbols which are loosely related to ancient Egyptian mysticism. And the depiction of Egyptians, worshippers of Isis and Osiris, as custodians of moral truths, was also compatible with Enlightenment views on the moral worth of pagans (again, it is important not to overstate the importance of this; these are not 'real' Egyptians, any more than they are real freemasons). References to Egypt first appear in the transformation before No. 6, which describes 'a splendid Egyptian room'. In the complete libretto, 'two slaves bring on beautiful cushions and a splendid Turkish table, and spread carpets', thus combining Egyptian and Turkish elements. (Egypt was still part of the Ottoman Empire when the opera was written.) In Act II, the Egyptian context of the brotherhood is more clearly defined, though in a way which is fantastic rather than realistic. At the opening of the act, Sarastro addresses the priests, who are later described specifically as Egyptian priests, as 'servants of the great gods Isis and Osiris'. The scene is set in a palm grove of silver trees with golden leaves. The priests enter carrying palm branches, and their seats are made of palm leaves. Beside each seat stands a pyramid, with a larger pyramid in the centre. The setting for Tamino's first trial (after No. 10) provides the basis for the frontispiece of the libretto (Fig. 11), with 'the ruins of fallen columns and pyramids' and 'tall ancient Egyptian portals'; and as Tamino approaches the final trials, the two Armed Men intone a 'transparent inscription which is written on a pyramid'. All this provides an atmosphere of exotic mystery, as well as a reference to the Egyptian elements of masonic ritual. It does not signify any great knowledge of Egyptian archaeology. Although Egypt had been visited by Europeans, and its monuments described, little was known about them in the eighteenth century.

One more specific Egyptian element is the oblique reference to sun worship. In ancient Egyptian religion, Isis and Osiris were the parents of Horus, the sun-god. In Act II, before No.14, we learn from the Queen of the Night that Sarastro holds the 'mighty Circle of the Sun'. In dialogue which is cut in this recording, we also learn that Pamina's father gave it to the brotherhood, and the Queen is desperate to get it back. It is described as 'all-consuming'. We never learn quite what this means, but it is presumably this which gives Sarastro the power to cast the Queen of the Night and her allies into 'eternal night' at the end of the opera. Immediately after the Queen's destruction, in the final moments of the opera, 'the whole scene changes to a sun', and Sarastro sings that the rays of the sun drive out the night. The splendour of the scene is underlined by the splendour of Mozart's music. Patricia Howard has written on composers' depiction of light earlier in the course (*Studies*, I, p.193 and AC 1628), and Tamino's symbolic journey from darkness to light is stressed at several points in the opera. You might describe it as part Enlightenment, part freemasonry, with a dash of Egyptian sun-worship, though masonic ideas of darkness and light are themselves informed by Enlightenment ideas.

10 Conclusion

You will have gathered that *The Magic Flute* is not a work about which it is possible to draw neat conclusions. But I hope this study has raised some questions which you find interesting, and which will lead you to ask some of your own. To end with, here are some other areas you might like to think about:

1   I have stressed Mozart's use of music for dramatic effect. How do you think *The Magic Flute* relates to ideas of Enlightenment music discussed by Patricia Howard in her essay in *Studies*, I?

2   Stephanie Clennell writes about *Nathan the Wise*: 'A dramatic poem, a modern morality play, a serious comedy? It is all of these, but defies strict categorization.' Having worked through *The Magic Flute*, how would you define its character? In particular, how would you assess the balance between the comic and serious elements?

3   There are other points of comparison with themes in *Nathan the Wise* – religion, tolerance, authority, ideas of humanity ('Mensch'), the treatment of women, the oriental. How much have the two works in common?

11 References

Anderson, E. (1985) *The Letters of Mozart and His Family*, 3rd edn, Macmillan, London.

Deutsch, O.E. (1966) *Mozart: A Documentary Biography*, 2nd edn, A. & C. Black, London.

Grove (1980) *The New Grove Dictionary of Music and Musicians*, vol. 20, edited by S. Sadie, Macmillan, London.

Landon, H. C. R. (1988) *1791: Mozart's Last Year*, Thames and Hudson, London.

Nettl, P. (1957) *Mozart and Masonry*, Philosophical Library, New York. (Also published by Da Capo Press, 1970.)

Porter, A. (trans.) (1980) Mozart's *The Magic Flute: Libretto by Emmanuel Schikaneder*, Faber, London.

Schikaneder, E. (1792) *Sämtliche Theatralische Werke (Complete Works for the Theatre)*, Alois Doll, Vienna.

12 Further reading

Anderson, E. (1985). (See 'References' above for full details. An invaluable primary source for Mozart's correspondence about *The Magic Flute* and its first production.)

Landon, H. C. R. (1988). (See 'References' above for full details. This book, also available as a Fontana paperback (1990), gives a most vivid account of the background to the writing of *The Magic Flute*.)

Nettl (1957; see 'References' above for full details) is more specifically a discussion of Mozart's involvement in freemasonry, and of his masonic music.)

Porter, A. (1980). (See 'References' above for full details. This is the most complete version of Schikaneder's dialogue available in English.)

Roberts, J.M. (1972) *The Mythology of the Secret Societies*, Secker and Warburg, London. (A general discussion of freemasonry in the eighteenth century.

Conclusion

Prepared for the Course Team by Robert Wilkinson

Contents

Conclusion

An important point concerning the religious outlook of the Englightenment emerges both from the texts in Part D, and from many others in the course, and it is that if many of the leading figures of the time are anti-clerical, they are rarely anti-religious. Noisy atheists like d'Holbach are untypical, more untypical than orthodox figures like Newton or Johnson, and far more so than deists of one sort or another. The commonest targets of attack for Voltaire or Lessing, for example, are what they took to be abuses fostered by established churches, Catholic and Protestant. These abuses were not only of a gross, political kind but also those, subtler but just as pernicious, which cramped the spiritual life of believers by imprisoning them in a rigid cell of beliefs claimed to be the unquestionable fruit of revelation. Sometimes their critics took these beliefs to be simply ridiculous, but more often drew attention to the pall they cast over the inner life, blighting spontaneity and inducing guilt where there need be none. This aspect of anti-clericalism is trenchantly epitomized in William Blake's (1757–1827) poem *The Garden of Love* from *Songs of Experience*, published in 1794:

> I went to the Garden of Love,
> And saw what I never had seen,
> A Chapel was built in the midst,
> Where I used to play on the green.
> And the gates of this Chapel were shut,
> And 'Thou shalt not' writ over the door;
> So I turn'd to the Garden of Love
> That so many sweet flowers bore;
> And I saw it was filled with graves,
> And tomb-stones where flowers should be;
> And Priests in black gowns were walking their rounds,
> And binding with briars my joys & desires.
> (Keynes, 1969, p.215)

Yet neither Lessing nor Blake nor many others would wish to deny the central importance of religion in human life. Indeed, their programmes of attack on established churches are based on the prior assumption that a satisfying religious experience is vital to our well-being, but that the churches hindered rather than promoted it.

However, the position most widely advocated throughout Enlightenment Europe as an alternative to the established orthodoxies, that is deism, failed to establish itself in the long term, and, as we shall see presently, faded as the century drew to a close. The root cause of this failure is that deism could not provide some of the satisfactions which a religion must provide if it is to attract adherents and endure. Deism was a neat and uncontentious form of belief. It cohered with the latest scientific discoveries, indeed seeming to complement them by supplying what science could not, namely a first cause for the universe. Again, by its very nature deism precluded sectarianism and so 'enthusiasm' and the conflict which, it seems, must often accompany the latter. But these virtues were bought at a high price. The god of deism is unspeakably remote: his sole intervention in the universe was to create it; he has never intervened and will never intervene in the running of the great machine ever again. Such a god can inspire neither fear nor love; he heard no prayers and sent no messages, and was in consequence as near indifferent to his creatures as any deity has ever been. Now one of the central functions of religion is to furnish a source of comfort and consolation to suffering and bewildered humanity, and the deist god cannot do that. This god is not a Father, neither compassionate nor justly wrathful, ready to console the good and punish the wicked, and provide a fixed point amid the unpredictable hurts of life. The deist god was merely an artificer and first cause, and no amount of double-talk by the deists, who continued to use the vocabulary of orthodoxy in a most unorthodox sense, could hide it. Deism cannot assuage our pain nor calm our bewilderment, and if a religion cannot do these things it will surely fail.

What happened as deism faded, and indeed partly as a result of which it faded, is of interest for many reasons, of which two are of direct relevance to our course. The first is that what occurred in the area of religious thought in the last two decades of the eighteenth century is a typical example of how ramified a phenomenon is cultural change in an advanced civil society. What I have in mind is summed up by one of the most penetrating analysts of cultural change, the Austrian writer and essayist Robert Musil (1880–1942):

> Progress… is not something that unfolds in a single line. Along with the natural weakening an idea suffers as it becomes diffuse, there is also the crisscrossing of influences from new sources of ideas. The innermost core of the life of every age, an inchoate, swelling mass, is poured into molds forged by much earlier times. Every present period is simultaneously now and yet millennia old. This millipede moves on political, economic, cultural, biological and countless other legs, each of which has a different tempo and rhythm. (Musil, 1990, pp.146–7)

Musil happened to be describing the thirty years before 1920, but what he says is applicable without modification to any part of our period: different aspects of a culture change at incommensurable rates and for changing sets of reasons, often different in different countries. What is true at the start of a decade of a given aspect of culture in a given place might be true ten years later, and it might not: one has to look and see in each case. This is exemplified perfectly by changes in the religious outlook of England, France and Germany in the generation which followed the death of Lessing, as I will try to show presently.

The second reason why this span of twenty or so years is of special interest in the present context is that during this period a number of key beliefs unquestioned during the Enlightenment are discarded or modified, and the changes make these beliefs, which give the Enlightenment its distinctive flavour, stand out with great clarity. It is no bad thing to begin to collect one's thoughts on the matter now, four-fifths of the way through the course. Let me now try to substantiate these general assertions.

The end of the eighteenth century was in many ways moulded and dominated by the French Revolution, and this is as true in the area of religion as elsewhere. In France itself, whilst the Gallican Church underwent profound changes during the Revolution, and recovered a degree of its pre-Revolutionary status under Napoleon, no new thinkers emerged to revitalize *ideas* about religion. Instead, the most eloquent work on religion to emerge from France in this period is *The Spirit of Christianity* (1802; *Le Génie du Christianisme*) by François-René de Chateaubriand (1768–1848), a major figure in French literature. This work is a long defence of orthodox piety. It breaks no new ground so far as thought about religion is concerned; rather, its chief aim is to repair the damage done by Voltaire, Rousseau and the Encyclopedists, who made piety ridiculous, with, in Chateaubriand's view, dire consequences:

> [Voltaire] had the baneful art of making unbelief fashionable among a capricious and friendly people... religion was attacked with every sort of arms, from the pamphlet to the folio volume, from the epigram to the sophism. A religious work had only to appear for its author to be covered in ridicule... This destructive system spread throughout France... Finally, it *came to be taken for granted* that Christianity was no more than a barbarous system whose fall could not arrive too soon for human liberty, the progress of knowledge, the quality of life and elegance in the arts... Each writer blessed his destiny for having been born in the century of Diderot and d'Alembert, in the century where the documents of human wisdom were arranged in alphabetical order in the *Encyclopédie*, that Babel of sciences and reason. (Chateaubriand, 1966, vol.1, pp.55–6)

Chateaubriand's rhetoric is impeccable, but one looks in vain in this work for a new idea about religion.

In England, the effect of the French Revolution and the Napoleonic Wars was to cement religion into insularity and to buttress the forces of conservatism, which made good use of the fears of upheaval generated by events across the Channel. The deist debate in England was over by the middle of the eighteenth century, leaving the field to Anglicanism and the various dissenting sects. The Church of England settled into a phase in which it was 'bad form' to exercise oneself too much over matters of dogma. The mood of the time was exactly captured by the Oxford historian James Anthony Froude (1818–94):

> [The Church of England] was orthodox without being theological. Doctrinal problems were little thought of. Religion...meant moral obedience to the will of God. The speculative part of it was accepted because it was assumed to be true. The creeds were reverentially repeated; but the essential thing was practice. People went to Church on Sunday to learn to be good... About the powers of the keys, the real presence, or the metaphysics of doctrine, no one was anxious, for no one thought about them. It was not worth while to waste time over questions which had no bearing on conduct, and could be satisfactorily disposed of only by sensible indifference. (*Short Studies on Great Subjects*, 1886, quoted in Vidler, 1961, pp.34–5)

Most shared the assumption of Froude's father Robert Hurrell Froude (1771–1859), Archdeacon of Totnes, 'that the way to heaven was to turn to the right and go straight on' (Vidler, 1961, p.36). England was isolated, and deliberately so, from any new ideas about religion. The debates of the first half of the century faded away, and the mood in orthodox circles was one of unintellectual, if very comfortable, belief. If by contrast one turns to Germany, one encounters a ferment of thought about religion, where ideas of a new kind were emerging in direct opposition to the prevailing outlook forged in the Enlightenment. For our purposes, the most illuminating work on which to focus is the first edition (1799) of *On Religion: Speeches to its Cultured Despisers (Über die Religion, Reden an die Gebildeten unter ihre Verächtern]* by the Protestant theologian and priest, Friedrich Schleiermacher (1768–1834).[1]

In this work, Schleiermacher seeks to defend religion from the views of two groups of people (the 'cultured despisers' of the title): one sub-set of these were the followers of a particular philosophical outlook developed late in the eighteenth century by J.G. Fichte (1762–1814), and with these we need not concern ourselves; the other sub-set were those who adhered to beliefs in natural religion of the kind favoured by the deists of the Enlightenment. What is of present interest are the grounds on which Schleiermacher attacks their beliefs.

One of the most fundamental presuppositions not only of deism but also of much of the thought of the Enlightenment in general is that the final, bedrock touchstone or guarantor of truth, and so of knowledge, is human reason. The ultimate test for any theory or fact or prescription is how it stands up under rational investigation. This was accepted by the Encyclopedists, by Hume, Gibbon, Lessing, indeed by almost every figure of note in this period, and it was in the name of reason that they opposed the other major contender to be the arbiter of truth, that is the authority of churches, claiming severally to be the unique custodians of divine revelation. To open Schleiermacher's text, which appeared less than twenty years after Lessing's death, is to find that, so far as religion is concerned, the rationalism of the Enlightenment has been put aside and declared irrelevant. The guarantors of religious conviction are neither reason nor authority, but intuition, feeling and imagination.

The core of religion, Schleiermacher contends, is not to be found either in holding the right set of beliefs, nor acting in accordance with a special set of moral precepts, but in a special intuition:

> Religion's essence is neither thinking nor acting, but intuition and feeling. It wishes to intuit the universe, wishes devoutly to overhear the universe's own manifestations, longs to be grasped and filled by the universe's immediate influences in childlike passivity …Everything must proceed from intuition, and those who lack the desire to intuit the infinite have no touchstone and indeed need none in order to know whether they have given any respectable thought to the matter. (Schleiermacher, 1980, pp.102–3)

This special intuition is pre-linguistic and so, strictly speaking, ineffable; but Schleiermacher must try to convey something of its character, since otherwise his assertions would be unlikely to convince the target audience. The rhetoric which he employs to describe it is well worth comparing with articles from the *Encyclopédie* or remarks by Gibbon or Hume or Lessing dealing with religious matters:

---

[1] I must stress that what I have to say concerns *only* the first edition of this book. Schleiermacher revised it twice, in 1806 and 1821, because the currents of belief he wanted to combat changed rapidly. Only the first edition is of relevance to our course, and this is itself another index of the pace at which change in belief can occur. The word 'Reden' in the title can also be rendered as 'Addresses': Schleiermacher did not intend these documents to be delivered as speeches, but only to be read.

> It [i.e. the religious intuition] is as fleeting and transparent as the first scent with which the dew gently caresses the waking flowers, as modest and delicate as a maiden's kiss, as holy and fruitful as a nuptial embrace; indeed, not *like* these, but it *is itself* all of these...I lie on the bosom of the infinite world. At this moment I am its soul, for I feel all its powers and its infinite life as my own; at this moment it is my body, for I penetrate its muscles and its limbs as my own, and its innermost nerves move according to my sense and my presentiment as my own. (Schleiermacher, 1980, pp.112–13)

Whether your intuition is of a god is relatively unimportant:

> ...for me divinity can be nothing other than a particular type of religious intuition...From my standpoint and according to my conceptions that are known to you, the belief 'No God, no religion' cannot occur...Whether we have a god as a part of our intuition depends on the direction of our imagination. (Schleiermacher, 1980, p.136)

It follows that for Schleiermacher the natural religion of the deists, both in method and content, has nothing to do with religion proper. Arrived at by rational reflection on the order of nature, it is unconnected with the pre-rational intuition which is the kernel of religious experience. The Savoyard Priest in Rousseau's *Émile* derives his convictions from reflection on the phenomena of nature; for Schleiermacher such phenomena and such reflection are an irrelevance:

> Neither fear of the material forces you see operating on this earth nor joy at the beauty of corporeal nature will or can give you the first intuition of this world and its spirit. Neither in the thunder of the heavens nor in the frightful rolling of the sea are you to recognize the presence of the almighty being; neither in the bloom of the flowers nor in the brilliance of the sunsets are you to recognize the lovely and benevolent. (Schleiermacher, 1980, pp.133)

Any attempt to found religion on scientific reflection – and the argument from design in the Enlightenment, as we have seen, is an example of precisely that – is equally an irrelevance. Religion is not a matter of belief at all: the domains of science and religion are incommensurable. Religion 'leaves you, your physics and, may it please God, your psychology inviolate' (Schleiermacher, 1980, p.133).

It is I hope clear by now that to read Schleiermacher is to find oneself in a world of ideas different from those of the Enlightenment in a number of profound and far-reaching ways. Much of the thought of the Enlightenment is the gradual working out of the implications of a number of deep convictions, notably the methods and findings of Newtonian science and a closely associated rationalism. When the figures of the time approached the apparatus of orthodox religion armed with these presuppositions, a great deal of that apparatus appeared to be irrational, and often merely superstitious. Those who retained a belief in God were generally pushed toward deism, as the only consistent and rational system of religious belief, that is the one which would square best with their bedrock assumptions. Of the deists, those who found the concept of a transcendent deist God remote or otiose tended to move toward a belief in immanentism. The only way out of these positions, other than atheism or the cosy practicality of many Anglicans, was to sacrifice or modify one of the bedrock presuppositions, and this is what Schleiermacher does: he takes religion out of the domain of the rational and makes it incommensurable with science, and this is a radical break with the thought of the Enlightenment.

In Germany then, to return to Musil's image, the legs of the millipede which moved religious thought were moving rather swiftly at the end of the eighteenth century; in France they were moving slightly backwards, and in England they had gone to sleep. And this is a quite typical state of affairs in cultural change, as in all dimensions of life: it was then, as it has always been, irreducibly untidy and various.

One more point: the radical shift we have found in Schleiermacher's text did not come, as it were, out of the air. There had been, for almost half a century in some cases, areas in which the Enlightenment outlook had been found wanting, and shifts of value had begun to take place. In subtle ways, attitudes to nature, to civilisation, to the importance of feeling in the economy of human nature, began to be questioned and modified. Some of these changes are dealt with in Part E of the course, to which you should now turn.

References

Chateaubriand, F.-R. (1966) *Le Génie du Christianisme*, edited by P. Reboul, Garnier, Paris.

Keynes, G. (ed.) (1969) *William Blake. Complete Writings*, Oxford Standard Authors, Oxford University Press, Oxford.

Musil, R. (1990) *Mind and Experience* (*Geist und Erfahrung*, 1921) translated by B. Pike and D.S. Luft in *Precision and Soul*, Chicago University Press, Chicago.

Schleiermacher, F. (1980) *On Religion: Speeches to its Cultured Despisers* (*Über die Religion, Reden, an die Gebildeten unter ihre Verächtern*, 1799) translated by R. Crouter, Cambridge University Press, Cambridge.

Vidler, R.F. (1961) *The Church in an Age of Revolution*, Penguin Group, London.

Part E
Nature, Feeling and Society

Contents

Study Timetable

The timetable below sets out the teaching materials you will need to have to hand for each unit of *Studies*, Part E.

Eighteenth-Century Poetry (Study weeks 24–25)

Studies/Texts	Radio	TV	AC	Set books
Studies, II	R6	TV13	AC1633 (green)	-
Texts, II				

Rousseau's Émile (Study weeks 26–27)

Studies/Texts	Radio	TV	AC	Set Books
Studies, II	-	TV14	-	-
Texts, II				

The Thought of Mary Wollstonecraft (Study week 28)

Studies/Texts	Radio	TV	AC	Set Books
Studies, II				
Texts, II	-	-	-	-

Diderot's Salon of 1765 (Study week 29)

Studies/Texts	Radio	TV	AC	Set Books
Studies, II	-	TV15	AC1632 (blue)	
Texts, II				
Illustration Book				

Laclos – Dangerous Acquaintances (Study weeks 30–31)

Studies/Texts	Radio	TV	AC	Set Books
Studies, II	Radio 7	TV 16		*Dangerous Acquaintances*
Texts, II	Radio 8			

Introduction

Linda Walsh

In this final part of the course you may find both a confirmation and a denial of the model of 'enlightenment' which you have constructed in your mind through your work on previous texts. You may have decided, for example, that reason, nature, scepticism, toleration, empirical scientific investigation and humanity (in the sense of a benevolent concern for the welfare of others) were key characteristics of eighteenth-century enlightened thought. If so, you may find that the status of these concepts alters in the texts you are about to study, or that they attain a new kind of complexity. The *Encyclopédie*, with which the course begins, commends a number of progressive ideals. As you read the work of British poets, of Jean-Jacques Rousseau, Mary Wollstonecraft, Denis Diderot and Choderlos de Laclos, you may draw your own conclusions about whether the programme of enlightenment outlined in the *Encyclopédie* was a success or a failure.

If you do detect differences in emphasis, new directions or failures of nerve, this may be due, in part, to chronological considerations. The poems you will study span the eighteenth century, covering the period from 1717 to 1786. Rousseau's *Émile* was published in 1762; Mary Wollstonecraft's *Vindication of the Rights of Woman* in 1792. Diderot's *Salon of 1765* was written in 1765 (though not published until much later) and Laclos's *Les Liaisons Dangereuses* (*Dangerous Acquaintances*) was published in 1783. Many of these texts, then, were produced in the later decades of the century, in Britain or France. If a belief in ideals such as nature, reason and humanity began to wane, or if there was a perceived need to debate these concepts within a new framework, this may have been related to social and economic developments in both nations and to the precipitation of revolution in one of them.

Nature, Feeling and Society have been selected as pivotal points in the debate on the fate of Enlightenment ideals. The texts you are about to study raise a much broader range of issues than those included in the title to Part E, but the elements of this title indicate areas of common concern for all of the texts in this part of the course and provide an organizing principle for the rich anarchy of the evidence before us.

1 Nature

In the *Encyclopédie* you met nature in the guise of a higher authority ready to redress the injustices of church and state if only mankind would reason effectively and discover her dictates (see *Texts*, I, *Woman-Natural Law*). At the same time she appeared, in her infinite variety, as the object of study for the scientist (*Experimental*) who, if prepared to practise first-hand observation of the natural world, would be able to discern her laws. To Reynolds she was both reality (the 'nature' of the sitter in the sense of a true likeness) and ideal (the selective and purified vision of natural forms transmitted by the Ancients). Diderot's *Salon of 1765* resumes this debate on the merits of observation and idealization in art. Indeed, all the texts you are about to study further exemplify the ways in which 'nature' represented both reality and something beyond reality for eighteenth-century writers and artists. Some of the poems you will read explore reactions to the pastoral idyll – an idealized and conventional view of the natural world – and to its escapist tendencies.

Writers and artists of eighteenth-century France tended to venerate nature as a source of truth, moral innocence (you've already encountered the 'noble savage' convention), liberty and wisdom. She was perceived as an antidote to falsehood, artifice and corruption. 'Nature' was viewed both on the human scale – human nature; human faculties, qualities and propensities both physical and mental – and on the larger scale of the world or environment inhabited by humankind, even up to the universe itself. To many thinkers who had forsaken the tutelage of orthodox religion, observation or contemplation of nature was seen as the only means of knowing God. As you read *Émile* you will recognize elements of the deist tradition discussed in Hume's *Dialogues*: according to Cleanthes, in the latter text, the natural world is 'one great machine' which irresistibly suggests the existence of a Designer. Some thinkers, like Diderot, eventually regarded nature as a substitute for God: their atheism led them to look to human nature and the wider natural world when establishing beliefs and principles on moral and aesthetic matters. Both eighteenth-century writers and modern commentators tend to capitalize the word Nature when it is used to denote this kind of elevated, abstract or august authority but there are no hard and fast rules here and caution must be exercised: it was common practice in many eighteenth-century texts to capitalize nouns (particularly abstract nouns) and adjectives worthy of emphasis or authority.

The confidence of the intelligentsia in their ability to discover universal laws of human nature (i.e. of behaviour and ethics) was matched only by their ability to disagree about what those laws were and whether any such laws were good, bad or morally neutral in essence and effect. While Voltaire gave serious consideration in *Candide* to the thesis that 'man's origin is evil', Rousseau vacillated between the view that man was born good and the view that he was born, at the very least, capable of good. In his *Discourse on Inequality* (1755) he described compassion as 'so much the more universal and useful to mankind, as it comes before any kind of reflection; and at the same time so natural, that the very brutes themselves sometimes give evident proof of it' (Rousseau, 1986, p.73). According to Rousseau, all depravity and vice have their source in society rather than in the nature of human beings as individuals. This concern lies at the heart of *Émile* and of Laclos's novel *Dangerous Acquaintances*, which offers a spine-chilling demonstration of the forces massed against the virtue of humanity. This novel might be read as a powerful affirmation of the bleak view of human nature presented in parts of Voltaire's *Candide*.

In many of the Part E texts the eighteenth-century view that 'human nature' can be sub-divided into 'female nature' and 'male nature' is implicit. *Émile* looks at the implications of gendered characteristics which are assumed to be innate and at the social expectations which shape male and female education, while *Dangerous Acquaintances* reveals the complex interaction of social convention with the male and female psyches. Mary Wollstonecraft questions stereotypical views of female nature and in particular, the conventional view that intellectual powers are not 'natural' to women. TV16 explores further the complex relationship between the eighteenth-century view of women and the concept of nature.

It is often suggested that, while in texts of the first half of the eighteenth-century, the term 'Nature' was associated with stability, order and the immutable laws of Newton, it was later coupled with the ideas of flux, asymmetry and disorder. This progression from order to disorder is epitomized in the landscapes sought and constructed by eighteenth-century travellers, writers and landscape gardeners. Throughout the century formal, rectilinear gardens slowly gave way to more informal and 'natural' vistas in landscape design. Classical formality was succeeded by the sinuous picturesque vistas carefully arranged by designers like Capability Brown (see TV7, 'Kedleston Hall'). The vogue for the new 'English gardens' spread to other countries, including France. It was only, however, in the final decades of the century that wilder mountain scenery was widely appreciated by the educated élite of Europe. Participants in the Grand Tour (see TV5, 'The Grand Tour and the Rediscovery of the Classics') who had to cross the Alps when travelling from France to Italy dreaded the dangers of the route with its 'Eternal Snow, Clouds hanging far below [their] feet, and the cascades tumbling down the Rocks with a confus'd roaring' (Halsband, 1965, p.99). This wilder Alpine scenery, much appreciated by Rousseau, was a late eighteenth-century taste expressed only by those who welcomed the full sublime force, the torrents and crags of Nature's power. Edmund Burke's treatise *A Philosophical Enquiry into the origin of our ideas of the Sublime and Beautiful* (1756), in which sublimity was associated with the feelings of terror and pain aroused by nature and art, was instrumental in this shift in taste. In TVs 5, 14 and 15 and in the dramatic shipwrecks painted by Vernet, freer, less formal landscapes are endowed with aesthetic, moral and political significance. The exaltation of Nature in its innocent, free and primitive state is an important theme in Part E texts and one which was to receive unprecedented attention in the cultural movement known as Romanticism, conventionally located by scholars in the period 1780–1850.

The concept of Nature, then, can be found anywhere along the lines that run between the polarities of reason and sublimity, order and freedom, reality and ideal, innocence and evil, tameness and wildness. 'Nature' could be cited in support of either extremity or pole of such conceptual pairings. Any attempt to interpret its meaning must take account of the specific context in which it occurs.

2   Feeling

It is wrong to regard the eighteenth century simply as an 'Age of Reason'. Despite the evident emphasis on independent intellectual and scientific enquiry and on the exercise of a humane, tolerant common sense, as the century progressed emotion (or feeling) was increasingly regarded as an important human faculty. This trend is discernible in thinking on morality, society, art and literature. It is because of this trend that the eighteenth century is often regarded as an age of pre-romanticism, or as an age in which 'classical' (or rational) and 'Romantic' ideas about art overlapped or merged: Romantic culture placed an unprecedented emphasis on the free expression of emotion.

'Sensibility' (*sensibilité* in French) was one of the key words of the century and carried a variety of meanings, but generally denoted a capacity for feeling (as opposed to reasoning) of some kind, ranging from crude sensory impressions to violent emotion. Although the word was sometimes used in a general and neutral sense, it often carried connotations of a *special* sensitivity, a capacity for particularly *keen* responses of the heart and senses. Scholars often use the word 'sensibility' to denote the *cult* of feeling which swept through the eighteenth century. 'Sensibility' was closely related in eighteenth-century texts to the words 'sensation', 'passion' and 'sentiment': types of feeling which could be experienced by sensitive (*sensible*) people. 'Sensation(s)', 'passions(s)' and 'sentiment(s)' (the French words were spelled in the same way as their English equivalents but pronounced differently) could all be used in a generic way to denote feeling(s) in general. Increasingly, however, they conveyed distinctive meanings. Thus 'sensation(s)' was used in reference to physical responses of the senses (subsequently conveyed to the brain) or crude and immediate feelings of pleasure or pain stimulated by reactions of the sense organs to external stimuli. We still speak of 'a sensitive skin' in this sense. It was common to speak of the *sensations* of light, colour, heat, cold, hunger etc. You will see, in Rousseau's *Émile*, how such impressions are regarded as an important source of knowledge, in accordance with the epistemological tradition developed by Locke. In the *Salon of 1765* Chardin's still lifes (mouth-watering peaches, for example) give Diderot 'pleasant sensations': sensation played an important part in eighteenth-century views on aesthetic taste.

'Sentiment' was used to denote a more refined kind of sensibility. Whereas seventeenth-century dictionary definitions of sensibility/*sensibilité* make the briefest reference to compassion, eighteenth-century entries devote much more space to this 'sensibility of the heart' or sensitivity to the ills of others: 'sensibility' and 'sentiment' were used increasingly to refer to feelings(s) of a virtuous kind and carried connotations of noble, elevated responses to one's fellow humans. The tendency of eighteenth-century thinkers to grade and differentiate between 'classes' of feeling in this way may seem strange to the twentieth-century reader but we must envisage a period in which the most sophisticated theories in psychology were those provided by Locke. Theorists like Shaftesbury (in his *Characteristicks of Men, Manners, Opinions, Times*, 1711), Hutcheson (in his *Inquiry into the original of our ideas of Beauty and Virtue*, 1738), Hume and Adam Smith popularized the idea that there is an 'inner sense' in human beings inclining them to acts of charity and beneficence and drawing them towards harmony of sound and beauty of form. In other words, humankind was capable of a kind of mental and moral sensitivity which facilitated responses to art and life and which distinguished humans from the beasts. The word 'sentiment' was often used to refer to a sensitivity of the mind as well as of the heart – a kind of 'correct' intuition or refined perception. (There was no equivalent in eighteenth-century French for our word 'intuition'.) Mary Wollstonecraft distinguishes between crude, 'mechanical' sensations and the kinds of feelings, achievable by humans, which are more compatible with reason and morality. The popularity of the three grand masonic principles of brotherly love, relief (assistance) and truth further testify to the importance of this belief in elevated, moral feeling in the eighteenth century.

Moral sensibility, grounded in a love of virtue and a capacity for compassion and suffering, enjoyed an unprecedented vogue in the eighteenth century. It became desirable to exhibit one's emotions: tears were interpreted as the sign of a virtuous heart. There have been several attempts to explain the origins of this phenomenon, which became more marked from the mid-century onwards. Some trace its origins to the medieval Christian notion of a 'vale of tears' and some state that it was a natural development in an age which increasingly cast aside religion: it was, for the enlightened, a secular alternative to Christian compassion and fervour. Others trace the origins of the phenomenon to Anglican Latitudinarianism (for a later comment on the broad-mindedness of the Anglican Church see the Conclusion to Part D, above, p.116) or to the spread of a more optimistic conception of human nature among some thinkers. The ills of French society (war, outbreaks of smallpox, religious discord, poverty, even rampant rationalism) have also been identified as catalysts. Some scholars relate the movement closely to the bourgeoisie, growing in importance economically and thus acquiring a voice in moral affairs; while others dismiss such explanations as 'Marxist' and inaccurate. Whatever the cause(s) it is a fact that art, literature and social life in eighteenth-century Britain, France and other nations (e.g. – the writings of Goethe in Germany: see *Studies*, II, p.283) attached increasing importance to the expression of feeling, and that in the middle decades of the century the emphasis was on feeling of a moral kind.

The novels of Marivaux, Samuel Richardson, Mackenzie, Sterne, Rousseau and Prévost enjoyed great popularity. Richardson's novels were widely translated into French: readers enjoyed their open expression of emotion and their appeals to the heart. The following extracts from eighteenth-century British novels offer a glimpse of the kind of writing which celebrated and sought to arouse emotion and which was produced within the cult of sensibility:

> Dear sensibility! source inexhausted of all that's precious in our joys, or costly in our sorrows! thou chainest thy martyr down upon his bed of straw – and 'tis thou who lifts him up to HEAVEN – eternal fountain of our feelings! – 'tis here I trace thee – and this is thy divinity which stirs within me – not that, in some sad and sickening moments, *my soul shrinks back upon herself, and startles at destruction –* mere pomp of words! – but that I feel some generous joys and generous cares beyond myself – all comes from thee, great, great SENSORIUM of the world! which vibrates, if a hair of our heads falls upon the ground, in the remotest desert of thy creation. (Sterne, 1967, p.141)

(Note that the word 'sentimental' was used in a more neutral fashion in the eighteenth century, denoting that which pertains to sentiments of the heart, whereas it carries today connotations of mawkishness. In Sterne's book sentiment is alleviated by humour.)

In this extract from Mackenzie's *Man of Feeling* Miss Atkins's father, enraged to discover she is a prostitute, finds her with Harley:

> His daughter was now prostrate at his feet. 'Strike,' said she, 'strike here a wretch, whose misery cannot end but with that death she deserves.' Her hair had fallen on her shoulders! her look had the horrid calmness of out-breathed despair! Her father would have

spoken; his lip quivered, his cheek grew pale! his eyes lost the lightening of their fury! There was a reproach in them, but with a min-
gling of pity! He turned them up to heaven – then on his daughter.
– He laid his left hand on his heart – the sword dropped from his
right – he burst into tears. (Mackenzie, 1987, pp.66–7)

The middle of the century saw in France the growth of a new theatrical
form, the *drame bourgeois* (see the Introduction to *Nathan the Wise*), which
presented on stage family quarrels, moving reconciliations and reunions
and other subjects close to the hearts of the bourgeoisie. Public weeping
in the boxes was taken as an indication of the moral well-being of the
audience: it was visible proof of their capacity for commiseration with the
hapless victims of life's tragedies. In her book on Greuze, Anita Brookner
(1972, p.26) tells the tale of a mother who could not decide which of two
suitors her daughter should marry. She asked them both to accompany
her daughter to a performance of Marmontel's play, *The Good Mother*. The
successful candidate was the more profuse weeper of the two as he was
assumed to be the more virtuous.

Such a climate of ideas naturally encouraged exhibitionism and
mawkishness, although many scholars argue that it also provoked much
practical philanthropy (e.g. the decline of public executions as a popular
recreation; a greater concern for the poor). It is certainly true that many
twentieth-century viewers regard the sentimental scenes of the artist
Greuze which you will be studying (e.g. *Young Girl Crying over Her Dead
Bird* (Col. Pl. 31) and *The Well-Beloved Mother* (Pl. 173)) as mawkish or
exhibitionist. Diderot, a man of his time, regards them, as you will see, as
valuable instruments in the school of virtue. In praising the sentimental
didacticism of Greuze's art he was typical of most art critics of the mid-
century.

This cult of moral feeling could become self-congratulatory and
hedonistic at times. A theorist named Lévesque de Pouilly (in his *Theory of
Agreeable Sentiments*, 1747) popularized the idea that feeling is, above all,
pleasurable. Many regarded it as a voluptuous or sensuous experience
and spoke of the 'ecstasies' of grief. This celebration of emotion *for its
own sake* was difficult to reconcile with the view that there exists a specific,
moral strain of feelings or emotions: Diderot's *Salon of 1765* wrestles with
this dilemma. Edmund Burke's treatise on *The Sublime and the Beautiful*
(1756) in which sublimity was associated with feelings of terror and pain,
helped to weaken the link between morality and emotion. Moral sensibility, popular as a cult of the mid-century, came increasingly under
threat as the cultivation of wilder, often sensuous feeling (including melancholy and terror) took its grip in later decades. Gray's *Elegy Written in a
Country Churchyard* is a relatively early expression of a melancholic sensibility more usually associated with the late eighteenth century.

In the second half of the century the vehemence of feeling sought
in art and life was closely associated with the term 'passion'. Passions were
'movements of the soul' stimulated by sense impressions. They included
love, hate, admiration, desire, joy, hope, anger, despair and sadness. Des-
cartes had classified the passions systematically in the seventeenth century. His view that the passions involved the movement of blood and
animal spirits (subtle particles of matter carried by the blood and
enabling it to act on the soul) continued to hold sway in the eighteenth
century, as did the Hippocratic view, deriving from ancient Greek medical

tradition, that the seat of the passions was the diaphragm. Small wonder then, that the passions were often viewed as purveyors of physiological anarchy, clouding the judgement, causing illness and militating against virtuous conduct. The *Encyclopédie* articles *Sensibility* (by Fouquet) and *Passions* (by de Jaucourt) outlined the pathological symptoms of passion: hatred could produce headaches; terror could provoke fever.

It became fashionable to suffer from such conditions and to speak of cures for emotional disorders: baths, mineral waters, change of diet, music, fresh air. Such disorders and cures were confined to the upper echelons of society, anxious to assert the delicacy of their nervous systems. Swooning and the vapours were particularly fashionable among upper-class women. The causes of such disorders were usually cited as tea, coffee, literature, the theatre, novels, city life, idleness.

D'Alembert's mistress, Julie de Lespinasse, has left us her correspondence, in which she describes the physical symptoms (affecting her heart beat and pulse) of her 'nervous' condition (Asse, 1876). She felt she had been 'made for unhappiness'. Proud that she had been chosen by fate as a sufferer, as part of a spiritual and compassionate elite, she could not withstand the pressures brought to bear upon her. She resorted to opium, which precipitated her death. Mary Wollstonecraft, weary of the view that women had particularly vulnerable nervous systems, exhorts women, in the *Vindication of the Rights of Woman* (Chapter III) to cease boasting of their 'exquisite sensibility' and to learn to use their intellect.

Paradoxically, however, the passions were also cited as a means to happiness, inducements to action and heroism and agents of self-preservation. Their relationship to happiness was obviously ambivalent, as they were associated so closely with the thrills and strains of the nervous system. Many theoreticians and novelists (including Rousseau) undertook what has come to be known as the 'rehabilitation of the passions' (i.e. a more positive view of them than that taken by traditional Christian thought) and emphasized that, as long as they were properly restrained by reason, they could make a positive contribution to happiness and virtue. Catherine the Great, seeking to excuse her love-life, argued that passion is both natural and irresistible: all arguments to the contrary indicate prudery and ignorance of the human heart (*Texts*, I p.75). Laclos's *Dangerous Acquaintances* can be read as a fictional exploration of the ambivalent status of passion. In this novel moral sensibility cowers. Mme de Tourvel, in whom it chiefly resides, is portrayed as a hunted animal eventually hounded into the ravages of love and passion while Valmont, her seducer, cynically mimics the tears of moral sensibility in order to gain her favour. Moral sentiments are ineffectual; the less moral yet domineering *passions* of love and aggression of Valmont and Mme de Merteuil are both admirable in their energy and power and destructive in their consequences. As Angus Calder shows in his study, the novel reveals the different types (lust, devotion and obsession) and intensities of feeling with which 'love' was associated in the eighteenth century.

In a century in which both reason and feeling were celebrated, it is inevitable that these two often came into conflict. The texts you are about to study dramatize and explore their rival claims. *Dangerous Acquaintances* examines a section of society in which the kind of reasoning advocated by the *philosophes* is dwarfed by reasoning of a more sinister kind and, above all, by the vehemence of the passion driving its protagonists. Mary

Wollstonecraft practises a kind of writing which provokes a re-evaluation of and reaction against the traditional opposition of reason and feeling. Diderot's *Salon of 1765* also offers insights into the debate on the relative merits of reason and feeling: which of these should predominate in taste, critical method and the creative process? You have already witnessed a similar debate in Hume's *Of the Standard of Taste* in Part B. As you read the texts of Part E, try to identify the *kinds* of feeling which are being discussed or exemplified, as well as their status in art, literature and morals.

3 Society

It is difficult to speak of 'eighteenth-century society' in general terms. Although many of the cultural concepts we have discussed so far crossed national boundaries and helped to define a European Enlightenment, they were rooted in different national and social contexts which explain, to some extent, the different priorities, perspectives and tone of the British and French texts you are about to study. In France, the widely differing privileges of the three estates outlined in Clive Emsley's *France in the Eighteenth Century* (*Studies*, I, pp.417–25), the very wide differences of life style which cut across all three estates and often blurred those older legal distinctions, the remnants of feudalism, the system of absolute monarchy and the powerful alliance of church and state, provoked more strident cries for liberty and more desperate investigations into the nature of God and the origins of humankind and the physical universe than were commonly expressed in British texts.

In Britain the powers of the monarch were checked by Parliament. In France, the powers of the monarch were absolute, but neither Louis XV nor Louis XVI were held up as models of enlightened absolutism in the same ways that Frederick the Great and Catherine the Great were. The Church of England was noted for its latitudinarianism or broad-mindedness (perhaps at the expense of zeal) while the Catholic Church in France was perceived by many intellectuals as a major source of intolerance and persecution. Each nation then, might produce a different agenda to be addressed with reference to a set of international Enlightenment values.

The relationship between the Enlightenment and the French Revolution is problematic. The causes of the Revolution were many and varied and included sectional interests, differences of privilege and taxation, the crisis precipitated by the sudden formation of a consultative assembly after centuries of absolutism and a national financial crisis caused by war debts. There is not space here to discuss the Revolution itself but you will find further comment in your study on Mary Wollstonecraft (below, pp.221–3). Although there is no clear causal relationship between the increasingly common discourse among intellectuals centred on notions of 'liberty' and 'rights' and the Revolution, it is generally accepted that this discourse was fully exploited by revolutionaries and by those sympathetic to their cause, as Catherine the Great complained. Political liberty and popular representation are themes which feature prominently in the exchange of views between Mary Wollstonecraft and contemporaries like Richard Price and Edmund Burke.

In the decades before the Revolution, while some *philosophes* looked towards a constitutional monarchy coupled with representative institutions in which the voice of the (educated) people might be heard, there was no call for the overthrow of the monarchy. Politics of the mid-century were very different from those of the Revolution. The events of the latter precipitated countless alignments and re-alignments of sectional interests. Rousseau was one of the bolder voices among eighteenth-century intellectuals, arguing, in his *Social Contract* (1762) that supreme sovereignty should rest with the general will, which expressed the common aspirations of all citizens. Despite the lack of evidence for any direct relationship between thinkers and political events, it is generally accepted that the 1789 Declaration of the Rights of Man and the Citizen, and the first Constitution in 1791, owed much to the ideas and vocabulary of Montesquieu, Voltaire, Rousseau, Diderot (who all died before 1789) and others in their attacks on feudalism, despotism and clericalism. We must be careful, however, to locate such debates within their eighteenth-century context. To an eighteenth-century reformer political 'liberty' meant something quite different from twentieth-century notions of democracy. It was associated with the idea of the rule of law, not the rule of the people. The only people with whom a monarch might share power were those subjects occupying the ranks of the wealthier bourgeoisie upwards: there were few impassioned pleas for universal equality or equal participation in the consultative process. The term 'democracy' was often used pejoratively, to signify an obviously undesirable government by rabble. The class which gained the most political power from the Revolution was the bourgeoisie.

If political equality was regarded by many thinkers as a pipe-dream, however, this does not mean that they paid little attention to the grosser inequalities perceivable in society. Quite the contrary. Rousseau was particularly critical of the vast disparities of wealth and privilege in eighteenth-century France. His suggestion in *Émile* that the well-to-do should learn a trade such as carpentry was part of his attempt to bring the upper echelons of society closer to the value of honest hard work: one has only to imagine the impact of such an ethic on Valmont in *Dangerous Acquaintances*. Rousseau's diatribe on luxury in *Émile* and other works suggests the desirability of a substantial redistribution of wealth as well as a re-evaluation of its merits. *Dangerous Acquaintances*, *Émile* and the aristocratic taste for rococo art discussed in the study on Diderot's *Salon of 1765*, demonstrate the 'unnatural' consequences of a society in which wealth, labour and leisure are so unevenly distributed. Most enlightened thinkers were alert to the extremes created by such discrepancies: contributors to the *Encyclopédie* campaigned for reform of the more unjust and burdensome taxes (such as the corvée – forced labour on the highways – a form of indirect taxation imposed on the peasantry).

In Britain the system of parliamentary monarchy did not, perhaps, provoke such strident pleas for liberty and justice. Nevertheless, your reading of poems by Burns, Crabbe and others will raise the possibility of profound social criticism aimed at a society in which the sharing of power and privilege was limited to a relatively small section of that society. Mary Wollstonecraft engages with the ideas of Richard Price, a champion of liberty and democracy, as she contemplates conservative reactions to the French Revolution. It would appear, therefore, that liberty and justice were ideals which crossed national boundaries in our period. They relate to many of the debates about what is natural or unnatural in previous and existing social orders. The theme of 'society', then, will involve an exploration of the ways in which social conventions influenced our texts or were challenged by them in the interests of moral regeneration.

You have already encountered the claim that many Enlightenment texts were elitist in nature or origin. Many of the texts and studies in Part E question, explicitly or implicitly, the relative value traditionally attached to the culture, behaviour and beliefs of different sections of society. Not least in this questioning process is the issue of gender. We have already seen both how women were believed, by some, to have a special capacity for feeling, and how restricted were conventional views of female nature. These views are central to the debates on the role and education of women which run through all Part E texts. Mary Wollstonecraft, Rousseau and Laclos respond in different ways to stereotypical views of female nature and of women's roles. Instinct (particularly the maternal kind) and feeling are weighed against claims to intellectual emancipation. 'Feminine' obedience and subservience are weighed against the claim for independence of mind, much as they were in the *Encyclopédie* articles on *Woman*. The importance of physical charm is as central to these debates on female education as it was to Reynolds's subjects for portraiture or to those seeking to paint Catherine the Great's portrait. The alliance of power and beauty in Mme de Merteuil and in the Russian monarch is rooted within the very different lives, roles and education of these two women: the personal and political empires in which they were involved provided very different opportunities for the exercise of power.

Education played a vital part in the definition of roles. While poor girls might, exceptionally, find an education in charity schools, where they would receive training in religion, housework, reading and writing, middle- and upper-class girls fared better only in so far as they would enjoy more comfortable conditions and see their curriculum extended to include singing, dancing and music. Mothers, governesses and (in France) convents were their main instructors. Drawing (and sometimes history and geography) might be permitted, but maths and physics were frowned upon until the late eighteenth century.

Despite this disadvantage and the difficulties caused by financial dependence on male relatives, the education and literary reputation of women writers, particularly in the middle and upper classes, improved slightly as the century progressed. Your reading of the work of British female poets will demonstrate the efforts made by women to enter a world of literary production and consumption which was male-oriented. The following anonymous Preface (1762) to the works of the playwright Susannah Centlivre (1667?–1723) illustrates this:

> She was even asham'd to proclaim her own great Genius, probably because the Custom of the Times discountenanced poetical Excellence in a Female. The Gentlemen of the Quill published it not, perhaps envying her superior Talents; and her Bookseller, complying with national Prejudices, put a fictitious name to [her play], thro' Fear that the work shou'd be condemned, if known to be Feminine …
>
> A pleasing Prospect I've lately had, viz. the Work of the ingenious Lord Corke, and the not less ingenious Mr Samuel Johnson, who have took Pains to translate a large Part of Father Brumoy's Greek Theatre, and were not ashamed that their Labours should be

joined to those of Mrs *Lennox*. This convinces me that not only the barbarous Custom of denying Women to have Souls, begins to be rejected as foolish and absurd, but also that bold Assertion, that Female Minds are not capable of producing literary Works, equal even to those of Pope, now loses Ground, and probably the next Age may be taught by our Pens that our Geniuses have been hitherto cramped and smothered, but not extinguished, and that the sovereignty which the male Part of the Creation have, until now, usurped over us, is unreasonably arbitrary: And further, that our natural Abilities entitle us to a larger Share, not only in Literary Decisions, but that, with the present Directors, we are equally entitled to Power both in Church and State. (Jones, 1990, pp.168–9)

From the 1730s it was increasingly possible for women to publish their work in the *Gentleman's Magazine* and increasingly common for them to publish their verse by subscription: a means of attaining some measure of financial security.

We must not impose twentieth-century conceptions of feminism on Enlightenment culture. Women's issues were not on the agenda of many 'enlightened' writers. By the end of the eighteenth century, little change had occurred in the way most women lived. In the realm of painting, for example, it remained very difficult for women to become professional artists. In 1770 the French Royal Academy of Painting and Sculpture decreed that no more than four women could be members at any one time. As mentioned in the Study on Reynolds (*Studies*, I, p.264), only two of the founding members of the British Royal Academy were women. No other female members were elected until the twentieth century. In practice, this meant that many women with an interest in art could aspire, at most, to the status of wealthy amateur. Women were also, of course, common subjects for artists.

The responses of Diderot to the lascivious nudes of Boucher and the wilting, virtuous heroines of Greuze in the *Salon of 1765* raise other important questions about eighteenth-century conceptions of female nature. Diderot is as bewildered by the alliance of virtue and sensuality in Greuze's heroines as is Valmont when possessed by the charms of Mme de Tourvel in *Dangerous Acquaintances*. Rousseau, in his demand that women should cultivate both virtue and coquetry, was even more tormented and provoked the scorn of Mary Wollstonecraft. This debate on the role and status of women relates to important assumptions about the 'natural' order of society and the 'natural' constitution, physical, mental and emotional, of the men and women within it. It is for you to decide whether these broader ideas on nature, feeling and society advance or undermine the concept of 'enlightenment'.

4   References

Asse, E. (ed.) (1876) *Lettres de Julie de Lespinasse*, Charpentier et compagnie, Paris.

Brookner, A. (1972) *Greuze*, Elek, London.

Halsband, R. (ed.) (1965) *The Complete Letters of Mary Wortley Montagu*, Clarendon Press, Oxford.

Jones, V. (ed.) (1990) *Women in the Eighteenth Century: Constructions of Femininity*, Routledge, New York.

Mackenzie, H. (1987) *Man of Feeling*, edited by B. Vickers, Oxford University Press, Oxford. (First published 1771.)

Rousseau, J.J. (1986) *The Social Contract and Discourses* (containing *A Discourse on the Origin of Inequality*), Everyman, London.

Sterne, L. (1967) *A Sentimental Journey Through France and Italy*, edited by G. Petrie with an Introduction by A. Alvarez, Penguin, Harmondsworth. (First published 1768.)

Eighteenth-Century Poetry
Prepared for the Course Team by
Michael Rossington

Contents

Eighteenth-Century Poetry (Study weeks 24–25)

Studies/Texts	Radio	TV	AC	Set books
Studies, II	R6	TV13	AC1633 (green)	-
Texts, II				

For this fortnight's work you will need this *Studies* volume and *Texts*, II. TV13 and AC1633, Sides 1 and 2 are also essential viewing/listening.

Eighteenth-Century Poetry

1   Introduction

1.1   Aim

The aim of the fortnight's work which follows is to introduce you to a selection of eighteenth-century poems mainly by English, but also by Scottish and Irish authors.

1.2   The structure of the Poetry Study

There are twenty-one poems (or parts of poems) by thirteen different authors reprinted, along with editorial notes, in *Texts*, II. In the course of reading the Poetry Study which follows, you will be instructed to read eighteen of these poems (those by Gray, Goldsmith, Crabbe, Swift, 'Miss W-', Duck, Collier, Leapor, Montagu, and Burns). In watching TV13, and doing the exercise in the Broadcast Notes which accompany the programme, you will be asked to read extracts from poems by Pope and Thomson. The poem by Macpherson is referred to in Angus Calder's 'Historical Background to Scotland', *Studies*, I, p.442–43.

In addition to using *Texts*, II and *Studies*, II, you will also be required to:

1   Watch TV13, in which Professor John Barrell discusses the relationship between the conventions of poetry and painting in the eighteenth century. As well as being important for the exercises you do on Pope and Thomson, this programme will be essential viewing for your work on Gray, Goldsmith, Crabbe, Duck, Collier, Leapor and Burns.

2   Listen to Audio-cassette, AC 1633, Side 1, where several poems by women poets of the eighteenth century will be read, and discussed by Dr Vivien Jones.

3   Listen to Audio-cassette, AC 1633, Side 2, where several poems by Robert Burns will be read by a professional actor.

In the first week of study, I suggest that you watch TV13, do the accompanying exercises in the broadcast notes, and read the first two sections of the Poetry Study, on Gray's *Elegy* and Goldsmith's *Deserted Village*.

In the second week, you should read the third section of the study on Crabbe's *Village*, the fourth section on poetry by women and the fifth section on Burns's poetry. While working on the fourth and fifth sections, you should also listen to the audio-cassette, Sides 1 and 2.

1.3   A note on the Poetry Study

In the course of reading the poems in *Texts*, II, and the Study which accompanies them, you will be invited to make your own connections between their language and themes, and the title of this part of the course, 'Nature, Feeling and Society'. The work you did on Johnson in Part A, and on eighteenth-century views of the 'classical' in Part B will be useful to refer to as you work through this Study.

The emphasis of each section of this Study varies according to the text, or texts, under discussion. In the section on Gray's *Elegy*, detailed attention is focused upon the language and argument of the poem. The sections on Goldsmith's *Deserted Village* and Crabbe's *Village*, in addition to exploring aspects of the language of the poems, emphasize the importance of the motivations of each author in terms of a wider debate about rural life, and the way poems represent it. The section on poems by women concentrates on the way the position of women in eighteenth-century society influences the language and themes of these texts, a subject which Vivien Jones elaborates in audio-cassette, AC 1633, Side 1. The final section on Burns's *Kilmarnock Poems* provides an introduction to the language and themes of Burns's poetry which is read on audio-cassette, AC 1633, Side 2.

This variety of critical approaches in the Study is meant to 'open up' different ways of reading poetry, rather than to impose upon each text the same approach with the expectation that similar results will be yielded. Nevertheless, poems tend to resist the confines of any criticism rather than comply dutifully with them. In the light of reading this Study you may think that one kind of approach is more useful than another in relation to a particular text. Arguing against readings which you find restrictive, and defending your own interpretations of texts is, of course, to be encouraged.

However, there are two issues referred to throughout this Study which lend it a loose coherence. Before you start reading the poems in detail, it's worth pausing briefly to draw your attention to the meaning and significance of the terms 'pastoral' and 'the canon'.

1.4 Pastoral

Many of the poems in the *Texts* engage with the literary convention of 'pastoral'. The word 'pastoral' derives from the Latin adjective meaning 'of, or pertaining to, shepherds or their occupation' (*OED*). As a literary term, it refers to writing about rural existence in an idealized way. From its earliest exponents, such as Theocritus (*c*.308–240 BC), whose *Idylls* adapted 'the popular songs and ballads of a Sicilian peasant culture for a sophisticated and literate urban public' (Barrell and Bull, 1982, p.4), pastoral was concerned with a representation of rural life designed to appeal to an urban audience. The emphasis on idealization was, from its origins, integral to the convention of pastoral.

You have already studied the reasons for the influence of Greek and Latin culture on the Enlightenment (in Part B). The pastoral tradition in classical literature would be one dimension of the education of most English eighteenth-century middle- or upper-class males (and, exceptionally, a few women too). But why, you may ask, should this particular convention be utilized, often for ironical as much as serious purposes, by poets writing in eighteenth-century England?

In some of the poems you will read in *Texts*, II, for example those by Gray and Goldsmith, it seems as if the countryside, and its inhabitants, are a means of escape for a troubled metropolitan consciousness. This function of the pastoral convention, to criticize 'civilized society', can be found in the second book of *The Georgics* of Virgil (70–19 BC), and in the second *Epode* of Horace (68–65 BC). In both these texts, idyllic and unsophisticated life in the countryside is contrasted favourably with the values of urban culture. Such a contrast could also be applied by educated poets to English society in the late eighteenth century. This was especially so when, as in the case of Goldsmith, the author perceived the values of commerce to be undermining the order of contemporary society. In the case of Goldsmith's *Deserted Village*, and other eighteenth-century poems, the pastoral is a means of associating the countryside with an *imagined* stable order in the past. Thus, as a convention, it often has elegiac connotations. While 'elegy' was originally a term used to describe a 'lament for the death of a fellow-shepherd', the elegy has been described with wider relevance to the pastoral convention as, 'a term ... applied to the nostalgic evocation of an Arcadian ideal in which the sense of the past-ness, the irrecoverability of that ideal, predominates' (Barrell and Bull, 1982, p.10). It is worth bearing this comment in mind, as you read the poems, in *Texts*, II.

1.5 The canon

The word 'canon' refers to the list of sacred books of the Bible accepted as genuine. Cultural historians, amongst others, have used the term metaphorically to refer to those texts which literary critics have in the past deemed to represent the highest qualities of English Literature, and therefore to merit study by students such as yourselves. Some of the texts you will read, for example those by Gray, Goldsmith and Crabbe are definitely within the canon of eighteenth-century poetry, and of English Literature itself. Others, for example those by 'Miss W-', Collier and Leapor, have hardly been re-read until recently, and therefore have not qualified.

Whatever the criteria for entry into the canon are, and whether or not you think the formation and defence of a canon of literary works is useful, the debate is essentially about the validity of studying certain kinds of writing either instead of, or in addition to, others. Even if you disagree with those criteria which make the canon an exclusive category, reading canonical texts is necessary and rewarding, in part to reflect on why their reputation endures. But the inclusion of non-canonical poems in *Texts*, II gives you a more accurate picture of the variety of poetry produced in the eighteenth century, as well as making you reflect on why these poems have remained buried for so long. Just as you began this course by being alerted to the varieties of Enlightenment, so it is worth considering for a moment your own expectations, if you have any, of eighteenth-century poems in English. One editor has commented wryly that 'the general reader seems to know all too well what to expect from the age of Good Taste and Common Sense' (Lonsdale, 1987, p.xxxiii). If, having read the selection of poems in *Texts*, II, you become aware that, like the term 'Enlightenment', 'eighteenth-century poetry' eludes a stable definition, then maybe that's for the better.

2 Gray, 'Elegy Written in a Country Churchyard' (1751)

Please read 'Elegy Written in a Country Churchyard' (*Texts*, II, p.131).

2.1 Introduction

Despite Matthew Arnold's view that it had received 'a too unmeasured and unbounded praise' (1973, p.191), Gray's *Elegy* ranks as one of the best-known of English poems. It has certainly been one of the most powerful influences on subsequent English poetry. Perhaps the most intriguing source of appeal for an English audience from the eighteenth-century to the present has been that it addresses the issue of the hierarchical division of society whereby those of modest economic means have usually been denied access to education and status. The fact that it was reputedly the favourite poem of the former Conservative Prime Minister, Margaret Thatcher, but also the model for the controversial poem *v.* (1985) by Tony Harrison (b.1937), and that it was selected by Tom Paulin for his *Faber Book of Political Verse* (1986) because 'it expresses a compassion for the rural poor which makes it a member of the popular tradition'(p.37), tells us much about how diversely its popularity has been tapped to serve distinct political ideologies.

The most celebrated reactions to the *Elegy* in the eighteenth century registered its implicit approbation of a hypothetical English peasantry as well as its critique of the powerful. General Wolfe is reputed to have declared, on the night before the capture of Quebec in 1759 in which he was killed, 'I would rather have been the author of that piece than beat the French tomorrow' (cited in Lonsdale, 1969, p.116). The irony of his celebrated anecdote is that a successful military commander is remembered as having contemplated forgoing his own glory for the authorship of a poem, part of whose purpose was to question the claims to greatness of him and his kind. This feature of the *Elegy* persuaded Samuel Johnson that the poem had a universal appeal:

> In the character of his *Elegy* I rejoice to concur with the common reader; for by the common sense of readers uncorrupted with literary prejudices, after all the refinements of subtlety and the dogmatism of learning, must be finally decided all claim to poetical honours. The *Churchyard* abounds with images which find a mirror in every mind, and with sentiments to which every bosom returns an echo. (from *Prefaces, Biographical and Critical, to the Works of the English Poets*; reprinted in the Johnson set text (Greene, 1984), pp.768–9)

2.2 A Study Guide to the Poem

Let's begin by considering the form of the poem (its rhyme and rhythm, verse divisions, alliteration and assonance). Please read the first three stanzas (ll.1–12).

You will have noticed that the poem consists of alternately rhyming lines of ten syllables each. The rhythm of each line is iambic (i.e. it consists of units, technically known as 'metrical feet', in which an unstressed syllable is followed by a stressed syllable); because there are five such 'feet', these lines are described as 'iambic pentameters', the basic line of much verse in English from Chaucer onwards. Gray's use of the iambic pentameter in the *Elegy* is stylistically innovative in the context of some earlier eighteenth-century poems in *Texts*, II; it differs from the 'blank verse' (*unrhymed* iambic pentameters) used by Thomson in *The Seasons*, as well as the 'heroic couplet' (iambic pentameters *rhymed in pairs*) used by Pope in the *Epistle to Burlington*, not only because he employs *alternately rhyming* iambic pentameters but because of the division of the poem into stanzas. Johnson's *Vanity of Human Wishes*, you will recall, uses heroic couplets.

While the way the first stanza is divided from the second accords with its sense (i.e. the stanza ends with a full-stop), the semi-colon in the final line of the second stanza indicates that the sense is being carried forward into the next stanza. Gray was sensitive to instances of such links called 'enjambements' (more emphatically apparent in lines 64–5 than in the first three stanzas); in his original instructions he asked that the poem be printed 'without any Interval between the Stanza's, because the Sense is in some places continued beyond them' (Lonsdale, 1969, p.110), although he dropped this stipulation in later editions. Perhaps he eventually realized that grouping the verse into four-line stanzas (known as 'quatrains') had the advantage of flexibility; the poem is both broken down into units which are concentrated and to some extent self-contained, but also can change direction, as it does dramatically at line 93, and develop cumulatively towards a different argument and mood.

Finally, there is much evidence of alliteration, in which consonants, especially at the beginning of words, or stressed syllables, are repeated, and assonance, in which similar vowel sounds are echoed. Alliteration is especially evident in the consonantal 'l' sounds, either simple or compound, in lines two and three of the first stanza: 'The lowing herd wind slowly o'er the lea,/ The ploughman homeward plods his weary way'. These lines also exhibit examples of assonance, particularly in the 'o' sounds. I'm sure you found further alliterative and assonantal effects in these lines (e.g. the 'w' and extended 'e' sounds) and elsewhere in these three stanzas and noticed that often the consonantal and vowel sounds are repeated close together, as in the above examples. The effect of such phonetic echoes which create rhymes, or near rhymes, within, as well as between, lines is to tighten the association of the sound of the words with their meaning; the closer they are bound together the more forcefully the effect is communicated. Using the above example, the softness of the 'l' s and the extended 'o' sounds contribute in significant ways to the evocation of a sleepy, peaceful landscape at dusk with which the *Elegy* begins.

Now let's investigate further the importance of the beginning of the poem with the aim of discovering whether there is more to these stanzas than mere description and scene-setting. Please now read on to the end of the seventh stanza (line 28), the moment at which the explicit moral theme of the poem is announced.

EXERCISE   Write brief notes in response to the following three questions:

1   Whom does the 'me' in the last line of the first stanza refer to?

2   How does the introduction of this personal voice influence the reader's response to these stanzas?

3   What is the subject of lines 13–28, and through what images are the 'rude forefathers' (l.16) described?

DISCUSSION   1   You might have answered that the 'me' in the last line of the first stanza is Gray himself. However, there is an important distinction to be made between the identifiable author of the *Elegy*, Thomas Gray (1716–71), and the generalized figure of the poet to which this line more accurately refers. From your first reading of the poem at the start, you will recognize that from line 93 to the end, and especially in its Epitaph, the poem is concerned with this generalized figure, rather than Gray in particular. However, this doesn't mean that this figure is impersonal or abstract. On the contrary, we are invited to identify the 'me' of line 4, as an individual who is addressing either us, or in line 93, himself.

2   The way that this personal voice is introduced is crucial. While the first three lines of the first stanza, which are similarly structured in form, appear to impart through images the information necessary to tell us that nightfall is imminent, the fourth line strikes a different note. 'And leaves the world to darkness and to me', suggests that there is a personal interest in what seemed to be merely neutral description. The figure of the poet wants to be left alone, to be detached from the daily round of rural life and labour and looks forward to impending night as the time when solitude can be achieved most effectively. So, in answer to the question, the verses that follow down to line 28 (but also through the rest of the poem), can be seen as arising out of the positioning of this personal voice; the scene is arranged so that its elements are metaphors (i.e. ways of describing one thing in terms of another) for the poet's own imaginative excursion. Thus the Gothic touches in the third stanza, 'the ivy mantled tow'r' (l.9) and the 'moping owl' (l.10), function as a metaphor for the poet's desire to be undisturbed, like the owl in 'her ancient solitary reign' (l.12).

3   The following four stanzas introduce the principal subject of the poem, the speculative musings on the lives which the former inhabitants of the hamlet lived, and those they didn't. They also introduce the characteristic tone of the poem's pathos, which is achieved through a series of contrasts and negations. First, the organic world of nature is seen as durable where human life is finite (ll.13–16); then the rhythm of the rude forefathers' working lives is evoked only to be denied (ll.17–20); then their domestic and familial love is glimpsed only to be lamented because enjoyed no more (ll.21–4); and finally they are shown to have been, while alive, in command of the natural world in which they are now interred and subsumed (ll.25–8).

The contemporary poet and critic Thomas Warton (1728–90) noted that Gray's opening lines are 'painted from books and not from the life' (in his edition of Milton's *Poems on Several Occasions* (1785), p.176n, cited in Lonsdale, 1969, pp.117–18), since his description of the ploughman returning at dusk bears no relation to rural habits in contemporary England, where ploughing was normally completed at noon. Although Warton was challenged at the time, and subsequently, about contemporary agricultural practice (see Lonsdale, 1969, p.118.), his point alerts us to the fact that his readership would have understood the poem to be based not in any real English time or place, but on sources in classical and English literature. Gray's *Elegy* also exploits the contemporary

Figure 14
*Richard Bentley and Charles
Grignion, Frontispiece to
Gray's 'Elegy Written in a
Country Church-Yard'.
(Published by permission of
the British Library Board)*

popularity of poems about the rituals associated with death; the title-page of the first edition was 'embellished by woodcuts of skulls, cross-bones and other symbols of mortality, commonly used for bourgeois funeral elegies since the sixteenth century' (Lonsdale, 1969, p.111). The frontispiece to the 1753 edition of some of Gray's poems which depicts the poet reading a tombstone behind a Gothic arch falling into ruin (see Fig. 14), and the tail-piece which shows the poet's grave as a hole in the earth waiting to be filled (see Fig. 15), demonstrate the force of the visual imagery which could be used to illustrate these themes.

Neither would an eighteenth-century audience have been surprised at the moralizing which begins in line 29, where the poet defends passionately those upon whose lives he has just been speculating. He uses the personification of abstract qualities such as 'Ambition' (l.29) and

Figure 15
Richard Bentley and Charles
Grignion, Tail-piece to Gray's
'Elegy'. (Published by
permission of the British
Library Board)

'Grandeur' (l.31) to undermine potential criticism of 'their useful toil' (l.29), and to pre-empt patronizing contempt for 'Their homely joys and destiny obscure' (l.30). This rebuke of those who would scorn to hear 'The short and simple annals of the poor' (l.32) has the immediate effect of challenging the values and aspirations of the socially sophisticated, likely to be amongst his readership, who ignore the equalizing effect of the common human lot: 'The paths of glory lead but to the grave' (l.36). Equally, in lines 37–40 there is scorn for those who seek to deny or resist mortality through elaborate funerals and memorials. In the light of the preceding argument, the rhetorical questions in lines 41–4 invite a response in the negative, but it should be noted that from line 73 onwards, the poem expresses sympathy for the desire to erect modest memorials to the dead. So, while the force of, 'Can storied urn or animated bust/Back to its mansion call the fleeting breath?' (ll.43–4), is registered in one sense as a fitting crescendo to this phase of the argument, the rest of the poem, especially the Poet's Epitaph in the final lines, appears to resist it.

The following four stanzas in which the poet reflects that, but for their circumstances, these humble labourers might have become celebrated, have provoked a good deal of controversy. There are of course evident ironies within them, particularly in lines 57–60 where it is made clear that in the case of Cromwell at least, the aspiration to emulate the great is suspect, if not better avoided altogether. In the original manuscript Gray used classical heroes, but in revising the poem changed them, partly it is argued, because he 'wanted examples of greatness which had proved dangerous to society (as opposed to the innocence of the villagers)...' (Lonsdale, 1969, p.128). Gray's trio, Hampden, Milton and Cromwell, were all key figures in the English Civil War; but in the *Elegy* they exemplify the hazards of fame as opposed to anonymity (all three suffered in various ways for their roles). The following three verses (ll.61–72) continue this theme, reinforcing the ironical idea that if on the one hand, the villagers were prevented by circumstances from becoming great leaders, they were also relieved of the temptations and corruptions to which those succumb who seek and obtain power. In particular, they did not abuse their poetic gifts for the purposes of self-advancement ('Or heap the shrine of Luxury and Pride/With incense kindled at the Muse's flame' (ll.71–2)).

Taking the imagery of nature in lines 53–56 as a metaphor for the affirmation of the social hierarchy, the critic William Empson argued that,

> By comparing the social arrangement to Nature he [Gray] makes it seem inevitable, which it was not, and gives it a dignity which was undeserved. Furthermore, a gem does not mind being in a cave and a flower prefers not to be picked; we feel that the man is like the flower, as short-lived, natural, and valuable and this tricks us into feeling that he is better off without opportunities. (Empson, 1935, p.4)

Empson thinks that here and elsewhere in the poem, the reader is made to feel that, 'we ought to accept the injustice of society as we do the inevitability of death' (Empson, 1935, p.4). But this view has been seen as ignoring both the ironic humour of lines 45–72, and the poet's attitude. The poet is both protective (perhaps paternalistic) towards the villagers, and, in wishing to identify with them, is genuinely envious of the freedom of their anonymous destinies.

From line 73, 'Far from the madding crowd's ignoble strife', the poem begins to acknowledge that even the simplest gravestone, 'With uncouth rhymes and shapeless sculpture decked' (l.79), which seeks to resist oblivion, invites a sympathetic response (ll.77–92). But the most dramatic development comes in the change of address in line 93 which has become the *Elegy's* most problematic crux. The most convincing interpretation of the 'thee' of line 93 is that it refers simply to the figure of the poet himself. The neatly constructed reversal of perspective in the subsequent lines confirms this view. Instead of the poet speculating on the population of the village, the 'hoary-headed swain' (l.97) is given an albeit improbably elaborate speech (ll.98–116) in which to ponder the mysterious figure of the poet. Please now read from line 93 to the end.

EXERCISE How is the figure of the poet represented in this final section of the poem and what effect is created at the end?

DISCUSSION First, there is an indication that the position of the poet is paradoxical. The preoccupation with relating the 'artless tale' (l.94) of 'th' unhonoured dead' (l.93) is in danger of excluding recognition of the poet's own life: 'If chance, by lonely Contemplation led,/Some kindred spirit shall inquire *thy fate*' (italics added); (ll.95–6). If the irony is that in remembering the hitherto unremembered villagers, he himself will be forgotten, then he has to imagine himself as a source of interest to a 'kindred spirit' (l.96). By this we might think he means a poet, whereas in fact, the 'hoary-headed swain' of line 97, signifies a figure like the villagers whose gravestones he has been reading (the elegiac tradition in pastoral whereby dead shepherds are commemorated in verse would have made the idea of the swain's being literate, let alone a poet, less problematical to Gray's audience). This creates a multi-layered perspective, whereby he imagines himself after he is dead being remembered by an imaginary figure, who is himself one of the unremembered, anonymous villagers to whom the poem has been dedicated so far. The swain's description of the poet (ll.101–16) as a figure beheld at a distance, essentially unknown (rather as the dead villagers remain a tantalizing source of mystery to the poet earlier on) and apparently unhappy (ll.105–8), suggests that it is the gravestone, not the memory of him in life, that will be the key to his identity. That wonderful touch, 'Approach and read (for thou canst read) the lay,' (l.115), seems both to admit and seek to overcome, the problem of credibility we have in believing that the rural folk will be able to read his epitaph in the way that he has been able to read theirs. The Epitaph itself concentrates much of the poem to a further level of irony where the much-deferred identity of the poet is again denied us, as the poem itself snaps shut, 'No farther seek his merits to disclose,/Or draw his frailties from their dread abode/(There they alike in trembling hope repose),/The bosom of his Father and his God' (ll.125–8). Part of the point here seems to be that instead of the poet's being elevated above the villagers through his ability to write poetry, his destiny is joined with theirs. The sense of mortality with which the poem ends has been glossed eloquently: 'The Poet is indeed equalled in death with the illiterate and the inarticulate, and we are moved because the poet's democratic exhortation within the poem is no mere preaching from a secure position. Of all poems, the *Elegy* most eloquently says that there is no secure position' (Doody, 1985, p.195).

The effect of this series of oblique manoeuvres which destabilizes the end of the *Elegy* is to make what we are led to at the end of the poem seem a paradoxical kind of self-revelation on the part of the poet. On the one hand, that he is a suffering and ultimately mortal individual like the rest of us, could be used as testimony to support Johnson's famous comment about the poem. On the other, to see the poem simply as a revelation of the mortality of the poet, as Doody suggests in the above comment, rather than his singularity, is to ignore the tortuous means by which its conclusion is reached. Part of the effect of the *Elegy* is to communicate the unique qualities necessary to be a poet (e.g. sensibility and melancholy) and to argue that such a figure is intrinsically valuable to society.

2.2.1   The two versions of the Elegy

The *Elegy* was probably written between 1746 and 1750. The earliest surviving version is entitled 'Stanza's Wrote in A Country Church-Yard'. This consists of eighteen stanzas which, with a few minor variants, correspond to the first 72 lines of the final version of the *Elegy,* followed by the four stanzas reprinted in the note to line 72 in the *Texts*. These four stanzas were omitted from the final version, although some of the lines were re-worked in it. Please read them now.

EXERCISE Compare the two versions of the poem, and summarize briefly how they differ.

DISCUSSION Apart from being much shorter, the earlier version has a symmetrical structure which has been summarized thus:

> The last three stanzas, balancing the opening three, return to the poet himself in the churchyard, making clear that the whole poem has been a debate within his mind as he meditates in the darkness, at the end of which he makes his own choice about the preferability of obscure innocence to the dangers of the 'great world'. (Lonsdale, 1969, p.114)

This makes the argument of 'Stanza's' compatible with classical models (especially poems by Virgil and Horace) in which rural retirement is shown to be morally and aesthetically preferable to city life. No doubt Gray had the sophisticated Augustan society of the metropolis in mind; in this respect, 'Stanza's' is comparable with Johnson's *The Vanity of Human Wishes* (1749) which you read in Part A.

The final version of the *Elegy* differs from 'Stanza's' in moving beyond the abstract personification of its rejected final stanzas; it imaginatively redresses the imbalance of perspective in the earlier version, by making the figure of the poet subject to the villagers' scrutiny and by introducing a distinctive argument about the role of the poet. Gray himself was clearly satisfied with the final version, as he explained to his friend Horace Walpole (1717–97): 'You will, I hope, look upon it in the light of a *thing with an end to it*; a merit that most of my writings have wanted' (Lonsdale, 1969, p.103).

The difference between the two versions has been summarized succinctly; 'a poem of Christian Stoicism is rewritten as a poem of Sensibility' (Jack, 1965, p.146). Indeed there was criticism of the *Elegy* for being too undisciplined in its emotional impact: 'Delicacy and Taste recoil at the publication of internal griefs. They profane the hallowedness of secret sadness, and suppose selected and decorated expression compatible with the prostration of the soul' (Young, 1783, p.11). This comment suggests that Gray failed to observe the proprieties of the elegiac, pastoral tradition. More recent critics have seen the exhibition of feeling in the poem as part of an incipient challenge to Augustan values:

> The 'ivy-mantled tow'r', the 'mopeing owl', the 'dark unfathom'd caves' all are parts of what is to become a familiar Gothic landscape, a decay which will come to all civilizations, however confident they are in their conviction that the movement of history is a progression towards perfection. The 'Elegy' is both the final synthesis of the Augustan culture – the poet as spokesman for his audience – and the first expression of a hesitant romanticism – the poet separated from his audience. (Barrell and Bull, 1982, p.300)

While in part absorbing and refashioning the values of the Enlightenment classical tradition, the *Elegy* also questions such values.

The emphasis on the ability of the poet to 'feel' in the *Elegy* (see, in particular the note on 'Melancholy' in line 120 of the text) shows the poem to exhibit a preoccupation with the poetic self, often associated with the Romantic period, but which can be more correctly seen in the light of Gray's increasing interest in the historical sources of the ancient mythical repository of British poetry, the Bard (the subject of his poem, *The Bard*, begun in 1754). But, as Susan Khin Zaw has pointed out to me, the *Elegy* also relates closely to other texts studied in Part E, in its subversion of the classical ideal of fame (cf. Laclos's *Les Liaisons Dangereuses*) and in its closeness in spirit to the title and content of some of Rousseau's writings.

3   Oliver Goldsmith's The Deserted Village (1770)

Please read *The Deserted Village* in *Texts* II, p.136.

3.1   Introduction

Like Gray's poem, *The Deserted Village* is partly indebted to the pastoral tradition for its elegiac mood and its defence of a notional English peasantry. But it is also an explicit attack on those values which threaten the idyllic innocence of village life in rural England. It challenges what Goldsmith regarded as contemporary perversions of the pastoral, such as landscape gardening (which is discussed in TV7, 'Kedleston Hall'), by pointing up the conflict between their aesthetic appeal and the effects of their imposition by the *nouveaux riches* on the material lives of those who worked the land. On a first reading of the poem, several questions arise about how to validate the poem's argument against luxury and commercial values. Where was Auburn? What was Goldsmith's relationship to it and is the nostalgic mood of parts of the poem motivated by personal feeling? What was the response to enclosure in contemporary England? Was *The Deserted Village* the expression of a common feeling towards the growing commercialism of contemporary society? We will consider these questions in detail in the section on the poem's background and context, but let's begin by looking at the text itself and how its effects are achieved.

3.2   A Study Guide to the Poem

Please re-read the first verse paragraph of the poem (ll.1–34).

EXERCISE   What effect do you think the poet is striving for in these lines and how do particular features of the form and diction of the poem contribute to that effect?

DISCUSSION   Put simply, the depiction of rural prosperity and festivity in these lines has the effect of creating a sense of unfettered and innocent joy. Several features of the form and diction of the poem contribute to this. There is the use of key words, repeated frequently throughout the poem, which describe the mood of Auburn (including 'sweet' (ll.1, 31, 32), 'smiling' (l.3), 'bowers' (ll.5, 33) and 'charm/s' (ll.9, 31)); and alliteration (especially the 's' sound in lines 1–8), which relates phonetic effect to the mood conveyed by the poem's diction. The use of transferred epithets (a figure of speech in which the epithet, often an adjective, is transferred from the noun to which it is appropriate to another to which it doesn't really apply, for example, 'smiling spring' (l.3), 'humble happiness' (l.8), 'decent church' (l.12)) demonstrates how far the relaxed and contented atmosphere with which this opening section brims, is a consequence of a profusion of adjectives being applied to elements of the scene. Further emphasis is given to the rhythm and structure of the first fifteen lines through the repeated use of the constructions 'Where' and 'How often' to begin six of those lines, and the similar structure of the series of relative clauses which make up the first sentence of fourteen lines. The heroic couplet (iambic pentameters in rhyming pairs) also contributes to this, its form facilitating such repeated phrases, and providing balance between elements in a line as well as between lines (e.g. 'The sheltered cot, the cultivated farm,/The never-failing brook, the busy mill', (ll.10–11).

The repetition of patterns of sound and structure in this section is vital to the poem's argument. The imagery of these opening lines suggests an unchanging state of affairs, a topography where all the detailed features of the scene are secure and assured of their place. Yet the buoyant stability of this vision is to be radically upset. What the formal elements of the opening section do is to affirm an idealized scene, natural and right, by using such features as the transferred epithets, noted above, in an unobtrusive way to persuade the reader that the vision of mutual support between nature's bounty and human fulfilment is not only plausible, but essential to the well-being of the nation. Notice how ideas usually held at least in tension, if not altogether antithetical, are here conjoined unproblematically (e.g. the 'innocence and ease' of line 5); how nature's largesse combines with physical well-being to sustain the labourer (l.2); how modest means are offset by 'happiness' (l.8), and how the natural world co-operates with the industry of Auburn's inhabitants, (ll.9–12). The culmination of the rhetorical strategy of these lines comes after the description of the festival (ll.31–4), where we realize that the vision has been evoked only to be exploded. The barely suppressed metaphor to describe Auburn in lines 31–4, appears to be that of a wronged woman (the corruption of its 'bowers' (l.33) alludes to literary adaptations of the story of the temptation of Eve by the serpent in the Garden of Eden).

Having suggested the way in which Auburn is feminized in lines 31–4, the following section (ll.35–50) depicts the fall of the village in terms of rapine and plunder. The perpetrator, imaged as 'the tyrant's hand' (l.37) who is the 'One only master' (l.39) has ruined the village and orphaned its inhabitants: 'Far, far away, thy children leave the land' (l.50). The contrast between the impulsive vagaries of the rich and the stable reliability of 'a bold peasantry' (l.55) is used to advance a mythical, rather than historically accurate, view of a golden age in which each individual lived satisfactorily off the land: 'A time there was, ere England's griefs began,/ When every rood of ground maintained its man' (ll.57–8). Now commerce has intervened and corrupted what Goldsmith sees as a 'natural' relationship between the people and the land: 'But times are altered; trade's unfeeling train/Usurp the land and dispossess the swain' (ll.63–4).

We shall return to the sections on Auburn as the poet's ideal retirement (ll.75–112) in the final exercise, but, without analysing in detail the sympathetic portraits of the widow (ll.129–36), the village preacher (ll.141–92), and the school-master (ll.193–216), I'd now like to return to the poem's main argument against commerce and luxury which is resumed at line 251. Goldsmith's defence of 'Spontaneous joys, where nature has its play' (l.255) as against aristocratic pleasure (ll.259–64) is developed into a wider challenge to the country's statesmen: 'Tis yours to judge how wide the limits stand/Between a splendid and an happy land' (ll.267–8). The argument that pleasure for the aristocratic few entails enclosure and the dispossession of the rural poor (ll.275–86), is presented in terms of an extended metaphor in which nature with its connotations of 'what is right', is contrasted with artifice. Just as 'some fair female unadorned and plain' (l.287) who, with the insecurities of age, 'shines forth, solicitous to bless,/In all the glaring impotence of dress' (ll.293–4), so with the countryside refashioned by the aristocracy: 'Thus fares the land, by luxury betrayed,/In nature's simplest charms at first arrayed;/But verging to decline, its splendours rise,/Its vistas strike, its palaces surprise' (ll.295–8). The future for the rural population, exiled either to the cities or to the hostile colonies, is presented with deliberate pathos, as in the portrayal of the destitute female (ll.325–36).

Please now read the final part of the poem (line 395 to the end).

EXERCISE   What do you think Goldsmith is asserting about the place of the poet in the moral argument of the poem?

DISCUSSION   As in Gray's 'Elegy', there is much evidence throughout the poem to suggest the poet's aspiration to represent those who cannot speak for themselves: 'I still had hopes, for pride attends us still,/Amidst the swains to show my book-learned skill,/Around my fire an evening group to draw,/ And tell of all I felt and all I saw' (ll.89–92). Goldsmith suggests that the poet is on the side of the common people and against luxury. Hence the symbolic abandonment of England and the values with which it was formerly associated by the personification of poetry, 'thou loveliest maid' (l.407). Unlike Thomson's *Seasons* in which commerce and poetry go hand in hand, in Goldsmith's *Deserted Village* poetry does battle with commercial values, wherever it is exiled, 'with thy persuasive strain/ Teach erring man to spurn the rage of gain' (ll.423–4).

3.3 Background

Let's return to some of the questions raised in the introduction. First where was Auburn and what was Goldsmith's relationship to it – is the nostalgic mood of parts of the poem motivated by personal feeling?

Some critics have dismissed the idea that the poem has any verifiable specificity in its location by asserting that the description of 'Auburn' is intentionally factitious and mythical, based upon fond memories of Goldsmith's childhood in the village of Lissoy in County Westmeath, Ireland. Such a view construes the nostalgia of the poem as a deliberately idealized meditation on Goldsmith's own past: 'he is lamenting the lost innocence and happiness of his own childhood as well as of the village' (Lonsdale, 1969, p.673). Lonsdale argues that 'Goldsmith 'concedes his friends' belief that he was reading his own problems into the landscape' (Lonsdale, 1978, p.23), and sees the poem as primarily expressing anxieties about the role and status of the poet. Other critics, however, use the evidence of Goldsmith's essay, 'The Revolution in Low Life' (first printed in *Lloyd's Evening Post*, 14–16 June, 1762) to argue that he had direct experience of the lives of the rural poor as described at the opening of the poem:

> I spent part of the last summer in a little village, distant about fifty miles from town, consisting of near an hundred houses. It lay entirely out of the road of commerce, and was inhabited by a race of men who followed the primeval profession of agriculture for several generations. Though strangers to opulence, they were unacquainted with distress; few of them were known either to acquire a fortune or to die in indigence. By a long intercourse and frequent marriages they were all become in a manner one family; and, when the work of the day was done, spent the night agreeably in visits at each other's houses. Upon those occasions the poor traveller and stranger were always welcome; and they kept up the stated days of festivity with the strictest observance. They were merry at Christmas and mournful in Lent, got drunk on St George's-day, and religiously cracked nuts on Michaelmas-eve. (Friedman, 1966, vol.3, p.195)

With this evidence in mind, some critics have taken Auburn to be modelled on the village of Nuneham Courtenay near Oxford which was physically removed by Lord Harcourt in 1760–1 to make room for the construction of his park (see Lucas, 1988, p.158). According to these critics, 'the sad historian of the pensive plain' (l.136) refers to the sole remaining inhabitant of Nuneham Courtenay who is said to have refused to leave her house. There is also anecdotal evidence that Goldsmith had witnessed the effects of enclosure:

> In one of his country excursions he resided near the house of a great West-Indian [i.e. merchant who had made his money in the West Indies], in the neighbourhood of which several cottages were destroyed, in order to enlarge, or rather to polish the prospect. This circumstance the Doctor [i.e. Goldsmith] often mentioned to evince the truth of his reasoning, and to this he particularly alluded [ll.65–6]. (Lonsdale, 1969, pp.670–1)

But did *The Deserted Village* voice an anxiety about enclosure and rural depopulation which was commonly held in contemporary eighteenth-century society? In his section on the historical background to eighteenth-century England (*Studies*, I, pp.426–35), Clive Emsley thinks not. Neither were many reviewers of the poem convinced by its argument:

> He who reads the *Deserted Village*, and is not acquainted with the face of our country, may imagine, that there are many deserted villages to be found in it, and many more tracts of uncultivated land than formerly. England wears now a more smiling aspect than she ever did; and few ruined villages are to be met with except on poetical ground. – Whatever is, must be ultimately right, and productive of universal good. When the author of nature formed us, he knew, that, by our constitution we must pass from barbarism to a more improved state; and that, in process of time, we should arrive at a state of opulence, luxury, and refinement; a state which, perhaps, is as productive of happiness as of misery, to mankind. (*Critical Review* (June 1770) vol.xiii, reprinted in Rousseau, 1974, p.77)

This and other robust defences of the Enlightenment view of progress, 'the absurdity of supposing that there was a time when England was equally divided among its inhabitants by a rood a man' (Hawkesworth in Rousseau, 1974, p.85), clearly opposed Goldsmith's nostalgic view of pre-commercial society. Goldsmith, however, anticipated such critical scepticism, in the Dedication to Sir Joshua Reynolds which preceded the text of the poem, from which the following excerpt is taken:

> I know you will object (and indeed several of our best and wisest friends concur in the opinion) that the depopulation it deplores is no where to be seen, and the disorders it laments are only to be found in the poet's own imagination. To this I can scarce make any other answer than that I sincerely believe what I have written; that I have taken all possible pains, in my country excursions, for these four or five years past, to be certain of what I allege; and that all my views and enquiries have led me to believe those miseries real, which I here attempt to display. (Lonsdale, 1969, pp.674–5)

Notice how Goldsmith, while anticipating not simply hostility but disbelief, sees the sincerity of his feeling about depopulation, rather than whether a genuine social problem existed as a result of it, as a justification for the argument of the poem. Elsewhere in the Dedication he undermines the idea that it is purely a poem of social protest:

> But this is not the place to enter into an enquiry, whether the country be depopulating, or not; the discussion would take up much room, and I should prove myself, at best, an indifferent politician, to tire the reader with a long preface, when I want his [sic] unfatigued attention to a long poem. (Lonsdale, 1969, p.675)

Was the poem expressing a common feeling towards the growing commercialism of contemporary society? The defensive tone of the Dedication again indicates that Goldsmith knew that it wasn't:

> In regretting the depopulation of the country, I inveigh against the increase of our luxuries; and here also I expect the shout of modern politicians against me. For twenty or thirty years past, it has been the fashion to consider luxury as one of the greatest national advantages; and all the wisdom of antiquity in that particular, as

erroneous. Still however, I must remain a professed ancient on that head, and continue to think those luxuries prejudicial to states, by which so many vices are introduced, and so many kingdoms have been undone. Indeed so much has been poured out of late on the other side of the question, that, merely for the sake of novelty and variety one would sometimes wish to be in the right. (Lonsdale, 1969, p.675)

Your work on Gibbon in Part B will have made you aware of the debates about the dangers of civilizations being corrupted by mercenary values, and the work on Rousseau which you do in the next study echoes the theme to which Goldsmith alludes here. But again, notice how the flippant and disingenuous tone of this passage undermines our sense that this is solely a poem of social protest. While the context of a dedication to a successful establishment patron by one who was always unsure of his status might account in part for its tone of ironic self-deprecation, Goldsmith also seems to set up a deliberate disjunction between a supposed historical actuality to which the poem alludes, and the more pressing need for it to appeal to, and entertain, a contemporary audience.

This brings us to other motives behind the writing of *The Deserted Village*. Certainly financial gain for the author, and therefore an understanding of current literary tastes were major factors in the background to the poem. Asked why he had not expressed his views on population in a prose pamphlet, Goldsmith replied, 'It is not worth my while. A good poem will bring me a hundred guineas, but the pamphlet would bring me nothing' (Lonsdale, 1969, p.671). Equally, he was praised by the *Critical Review* in the article cited above for his exploitation of the fashion for the sentimental (discussed in this volume, pp.125–30), to further his argument, '[he] deserves the highest applause for employing his poetical talents in the support of humanity and virtue, in an age when sentimental instruction will have more powerful influence upon our conduct than any other' (Rousseau, 1974, p.82).

Much of the praise of *The Deserted Village* was expressed in terms of metaphors from the visual arts: 'fine painting' (John Hawkesworth, *Monthly Review* (June 1770), vol. xiii, reprinted in Rousseau, 1974, p.85); 'particularly picturesque' (*London Magazine*, June 1770, no.xxxix, reprinted in Rousseau, 1974, p.87); 'descriptions of local scenery as rich and as appropriate as any thing that ever came from the pen of Shakespeare or the pencil of Claude' (Edward Mangin, *An Essay on Light Reading* (1808) reprinted in Rousseau, 1974, p.109). While detailed discussion of landscape in painting and literature takes place in TV13, here it's worth noting the irony of such language. While Goldsmith condemns the effect of the aesthetics of landscape gardening on the lives of rural folk, the very style in which he evokes village life is praised as picturesque. Goldsmith can thus be seen as exploiting a genre which clearly appealed to the marketplace while at the same time launching a stinging attack on the way that genre corrupts the pastoral ideal.

It's also important to consider the place of the poet in the poem. The critic Raymond Williams has argued that 'what is in question ... is not only the life of the village, but the independence of the poet who had hoped to retire there... It is that the social forces which are dispossessing the village are seen as simultaneously dispossessing poetry' (Williams, 1985, p.77). The irony is that what Goldsmith is really writing about, to put it simply, is the danger of the poet, like the villagers, being displaced, since the dominant mode of expression for a pastoral poet like him is elegy, in which the loss of a past ideal is lamented. So in *The Deserted Village*, it could be argued that whereas Goldsmith claims to be writing out of a social conscience about the threat to the livelihood of rural labourers, in fact the literary sensibility, or feeling of the poem, is directed towards a lament for his own endangered métier.

4   George Crabbe's **The Village** *(1783) (Book I)*

Please read *The Village* (Book I), reprinted in the *Texts* II, pp.145–53.

4.1   Introduction

In his poem 'The Parish Register' published in *Poems* (1807), Crabbe condemned *The Deserted Village* as pure make-believe:

> Is there a place, save one the Poet sees,
> A Land of Love, and Liberty and Ease:
> Where labour wearies not, nor cares suppress
> Th'eternal flow of Rustic Happiness;
> Where no proud Mansion frowns in aweful State,
> Or keeps the Sunshine from the Cottage-Gate;
> Where Young and Old, intent on pleasure, throng,
> And half man's life, is Holiday and Song?
> Vain search for scenes like these! no view appears,
> By sighs unruffled or unstain'd by tears;
> Since Vice the world subdued and Waters drown'd,
> *Auburn* and *Eden* can no more be found (15–26).

(Dalrymple-Champneys and Pollard, 1988, vol.3, p.213)

The final couplet, which announces ironically that the existence of Auburn is about as likely as the recovery of the lost Eden, strikes the characteristic note of Crabbe's verse which, by contrast with Goldsmith's poem, insists 'upon factual accuracy in verse, a criterion which demands that poetic details be presented in contexts that are time- and place-specific' (McGann, 1985, p.306).

4.2   A Study Guide to the Poem

Please re-read the first sixty-two lines of the poem, then do the following exercise.

EXERCISE   Summarize the argument of this section of the poem briefly, and then show how each verse paragraph contributes to it.

DISCUSSION   This opening section is a critique of the literary convention of pastoral whereby rural life is idealized. In pastoral verse those who work the land – and the land itself – have traditionally been conceived of in terms of improbable stereotypes.

By contrast this poem opens by asserting that it will present an accurate account of the hard work and meagre rewards of rural life, while recognizing that a poem conveying such facts will, in itself, not alleviate the suffering of the labouring poor: 'What forms the real picture of the poor,/Demands a song – the Muse can give no more' (ll.5–6). The inappropriateness of the characteristic idiom of conventional verse is wryly lamented: 'And shepherds' boys their amorous pains reveal,/The only pains, alas! they never feel' (ll.13–14).

Crabbe allowed the 'correction' of lines 15–20 by Johnson (which contains more classical allusions than his own version), to stand, even though both Crabbe's original lines (reprinted in the *Texts*, II, p.146 fn.) and Johnson's argue the same point against modern poets slavishly imitating Virgil rather than following their own poetic inspiration: 'From truth and nature shall we widely stray,/Where Virgil, not where Fancy, leads the way?' (ll.19–20). In lines 21–30, it is argued that few country folk, with the exception of Stephen Duck (whose *The Thresher's Labour* (1730) and Mary Collier's reply, *The Woman's Labour. An Epistle to Mr Stephen Duck* (1739), reprinted in *Texts* II, p.111 and p.121, we shall examine in the next section), have the time to challenge the idealized myth of rural labour perpetuated by poets. Having argued that poetic clichés can happily charm those who have leisure or own land, 'For him that gazes or for him that farms' (l.40), the poet argues that he has a responsibility to contradict their delusions by describing what he witnesses ('Then shall I dare these real ills to hide/In tinsel trappings of poetic pride?') (ll.47–8). The deficiencies of his local environment in terms of a Virgilian ideal are then noted (l.49 ff.)

Crabbe was born and raised in Aldborough (as it was then spelt) on the Suffolk coast, 'Which can no groves nor happy valleys boast' (l.50), and this bleak heath and marshland area forms the setting of his critique: 'By such examples taught, I paint the cot,/As truth will paint it, and as bards will not' (ll.53–4). The rhetorical questions of lines 55–62 invite the poor to consider the poet as doing them a greater favour by presenting the real squalor of their lives than by churning out derivative literary pastoral which does nothing to redress their grievances.

Let's now look at how Crabbe presents the natural world in *The Village*. Please read lines 63–84.

EXERCISE   Compare the description of the natural world in lines 63–84 of *The Village* with lines 1–34 and 287–302 of *The Deserted Village.*

DISCUSSION   Without revising your study of *The Deserted Village* in detail, you will remember the opening of the poem as a perfect idyll in which nature is fertile, protective, morally sound (as in the literary/biblical reference to 'bowers' in lines 5 and 33) and in harmony with the lives of the inhabitants of Auburn. By contrast the passage from *The Village* focuses on the ways in which climate, soil and vegetation are inimical to the efforts of those seeking to make a living from the land. Whereas it is the landowner in Goldsmith's poem whose tyranny deprives the villagers of their livelihoods, here it is nature: 'Rank weeds that every art and care defy,/Reign o'er the land and rob the blighted rye' (ll.67–8). Whereas the opening of *The Deserted Village* is a distant, generalizing perspective, similar to that of a landscape painting, *The Village* concentrates in detail on individual species of vegetation and the collective effect of their constriction: 'O'er the young shoot the charlock throws a shade,/And the wild tare clings round the sickly blade;/With mingled tints the rocky coasts abound,/And a sad splendor vainly shines around' (ll.75–8).

Goldsmith uses the image of a woman trying to disguise her age and declining beauty as a metaphor for the artificiality of the landscape garden: 'Thus fares the land, by luxury betrayed,/In nature's simplest charms at first arrayed' (*The Deserted Village*, ll.295–6). Whereas Goldsmith's metaphor (which is designed to condemn the corruption of nature by artifice) has a familiar moral ring to it, Crabbe inverts its logic. His image of 'the nymph whom wretched arts adorn' (l.79), is a metaphor for the paradox of a natural habitat which is on the one hand gay and colourful, but on the other, in terms of agricultural potential, is sterile and empty. For Crabbe the elaborately made-up maiden, 'Betrayed by man, then left for man to scorn' (l.80), 'Whose outward splendour is but folly's dress' (l.83) is a metaphor for the deceptively colourful appearance of the vegetation in these parts. There is then a sad pathos about the flourishing plant-life, incongruous with productive nature, which the image of the vulnerable woman captures, 'Exposing most, when most it gilds distress' (l.84).

There are other occasions in the poem where imagery of the natural world symbolizes, or functions as a metaphor for, constriction and destitution rather than, as in conventional pastoral verse, hope and release. Take, for example, the old man who, 'looks up to see/The bare arms broken from the withering tree'/On which, a boy, he climbed the loftiest bough,/Then his first joy, but his sad emblem now' (ll.186–9).

This bleak view of the natural world influences the portrayal of the inhabitants of the village (ll.85–130). Crabbe denies the innocent, vigorous mirth of the villagers in *The Deserted Village*, pointing instead to the unscrupulous practice of smuggling liquor in which the villagers engage (ll.93–108). The moral antithesis between town and country, resorted to rather tritely by Goldsmith, is flatly denied in lines 109–12. That Crabbe is not interested in romanticizing the poor is confirmed in the depressing litany of their behaviour in the first part of Book II of *The Village* (unfortunately there is no space to reprint Book II in *Texts*, II). But, significantly, he goes on in Book II to answer his own question, 'Yet why, you ask, these humble crimes relate/Why make the poor as guilty as the great?' (II, ll.85–6) by giving an object-lesson to the affluent and complacent, implicitly amongst his readership:

> To show the great, those mightier sons of Pride,
> How near in vice the lowest are allied;
> Such are their natures and their passions such,
> But these disguise too little, those too much:
> So shall the man of power and pleasure see

In his own slave as vile a wretch as he;
In his luxurious lord the servant find
His own low pleasures and degenerate mind;
And each in all the kindred vices trace
Of a poor, blind, bewildered, erring race;
Who, a short time in varied fortune passed,
Die, and are Equal in the dust at last.

(Book II, ll.87–98; text from Edwards, 1991, pp.15–16)

This is the language and tone of a sermon, the idiom of Crabbe's second-ary profession, that of a curate and chaplain. Even as the shortcomings of all classes, no matter what their position in the social hierarchy, are emphasized, Crabbe nevertheless directs his strongest criticism towards those who see themselves as superior to the poor.

EXERCISE   What particular aspects of the pastoral convention is the reader invited to criticize in lines 131–81? Who do you think the poet is addressing in his questions in lines 140–1, 154–5, 168–73, 174–5?

DISCUSSION   Having demystified the potent pastoral myth of Nature's bounty (ll.131–4), Crabbe now turns to the unequal distribution of the profits of agricultural labour, even where farming is easier (ll.136–9). Similarly, he dispenses with the idea that penury is compensated by the healthy effects of physical work, itemizing the discomforts to which labourers are subject (ll.142–55), the sickness to which they are prone (ll.156–65) and the poor quality of their nutrition (ll.166–73).

Crabbe's rhetorical questions, (ll.140–1, 168–9) and forthright answers seem directed squarely at what he perceives to be the complacency of the educated reader, whose misplaced moral judgements show no understanding of the material conditions of rural life for the labourer. His tone ranges from the haranguing of the pulpit, 'Then own that labour may as fatal be,/To these thy slaves, as luxury to thee', (ll.154–5); to the aggrieved tone of social protest, 'Oh! trifle not with wants you cannot feel,/Nor mock the misery of a stinted meal' (ll.170–1) and to his familiar disdain for literary self-indulgence: 'Ye gentle souls, who dream of rural ease,/Whom the smooth stream and smoother sonnet please' (ll.174–5).

The second half of Book I is structured in terms of a series of detailed portraits: the old man (ll.184–227); the Parish Poor (ll.230–51, 264–75); the apothecary (ll.276–97) and the village priest (ll.298–319). There were literary precedents for these characterizations, some of which Crabbe imitates (e.g. the contemptible parish officer in John Langhorne's *The Country Justice*, (ii, 43–66)) and others which he challenges, (e.g. the endearing village preacher in Goldsmith's *Deserted Village*, l.141 ff.). But Crabbe vividly describes what he knows to be absent from such portrayals of village life, in particular the indignities wrought on the old and destitute (ll.196–201). His singular skill in the second half of Book I is not simply to provide such material, authenticated by his own experience, but to structure it for maximum effect. The catalogue of constituents of the Poorhouse (ll.234–41), including the sick (ll.242–251), is contrasted with his imaginary reader whom he once again assaults, 'How would ye bear in real pain to lie,/Despised, neglected, left alone to die?' (ll.260–1), while the portrayals of the apothecary and the village priest, both pre-posterous but entirely believable characters, soften us for the emotive end to Book I. In this final passage even death does not accord the old man peace and dignity; he is buried hurriedly in a common grave without the attendance of 'the busy priest' (l.345). Whereas the allusions to the moral and literary conventions of eighteenth-century verse (line 343 is a direct borrowing from Gray's 'Elegy') demand pathos and respect even for the pauper dead, there is no sense of this particular burial being a fitting end to a life.

4.3 Background

The reception of *The Village* was largely favourable, though it was criti-cized for being as exaggerated in its gloom as the idyllic view of rustic happiness which Crabbe rejected:

> For it may be questioned whether he, who represents a peasant's life as a life of unremitting labour and remediless anxiety … gives a juster representation of rural enjoyments than they, who, running into a contrary extreme, paint the face of the country as wearing a perpetual smile … ([Edmund Cartwright], *Monthly Review*, vol.lxix (Nov., 1783), reprinted in Pollard, 1972, p.43)

Likewise, the *Gentleman's Magazine*, though complimentary, noted Crabbe's insistence on 'only the dark side of the landscape' (Unsigned Notice, *Gentleman's Magazine*, vol.liii (Dec., 1783), reprinted in Pollard, 1972, p.44). Thus the visual metaphors used to describe *The Deserted Vil-lage* in terms of the picturesque are, in Crabbe's case, expressed in terms of pictorial realism. The literary establishment particularly enjoyed this feature of his work; Boswell observed to Samuel Johnson, that, its 'senti-ments as to the false notions of rustick happiness and rustick virtue' were 'quite congenial' (cited in Dalrymple-Champneys and Pollard, 1988, vol.i, p.663), and Johnson himself commented to Reynolds that *The Village* was, 'original, vigorous and elegant' (letter of 4 March 1783, reprinted in Pol-lard, 1972, p.41).

However, the final hundred lines of Book II were perceived rightly to be incongruous with the rest of the poem; The *Critical Review* noted that 'The subject is broken off rather abruptly towards the conclusion' (*Critical Review*, vol.lvi (July, 1783), reprinted in Pollard, 1972, p.42). These lines take the form of a respectful dedication to Lord Robert Man-ners, younger brother of Crabbe's patron, who died in combat in April 1782, as the poet was making final revisions to *The Village*. Here is a sam-ple from the rather derivative passage:

> Oh! ever honoured, ever valued! say
> What verse can praise thee, or what work repay?
> Yet Verse (in all we can) thy worth repays,
> Nor trusts the tardy zeal of future days; –

> Honours for thee thy Country shall prepare,
> Thee in their hearts, the Good, the Brave shall bear;
> To deeds like thine shall noblest chiefs aspire,
> The Muse shall mourn thee, and the world admire.
> (Book II, ll.135–42; cited in Edwards, 1991, p.17)

Crabbe's career as a writer forms a necessary context to this final section of Book II of *The Village*, although details of his biography can be discussed only briefly here. His first poem, *Inebriety* on the evils of drink, was published in 1775 while he was working as an apothecary, but after this career failed he attempted unsuccessfully to support himself through writing verse. He went to London in 1780, to seek his literary fortune but had no contacts and little money with which to make a living. Early in 1781, however, Edmund Burke rescued him and with some charity agreed to see his poem *The Library* (1781) through the press, and enabled him to be ordained in the Church – a common way to secure a modest livelihood. And in 1782, after having been a curate at Aldborough for a year, he was made domestic chaplain to the Duke of Rutland at Belvoir castle, a position which by some accounts he did not enjoy, but where he completed *The Village* (1783), which was probably begun in 1781. The success of *The Village* enabled him to marry and in 1784 he moved to Leicestershire as a curate.

Your work on Samuel Johnson and his circle in Part A will have given you some idea of the importance of patronage to a writer's career and its influence on the content and success of their verse. One recent critic thinks that the encomium at the end of *The Village* shows Crabbe to be revealing himself to his readership as 'complicit in a social structure that would remain unjust':

> In bringing his first and most radical poem formally under the shelter of patronage he confessed, symbolically, to the economic necessity that drove him originally to seek help from Burke and therefore kept him in attendance on the Duke and Duchess of Rutland. (Patterson, 1988, pp.232–3)

But the idea that Crabbe was testifying to an unwilling acceptance of the constraints of patronage is contradicted both by his genuine gratitude to his literary patrons to whom he arguably owed the publication of *The Village* and to the ways in which the moral tone of the poem (especially in the 'Dedication to Manners') is as important as its social criticism.

The Village is a clear example of what has been termed 'counter-pastoral' (Williams, 1973, p.92), but it is worth noting that we need to be cautious about seeing Crabbe as simply a 'realist' poet. Gavin Edwards, editor of a recent Penguin selection of Crabbe's poems has commented that:

> The concept of realism has dominated and depressed the discussion of Crabbe not only by literary critics but also by social historians, who ... have rifled his poetry for descriptions of English life in the eighteenth and early nineteenth centuries. (Edwards, 1987, p.303)

Cartwright's criticism in the *Monthly Review* cited above, alerts us to the fact that Crabbe's 'real picture of the poor' (l.5) is in fact exaggerated in an attempt to redress the rhetorical excesses of other poets; in addition, we should be wary of thinking that the literary strategy of *The Village* is a means to substantiate historical evidence.

5   Eighteenth-Century Poems by Women

5.1   Introduction

> Shall lordly man, the theme of ev'ry lay,
> Usurp the muse's tributary bay;
> In kingly state on *Pindus'* summit sit,
> Tyrant of verse, and arbiter of wit?
> By *Salic* law the female right deny,
> And view their genius with regardless eye?
> Justice forbid! and every muse inspire
> To sing the glories of a sister-quire!
> Rise, rise bold swain; and to the list'ning grove
> Resound the praises of the sex you love;
> Tell how, adorn'd with every charm, they shine,
> In mind and person equally divine,
> Till man, nor more to female merit blind,
> *Admire* the person, but *adore* the mind. (ll.1–14; Cited in Jones, 1990, p.170)

This is the opening of *The Feminiad. A Poem* (1754) (by John Duncombe, a friend of the novelist Samuel Richardson and contributor to *The Gentleman's Magazine*), one of several poems by men in the 1740s and 1750s in which the achievements of women writers were noted. While *The Feminiad* promoted the literary skills of a range of women from different backgrounds in the period since the Restoration, Duncombe nevertheless condemned those authors such as Aphra Behn (1640–89) and Delarivière Manley (1663–1724) who wrote sexually explicit or risqué drama and fiction:

> The modest Muse a veil with pity throws
> O'er Vice's friends and Virtue's female foes;
> Abash'd she views the bold unblushing mien
> Of modern Manley, Centlivre, and Behn;
> And grieves to see One nobly born disgrace
> Her modest sex, and her illustrious race.
> Tho' harmony thro' all their numbers flow'd,
> And genuine wit its ev'ry grace bestow'd,
> Nor genuine wit nor harmony excuse
> The dang'rous sallies of a wanton Muse. (ll.139–48; cited in Jones, 1990, p.173)

Duncombe's distinction between the 'modest Muse' and the 'wanton Muse' suggests a prescriptive element in literary criticism (which, it should be said, was shared by some women writers and critics as well), an unease towards those writings by women which either transgressed the boundaries of decorum or challenged the traditional idea that a woman's proper role was to be dutiful and virtuous in the private, domestic sphere. Thus, for example, Duncombe disapproves of those aspiring women whose wit and learning threatens their eligibility for becoming wives:

> And husbands oft experience to their cost
> The prudent housewife in the scholar lost:
> But those incur deserv'd contempt, who prize

Their own high talents, and their sex despise,
With haughty mien each social bliss defeat,
And sully all their learning with conceit:
Of such the parent justly warns his son,
And such the Muse herself will bid him shun. (ll.85–91; cited in Jones, 1990, p.172)

In the end, according to Duncombe, to be a suitable marriage partner is, for a middle-class woman especially, a greater priority than the ambition to write or to publish. Yet, many women did write, have their verse (and drama and fiction) published and enjoy the support and patronage of powerful literary figures of the day including Richardson and Johnson. Richardson, himself a publisher, enjoyed a circle of female acquaintance who commented on his work and asserted the importance of female literary taste; Johnson was both impressed and bemused by what he termed 'a generation of Amazons of the pen' (*The Adventurer*, no. 115, 11 Dec., 1753; cited in Lonsdale, 1990, p.xxx).

Twenty years later, the poet Mary Scott (1752?–93) took up the spirit of Duncombe's poem in *The Female Advocate* (1774), a survey of British women writers from the Renaissance. In the Preface, she expresses indignation at men for discouraging women to become educated: 'Do they not regard the woman who suffers her faculties to rust in a state of listless indolence, with a more favourable eye, than her who engages in a dispassionate search after truth?' (cited in Jones, 1990, p.181). Scott's poem looks forward to a time when this imbalance in opportunities and achievements will be redressed:

From sense abstracted, some, with arduous flight,
Explore the realms of intellectual light;
With unremitting study seek to find,
How mind on matter, matter acts on mind:
Alike in nature, arts, and manners read,
In ev'ry path of knowledge, see they tread!
Whilst men, convinc'd of Female Talents, pay
To Female Worth the tributary lay. (ll.457–64, cited in Jones, 1990, p.183)

The confidence that 'Female Worth' would be increasingly recognized is reflected in some critical journals of the second half of the century. A (male) critic reviewing poems by Elizabeth Carter (1717–1806), a friend of Johnson, prophesied a revolutionary change in the profile of women writers:

The men *retreat*, and the women *advance*. The men prate and dress; the women read and write: it is no wonder, therefore, that they should get the upper hand of us; nor should we be at all surprised, if, in the next age, women should give lectures in the classics, and men employ themselves in knitting and needlework. (*Critical Review*, vol.13 (1762); cited in Jones, 1990, p.175)

As it turned out, such expressions of confidence were misplaced. Many of the poems and their authors were forgotten and not re-published until very recently. The result of this unwarranted neglect has meant a hitherto distorted sense of eighteenth-century poetry, and even now the effect of separating female from male poets (which the arrangement of the poems in *Texts*, II avoids), has had mixed consequences for our sense of eighteenth-century poetry:

> The work of the women poets became increasingly part of the literary atmosphere; any reader who regularly read contemporary poetry would have read a number of the women's works. In setting them apart, we still subscribe to the notion that they are a decided subset, a party enclosed in a carriage running on a different if parallel road. (Doody, 1989, p.3)

We will now look in detail at some of the poems by women in the *Texts*.

5.2 Miss W–'s 'The Gentleman's Study'

First, please read Swift's 'The Lady's Dressing Room' (*Texts*, II, p.113),and then Miss W–'s reply, 'The Gentleman's Study' (*Texts*, II, p.117).

EXERCISE   What are the similarities and differences between the two poems?

DISCUSSION   The poems are similar in both form and content. Both are written in iambic tetrameter (iambic metre with four metrical feet in each line), a form which discourages the high style of the poems by Pope and Thomson in *Texts*, II, and both are explicitly scatological. ('The Lady's Dressing Room', though, was one of the most popular poems of its time; much reprinted in pamphlet form and in the newspaper press, it occasioned many replies, including one from Lady Mary Wortley Montagu.) While both poems are obsessed with bodily functions, they also share a similar emphasis in exposing what goes to 'make up', quite literally, a representative society lady, Celia, and a gentleman, Strephon.

The poems differ in that their perspectives of class as well as gender are distinct. Whereas in Swift's poems, it is the 'gentleman' Strephon who creeps into Celia's dressing-room while her servant isn't looking, in 'Miss W–''s poems it is Mrs South, the milliner, invited into Strephon's study by his valet, whose perspective we share, thus emphasizing forcefully the alienation of the lower class from the profligacy of the gentry and aristocracy. But it is clearly impossible to read either poem exclusively through the perspective of class. Swift's poem is deeply misogynistic; the criticism of society ladies which is expressed with heavy irony in lines 119–44, is inseparable from a general attack on women, particularly noticeable in the final couplet, 'Such order from confusion sprung,/Such gaudy *tulips* raised from *dung*'. Furthermore the two titles express a crucial difference; the status of dressing room and study indicate distinct resources of power in men and women of comparable social status. The vindictiveness of Swift's attack could be said to reveal an acknowledgement of the power that dress and make-up lend to women; while 'the strange confusion' (l.34) of the gentlemen's study reveal not just disgusting personal habits, but the abuse of wealth and education, privileges denied to many women. In this regard, 'Miss W–''s poem seems altogether less restrained in its language and the savagery of its condemnation of the opposite sex, especially in the first and last verse paragraphs, which are less oblique and more moral than Swift's.

5.3   Mary Collier's 'The Woman's Labour'

Mary Collier's *The Woman's Labour* is a notable text on this course because she 'appears to have been the first published laboring-class woman poet in England' (Landry, 1990 p.56). It was inspired by Stephen Duck's *The Thresher's Labour*, in particular his scorn for women farm labourers in a passage which we have not had space to reprint in *Texts*, II of which the following lines are an excerpt:

> Our Master comes, and at his Heels a Throng
> Of prattling females, arm'd with Rake and Prong,
> Prepar'd, whil'st he is here, to make his Hay,
> Or, if he turns his back, prepared to play.
> But here, or gone, sure of this comfort still,
> Here's Company, so they may chat their fill:
> And were their Hands as active as their Tongues,
> How nimbly then would move their Rakes and Prongs?
> (Thompson and Sugden, 1989, p.8)

You may find it useful to read the extract from Stephen Duck's *The Thresher's Labour* in *Texts*, II (though it predates the poems by Goldsmith and Crabbe which we have looked at, it arises, as they do, out of a critical engagement with the pastoral tradition in verse). Then read the extract from Mary Collier's *The Woman's Labour* and the accompanying footnote.

EXERCISE   Compare the way that labour is represented in each of the poems. In what sense is Collier's poem different from Duck's?

DISCUSSION   The passage from Duck's poem in *Texts*, II describes threshing at harvest time, while the rest of *The Thresher's Labour* describes summer work and laments that 'as the Year's revolving course goes round,/ No respite from our Labour can be found' (Thompson and Sugden, 1989, p.12). Duck's poem describes the pressures on farm labourers who work for a tenant farmer so intent on quick profit (ll.1–8) that the corn is cut too soon, making it difficult to thresh properly (l.71). Even in this pre-industrial age, threshing comes across as a mechanical task (ll.19–35), though the classical allusions and martial diction of lines 26–31, lend an epic heroism to the men who perform it. There is a possible reference to the women in 'Their master absent, others safely play' (l.36), but paradoxically in relation to the passage cited above, Duck is nostalgic about the time when conversation was possible while working (ll.38–41). Here, like Crabbe after him, he emphasizes the incompatibility of the aesthetics of the pastoral convention with the actual place of a labourer's work (ll.42–51).

   In contrast to the sense of the impotence which the male labourers feel after being rebuked by the master, 'we just like schoolboys look,/ When th'angry master views the blotted book' (ll.68–9), Collier's poem emphasizes the resourcefulness of women in the face of childcare and housework as well as wage labour. In this extract, the washerwoman sets to work with vigour, 'Briskly with courage we our work begin' (l.14) and is compliant with the demands made upon her (ll.40–1), even though the Mistress is an even more exacting employer than the threshers' Master:

'Not only sweat but blood runs trickling down/Our wrists and fingers' (ll.43–4). Whereas sunrise and sunset define the agricultural labourers' outdoor work, the women house servants, though anxious to complete their duties, 'know not when 'twill end' (l.53) and 'till our work is done, are forced to stay' (l.55).

When *The Thresher's Labour* first appeared in 1730, Mary Collier 'got the poem by heart' until 'fancying he had been too Severe on the Female Sex ... brought me to a Strong propensity to call an Army of Amazons to vindicate the injured Sex' (cited in Thompson and Sugden, 1989, p.x). The complete text of Collier's poem shows her to match Duck's poem in content and technique. With reference to Duck's aspersions about female sociability and solidarity during work, she remarks 'For none but *Turks,* that I could ever find,/Have mutes to serve them, or did e'er deny/Their slaves, at Work, to chat it merrily' and regards talk as 'the only Privilege our sex enjoy' (Thompson and Sugden, 1989, p.17). She also shows that as a woman poet, she is as capable as he is, of employing apposite classical allusions, 'While you to Sysiphus yourselves compare,/With Danaus' Daughters we may claim a Share' (Thompson and Sugden, 1989, p.23). (Sisyphus was condemned in Hades to roll a huge stone up a hill that would always roll down again, while Danaus' daughters were condemned to collect water in leaking vessels.) But the most revealing comparison which she makes between herself and Duck concerns education. Her poem opens by praising Duck who, though largely self-taught, was also educated by his patrons, and then contrasts her own position: 'No Learning ever was bestow'd on me;/My life was always spent in Drudgery;/And not alone; alas! with Grief I find;/It is the Portion of poor Woman-kind' (Thompson and Sugden, 1989, p.15).

The biographical details of the poets also supply instructive contrasts. Duck got patronage from the Establishment in the late 1720s, after Queen Caroline, on hearing his verses, granted him an annuity of £30 and a small house in Richmond; the list of subscribers to the 1736 edition of his *Poems on Several Occasions* included royalty as well as nobility. Many critics have argued that with increasing patronage, Duck's poetry lost its way; as he became pressurized into conforming to conventional models in poetry, so his verse became increasingly derivative (see Thompson and Sugden, 1989, pp.i–ix). In 1746 he was admitted to the Church of England, eventually becoming Rector of Byfleet; he committed suicide in 1756. Mary Collier's poetry, as the footnote indicates, brought neither social elevation nor its catastrophic consequences. But 'The Advertisement' to the volume in which her poem appeared reveals motives and aspirations which suggest that she was fully conscious of Duck's precedent:

> ... Though she pretends not to the Genius of Mr Duck nor hopes to be taken Notice of by the Great, yet her Friends are of Opinion that the Novelty of a *Washer-Woman's* turning Poetess, will procure her some Readers.
>
> If all that follow the same Employment would amuse themselves, and one another, during the tedious Hours of their Labour,

in this, or some other Way as innocent, instead of tossing Scandal to and fro, many Reputations would remain unwounded, and the Peace of Families be less disturb'd.

I think it no Reproach to the Author, whose Life is toilsome, and her Wages inconsiderable, to confess honestly, that the View of her putting a small Sum of Money in her Pocket, as well as the Reader's Entertainment, had its Share of Influence upon this Publication ... (cited in Thompson and Sugden, 1989, pp.25–6).

In this passage issues of gender are once again linked with those of class. First, while not regarding herself as suitable to emulate Duck's abilities, she nevertheless sees him as a role model for her literary ambitions; her profession could publicize her poetry as Duck's did his. Secondly, in seeing the act of writing itself as a means of preserving the moral welfare of women of her class, Collier echoes Catherine Cockburn, a writer whose verses sent to the *Gentleman's Magazine* in 1737, suggested that 'royal patronage of Duck should be extended to studious women, less to encourage more women to become writers than to help to wean them from frivolous 'feminine' amusements, and so to make them better wives and mothers' (Lonsdale, 1990, p.xxviii). Finally, Collier confesses that part of her ambition which, as the footnote (*Texts*, II, p.121) explains, was not fulfilled, is to use any profits from the sale of the volume to avoid the washerwoman's fate described in the last lines of the extract in *Texts*, II 'For all our pains no prospect can we see/Attend us, but old age and poverty' (ll.58–9). Collier did not seek fame; though unsuccessful, her self-deprecation and endorsement of prevailing views about the position of women, were expressed to encourage the sale of her books.

5.4   *Mary Leapor's poetry*

Please now read the three poems by Mary Leapor in the following order: the extract from 'An Epistle to Artemisia' (note that 'Mira' refers to Leapor herself, and 'Artemisia' to Bridget Freemantle, her local patron (see footnote, *Texts*, II, p.125)); 'Man the Monarch' and 'An Essay on Woman'.

EXERCISE   What attitudes do the characters in the 'Epistle' express towards Mira's poetry? How do these attitudes relate to the arguments of the other two poems?

DISCUSSION   The ironic sub-title of the poem, suggests that she received no help with her poetry from anyone except Artemisia. First, the male critic's oracular judgement turns out to be so vague as to be useless (ll.1–12); then her friend Cressida, more interested in her own appearance than in reading her friend's work is eventually dismissed with relief (ll.13–46); the superficial flattery of Vido does nothing to increase Mira's self-esteem (ll.47–62); Codrus turns out to be more interested in harassing her than in hearing her verse (ll.63–70); finally Parthenia and Sophronia condemn the way that poetry has led her to neglect her appearance and her work. Eventually she is dismissed from service (as Leapor herself was), and is only rescued from misery by Artemisia.

The other two poems are less preoccupied with the specific hazards of a woman writing, more with the general obstacles to her advancement in any sphere. In 'Man the Monarch' Leapor presents an ironic version of Genesis; man is created as a tyrant who intimidates the beasts of nature into submission whereas woman is fashioned by mother nature who 'Beholds a wretch, whom she designed a queen,/And weeps that e'er she formed the weak machine' (ll.32–3). Those qualities which enhance women in the eyes of men in fact assure their subordination (ll.34–49) which has been perpetuated through history amongst all classes (ll.58–65). In 'An Essay on Woman' the deification of the woman prior to marriage is followed by mortification (ll.15–18); even those women such as Pampilia and Sylvia who have the advantage of wisdom and beauty are despised as much by their own sex as by men (l.29 ff.); Mira's defiance, 'Still give me pleasing indolence and ease,/A fire to warm me and a friend to please' (ll.51–2) seems the only compensation in a world in which 'Unhappy woman's but a slave at large' (l.60).

In the poems examined above, we have considered the intertwined issues of gender and class, the question of patronage and, in the case of Leapor, an argument against male power which is articulated in terms recognizable to modern feminism.

5.5 Lady Mary Wortley Montagu's poetry

Please now read the three poems by Lady Mary Wortley Montagu reprinted in *Texts*, II.

EXERCISE   What do the form and content of the poems suggest about the position from which Montagu is writing? Find examples from one or more of the poems to illustrate your view.

DISCUSSION   The poems reflect a privileged perspective. Montagu is fascinated by the Orient in 'Verses', frank about sexual love in 'The Lover' and unafraid in her satirical attack on Pope. Her writing expresses a confidence that can be attributed in part to her wealthy background, a fact which distinguishes her from the other women poets whose work you've read. But equally, it emphasizes that women could and did write in the same idiom, and with the same force as male authors.

The fact that 'she considered it ill bred to seek literary fame, so that much of her writing was published anonymously and almost accidentally' (Lonsdale, 1990, p.xxv) once again emphasizes that obstacles to recognition came in part from women poets themselves as well as from male literary culture.

6 *Robert Burns (1759–96), Selections from* The Kilmarnock Poems (Poems, Chiefly in the Scottish Dialect, *1786*)

Using the glosses and notes provided in *Texts*, II, please read the five poems by Burns from *The Kilmarnock Poems* (1786). If you find this task daunting initially, try following the recommendation of the editor whose text we are using: 'possibly the best single piece of advice for anyone coming to Scots poetry for the first time is to try reading the words aloud' (Low, 1985, p.xxi).

One eager contemporary reader was the English poet, William Cowper, whose anecdote may reassure those who experience problems with a first reading:

> Poor Burns loses much of his deserved praise in this country through our ignorance of his language. I despair of meeting with any Englishman who will take the pains that I have taken to understand him. His candle is bright, but shut up in a dark lantern. I lent him to a very sensible neighbour of mine; but his uncouth dialect spoiled all; and before he had half read him through he was quite *ram-feezled* [exhausted]. (Letter to Samuel Rose, 27 August 1787, cited in Low, 1985, p.xviii)

But my colleague Angus Calder offers a different explanation of the supposed difficulty of Burns's language:

> His dialect had no terrors for working people in England. It is twentieth-century ideology that has marginalized Burns as a 'regional exception' in 'English' literature and has made him seem, to nationalistic Scots like MacDiarmid [C.M. Grieve, 'Hugh MacDiarmid', poet (1892–1978)], charming but brainless, like a nice old dog. (Calder and Donnelly, 1991, p.xiii)

It is worth noting that by the eighteenth century, due to the historical factors which Angus Calder has outlined in his 'Historical Background to Scotland' (*Studies*, I, pp.436–44), the status of 'Scots' (which was spoken in Lowland Scotland) as a national language had been undermined. Given the fragmentation of the language into a variety of dialects, Burns was conscious that some of his poetic diction would be obscure even amongst his Scots readers, so he published a glossary at the end of the 1786 edition which was expanded in 1787. But Burns's father had ensured that his family acquired skills in the reading and writing of English as well, and this modulation between linguistic idioms, English and Scots, in, for example, 'The Cotter's Saturday Night', is an important aspect of Burns's poetry to which we shall return later (see Low, 1985, pp. ix–xx).

6.1 Introduction

The brief survey which follows of some poems from Burns's earliest published collection is related, through the themes of pastoral and 'counterpastoral', to the earlier sections of this Study, but it also introduces a recognizably distinct dimension to both this essay and the Part as a whole. These poems, written and published in the 1780s, are undoubtedly influenced by Sensibility, that emphasis on a combination of emotional feeling and moral responsibility which functions as the ethical basis of much literature written in Britain in the period *c*.1760–90. Each of the

poems selected for *Texts,* II represents a different aspect of Burns's the-
matic range, his dislike of rigid Calvinism, his patriotic promotion of the
Scottish rural labourer, his critical engagement with poetic traditions, but
each also gives a sense of the range of his techniques, from satire to
comic elegy, to adaptations of vernacular Scots verse, to Spenserian imitation, to poetic epistle. Needless to say, this is a small sample from only
one collection (five out of thirty-six poems). But while much information
is necessarily excluded for reasons of space (e.g. the details of Burns's life
and reputation, the detailed context of eighteenth-century literary culture in Scotland, the history of the Lowland Scots dialect in which Burns
wrote some of his poems), there are supplementary materials in the
course to which you can turn for enlightenment. Indeed, even if you read
it in *Studies,* I, you **must** now carefully re-read Angus Calder's section entitled 'Historical Background to Scotland' which forms a suitable starting-
point for this section. You should also listen to a reading of the five
poems on audio-cassette, AC 1633, Side 2.

6.2   *Background*

The publication of *The Kilmarnock Poems* in July 1786 came at a point in
Burns's life when his future seemed uncertain. His father had died in
1784, and Robert, and his brother Gilbert, were experiencing practical
and financial difficulties in managing the farm which they had leased.
Moreover, his marriage to a girl from the local village who was pregnant
by him, was prevented by her parents, causing emotional distress to them
both. Given these circumstances, Burns was tempted to emigrate to
Jamaica to manage an estate owned by a Scotsman from Ayr, and publication of some of his poems seemed a fitting valediction to his troubles:

> Before leaving my native country for ever, I resolved to publish my
> Poems. – I weighed my productions as impartially as in my power: I
> thought they had merit; and 'twas a delicious idea that I would be
> called a clever fellow, even though it should never reach my ears a
> poor Negro-driver, or perhaps a victim to that inhospitable clime
> gone to the world of Spirits ... I was pretty sure my Poems would
> meet with some applause; but at the worst, the roar of the Atlantic
> would deafen the voice of Censure, and the novelty of west-Indian
> scenes make me forget Neglect. (Letter to Dr John Moore, August
> 1787, cited in Low, 1985, p.xii)

Burns deliberately accentuated the distinctiveness of his own relationship
with the natural world by stressing how different it was from the conventions of pastoral employed by other eighteenth-century poets:

> The following trifles are not the production of the Poet, who, with
> all the advantages of learned art, and perhaps amid the elegancies
> and idlenesses of upper life, looks down for a rural theme, with an
> eye to Theocritus or Virgil ... Unacquainted with the necessary
> requisites for commencing Poet by rule, he sings the sentiments and
> manners, he felt and saw in himself and his rustic compeers around
> him, in his and their native language. (Low, 1985, p.175)

Your reading of his poetry might make you read these words with some
scepticism since it is clear that Burns was neither uneducated in any
sense, nor indifferent to literary tradition. The important point is that, in

an oblique and deferential way, he is resisting pastoral here because he does not have to 'look down for a rural theme' – it is his own experience of the physical and social circumstances of rural life which form the basis of his verse.

Having obtained 350 subscribers for the volume, Burns had the poems published by a local printer in Kilmarnock, John Wilson. A measure of their success is that of 612 copies printed, only 13 remained six weeks after publication (an expanded edition of the *Poems* appeared in Edinburgh in April 1787). Many subsequently famous poems did not find their way into print in the 1786 edition. For reasons of caution, the famous 'Holy Willie's Prayer', a verse satire on a church elder in his local village, was not published until after Burns's death.

The image of the 'ploughman poet', which Burns to some extent cultivated himself, was attractive to reviewers, and no doubt influenced the way he was lionized later by literary society in Edinburgh:

> The author is indeed a striking example of native genius bursting through the obscurity of poverty and the obstructions of laborious life. He is said to be a common ploughman; and when we consider him in this light, we cannot help regretting that wayward fate had not placed him in a more favoured situation. (*Edinburgh Magazine*, iv, October 1786; reprinted in Low, 1974, p.64)

But those who read his works clearly also saw him as representative of his age, not simply in terms of his espousal of the values of the Enlightenment, but as one who embraced the language of feeling too:

> His language is nervous, and his sentiments would do honour to a much more enlightened scholar. In short, he appears to be not only a keen satirist, but a man of great feeling and sensibility. (Letter by 'Allan Ramsay', *Edinburgh Evening Courant*, 13 November 1786; reprinted in Low, 1974, p.65)

Finally, it is worth noting the claim that *The Kilmarnock Poems* is the first identifiable text of Romantic poetry published in Britain. In the versatility of its literary form and technique, in its advancement of a literary language which challenged the supremacy of 'Standard English', in the way it projected human and social preoccupations on to nature and challenged religious orthodoxy, it could indeed be said to share features with the early published works of the late 1780s and 1790s by Blake, Wordsworth and Coleridge. Burns was certainly an important influence on Wordsworth. In December 1787, Dorothy Wordsworth wrote that her seventeen-year old brother, William, had 'read [the Kilmarnock edition] and admired many of the pieces very much' (Low, 1985, p.xviii).

6.3   The Poems

EXERCISE   Please now re-read 'Address to the Deil'. First, think about the tone of the poem, and its overall effect. Does it express Enlightenment values, of the kind discussed in the rest of the course, particularly Part D? How does the form of the poem contribute to its effect? Find examples to illustrate your views.

DISCUSSION To the extent that it offers an ironical view of Calvinism, the poem can be usefully compared to the many texts you've read on this course which attack religious institutions and the popular superstitions they foster in order to secure their power. But it should be emphasized that 'Address' mocks one dimension of orthodox belief in Burns's own country, Scotland, without employing 'reason' as the *philosophes* did, to undermine Christianity.

But, as well as giving details of folk tales and popular beliefs, the poem also announces itself as indebted to a variety of literary traditions. There were, for example, medieval poems in the vernacular Scots, 'flytings', where the devil was scolded, but most significant is the debt to the portrayal of Satan in Milton's *Paradise Lost* acknowledged in the poem's epigraph. Burns inaugurates a revisionary reading of the figure of Satan in Milton's poem, of a kind made most famously by Blake and Shelley in later decades, when he comments to a friend:

> I have bought a pocket Milton, which I carry perpetually about with me, in order to study the sentiments – the dauntless magnanimity; the intrepid unyielding independance; the desperate daring, and noble defiance of hardship, in that great Personage, Satan. (Low, 1985, p. 141)

But whereas such sentiments led some of the Romantic poets towards reading an explicitly political allegory on to Milton's poem, Burns's aim to ridicule the seriousness with which the Devil's powers are believed in by ignorant and orthodox alike, is best achieved through satire. Look, for example, at the way the sublime poetry of the Bible and Milton is subject to burlesque in lines 85–102. While the poet takes on the Devil and those who are deceived into believing he exists, and dismisses him lightheartedly, his most devastating blow is aimed squarely at the religious.

The confident tone of the poem is clearly comic, and results in part from the effect of its metrical and stanzaic form. The demonstrative rhyme-scheme, *aaabab*, and the uneven rhythm (the first, second, third and fifth lines of each stanza are of nine syllables and the fourth and sixth are of five) contribute crucially to its pace, which is both exhilarating to read aloud but also suitably uneven, lurching forwards in a kind of disrespectful swagger. Even if you were to ignore the glosses and notes, the sense of irreverent mirth would be conveyed through its form.

The important thing to note is that the Devil is treated essentially as a rogue figure with whom we're all familiar rather than as an intimidating and insidious spiritual essence. Thus the cumulative effect of the first four stanzas is to build up a sense of his power over us while also exposing our fanciful and exaggerated sense of how that power is deployed. For the poet to use his grandmother as an authority for the authenticity of the devil (ll.25–36), and to back this up with his own spooky anecdote (ll.37–48) makes it obvious, as in Hume's *Dialogues*, that belief in the supernatural is often a result of the projection of human fears on to the physical world. The tone of lines 49–84 is of a slightly different order, for Burns uses these stanzas as an opportunity to recount the bizarre and wonderful array of popular superstitions concerning witches and spirits which he had absorbed from his own childhood, and it demonstrates his loyalty towards his local culture even when, in the case of the Masonic handshake, it involves an irony directed at himself (see Low's note to line 69, *Texts*, II, p.155).

The last three stanzas achieve a fine balance between a touch of self-conscious sentimental pity, and the culmination of the poem's satirical edge. Angus Calder puts it eloquently: 'the 'Address' jibes once again, at the belief of the Auld Lichts, by inverting the Calvinist idea that all are damned save the elect: even the Devil, Burns suggests, might change his ways and be saved' (Calder and Donnelly, 1991, p.359). By employing 'a satiric thrust at the Calvinist view adroitly disguised as a piece of sentimentalism' (Daiches, 1966, p.126), Burns can evade accusations of a direct attack on religion – a technique familiar to you from the very first study in the course on the *Encyclopédie*.

Please now read 'Epistle to J. L–k, An Old Scotch Bard'. As in 'The Cotter's Saturday Night', the inspiration for the theme of the poem is a popular, *social* event, the 'rockin' of line 7 which is glossed in the *Texts*. Its central theme is the validity of Burns's local culture. John Lapraik, a tenant farmer like Burns himself, becomes, along with Allan Ramsay and Robert Fergusson (both eighteenth-century Scottish poets who influenced Burns significantly), representative of poetic skills which are seen as more durable and valuable than the canons of poetic taste as established by English or Anglicized Scottish poets and critics such as Pope, Steele and Beattie (ll.21–2). Burns in the rest of the poem gives an account of the origins of his own interest in writing verse, as well as telling Lapraik of his reputation (see, for example, lines 97–102). He presents his own as an unpretentious talent, and looks upon himself as a rhymer rather than a poet, aware that his interest in song may be frowned upon as inferior (ll.43–60). In general this is part of the democratic impulse of Burns's verse – a man's a man 'for a' that and a' that' – but it is also part of a significant shift in literary taste in the late eighteenth century which had far-reaching consequences for conceptions of poetry. Perhaps one of the reasons why Burns was popular with an English as well as Scottish audience was that he extended and developed the interest in ballads and popular songs inaugurated in 'high' English literary culture by Percy's *Reliques of Ancient English Poetry* (1765), a fashion which culminates in Wordsworth's unwarranted claim for the originality of his and Coleridge's *Lyrical Ballads* (1798), which were advertised as 'experiments' with public taste (Brett and Jones, 1963, p.7).

Yet for all Burns's flamboyant rejection of formal educational training of the kind received by critics (and academics), and his espousal of experience instead, ('Gie me ae' spark o' Nature's fire,/That's a' the learning I desire' (ll.73–4)), we should remember both his debts to such poets as Pope, and his admiration of them.

Regrettably, there is insufficient space to discuss the rest of Burns's poems in detail, so I shall simply highlight some important issues which you should consider in reading them.

'The Cotter's Saturday Night' has enjoyed an ambivalent status in the Burns canon, and has been deemed a failure by many recent critics. The reasons are not hard to see. The combination of vernacular Scots with English, though plausible because 'the accepted language for religious and moral reflection in poetry in eighteenth-century Lowland Scotland was not Scots but English' (Low, 1985, p.150), is awkward, particularly in the highly sententious stanzas IX and X. Equally, this is the only poem of the five you have read in which Burns does not employ his six line stanza, and uses instead the Spenserian stanza, a form with which he is not at ease, and in which he cannot be flippant. But the poem has been included for the way in which it answers the sentiments of both Gray's 'Elegy' and Goldsmith's *Deserted Village*, both in themes and in specific literary echoes, and you should be able to see how his defence of the Scottish rural labourer engages with the earlier English poems you have read.

Written to accompany 'The Death and Dying Words of Poor Mailie' which was based on an incident witnessed by Burns when a ewe had entangled herself in a tether, 'Poor Mailie's Elegy' comes from a Scots tradition of comic elegy in which the six line stanza, called 'Standard Habby' (used by Ramsay and Fergusson) is used. Both this poem and 'To a Mouse' indicate the fine balance Burns maintained through style and tone, between *sentimentality* with regard to the lesser species of the animal world, and an implicit identification of 'man' with their vulnerability. The influence of the Bible on 'To a Mouse', and the influence of the passage from Johnson's *Rasselas* (cited in the notes to *Texts*, II, p.164) alert the reader to the moral significance which Burns extracts from the incident described.

The work of Burns is a fitting way to end this essay on the selection of eighteenth-century poems in *Texts*, II. Burns answers the poet's curiosity about the lives of rural labourers in the 'Elegy' in a way that Gray could hardly have imagined. Equally, if the sentiments of 'To a Mouse' and the 'Epistle' make Burns a poet of democratic impulses, at one with the people (which the poet in Gray's 'Elegy', to his consternation, is not), this also suggests how by the mid-1780's, the form and content of poetry read in England, as well as Scotland, had changed radically. Burns's poetry represents not simply a forceful critique of the conventions of pastoral at a point when, with Crabbe's *Village*, it seemed to have exhausted itself, but a transcendence of it. Pastoral is abandoned, or at least revised, in a different mode of writing about rural life and labour, which is most vividly apparent in the poetry of Wordsworth and Clare. Along with the re-evaluation of many other themes and issues which you have studied on this course, this radical re-interpretation of the world of 'nature' in these later poets marks one of the most significant challenges to Enlightenment thinking.

7   References

Arnold, M. (1973) 'Thomas Gray', in *The Complete Prose Works of Matthew Arnold*, vol.9, University of Michigan Press, Michigan, pp.189–204. (First published 1888.)

Barrell, J. and Bull, J. (eds) (1982) *The Penguin Book of English Pastoral Verse*, Penguin, Harmondsworth.

Brett, R.L. and Jones, A.R. (eds) (1963) *Wordsworth and Coleridge: Lyrical Ballads*, Methuen, London.

Butt, J., ed. (1985) *The Poems of Alexander Pope: A One-Volume Edition of the Twickenham Text with Selected Annotations*, Methuen, London.

Calder, A. and Donnelly, W. (eds) (1991) *Robert Burns: Selected Poetry*, Penguin, Harmondsworth.

Daiches, D. (1966) *Robert Burns*, Deutsch, London.

Dalrymple-Champneys, N. and Pollard, A. (eds) (1988), *George Crabbe: The Complete Poetical Works*, 3 vols, Clarendon Press, Oxford.

Doody, M. A. (1985) *The Daring Muse: Augustan Poetry Reconsidered*, Cambridge University Press, Cambridge.

Doody, M.A. (1989) *London Review of Books*, vol. 11, no. 24, 1989, pp.3–5.

Edwards, G. (1987) 'Crabbe's So-Called Realism', *Essays in Criticism*, vol.37, pp.303–20.

Edwards, G. (1991) *George Crabbe: Selected Poems*, Penguin, Harmondsworth.

Empson, W. (1935) *Some Versions of Pastoral*, Chatto and Windus, London.

Friedman, A. (ed.) (1966), *Collected Works of Oliver Goldsmith*, 5 vols., Clarendon Press, Oxford.

Greene, D. (1984) *Samuel Johnson*, The Oxford Authors, Oxford University Press, Oxford.

Jack, I. (1965) 'Gray's *Elegy* Reconsidered', in H. Bloom and F.W. Hilles (eds) *From Sensibility to Romanticism: Essays Presented to Frederick A. Pottle*, Oxford University Press, Oxford, pp.139–69.

Jones, V. (ed.) (1990) *Women in the Eighteenth Century: Constructions of Femininity*, Routledge, London.

Landry, D. (1978) '"A Garden, and A Grave": The Poetry of Oliver Goldsmith', in *The Author in His Work: Essays on a Problem in Criticism*, edited by L. L. Martz and A. Williams, Yale University Press, pp. 3–30.

Landry, D. (1990) *The Muses of Resistance: Laboring-Class Women's Poetry in Britain, 1739–1796*, Cambridge University Press, Cambridge.

Lonsdale, R. (ed.) (1969) *The Poems of Thomas Gray, William Collins and Oliver Goldsmith*, Longman, London.

Lonsdale, R. (1987) *The New Oxford Book of Eighteenth-Century Verse*, Oxford University Press, Oxford.

Lonsdale, R. (1990) *Eighteenth-Century Women Poets: An Oxford Anthology*, Oxford University Press, Oxford.

Low, D.A. (ed.) (1985) *Robert Burns: The Kilmarnock Poems* (Poems, Chiefly in the Scottish Dialect, 1786), Dent, London.

Low, D.A. (1974) *Robert Burns: The Critical Heritage*, Routledge and Kegan Paul, London.

Lucas, J., (ed.) (1988) *Oliver Goldsmith: Selected Writings*, Fyfield, Manchester.

McGann, J.J. (1985) *The Beauty of Inflections: Literary Investigations in Historical Method and Theory*, Clarendon Press, Oxford.

Paulin, T. (1986) *Faber Book of Political Verse*, Faber, London.

Pollard, A. (ed.) (1972) *Crabbe: The Critical Heritage*, Routledge and Kegan Paul, London.

Rousseau, G.S. (ed.) (1974) *Goldsmith: The Critical Heritage*, Routledge and Kegan Paul, London.

Thompson, E. P. and Sugden, M. (eds) (1989) *The Thresher's Labour by Stephen Duck and The Woman's Labour by Mary Collier. Two Eighteenth Century Poems.* Introduction by E. P. Thompson, illustrations by Marian Sugden, Merlin Press, London.

Williams, R. (1985) *The Country and The City*, The Hogarth Press, London.

Young, J. (1783) *A Criticism on the Elegy Written in a Country Church Yard*, London.

8   Further reading

8.1   Texts

Barrell, J. and Bull, J. (eds) (1982) *The Penguin Book of English Pastoral Verse*, Penguin, Harmondsworth.

Lonsdale R. (1987) *The New Oxford Book of Eighteenth-Century Verse* Oxford University Press, Oxford.

Lonsdale, R. (1990) *Eighteenth-Century Women Poets: An Oxford Anthology*, Oxford University Press, Oxford.

8.2   Background and criticism

Barrell, J. (1983) *English Literature in History 1730–80: An Equal, Wide Survey*, Hutchinson, London.

Copley, S. (ed.) (1984) *Literature and the Social Order in Eighteenth-Century England*, Croom Helm, London.

Jones, V. (ed.) (1990) *Women in the Eighteenth Century: Constructions of Femininity*, Routledge, London.

Lonsdale, R. (ed.) (1986) *Sphere History of Literature: Dryden to Johnson*, Sphere Books, London.

Nussbaum, F. and Brown L. (eds) (1987) *The New Eighteenth Century: Theory, Politics, English Literature*, Methuen, London.

Sambrook, J. (1986) *The Eighteenth Century: The Intellectual and Cultural Context of English Literature, 1700–1789*, Longman, London.

Todd, J. (1986) *Sensibility: An Introduction*, Methuen, London.

Watson, J.R. (ed.) (1989) *Pre-Romanticism in English Poetry of the Eighteenth Century: The Poetic Art and Significance of Thomson, Gray, Collins, Goldsmith, Cowper and Crabbe, A Casebook*, Macmillan, London.

Willey, B. (1986) *The Eighteenth Century Background: Studies in the Idea of Nature in the Thought of the Period*, Ark, London. (First published 1940.)

Rousseau's Émile: the reconciliation of nature and society

Prepared for the Course Team by Linda Walsh

Contents

Rousseau's Émile *(Study weeks 26–27)*

Studies/Texts	Radio	TV	AC	Set Books
Studies, II	-	TV14	-	-
Texts, II				

1 Introduction

1.1 Production, publication and reception of Émile

Rousseau worked on his educational treatise *Émile* in the late 1750s, completed the book in the autumn of 1760 and saw it published in May 1762. It was condemned and publicly burned by the Paris *Parlement*. He had to flee from France to Switzerland to avoid arrest, turning down advice to go to England on the grounds, stated in his *Confessions*, that he 'never liked England or the English' (Rousseau, 1988, p.537). The book was subsequently condemned by the authorities of Geneva, Amsterdam, St Petersburg, Berne and Rome and by the Archbishop of Paris. Consequently, Rousseau was forced to flee from haven to haven (including, eventually, a reluctant year in England and an unsuccessful sojourn with Hume),[1] returning to France only in 1767, under an assumed name.

The main source of controversy was that section of the book dealing with religious education: 'The Profession of Faith of a Savoyard Priest',[2] in which Rousseau implicitly rejected the authority of the church by advocating a natural or deistic religion in which reason, observation of nature, human judgement and feeling should form the basis of faith: little importance was attached to conventional and institutionalized modes of worship. There was something extremely ironic about Rousseau's persecution, as he was an eloquent defender of religious belief in an increasingly anti-religious age: the 'Profession of Faith' attempted to deny the materialist conclusions of many *philosophes*. Rousseau wrote reverently, rather than ironically, about Christ and the Scriptures, and at this point in his life his regular bedtime reading was the Bible. Little wonder, then, that he felt his book was less likely to incur the wrath of the authorities than the openly atheistic and materialistic works of his contemporaries. Later, we'll look at some of the reasons for the alarm (and increased sales of the book!) caused by the 'Profession of Faith'.

Rousseau worked on *Émile* while living at Montmorency, (north-west of Paris), on the estate of the Maréchal de Luxembourg and his wife. He moved there after quarrelling with Mme d'Épinay, a close friend of some of the *philosophes*, who had previously offered him hospitality and accommodation (see Fig. 17). Mme de Luxembourg took a great interest in the publication of *Émile*, but Rousseau's autobiographical *Confessions* display little gratitude. Having entrusted all the necessary papers to his patroness, Rousseau left matters largely in her hands but continued to communicate with Malesherbes, Director of Publications (the minister in charge of censorship, well known for his liberal views). However, the *Confessions* reveal a complex tale of negotiations between his publisher, Duchesne, and a Dutch publishing house. Rousseau was anxious that the work should be printed in Holland in order to avoid any potential censorship problems – a common ploy in the eighteenth century. Slowly he became aware that his publisher was arranging for the book to be printed in Paris, while

Figure 16
Maurice Quentin de la Tour, Portrait of Jean-Jacques Rousseau, *pastel 1'6" × 1'3", Geneva Museum of Art and History. (Mansell Collection)*

---

[1] Frederick the Great also extended hospitality to Rousseau in Prussian Neuchâtel, 1762–5. See *Texts*, I, p.65 and TV14, 'Jean-Jacques Rousseau: Retreat to Romanticism'.

[2] You have already encountered this in the study on Lessing, (*Studies*, II, pp.43–80).

Figure 17
Rousseau's house at Mont-
Louis, Montmorency. (Musée
Jean-Jacques Rousseau,
Montmorency)

sustaining only the pretence of publication in Holland. Despite Malesherbes's reassurances about the improbability of any fuss over the 'Profession of Faith', Rousseau's anxiety grew as publication was delayed: he even suspected a Jesuit plot. He claimed that Malesherbes wrote to him immediately before publication, asking for the return of all the letters he'd written to Rousseau concerning the book. He also claimed that 'friends' who read the book when it appeared sent him appreciative notes, which they left unsigned. It was not long before the storm over the book's publication burst and Rousseau was forced to flee, in order, he said, to avoid compromising Mme de Luxembourg, although his gratitude for her hospitality was now strongly tinged with suspicion (see Rousseau, 1988, pp.494–5, 516–33).

In the preface to *Émile* Rousseau states that the work began as a random collection of ideas on education, designed to 'give pleasure to a good mother who thinks for herself'. The lady concerned was Mme de Chenonceaux, the daughter-in-law of Mme Dupin, a lady resident in Paris for whom Rousseau had worked as secretary and assistant. Rousseau described Mme de Chenonceaux as 'a very charming young person', of 'a metaphysical and reflective turn of mind, if somewhat given to sophistry. Her conversation, which was not what one would expect of a young woman fresh from the convent, was very appealing to me. Her complexion was marvellously fair, and her figure would have been tall and splendid if only she had held herself more gracefully ...' (Cranston, 1983, pp.215–16).

Clearly the project quickly outgrew the initial brief of a favour for an acquaintance. The book developed into a hybrid literary form interweaving elements of philosophical treatise, educational treatise, novel and autobiography, as Rousseau drew up guidelines for the education of an imaginary pupil, Émile. Later parts of the book deal with the love story of Émile and Sophie, his future marriage partner. These sections revive themes already explored in Rousseau's hugely successful novel, *La Nouvelle Héloïse* (*The New Eloïsa*), published in Paris in 1761. He was working on this novel, as well as on his important political work, *The Social Contract* (published in 1762) at Montmorency, at the same time as he was working on *Émile*. All three works explore the tension between what Rousseau perceives as the 'natural' or the just and eighteenth-century religious and political institutions and social conventions, perceived as sources of tyranny, artifice and injustice.

Given the strange hybrid form of *Émile*, it is not surprising to discover that Rousseau was anxious about the practicability of many of his ideas (see *Texts*, II, pp.184–5). He was well aware that many of his general points about education lacked concrete exemplification and in 1764 he wrote to a correspondent:

> You are quite right to say that it is impossible to form an Émile, but I cannot believe that you take the book which bears this name for a true treatise on education. It is rather a philosophical work on the principle ... that *man is naturally good*. (quoted in Rousseau, 1974, p.ix)

This principle in itself would, of course, appear as heresy to a nation subscribing to the doctrine of original sin. Some years later, in his *Dialogues*, he again described *Émile* as 'merely a treatise on the original goodness of man, intended to show how vice and error, alien to his constitution, are introduced into it from outside and imperceptibly distort it' (quoted in Rousseau, 1974, p.ix).

It is this central tension between man's[3] natural ('original') goodness and the vices of society, to which I would now like to turn. The main focus in this study will be on the concept underlying and informing not

---

[3] Rousseau, like most of his contemporaries, used the term 'man' to apply to *all* human beings.

only the religious ideas of *Émile*, but also its views on education and on the precarious relationship between man and society: the concept of Nature. I shall structure this analysis by looking at the following issues:

A natural education – How does Rousseau describe and define such an education in Book I of *Émile*?.

The acquisition of knowledge and faith – How does Rousseau think children learn? What, in his view, is the origin of religious faith?.

The broader context of Émile – Can we read *Émile* as part of a sustained philosophical programme within Rousseau's *oeuvre*? Are biographical factors significant?.

The education of women – Is Rousseau's concept of natural education applied consistently to both sexes?.

The legacy of Émile – What was the impact of *Émile* on eighteenth-century France and on subsequent educational theory?.

An examination of these issues will reveal some contradictory notions and unanswered questions. It is hoped, however, that you will gain a useful framework through which to approach a profound, complex and provocative writer, who was as much of an enigma to his own contemporaries as he is to twentieth-century commentators.

2   A Natural Education

EXERCISE   Please read the first paragraph of Book I of *Émile* (*Texts*, II, pp.171–2) and identify the main grounds of Rousseau's quarrel with the way in which the human race has developed.

DISCUSSION   Rousseau's complaint is that man 'is not content with anything in its natural state'. He has constantly meddled with the forces of nature both in his physical environment (trees, animals) and in himself.

This first paragraph of *Émile* contains the gist of the argument of the rest of the book: any useful and valid system of education must work with nature rather than against it.

EXERCISE   Now read the next few pages of Book I, up to '...after having perused this treatise' (*Texts*, II, p.176). How is a conflict between natural man and social man established in the text? As you read, note any metaphors, analogies or examples which convey Rousseau's ideas effectively.

DISCUSSION   On p.173 Rousseau says that nature operates in man through the 'internal development of our organs'. Our physical and mental faculties have their own internal rate and type of development, independent of any changes we can impose upon them ('entirely independent of us'). This is another way of saying that, for example, we can grow only as tall as nature allows, or develop any skills and abilities within the limits nature has set us. The distinction between habits 'conformable to nature' (p.173) and those, implicitly, which are not, then reinforces the message that we ignore nature at our peril: 'the force of … nature exerts itself' (p.173). Nature is viewed as a beneficent force which has endowed mankind with the capacity to feel pleasure and pain ('sensations… agreeable and displeasing') and, when reinforced by reason (rather than betrayed or distorted by prejudice), this capacity for feeling is a basis on which to construct 'happiness or perfection' (p.174) (see the Introduction to Part E, pp.125–30 on the importance of Sensibility).

Figure 18
Frontispiece of Émile, *engraved by Cochin. The French caption reads, 'Man's education begins at his birth'. The engraving shows a bust of Rousseau, beneath which the Latin inscription 'Vitam Impendere Vero' (To live life in truth) appears. (Bibliothèque Nationale, Paris)*

In the paragraph beginning 'It is to these original dispositions ...' the conflict between nature and society is crystallized: it is impossible to train man to be *equally* true to his inner nature *and* to the demands of society. The very attributes which equip man for successful existence within a group or society are the same attributes which lead him to ignore natural, innate impulses. Hence the resulting inner conflict, which Rousseau attributes to a society which is particularly effective (e.g. in its 'ridiculous...colleges' and 'education acquired by an intercourse with the world', p.175) in generating self-contradictions in man. The solution must lie in gaining a clearer picture of natural man so that society works with him rather than against him.

It is difficult to predict which of Rousseau's metaphors, analogies and examples, if any, you found effective. Were you struck by the image of the sap rising within a plant, or by the example of the Spartan mother, so stoical in her acceptance of her sons' deaths? The important point to note here is that Rousseau, like a good orator, appeals to our imagination and feelings as well as to our powers of reasoning.

EXERCISE   Read the rest of Book I of *Émile* (*Texts*, II, pp.176–202) and note examples of (1) natural and (2) unnatural aspects of childcare and education identified by Rousseau.

DISCUSSION   **1   *Natural childcare or education***
I noted the following examples (you may have additional or different ones):

> (a) an education for manhood rather than for any particular station in life (since 'according to the order of nature, all men [are] equal'), p.176;
>
> (b) freedom of movement for babies in order to aid the natural process of growth, pp.177–8;
>
> (c) mothers nursing their own children ('the sentiments of nature would revive in our hearts'), p.180: Rousseau stated earlier, in his first footnote to Book I (p.172), that such work is assigned to women by the 'author of nature' and on pp.180–1 he refers to the 'young persons ... of a good natural disposition' who 'discharge ... the most delightful obligation nature can impose' by breast-feeding their own children;
>
> (d) hardening children against pain and grief ('Observe nature...'), p.181;
>
> (e) mothers and fathers adopting personal responsibility for the upbringing and education of their child (p.182), in order to keep his 'original [i.e. natural] form';
>
> (f) the entire process of breast-feeding is natural because nature changes the milk in females according to a child's age, p.190;
>
> (g) a childhood spent in the fresh air of the countryside rather than in towns, in consideration of 'the constitutions of children', p.192;
>
> (h) the 'native [natural] vigour' promoted by cold baths, p.192;
>
> (i) an acknowledgement that 'every new object is naturally interesting to a child' (p.196) and that children should be encouraged to follow their interests;

(j) respect for the natural language of children, based on intonation, expression and gesture, pp.197–8;

(k) respect for the love of activity given to children by the 'author of nature', p.200.

2 Unnatural childcare or education

Examples I have:

(a) the use of swaddling-clothes, which alter a child's 'natural constitution' (p.178) (cf. Reynolds's *Discourse III* on unnatural fashions in *Texts*, I, p.214);

(b) the custom of farming one's children out to a wet-nurse, 'without the ties of nature' (p.178) – and see p.180 – 'the natural, quite subverted in our hearts';

(c) withdrawing children from the 'laws of nature' by shielding them from pain (p.181) – and also on p.181 – 'This is the rule of nature. Why should you act contrary to it?';

(d) encouraging tyranny (falsely attributed to nature) in children, p.182;

(e) the employment of a tutor, who adopts 'an obligation which nature has not imposed' (p.187) in the place of a father;

(f) medicine ('Man, by nature, is formed to suffer with patience'), p.188;

(g) the employment of a nurse, p.189;

(h) the 'stinking atmosphere of a city', p.192;

(i) the use of fermented liquors in baths, p.192;

(j) pandering to obstinate tears, p.199;

(k) the use of hard teething toys, p.201.

It is easy to see from Book I why Rousseau's chief concern in *Émile* is the issue of education. If society has created inner conflict in mankind, what better way to counteract this and induce reform than through the education and upbringing of children, particularly if this education can be brought closer to nature? The implication is that society warps natural inclinations by introducing people to unnecessary desires (do babies really need toys?), prejudices and bad habits which damage their well being. Does this really help us, however? Did you feel, as you read Book I, that there were any clear criteria guiding Rousseau's classification of the natural and unnatural? Is 'nature' reality or utopia? Is it really that easy to say when a baby's tears are an exercise in tyranny? In the end, does Rousseau's assertion that nature should be our guide amount to anything more than the circular argument that whatever he considers to be good must be natural and that whatever is natural must be good?

The conditions of Rousseau's experiment in natural education may have struck you as particularly harsh. His pupil must inhabit a temperate climate (pp.185–6) and have no disability (p.187). Is he constructing a utopia resistant to inconvenient realities or simply ensuring that his experiment avoids extremes and remains within the bounds of the familiar, in the interests of credibility and accuracy?

As you read Book I, you may have noticed that nature is sometimes accorded considerable reverence, for example in the use of the kind of personification often reserved by literary men for Greek goddesses (see p.181 – 'the track she has delineated'). This would seem to imply that Nature represents an ideal world or standard to which we should all aspire: a nexus of values which would be upheld by all in a world governed by reason and right feeling.[4] Defined by Rousseau as the creation of God, (the 'author of nature' – p.200), Nature itself is almost a deity. An eminent scholar of the concept of Nature in French eighteenth-century literature (see Ehrard, 1950, pp.421–3) found that the word 'Nature' was often found in close proximity to the following words in the texts he studied: law, reason, sentiment, virtue, happiness, innocence, society, necessity, providence, order, liberty. A semantic climate of this kind could generate a reassuring optimism with regard to an attainable, rational, social order. The *philosophes* often capitalized on this web of associations in order to exploit the polemical potential of the word: it was often placed in opposition to the abuses and injustices they sought to redress. (See *Encyclopédie* articles *Natural Equality* and *Woman (Natural Law)* and compare Lessing's *Nathan the Wise* Act I. 5: 'Nature, you do not lie!'.)[5]

'Nature' was often used in eighteenth-century texts in opposition to grace, miracle, revelation, superstition, custom, prejudice. Indeed, it is often easier to detect what 'nature' *doesn't* mean than what it does signify in eighteenth-century texts. Is Rousseau guilty of obscurity or do you think he relies on genuinely observed, empirical facts?

EXERCISE   Look again at *Texts*, II, pp.180–1 . Does Rousseau advance his arguments about what is natural by (a) an appeal to experience or observable fact or (b) by rhetorical (persuasive) flourishes and supposition?

DISCUSSION   I am inclined to distrust anyone who claims, in the name of nature, that women who suckle their own children will experience 'happy delivery, speedy restoration to constant and vigorous health' at childbirth. This appears to assume much on nature's behalf. Rousseau's promise that women 'of a good natural disposition', who take charge of the upbringing of their own children, will gain the undying love and respect of their husbands, children and the whole world, also seems to have a hollow ring to it. This phenomenon could not have been widely observed by him as he is aware only of '*some* young persons' who fulfil such a role. It seems to

---

[4]   There is not, in Kenrick's translation however, the systematic capitalization of abstract nouns typical of eighteenth-century texts: we perceive the status of nature as an elevated force or abstract ideal from the contexts in which it is used.

[5]   Hume's *Dialogues Concerning Natural Religion* present an interesting debate on the 'goodness' of Nature. See *Texts*, II p.49: '... nor has nature guarded, with the requisite accuracy, against all disorder or confusion'.

me that there is powerful supposition, rather than a scientific or strictly logical argument, that we can chart the 'path of nature' and the advantages which it brings.

Although there is no explicit claim here to have observed or experienced the chain of cause and effect of the natural/unnatural modes of behaviour and consequences described, there is an *implicit* claim that the arguments are based on common sense ('most obvious reasonings') and real fact ('observations I have never seen disputed'). Your acquaintance with other examples of eighteenth-century polemical writing (e.g. the *Encyclopédie*) will have familiarized you, however, with the ways in which a conspiratorial relationship with the reader can be established by such appeals to 'reason' and 'common sense'. Appeals to classical examples which were invested with great authority and significance (in this case the story of Thetis and Achilles) were another such ploy to arouse the sympathies of the educated. Some of these examples have been lost in the cuts made to our text.

It must be stated, however, that there are other parts of Book I where Rousseau's appeals to experience and observation appear to be both more explicit and more convincing. The anecdote recounted on p.198, for example, in which a woman beats a crying child, appears to conform more closely to an authentic witness account. Perhaps, then, some attempts to argue from experience are rooted in highly subjective experience, while others are based on more widespread experience. Perhaps, also, many attempts to argue from experience are coloured by personal polemic. The study on Wollstonecraft in this volume will shed further light on this interesting relationship between rhetoric, reasoning and experience.

Rousseau's programme of natural education does not conceal the harshness of nature, which sits uneasily between the realm of ideal values and that of physical reality and rigour. This harshness, however, is considered more pure and healthy than many aspects of civilized society. In subscribing to this view Rousseau established a relationship with a long-standing tradition of thought in European literature. It is believed that Montaigne, the sixteenth-century essayist, was among those who influenced Rousseau (see John, 1981, p.20). In his essay *On Cannibals*, Montaigne re-examines the alleged superiority of western European societies over so-called barbaric and cannibalistic societies. He stresses the innocence and healthy life style of some of the latter. The valour and martial honour of the people of Brazil are indicated as proof of the superiority of 'the great and mighty mother nature' over the 'art' of European societies. You have already met the concept of the 'noble savage' in earlier parts of the course. This concept accords with the view that 'nature knows best', so forcibly expressed in *Émile*. (See the example of the 130-year-old Patrick O'Neil, *Texts*, II, p.189.)

Pain and suffering, cold air and cold baths are among the rigours of nature to which in Rousseau's view, infants should be exposed. These ideas also belong to a tradition of stoical endurance established by earlier writers, including Montaigne in his essay 'On the Education of Children'.

Locke's *Thoughts on Education,* first translated into French in 1695, are also thought to have influenced Rousseau (Locke, 1989, pp.84, 85, 98,108–9, 164, 171–2, 175). Leaking shoes, wet feet, cold baths and hard beds were prescribed by Locke for the education of seventeenth-century English gentlemen. He urged caution against 'stubborn and domineering' tears, and the cultivation of Spartan endurance in children. (Cf. the Russian Cadet Corps under Catherine the Great, described in *Texts,* I, p.84.)

Rousseau's natural education was, then, to some extent rooted in tradition.[6] Equally, it was a reaction against established traditions, particularly in the view of human nature it conveyed. Unlike many of the religious thinkers of his day, he rejected the view that a system of education should be devised on the premise that human nature is tainted by original sin. On the contrary, argues Rousseau, any flaws in human nature are more likely to arise from the artificial constraints imposed by society. (Look again at the opening sentence of Book I.) He sees the wickedness of man as the product of particular historical, social and political developments. In *Émile* a new blueprint for society and citizenship is proposed in order to erase the awful mistakes of the past and to produce a healthier order. Nature and society (or culture), Rousseau proposes, can be harmonized much more successfully than in the past.[7] Many Rousseau scholars agree that *Émile* combines a bleak account of human nature with a more optimistic prognosis for its future.[8]

The irony of this reformism, however, lies in the fact that Rousseau's new order operates largely on the negative principle of 'letting well alone', or avoiding all unnecessary intervention in a child's development. On p.176 Rousseau introduces the metaphor of an anchor cast in a rough sea in order to reinforce the idea that any progress made *against* the swell of nature is not true progress at all. This principle is repeated at regular intervals throughout *Émile,* as Rousseau settles down to describing in detail the principles which must guide his imaginary pupil's curriculum. The implication is that whenever in doubt, a tutor or parent should refrain from interfering in the spontaneous natural development of a child.[9] In reality, however, the tutor in *Émile* plays a significant part in stage-managing various learning situations in response to his pupil's interests. (As an example of this stage-managing, see the section on the desensitization to face masks, *Texts,* II, p.196.) The key to success, for

---

[6] Montaigne's essays 'On Cannibals' and 'On the Education of Children' are studied in the Open University course, A205 *Culture and Belief in Europe, 1450–1600.* Other influences on the views Rousseau expresses in Book I of *Émile* include Boerhaave, a Dutch doctor and botanist (1668–1738), who was a major influence on Lind and Edinburgh medicine generally.

[7] Those who would like to pursue this argument in more detail may find the following of interest: Broome (1963) and Horowitz (1987, pp.xi–49, 207–53).

[8] On the political implications of this view and on Rousseau's dedication to the ideals of liberty, fraternity and equality, see Jordan (1979, pp.59–71).

[9] Claydon (1969, p.26), argues that the ideas of 'negative education' and 'natural education' are paradoxes. If all we have to do is stand back and let nature do her work, what need have we of the concept of education?

Rousseau, lies in taking the lead from the pupil and never forcing him to work on anything for which he has neither the interest nor the ability. Any active interest (e.g. the baby's will to explore, p.196) should be encouraged. Such ideas on 'child-centred education' have stimulated debates on teaching methods which remain alive in educational institutions today.

Figure 19
Illustration for Émile, *engraved by J. M. Moreau. The French caption reads, 'This is the rule of nature. Why should you act contrary to it?' (*Émile, *Book I). (Bibliothèque Nationale, Paris)*

J. M. Moreau, inv. 1777.   *J. B. Simonet, Sculp. 1778.*

Voila la règle de la nature, pourquoi la contrariez-vous?

3   The acquisition of knowledge and faith

In this section I'd like to look at Rousseau's ideas on how children learn – at some of the more specific details of his scheme of natural education, the general principles of which were examined in the previous section. Rousseau's views on epistemology (theory of the method for acquiring knowledge) will also be examined in relation to his views on religious education: how should faith be acquired?

3.1   How knowledge is acquired

EXERCISE   Please re-read the following short extracts from Book I of *Émile* (*Texts*, II, pp.195–6) from 'I say it again, the education of a man ...' to 'this must, by all means, be prevented'; pp.196–7 from 'In a state of infancy ...' to 'it may require some explanation'. How do children learn, according to Rousseau?

DISCUSSION   At first, children's responses to the world around them are purely 'affecting' or emotional: they learn that some things cause pleasure, others pain. Then sense experiences (of touch, sight and sound) or 'sensations' give them information (e.g. 'magnitude and figure') about the objects around them. Care must be taken to regulate a child's responses to pain (e.g. fear of the dark) and pleasure so that these responses do not encourage the formation of habits contrary to nature and to a healthy learning situation. The kind of knowledge a child acquires in early life is very crude and no complex thinking occurs at this stage: only the accumulation of sense data. Rousseau is anxious to stress, however, that a great *amount* of knowledge is gained in this way, and it is only prejudice which makes us grant greater status to later and rarer forms of knowledge, such as the ability to handle complex algebraic equations. Infants require liberty and encouragement ('walk him about often') in order to carry out this exploration of the physical properties ('heat and cold ...' etc.) of the objects around them.

The epistemological principle that all our ideas and knowledge come to us from information gathered by the five senses or by introspection on the mind's own operations had already been developed and popularized by Locke.[10] In his *Essay Concerning Human Understanding* he rejected the idea that there are innate ideas in the mind, prior to sense experience:

> The senses at first let in particular *Ideas* and furnish the yet empty cabinet: and the Mind by degress growing familiar with some of them, they are lodged in the Memory, and Names got to them. (Locke, 1694, ch. II, p.15)

---

[10]   This general approach had already been advocated, however, by much earlier writers, particularly Aristotle.

At birth, says Locke, the infant's mind is a *tabula rasa* ('blank sheet') on which various sensations subsequently leave an impression. Sensation is defined as ' ... the actual entrance of any Idea into the Understanding by the Senses' (Locke, 1694, ch. XII). Any 'simple or unmixed' sensations such as coldness or hardness, which are irreducible to any other sensations or experiences, constitute what Locke calls 'simple Ideas'. It is only later that the mind learns to combine and compare these simple ideas in order to form 'complex Ideas' such as beauty, gratitude, man.[11]

In *Émile* Rousseau follows closely Locke's model of a child's intellectual development and asserts that children should be asked to attempt only mental and physical tasks for which their current mental and physical development equips them. Furthermore, he upholds the view that children will learn effectively only when highly motivated.[12]

If you now read *Texts*, II, pp.202–5, taken from Book II (which covers the education of a child between the ages of 5 and 12), you will see how Rousseau sets about training his imaginary pupil to use the sense of sight so that his responses to sense impressions become more accurate, thus preparing him for the more complex mental operations of later life. Note also how he carefully manipulates the situation so that his pupil *wants* to learn, by making sport more attractive to him than cakes – a lesson provided by Nature? Or stage-managed by the tutor? It is Rousseau's opinion that the sense of sight is more sophisticated in the information it gives us than the other senses, hence its development brings a child closer to a fully functioning intellect.

3.2 Émile's education: a structured programme of development

An outline of the educational programme mapped out for Émile in Books I–IV of Rousseau's educational treatise is given below. As you look at this, note how different phases of Émile's education are timed so that they coincide with his physical and mental capacities and with his interests. (Page references are to the Dent/Everyman 1974 edition of *Émile*. You may wish to follow these up if you have time and opportunity; there is not space here to provide any further substantial extracts.)

3.2.1 Age 0–12 years

Books I and II cover the 'age of nature', in which a child learns mainly from experience and very little from books. At this age a child should be educated in the countryside, away from the corrupting influence of society, and education should be negative rather than positive: it is more important to preserve him from vice and error than to make him learn facts. It is too early to teach geography, history, literature and languages at this stage, as they are beyond a pupil's understanding (Rousseau, 1974, p.73). Only those facts and phenomena which can be grasped by the senses should be approached. Children should be treated as children and not as miniature adults (Rousseau, 1974, pp.43–4). Rational arguments

---

[11] Hence, in his *Thoughts Concerning Education*, Locke feels that the children of seventeenth-century English gentlefolk are made to read and study Latin and the Bible far too early.

[12] Locke's treatise on education emphasized the importance of learning through play and moulding education to pupils' interests.

about right and wrong are beyond most children of this age (Rousseau, 1974, p.54). The only way to encourage them to adopt right behaviour is to allow them to experience harsh consequences for wrong actions. If your child breaks his bedroom window, advises Rousseau, let 'the cold wind blow upon him night and day' (Rousseau, 1974, p.64). If he persists in breaking windows he must be locked in 'a dark place without a window' until he agrees formally to desist from such activity.

Reading is described as the 'curse of childhood', and Rousseau asserts that Émile, at the age of twelve, 'will hardly know what a book is' (Rousseau, 1974, p.80).[13] Writing is dismissed as a 'trifle'. He is adamant that 'education' should be understood in its broader sense of the development of the whole individual, and fails to be impressed by many of the childhood achievements which impressed his contemporaries, for example early and precocious chatter:

> If you want to say something clever, you have only to talk long enough. May Providence watch over those fine folk who have no other claim to social distinction. (Rousseau, 1974, p.70)

Book II also deals with the problem of a child's fear of the dark, and despite Rousseau's protests that he is more concerned with general principles than with specific guidelines ('Do not read my book if you expect me to tell you everything', Rousseau, 1974, p.102), he describes in detail some games which lessen this fear through habit (Rousseau, 1974, pp.98–101). Much attention is also devoted to diet. There is an extensive defence of plain food (about which he seems to think the French know little) and of vegetarianism (Rousseau, 1974, pp.115–20).

Perhaps the most striking aspect of Book II is the emphasis on physical freedom and education. Contrary to contemporary manners which would limit the movement and activity of children and enforce a restrictive mode of dress upon them, Rousseau's scheme builds on Locke's arguments that their physical activity should be increased:

> The French style of dress, uncomfortable and unhealthy for a man, is especially bad for children. The stagnant humours, whose circulation is interrupted, putrify in a state of inaction, and this process proceeds more rapidly in an inactive and sedentary life; they become corrupt and give rise to scurvy;[14] this disease, which is continually on the increase among us, was almost unknown to the ancients, whose way of dressing and living protected them from it. (Rousseau, 1974, p.91)

Elsewhere (Rousseau, 1974, pp.96, 104, 111) he stresses the importance of learning to swim (so that Émile may learn to 'live in every element'); of exercising barefoot outdoors (Émile should 'emulate the mountain goat, not the ballet dancer') and of instilling 'manly strength' through ball-games. We are reminded of the Cadet Corps as reorganized under Catherine the Great (*Texts*, I, p.84).

---

[13] Rousseau was an early reader himself and tells, in his *Confessions*, of his early initiation into classical literature. His early reading included Plutarch and he 'wept hot tears' over novels at the age of six.

[14] Compare the widely varying theories on the cause of scurvy discussed in *Studies*, I, pp.372–4.

By the age of twelve, Émile is a picture of glowing health. His manner is 'free and open'; he shows no insolence and speaks nothing but the 'plain, simple truth, without addition or ornament and without vanity':

> His ideas are few but precise, he knows nothing by rote but much by experience. If he reads our books worse than other children, he reads far better in the book of nature; his thoughts are not in his tongue but in his brain; he has only one language, but he understands what he is saying, and if his speech is not so good as that of other children his deeds are better. (Rousseau, 1974, p.124)

3.2.2   *The approach of adolescence (12–13 years)*

Book III deals with this period of Émile's education. He now becomes capable of sustained mental attention and can compare and reason about the phenomena within his experience. He begins to appreciate the use of things. He can now apply himself to science and handicraft but remains too immature intellectually for art, history, literature and religion. He learns the skills of self-sufficiency, and *Robinson Crusoe* is named as the one book which is of real use and interest to children (Rousseau, 1974, p.147). Like Crusoe, Émile explores his immediate surroundings. But his study of science (e.g. simple experiments in physics, cosmography, magnetism and topography) must be limited to what he discovers for himself: he should, for example, observe a sunrise closely and puzzle out for himself what it tells him about the relative positions and movements of the earth and sun (Rousseau, 1974, p.132).

It is now that Émile should be introduced to a rudimentary study of social relations. The concept of utility is central to this study. In his games based on *Robinson Crusoe* he learns the utility of things to a *solitary* man. But Émile must also now learn how men can be useful to one another: the 'natural' Émile having been effectively developed, 'social' Émile must now emerge. In a spirit of realism Rousseau recognizes that the division of labour is an irreversible fact which has influenced social relations and the interdependence of men (Rousseau, 1974, p.148). As men have specialized in different trades and occupations and produced goods surplus to their own requirements, they have need of one another's services and goods. Émile must become accustomed to the idea of a labour market and a system of barter and exchange. He must learn a trade. Rousseau eloquently defends manual trades and attacks contemporary prejudices against the mechanical or useful arts in favour of the fine arts:

> The value set by the general public on the various arts is in inverse ratio to their real utility. They are even valued directly according to their uselessness. (Rousseau, 1974, pp.148–9)

Rousseau would prefer Émile to be a shoemaker rather than a poet, a paver of streets rather than a painter of flowers on china (Rousseau, 1974, p.160). Those arts or trades which deal most closely with raw materials (e.g. agriculture, metalwork, carpentry) are to be most respected, but men should be educated for whichever occupation accords with their natural aptitude.

Sickened by the gross inequalities of wealth and privilege which he observes in his own society, Rousseau asserts that there is a 'natural equality' common to all men: after all, their stomachs, digestive systems, limbs and other physiological characteristics and needs are often very similar (Rousseau, 1974, p.157). Why then, should some members of society have their needs met much more easily than others? Beneath all this preoccupation with wealth and status, he argues, are buried the remains of natural man, immune to the vicissitudes of fortune:

> The crisis is approaching, and we are on the edge of a revolution. Who can answer for your fate? What man has made, man can destroy. Nature's characters alone are ineffaceable, and nature makes neither the prince, the rich man, nor the nobleman. This satrap[15] whom you have educated for greatness, what will become of him in his degradation? This farmer of taxes who can only live on gold, what will he do in poverty? (Rousseau, 1974, p.157)

Émile has learned to be guided by nature and to strengthen his natural abilities: he will be less vulnerable to the vicissitudes of fate than those 'educated for greatness'. He learns to despise luxury (Rousseau, 1974, pp.153–4). As manual labour is the form of work closest to the 'state of nature' he learns carpentry. (Some trades, such as wig-making, are rejected on the grounds that they are useless; others, such as stocking-knitting and stone-cutting, on the grounds that they do not suit an intelligent man; and others, such as tailoring, in the belief that they are better suited to women.) Rousseau would have all the upper classes learn a trade so that their lives become less dominated by the vicissitudes of fortune and patronage.

3.2.3   Adolescence (13 years onwards)

Book IV deals with adolescence. Émile is now ripe for a more academic and intellectual education and is ready to consider religion. His education grows closer to that of all young men of rank in France. He concentrates on the study of languages and literature and later goes on the grand tour in order to learn the ways of the world and the tastes of a gentleman. Rousseau sees Émile's chief motivating force at this point as the urge to find a mate. Consequently, the search for a suitable marriage partner becomes the driving force behind his education, rather than preparation for any specific career. It is considered important that Émile's sexual urges should be restrained for as long as possible so that they are not corrupted by the artificial ways and prejudices of contemporary society. Nature will reward continence:

> ... the writers justly attribute the vigour of constitution and the number of children among the Germans to the continence of these nations during youth. (Rousseau, 1974, p.282)[16]

The behaviour of society women who 'profess to educate young men and make them pay so dear for their teaching' (Rousseau, 1974, p.294) is seen as a particularly undesirable influence.

Between the ages of 13 and 18 Émile's emotions begin to develop. Rousseau has little patience with those who would stifle the passions. He argues that they are God-given and that the few *natural* passions in man are essential to his happiness and preservation. Any which appear to be harmful, must be unnatural:

---

[15]   Word of Persian derivation: subordinate ruler or governor; often used rhetorically with an implication of luxury or tyranny.

[16]   Compare Gibbon's comments on the ancient Germans in *Texts*, I, pp.245–65.

> Their source, indeed, is natural; but they have been swollen by a thousand other streams; they are a great river which is constantly growing, one in which we can scarcely find a single drop of the original stream. Our natural passions are few in number; they are the means to freedom, they tend to self-preservation. All those which enslave and destroy us have another source; nature does not bestow them on us; we seize on them in her despite. (Rousseau, 1974, p.173)

In fact, says Rousseau, the only original passion, the one from which all others stem, is self-love. This is not the same thing as selfishness. Self-love, which urges us towards our own preservation and happiness, also leads us to love of others:

> So a child is naturally disposed to kindly feeling because he sees that everyone about him is inclined to help him, and from this experience he gets the habit of a kindly feeling towards his species ... (Rousseau, 1974, p.174)

Children then have a natural capacity for humanity. It is the mishandling of their education by society which perverts their natural feelings and makes them spiteful, jealous, selfish etc. In adolescence Émile's 'dawning sensibility'[17] must be delicately handled so that he learns friendship and concern for others before facing the demands of a sexual relationship. Thus Rousseau proposes ways in which Émile's capacity for pity might be nurtured (Rousseau, 1974, pp.181–7): 'let him see and feel the calamities which overtake men' (Rousseau, 1974, p.186). In this way, natural feeling or sensibility and society can work together.

As Émile's emotional life develops, so does his conscience, and he becomes capable of moral discourse. It is at this point that Rousseau feels that he may be awakened to moral and political realities through the study of society and history. Rousseau's own perspectives on these issues emerge clearly:

> ... hence it follows that the higher classes which claim to be useful to the rest are really only seeking their own welfare at the expense of others. (Rousseau, 1974, p.198)

Thus Émile learns to live by 'nobler feelings' and to fight against 'the lesser passions'. But Rousseau's 'natural man' is not banished to the woods:

> But remember, in the first place, that when I want to train a natural man, I do not want to make him a savage and to send him back to the woods, but that living in the whirl of social life it is enough that he should not let himself be carried away by the passions and prejudices of men ... (Rousseau, 1974, p.217)

In this way, nature and society can be truly reconciled. It is also in Book IV that Rousseau outlines Émile's religious education.

---

[17] See Introduction to Part E, pp.125–30 on Sensibility.

3.3 The religious education of Émile

It is not until Émile is about 18 years of age that he is ready for religious education, in Rousseau's view. God is such an incomprehensible and complex being that our mental development must be quite advanced before we can even begin to think about him:

Figure 20
Illustration for Book IV of Émile, *engraved by J. M. Moreau. The French caption reads, 'Nature was displaying all her splendour before our eyes'. (Bibliothèque Nationale, Paris)*

La nature étaloit à nos yeux toute fa magnificenc

> Since our senses are the first instruments of our learning, corporeal and sensible[18] bodies are the only bodies we directly apprehend. (Rousseau, 1974, p.218)

Statements such as this provoked the uproar over *Émile*. Rousseau's epistemology, derived from Locke, was related to a rigorous questioning of conventional attitudes to religion and religious education: we should only concern ourselves with whatever our brain can cope with, religion being no exception. To a state which relied on the power of the church to bolster its own power, this was unacceptable.

The 'Profession of Faith of a Savoyard Priest' is presented by Rousseau in Book IV of *Émile* as the work of an author 'whose writings I am about to transcribe' (Rousseau, 1974, p.223). In fact, it is heavily autobiographical. The priest who offers his views so eloquently in this section is based on two real-life priests whom Rousseau had met on his travels: the Abbé Gaime in Turin and the Abbé Gatier in Savoy.[19] The 'Profession of Faith' is introduced as a fictional event: 'Thirty years ago there was a young man in an Italian town ... an exile from his native land ... reduced to the depths of poverty' (Rousseau, 1974, p.223). Rousseau quickly admits that this young man was himself, and proceeds to 'reproduce' the spiritual advice he received when in trouble.

The priest conveyed his advice in a suitably beautiful and inspiring location:

> It was summer time; we rose at daybreak. He took me out of town on to a high hill above the river Po, whose course we beheld as it flowed between its fertile banks; in the distance the landscape was crowned by the vast chain of the Alps; the beams of the rising sun already touched the plains and cast across the fields long shadows of trees, hillocks, and houses, enriching with a thousand gleams of light the fairest picture which the human eye can see. You would have thought that nature was displaying all her splendour before our eyes to furnish a text for our conversation. (Rousseau, 1974, p.228).

And indeed this is exactly what 'Nature' *was* doing.

EXERCISE   Please read *Texts*, II pp.205–10. As you read through these extracts from the 'Profession of Faith', try to analyse the way in which Rousseau uses Nature to combat *both* the materialist views of many of the *philosophes* (according to which both human kind and the universe are made up entirely of physical matter – there is no room for talk of a non-corporeal or spiritual soul or God) *and* the proceedings of contemporary churches.

---

[18]   i.e. accessible to, or perceivable by, the senses.

[19]   The latter is described in Rousseau (1988, p.118) as sensitive and affectionate: 'in his large blue eyes there was such a mixture of sweetness, tenderness and melancholy ...'.

DISCUSSION   First, Rousseau uses his observation of the beauty and order of the natural world to prove that the universe cannot be the result of chance combinations of matter. The matter of which it is composed must have been set in motion, initially, by a non-material being: matter itself is not capable of action or of *causing* motion. Furthermore, the world as he sees it shows evidence of a benign Providence, of a wise and benevolent creator: 'I admire the artist for every part of his performance' (p.206).[20] He therefore uses natural evidence available to the senses to draw conclusions about the nature of God: this is the 'argument from design' commonly used by eighteenth-century deists.[21] Nature is used by Rousseau as a force against materialism. It is also used, however, as a force against conventional Christianity: 'natural religion' reduces the importance of the church as a place of worship and of the Scriptures as a 'revelation' of God's word. Its emphasis on 'involuntary sentiment' in the face of Nature (p.206) undermines the need for any complex theological or institutional framework of worship. (See also pp.226–9, where he adopts a similar response to the religious education of women.)

The footnote on fanaticism and atheism (pp.209–10) would further alienate Rousseau from many contemporary *philosophes*. (There is further evidence of this alienation in TV14, 'Jean-Jacques Rousseau: Retreat to Romanticism'.) His attack on the 'indifference of the philosopher' (p.209) or on atheism constitutes a serious challenge to the social and moral role of non-believers. Unforgivably, from a *philosophe*'s point of view, Rousseau also dares to suggest that there is a large part for feeling, as well as for empirical observation and reasoning, in faith: 'I see it, or rather I feel it' (p.207).

For Rousseau religion and worship become a matter of private communication with the natural world. In his *Confessions* he recounts:

> I got up every morning before sunrise and climbed through a nearby orchard on to a road above the vineyard which ran along the hill as far as Chambéry. As I walked up there I said my prayers, which did not consist merely of a vain motion of the lips but of a sincere raising of the heart towards the Creator of that beauteous Nature whose charms lay beneath my eyes. I have never liked to pray in a room; walls and all the little works of man come between myself and God. I love to contemplate Him in His works, while my heart uplifts itself to Him. (Rousseau, 1988, p.28)

Nature (the observable world) became his church and almost his deity. If the only way to know God is through nature, the rules dictated by religious authorities become less important than a subjective reverence for the natural world: a conclusion which the establishment would find ideologically and politically threatening. Rousseau's arguments were regarded as particularly dangerous to the church because he *did* profess to believe in God, unlike his openly atheistic or materialist contemporaries, whose arguments

---

[20]   In his *Letter from J.J. Rousseau to M. de Voltaire* (1756), Rousseau was upset by the attack on Optimism in Voltaire's *Poem on the Lisbon Disaster* and argued that evil is man's doing rather than God's.

[21]   See the Introduction to Part D pp.4–9, above and the study on Hume, pp.11–42, above.

could be dismissed on the grounds that they were anti-religious. His belief was untrammelled by the regulations of church or state.

Émile's religious education was to consist of a nurturing of his conscience, a faculty of great importance to Rousseau (Rousseau, 1974, pp.252, 254) and of the virtues of austerity, charity and tolerance (Rousseau, 1974, p.274). Rousseau does not rule out conventional worship[22] but concludes:

> ... remember that the real duties of religion are independent of human institutions; that a righteous heart is the true temple of the Godhead; that in every land, in every sect, to love God above all things and to love our neighbour as ourself is the whole law; remember there is no religion which absolves us from our moral duties; that these alone are really essential, that the service of the heart is the first of these duties, and that without faith there is no such thing as true virtue. (Rousseau, 1974, p.276)[23]

Like the rest of Rousseau's programme of natural education, religion is to be freed from unnecessary and premature theorizing. Faith is to be built on empirical reasoning and emotion, on conclusions deduced from close observation of the natural world and on the feelings that the world inspires in the contemplative individual.

3.4 The eighteenth-century context of Rousseau's educational programme

Most young boys in eighteenth-century France did not receive the kind of education outlined by Rousseau. Émile's education is organized on the basis that he progresses from an age of nature (up to 12 years) to an age of reason (12–15 years) to an age of force (15–20 years) to an age of wisdom (20–25 years). (The rest of his life was to be an 'age of happiness'.) Most boys in Rousseau's time were assumed to have reached the 'age of reason' much sooner; hence their education made extensive, early demands on their intellect. The Ancien Régime entrusted education almost entirely to the clergy. Religious orders such as the Jesuits established 'colleges' as well as conventual schools. The colleges were schools (some of which were incorporated into universities) for older boys, who had usually been taught previously by private tutors, and they concentrated on proficiency in classical languages and literature, mathematics and theology.[24] On p.186 of *Texts*, II, Rousseau says that, as far as the poor man is concerned, the education of his own station in life is forced upon him. There was no system of primary education (a few charity schools

---

[22] He had been both a Protestant and a Catholic at different stages of his life.

[23] This emphasis on the moral obligations of faith was common among exponents of deism. Compare the claims to moral perfection asserted by the quasi-masonic brotherhood in *The Magic Flute*.

[24] On the lack of impact of Enlightenment writings on the secondary or 'collège' curriculum in France see Leith (1977, pp.105–24).

provided this) and the colleges were mainly for the sons of the prosperous (i.e. the sons of noblemen, merchants and the liberal professions). Education was not even among the rights of man to be claimed in 1789, nor was it so claimed until 1793. Illiteracy was therefore normal for the poor throughout the century, especially in the south, though it was by no means universal.

Rousseau's programme of educational reform is therefore aimed, realistically, at those classes which received education. For those who did enter the colleges there were opportunities for educational advancement. Following a decision taken by the Paris *Parlement*, the Jesuits lost control of their colleges in 1762 (coincidentally, the same year in which *Émile* was published) but many of their colleges remained open and it is estimated that in 1789 one in every 392 men in France or one in every 31 of (college) student age, was in a college of some kind. On the eve of the Revolution there were 22 universities in France. Rousseau's innovation, in *Émile*, lay primarily in his unconventional views on raising young children and in the priority he attached to physical education for children under 12. He argued that conventional college education introduced an academic curriculum too soon and worked against the natural growth and rhythm of pupils' capabilities. If Nature were allowed a more powerful hold over children, the basis of a healthier society would be formed.

4   The broader context of Émile

So far we have been looking at the detailed arguments of *Émile* and examining its internal logic, touching only briefly on its relationship with other works by Rousseau or with eighteenth-century society and culture. In this section I would like to problematize more explicitly various approaches to reading the work. In particular, I'd like to consider whether it is legitimate to read *Émile* as part of a continuum of thought spanning other works by Rousseau or as the product of biographical factors.

4.1   Émile *as part of Rousseau's philosophical programme*

There is evidence to suggest that *Émile* can be read as an answer to a philosophical problem which had haunted Rousseau for many years. The central problem addressed in *Émile* is what Rousseau perceives as the corrupting influence of contemporary society and culture on man's natural impulses or 'primitive' nature. By the time he wrote *Émile*, however, Rousseau had already established a reputation for his unconventional opposition to eighteenth-century civilized city life. His *Discourse on the Moral Effects of the Arts and Sciences* (1751) and his *Discourse on the Origin of Inequality* (1755)[25] are fascinating in their attempts to shoot down the claims to achievement and progress made by many of his contemporaries, including the *philosophes*.[26]

---

[25]   All page references to the *Discourses* are to *The Social Contract and Discourses*, Everyman, 1986.

[26]   For Frederick the Great's counter-argument, directed against Rousseau, see his *Discourse on the Usefulness of the Arts and Sciences in a State* in *Texts*, I, pp.66–7.

In the first of these *Discourses*, Rousseau argues that the spread of learning which has characterized western civilization since the times of the Ancient Greeks and Romans has had a pernicious effect on the morals of those societies concerned.[27] He blames the arts and sciences for generating political and moral bankruptcy, encouraging a veneer of urbanity and a taste for luxury, and stifling, through the forms of government they have spawned, 'that sense of original liberty' (p.5) in men's breasts. Western civilization is characterized as inferior to the freedom and vigour of 'primitive' American savages, and Rousseau sees his own society as a hotbed of 'jealousy, suspicion, fear, coldness, reserve, hate and fraud' (p.7), concealed beneath a 'deceitful veil of politeness'. The arts and sciences, claims Rousseau, have their origins in the human vices of superstition, ambition, falsehood, avarice, flattery, idle curiosity and pride.

In his second *Discourse*, Rousseau looks at the causes of the vast inequalities of wealth, status and privileges which he perceives in eighteenth-century society. He postulates a hypothetical 'state of nature' – a pre-civilized age which was not plagued by such inequalities. Once again, man has ignored the 'voice of nature' and fallen victim to his own pernicious social conventions. In this work Rousseau vacillates between the claims that man is naturally good (p.118) and that he is neither good nor bad in his natural state (p.71) but has the potential to become good. This potential to become good is central to Rousseau's faith in human nature. Compassion is, he believes, 'a natural feeling, which, by moderating the activity of love of self in each individual, contributes to the preservation of the whole species' (p.76).

The only natural source of inequality, claims Rousseau, is bodily strength and natural aptitude. The growth of metallurgy, agriculture, property law and commerce has generated other, less natural inequalities between men:

> ... it is plainly contrary to the law of nature, however defined, that children should command old men, fools wise men, and that the privileged few should gorge themselves with superfluities, while the starving multitude are in want of the bare necessities of life. (p.117)

Rousseau is adamant, however, that he is not advocating that we 'destroy society, abolish *mine* and *yours* and go back to living with the bears' (p.125). Rather, he would like society to go back to first principles, attend to the voice of nature, and reform itself.

It is possible to see *Émile* as a programme of reform aimed at solving this problem. In the first *Discourse* Rousseau does not launch an attack on learning *per se*: only on the form which learning had taken in western civilization. College education comes under fire:

> We see, on every side, huge institutions, where our youth are educated at great expense, and educated in everything but their duty.

---

[27] See Appendix (p.214). Rousseau was inspired to write this *Discourse* while on his way to visit Diderot in prison. In answer to the question posed by the Academy of Dijon as part of an essay competition, 'Has the progress of the arts and sciences done more to corrupt or to purify morals?' he decided to set out the controversial argument for corruption. The extent of Diderot's influence on Rousseau's chosen approach remains uncertain.

Your children will be ignorant of their own language, when they can talk others which are not spoken anywhere. They will be able to compose verses which they can hardly understand; and, without being capable of distinguishing truth from error, they will possess the art of making them unrecognizable by specious arguments. But magnanimity, equity, temperance, humanity and courage will be words of which they know not the meaning. The dear name of country will never strike on their ears; and if they ever hear speak of God, it will be less to fear than to be frightened of Him. I would as soon, said a wise man [Montaigne] that my pupil had spent time in the tennis court as in this manner, for there his body at least would have got exercise. (pp.22–3)[28]

He also cites the rhetorical materialist publications of the *philosophes* as examples of intellectual vandalism, which have brought moral ills to society.

Apparently bowing to paradox, Rousseau criticized the education, publications and 'prizes for discourses' (p.24) sought by his contemporaries, and went on to indulge similar interests himself. (His two *Discourses* were submitted for Academy competitions.) Proclaiming that the spread of printing had done society great harm, he went on to write and publish prolifically himself. This underlines, I think, his view that *Émile* (as well as the works on which he was writing simultaneously – *The Social Contract* and *La Nouvelle Héloïse*) was a new and legitimate use of the pen and the intellect: he would reassert man's natural goodness and demonstrate how, through education, this could be preserved within a more natural society.

It could be argued, however, that all discussion of a philosophical 'plan' or 'scheme' spanning Rousseau's works is, at best, conjectural. Is it helpful at all to speculate about a writer's intentions? Even where authors provide explanatory prefaces (as Rousseau did for *Émile*), can we be sure that the intentions laid out in such prefaces are carried out in the work itself, or that they help to explain it in any way? And in any case it could be argued that the concepts and arguments of *Émile* are not sufficiently coherent or structured to qualify them, in our day, as 'philosophy'. I leave you to consider your own views on this before going on to another contentious way of looking at *Émile*.

4.2   The role of biographical factors

So far little has been said of the biographical backdrop to *Émile*. In this section I would like to set out some of the details of Rousseau's life which might be considered relevant to the work and invite your views on how much, if at all, these details inform and enrich your responses to the text. You will find a selective outline of Rousseau's life and works in the Appendix. You might like to read this before going on to the more specific points below. You should also gain a more detailed knowledge of Rousseau's life and works from TV14.

---

[28]   Those of you who have studied Open University course A205 will find further echoes here of Montaigne's 'On the Education of Children' discussed in Block VII, p.41ff.

Émile was one of Rousseau's last attempts to engage constructively with the society in which he lived. He had already fallen out with many of the *philosophes* (mainly because of his attacks on civilization) when he wrote it. After the furore caused by its publication, he devoted most of his literary energies to autobiographical works of self-justification (*The Confessions, The Dialogues* and *Reveries of a Solitary Walker*) which expressed a strong preference for the company of verdant meadows, plants, rabbits and mountain streams over that of his fellow men. His life became dominated by introspection and fear of persecution:

> 1762 Here begins the work of darkness in which I have been entombed for eight years past, without ever having been able, try as I might, to pierce its hideous obscurity. In the abyss of evil in which I am sunk I feel the weight of blows struck at me ... Disgrace and misfortune fall upon me as if of themselves and unseen. When my grief-stricken heart utters groans, I seem like a man complaining for no reason. The authors of my ruin have discovered the unimaginable art of turning the public into the unsuspecting accomplice of their plot, who does not even see its results. (Rousseau, 1988, p.545)

If this picture of despair hardly accords with our image of a resilient reformer, the information given to us by Rousseau concerning his experiences of teaching and parenthood appear to add even less to our understanding of *Émile*. He had previously, in 1740, held the post of tutor to the children of M. de Mably in Lyons and had proved an outright failure. Rousseau is remarkably frank about the reasons for his failure, which he attributes to his excitability:

> When my pupils did not understand me I raved; and when they showed signs of disobedience I could have killed them. That was not the way to make them good and wise. (Rousseau, 1988, p.253)

Undaunted by failure, Rousseau went on to present his employer with a memoir on education which borrowed heavily from Montaigne and Locke and said little startling or new about education.

Rousseau's experience of parenthood was disastrous. When Thérèse Le Vasseur, his mistress, (and, eventually, wife) had his first child, he took advice from fashionable friends (for in the late 1740s he was still enjoying a busy social life in Paris) and had the child taken to the Foundling Hospital. The same remedy was adopted, against the mother's wishes, for all the other children subsequently born to Rousseau and Thérèse (five in all). Rousseau (1988, pp.320–2) tells the sad tale in *The Confessions*. Recently some scholars have doubted the authenticity of Rousseau's account of the existence and fate of his children, but this only leaves us with a much larger problem: why on earth should anyone make up a story like that? Whatever the truth of the situation, it's clear that Rousseau felt no pride in his actions (he later tried, unsuccessfully, to trace one of his children) and in *The Confessions* (Rousseau, 1988) there were certainly no attempts to argue his merits as a potential parent. He merely claimed that he gave his children away in order to give them a better chance: ' ... in handing my children over for the State to educate, for lack of means to bring them up myself, by destining them to become workers and peasants instead of adventurers and fortune hunters, I thought I was acting as a citizen and a father, and looked upon myself as a member of Plato's Republic' (Rousseau, 1988, p.333). He later admitted (Rousseau, 1988, p.549) that working on *Émile* made him conscious of his own neglect of parental duty. For Rousseau, writing often seems to be a means of compensation for his inadequacies or failures in life: a somewhat perverse relationship between biography and text can result. (See p.184 of *Texts* II: 'I shall not set my hand to the work, but to the pen.')

I am strongly tempted to acknowledge that Rousseau's personal difficulties, philosophical problems and written texts are interdependent. With regard to his views on physical health and medicine in Book I of *Émile*, this certainly seems to be the case. He had extensive experience of health problems and doctors, having suffered from bladder problems (a blocked urethra) for many years. At first waxed catheters (recommended by Daran, a surgeon), painfully inserted, helped to relieve the problem. Later, however, they ceased to be effective. This remained a life-long problem for Rousseau and eventually he gave up consulting doctors and lost faith in the only common remedies available: baths and diuretics.

In *The Confessions* (Rousseau, 1988, pp.245, 340, 508) he frequently expressed a vehement distrust of the medical profession, for in addition to his main problem he also suffered from pleurisy and from the effects of a kidney stone (Rousseau, 1988, pp.275, 337). Thus he formed the opinion that nature (in the form of careful attention to diet and life style) was the best healer. This was perhaps an understandable reaction in an age when doctors remained ignorant of many diseases and their treatment, often recommending bleeding as a cure-all – even in cases of anaemia.

Rousseau often blamed his condition for his social awkwardness (he often complained of his inability to shine in the learned salons of Paris) and for his poor relationships with women. One of the consequences of his affliction was that he always sought comfortable clothes. He began to dress in Armenian 'caftan and fur cap', which made him conspicuous to local people and increased his reputation for eccentricity. (In *The Confessions* (Rousseau, 1988, p.579) he recounts how he was regarded as a 'were-wolf'.) It seems, then, that he *could* argue, on the basis of experience, that nature brings pain and suffering and that it demands temperance and endurance.

How, then, should we treat this biographical information? Earlier (pp.184–5) we examined the way in which attempts to 'argue from experience' or 'plain facts' can be misleading or directed by polemic. Are such attempts made any more convincing when his own personal experience, rather than his observation of other people's, is what produces Rousseau's opinions? I find that, on an intuitive level, the biographical details outlined above greatly enrich my appreciation of *Émile*. I do perceive a link between his personal difficulties, his cult of Nature and his growing alienation from society. It might be argued, however, that such an approach is fraught with difficulties. Are Rousseau's *Confessions* an authentic account of his experience? Are they as reliable as objective biography? Or are they filtered through a lively imagination and a selective memory?

Any study which has the task of examining the nature, structure or validity of the arguments and concepts of *Émile* should make little, if any, use of biographical detail: it is very difficult, perhaps impossible, to prove any link between specfic 'facts' of Rousseau's life and the direction his arguments take.[29] Even when solid links are established they are logically irrelevant to the soundness of his arguments. Nevertheless, biographical knowledge can help us to establish a *context* for a work like *Émile* and help to locate it in a climate of ideas and experience. It can illuminate a text obliquely rather than directly, by making us aware of the factors which *may have* nourished its growth. (A strong tradition of Freudian criticism of Rousseau's works has emerged from such an approach.) Those of you who go on to study the arts disciplines at third level will have the opportunity to ponder these problems of reading and interpreting texts in greater depth.

5   The education of women

In this section I should like to look at Rousseau's ideas on the education of women, outlined in Book V of *Émile*, and to ask whether these views rest on the same premise about the need for education to respect nature as those expressed previously on the education of the male sex. If this *is* the case, how can we account for any differences in the educational programmes outlined for the two sexes? This time I would like to begin with some of Rousseau's own account of his experiences.

His *Confessions* abound with tales of unsuccessful relationships with women. He blames this partly on his physical affliction (the problem with his urinary tract) and partly on Mlle Lambercier, the sister of a pastor to whose care Rousseau and his cousin were entrusted at an early age. (Rousseau's mother did not survive his birth and his father fled Geneva some years later after an alleged duel with a French captain.) Mlle Lambercier beat the boys and Rousseau says this gave him a life-long taste for flagellation which made him find most subsequent sexual experiences disappointing (Rousseau, 1988, p.27). Generally, he recounts his shyness and awkwardness with women (Rousseau, 1988, pp.77, 80) and, apart from a few pleasant and flirtatious outings with the opposite sex (Rousseau, 1988, pp.134–5, 141, 241), there are many tales of unhappiness and unrequited love. His sexual desire and timidity combined to fuel his frustration and he resorted as a youth to exposing himself to women in dark alleys 'from afar off' (Rousseau, 1988, p.90) and wrote of his addiction to masturbation (Rousseau, 1988, p.161).

At the age of 16, after running away from his native Geneva, he went to live with Mme de Warens at Annecy. A Protestant, she was supposed to oversee Rousseau's spiritual welfare, as he contemplated conversion to the Catholic faith. (He later went through with this in Turin and later still renounced Catholicism and re-converted to the Calvinism of Geneva.) For a while they lived in great happiness and Rousseau regarded her as a mother, 'Maman'. She later became his mistress (Rousseau, 1988, p.186), so that he always remembered his first significant

---

[29]   Rousseau himself was convinced that such links existed however: 'Imagine a person timid and docile in ordinary life, but proud, fiery and inflexible when roused, a child who has always been controlled by the voice of reason, always treated with kindness, fairness, and indulgence, a creature without a thought of injustice, now for the first time suffering a most grave one at the hands of the people he loves best and most deeply respects. Imagine the revolution in his ideas, the violent change of his feelings, the confusion in the heart and brain...' (Rousseau, 1988, p.29).

Figure 21
*Illustration of Book V
of* Émile, *engraved by
J. M. Moreau in 1779. The
French caption reads, 'Sophie,
control yourself'. The image
depicts the occasion of Sophie's
first meeting with Émile.
Sophie is overcome by her
parents' account of their own
love and marriage.
(Bibliothèque Nationale,
Paris)*

sexual experience with the feelings of sadness and guilt associated with
incest (Rousseau, 1988, pp.186–9). Later, in Paris, he met Thérèse Le
Vasseur, a linen maid; he lived with her and had five children by her. He
seems to have enjoyed her companionship but found the relationship
unfulfilling in many ways (Rousseau, 1988, pp.309, 385), although he did
eventually marry her.

If we are to believe Rousseau's *Confessions* (Rousseau, 1988) – and some scholars have already identified factual errors in some of his accounts – Rousseau's relationships with women were fraught with the same suspicion, shame, guilt and paranoia which plagued all aspects of his life in his later years. When working as secretary to an ambassador in Venice he encountered prostitutes and courtesans (Rousseau, 1988, pp.296–302) but had a deep distrust of women who made themselves too readily available to him (Rousseau, 1988, pp.300–1). Although he claimed he had 'never been inside a house of ill-fame in his life' (Rousseau, 1988, p.584), on two separate occasions he shared (or planned to share) the favours of young girls of 11–12 years of age with friends (Rousseau, 1988, pp.302–3, 331). These occasions were attended with remorse however. In one case he contributed towards a spinet and singing lessons for the girl (as it was necessary to 'sow' before he could 'reap') but finally realized that he could not go through with corrupting her innocence. (He had developed a fatherly attitude to her and felt in danger of committing incest.)

The Confessions abound with examples of women whom Rousseau considers to be *unnatural* or, as he puts it on one occasion, '... some kind of monsters, rejected by Nature, men and love' (Rousseau, 1988, p.301). Leaving aside these autobiographical factors for a while, let us now consider Rousseau's views on *natural* womanhood in *Émile*.

EXERCISE   Please read *Texts*, II pp.210–36. Make notes on the qualities and abilities bestowed on women by nature, according to Rousseau.

DISCUSSION   He argues that Nature has made women for man's delight (p.211). Women must learn to 'render [themselves] agreeable' to men (pp.211,217). Nature has made woman the 'weakest party' (p.212): this enhances attraction between the sexes. The modesty of woman is a quality bestowed on her by 'the Supreme Being' and destined to make the course of love run more smoothly (p.212). By seeking to please a man, a woman eventually makes her love and support indispensable to him and makes him dependent on her (p.212). This is all part of nature's plan. Woman is bestowed by nature with a special constitution which equips her for a life of gentle domesticity. Nature has entrusted woman with the care of children (p.213). Girls should be trained to be good women rather than surrogate men, as in Rousseau's view education must respect 'whatever is characteristic of the sex' (pp.215–16). Nature has destined women to be 'shut up in their houses' (p.218). She has graced them with politeness (p.225), delicate powers of observation (p.231) if not of intellect (p.232), with cunning and gentleness. Women must treat their natural constitution with respect in all things, including dress (p.218): tight corsets are an abuse of nature.

Rousseau defines women's strength in terms of their ability to submit to men and duty. Julie, the heroine of his great novel *La Nouvelle Héloïse*, placed domestic and family duties above all personal gratification and sexual desire. His view of women as guardians of home and morality was also strongly expressed in the earlier *Discourse on the Arts and Sciences*, in which he argued that it is precisely *because* women have such influence in the domestic sphere that they should be schooled in virtue:

> If you wish then that they should be noble and virtuous, let women be taught what greatness of soul and virtue are. (Rousseau, 1986, p.19)

In the *Discourse on Inequality*, he explains how the lives of men and women became naturally differentiated as 'the women became more sedentary, and accustomed themselves to mind the hut and the children, while the men went abroad in search of their common subsistence' (Rousseau, 1986, p.88). Such was the state of affairs as mankind began to group into family units.

EXERCISE Do you think Rousseau's views on the natural role and education of women present a coherent and logical development of his conception of natural education for men? Do you consider that the biographical factors outlined above (pp.203–5) were more significant in motivating his views on women?

DISCUSSION It seems to me that Rousseau is contradicting the message he delivered in earlier parts of *Émile*. Émile was encouraged to be himself; to discover his natural abilities and inclinations before bowing to the demands of society. A good woman, however, is described as one who learns early to bear 'constant and severe restraint' (p.220). Sophie must be trained to submit to the will of others – even to that of an unjust husband. Women must learn to live within the bounds of male values, and if they are raped it is their own fault for frequenting lonely places (p.213). In matters of religion women must take the lead from fathers and husbands. This hardly corresponds to the emphasis placed on the role of conscience in the formulation of belief in earlier parts of the book. Although Rousseau repeats his plea that we must all 'observe constantly the indications of nature' (p.215), nature seems to have a less significant role in the educational programme and life style he outlines for girls than social control and convention. His attitude switches from the polemical to the conservative, with the exception of his attack on the artifice and superficiality of upper-class women (p.223) and lack of opportunities for singing, dancing and physical exercise for girls (pp.217, 224). It could be argued, however, that this change of approach is justified by him on the grounds that *nature* has created differences between men and women (see p.212 – 'an invariable law of nature'). Women, like men, should develop the attributes bestowed on them by nature: the same premise applies in both cases. Perhaps, then, Rousseau *is* consistent in his adherence to the principle of Nature and to his belief in its importance as the primary reference point when he discusses female education, but makes false claims about the 'nature' of women? Has he convinced you (a) that nature has created differences between men and women and (b) that he has correctly identified these 'differences'?

It is possible to see this ideal construct of womanhood as a consequence of Rousseau's fear of women and sex. In both *Émile* and *The Confessions* Rousseau despises the exaggerated coquetry of women and attacks the wiles of upper-class women, particularly those in Paris, who 'have ceased to believe in honour' (Rousseau, 1974, p.320): he claims that it was not possible to advance in Parisian society without the help of influential hostesses (Rousseau, 1988, p.272). Such a situation was a minefield for young, innocent men seeking their fortune (Rousseau, 1974, pp.154, 192).

He was consistent in preferring the less threatening demeanor of women devoted to domesticity, if not domestic servants themselves:

> Besides, seamstresses, chambermaids, and shop girls hardly tempted me; I needed young ladies ... However it is certainly not pride of rank or position that attracts me. It is a better preserved complexion, lovelier hands, greater elegance in jewellery, an air of cleanliness and refinement about a woman's whole person, better taste in her way of dressing and expressing herself, a finer and better made gown, a neater pair of shoes, ribbons, lace, better done hair ... (Rousseau, 1988, p.132)

Such aids to beauty are entirely natural as long as they are not carried to extremes, for they please men. His own wife, of lower station, was often an embarrassment to him and he shared jokes at her expense with his friends. While she was still his mistress he commonly referred to her as his 'housekeeper'. Perhaps, then, knowledge of Rousseau's life (and of the society in which he lived) can illuminate his views on women or, at the very least, explain his failure to apply his concept of natural education in any coherent or consistent way to both genders. Is this a valid conclusion?

Elsewhere in *Émile* Rousseau reinforces the notion of separate spheres for men and women, who must be treated as *different* creations of Nature (Rousseau, 1974, p.172): 'Kite-flying is a sport for women, but every woman will run away from a swift ball. Their white skins were not meant to be hardened by blows and their faces were not made for bruises.[30] But we men are made for strength ... '(Rousseau, 1974, p.111). Later (Rousseau, 1974, p.400) he states that 'Women were not meant to run; they flee that they may be overtaken'. They should steer clear of intellectual matters (Rousseau, 1974, p.306). Rich women are particularly at risk from 'tedium' or 'the vapours' (Rousseau, 1974, p.316) and little hope is offered of remission from this condition. Sewing and tailoring – work fit for 'women and cripples' (Rousseau, 1974, p.162) – are described as occupations more suitable for women than for men. As in Catherine the Great's Smol'ny Institute, the education of women is seen as a distinct, specialist enterprise.

---

[30] Contrast the trials faced by Pamina in *The Magic Flute*. See *Studies*, II pp.104–7.

But perhaps Rousseau was neither a bad philosopher nor a misogynist: his views *could* merely demonstrate that he was a man of his times, his ideas framed by contemporary conventions.[31] Convention in eighteenth-century France dictated that girls should receive a specifically feminine form of education. The *Memoirs* of Mme Roland (1754–92) offer an interesting insight into the education and life style of a bourgeois woman (her father was a master engraver and small-time art dealer). She relates how she was brought up mostly by her mother. She received tuition at home in writing, history, geography, dancing and music. Much of her time was devoted to needlework. On Sundays she attended Sunday school, where she learned by rote passages from the Old Testament, the Gospels, the Epistles, and the catechism. She was allowed very few outings outside the home and these consisted mainly of visits to elderly relatives, to church or to market. Her life was a secluded preparation for the domestic duties of marriage.

There were, of course, particularly in the capital, women who succeeded in leading a more worldly life.[32] Those in possession of some wealth ('ladies of quality') might eventually set themselves up as society hostesses dedicated to extravagant dress and dinner parties. A particular form of such hostessing was the opportunity to run a salon, where gatherings of the learned men of Paris produced discussions on philosophy, science, literature, music and art. Such was Mme d'Epinay, whose patronage of the *philosophes* is discussed in Rousseau's *Confessions*.

Girls born into the upper classes might be sent to college at the age of 10–12 years. Most of the college education in Paris was dependent on the Catholic church for funding or subsidy. The cathedral chapter of Notre Dame, for instance, regulated the small, fee-for-service schools inside the capital and granted teachers certification (see Sonnet, 1987). There were also some free, charitable schools set up by priests and run by nuns. Some religious orders (e.g. the Ursulines) set up boarding schools for the daughters of wealthy families. At most of these institutions the emphasis was on preparation for the first communion. The memorizing of prayers and the Scriptures were given precedence over reading and writing. Needlework always occupied much of the time-table.

In this context it is possible to see Rousseau's emphasis on physical exercise for girls, and his more relaxed attitude to religious education, as somewhat liberal; the same could be said of his encouragement to

---

[31] On the inappropriate and anachronistic application of the terms 'feminist' and 'anti-feminist' to Rousseau's thought see Le Bouler (1981, pp.225–36). On the dangers of confusing 'misogynist' with 'anti-feminist' see Piau-Gillot (1983, pp.169–82), where she argues that Rousseau was not a misogynist: there are too many favourable references to women in his works as a whole. See also Graham (1976, pp.127–39) where she discusses the more positive aspects of Rousseau's view of women, including the moral ascendency of the latter over men. Graham states that Rousseau saw women as man's companion rather than his slave (p.128): his writings inspired women to campaign for greater social and political rights during the Revolution. Wilson (1976, pp.89–104) outlines the different ways in which enlightened writers responded to women's status, from the reactionary to the liberal.

[32] Compare, later, the Marquise de Merteuil in *Les Liaisons Dangereuses* (*Dangerous Acquaintances*).

women to be 'natural' mothers rather than society hostesses. Perhaps, in the case of women, the attempt to reconcile nature and society simply encountered larger barriers of convention? He does (*Texts*, II, p.224) express a wish to move away from conventional prejudice in his views on women. We are still left, however, with the problem of why he bowed to convention in his ideas on the education of women and not in his views on that of men. Was this because he felt that conventional views of female nature were true; those of men false? Mary Wollstonecraft was later to express frustration and dismay at the slackness of Rousseau's arguments about women (see *Studies*, II p.227 and *Texts*, II pp.242, 244–8.) Later you will see how the issue of female education is approached in the work of Laclos.[33]

6 The legacy of Émile

In this section I'll look briefly at the impact of *Émile* on eighteenth-century France and on subsequent educational theory.

It is claimed that *Émile* exerted a strong influence on eighteenth-century child-rearing practices and encouraged a widespread re-examination of contemporary assumptions about the kind of existence for which young people should be moulded. Most literate Europeans seem to have read the book, so often was it translated, pirated, quoted, imitated, praised and attacked. Approximately ninety French-language editions were published before 1800 (McEachern, 1989). The *philosophes*, with whom Rousseau had fallen out, ridiculed the book and highlighted its weaknesses, though Catherine the Great shared his belief in fresh air and exercise.

The book had no immediate impact on public instruction. Speeches addressed to the National Convention in July 1793 on educational reform show little understanding of it and it was not until the nineteenth century that its impact on the sphere of public education became significant. Rousseau's ideas on the upbringing of infants had a more immediate impact, however, on contemporaries. In the early eighteenth century it had become increasingly fashionable in France to employ wet-nurses to feed and rear babies. This was partly due to the common belief that sexual intercourse would stop or at least spoil the mother's milk so that many women felt they had to choose between their husband and their child. As some wet-nurses took children away to their homes in the country until weaning (12–18 months) and many children remained in their care for an even longer period (3–4 years), there was often little contact with the parental home. Some children allocated to wet-nurses died or were lost. Hence the recurrence of the romantic theme of the reunion in eighteenth-century novels. For children of the rural poor, foundling hospitals were often the alternative to parental care, and baskets of four or five babies would arrive in the capital strapped on to donkeys after a slow and often fatal journey from the provinces.

---

[33] See *Studies*, II, pp.291–3 and *Texts*, II pp.297–301. While elevating the domestic and child-bearing role of women, Laclos's *Discourse on the Education of Women* shifts the emphasis towards the importance for women of developing their intellect through the study of history, literature and languages. Laclos's views on early childcare are very reminiscent of those of Rousseau.

Rousseau was not the first to challenge the convention of using wet-nurses but was the first to do so with eloquence and impact. After *Émile*, it became fashionable for mothers to enjoy feeding their own children. (Doctors reinforced this trend by recommending breast-feeding as a contraceptive measure.) In 1788 the novelist Restif de la Bretonne offers a disapproving view of the new generation reared à la Rousseau:

> Their hair straggles in a hideous and disgusting way ... They are no longer checked, but clamber on to you with their muddy feet. When you visit their parents, they deafen you with their noise, and just when their father or mother is about to reply to you on some important matter, you see them choose instead to answer some childish question of their darling son or daughter ... It is *Émile* which is responsible for this provoking, obstinate, insolent, imprudent, arrogant generation ... (quoted in Rousseau, 1974, p.xxv)

Similar complaints are made today, of course, about 'liberal' methods of child-rearing. The increased freedom, particularly of a physical kind, enjoyed by children in the late eighteenth century, is often regarded as a legacy of *Émile*. The book overturned preceding views, prevalent in early eighteenth-century medical and orthopedic literature, that children were bestial, savage, lacking in intelligence and in need of corsets and swaddling-clothes in order to control their puny, animal-like bodies.

Rousseau strengthened the tradition formulated by Locke and other writers according to which children should be seen as individuals with potential for goodness. In the nineteenth century such views infiltrated the educational establishment of Europe and have remained influential (and controversial) to the present day. Educationists like Pestalozzi, Froebel and Montessori are thought to have been stimulated by *Émile*, although its influence on them was not always sustained. (Pestalozzi, in 1792, denounced it as an 'impractical dreambook'.)[34] Twentieth-century commentaries on *Émile* are numerous and the book is often on the reading list of student-teachers.

In the force of its reputation, if not through detailed knowledge of its content, *Émile* has become associated with the cause of 'child-centred education', a mid-twentieth-century challenge to traditionalism in the classroom in Britain. The principles behind this approach are simple. Education must serve the distinct phases of development characteristic of the individual child's mind and interests. Children must learn from first-hand experience.

7 Conclusion

Émile receives an education from nature before he embarks on his initiation into citizenship, and in this way the precious balance between nature and society is preserved. He and Sophie listen to the voice of nature and contribute in a positive way to society. They eventually marry and have a child of their own. *Émile* then becomes an educator and the cycle repeats itself. He becomes a patriarchal landowner who looks after

---

[34] On Pestalozzi and Rousseau see Kessen (1978, p.162). Johann Heinrich Pestalozzi (1746–1827), a Swiss educationist, is often described as a disciple of Rousseau. He attempted to reform the education of poor children.

the peasants on his land and permits no injustice or gross inequality of privilege. His own life style is modest. I must re-emphasize, however, that it is far from easy to grasp the essence of this 'natural', rational reform of society. What, for example, are we to make of the following:

> Now all that is not from nature is contrary to nature, as I have proved again and again. (Rousseau, 1974, p.368)

This nebulous reconciliation of nature and society was not matched by events in Rousseau's life. As TV14 shows, he became increasingly convinced that in order to remain faithful to *his* own nature and to his love of the natural world, alienation from contemporary society was essential. In this programme Professor Maurice Cranston argues that Rousseau distanced himself from the Enlightenment and became the first of the Romantics. *Émile* sketched perhaps, an ideal society for the future based on a hypothetical pupil. Rousseau's recognition that contemporary reality was lagging behind this ideal contributed to his search for solitude in his later years.

Rousseau began, but never completed, a sequel to *Émile* (*Émile and Sophie*) which was published postumously in 1780. Described as an exercise in 'fantasy gratification' this unfinished novel tells of the misery which eventually befalls the couple: Sophie commits adultery; they lose their children; Sophie, after a period of expiation and redemption, is reunited with her husband who has, in the meantime, fallen victim to piracy and slavery on his travels. This somewhat gloomy prognosis for human relationships underlines the fragility of the reconciliation between nature and society to which *Émile* aspires. Perhaps, however, this should not detract from the whole-hearted attempt made by Rousseau to effect such a reconciliation. In attempting to reform society in accordance with the demands of reason and nature, he was engaging with problems which lay at the heart of Enlightenment thought.

8 References

Broome, J.H. (1963) *Rousseau: A Study of his Thought*, Arnold, London.

Claydon, L.F. (1969) *Rousseau on Education*, Collier-Macmillan, London.

Cranston, M. (1983) *Jean-Jaques: The Early Life and Works of Jean-Jaques Rousseau 1712–1754*, Penguin Books, Harmondsworth.

Ehrard, J. (1950) *L'idée de Nature en France à l'aube des lumières*, Flammarion, Paris.

Graham, R. (1976) 'Rousseau's sexism revolutionised' in P. Fritz and R. Morton (eds), *Woman in the Eighteenth Century*, A. M. Hakkert, Toronto and Sarasota.

Horowitz, A. (1987) *Rousseau, Nature and History*, University of Toronto Press, Toronto.

John, G. (1981) 'The moral education of Émile', *Journal of Moral Education*, vol.II, no.1.

Jordan, R.J.P. (1979) 'A new look at Rousseau as educator', *Studies on Voltaire and the Eighteenth Century*, vol.182.

Kessen, W. (1978) 'Rousseau's children', *Daedalus*, Summer edn, pp.155–66.

Le Bouler, J.P. (1981) 'Sur les écrits "féministes" de Rousseau', *Studies on Voltaire and the Eighteenth Century*, vol.199, pp.225–36, Voltaire Foundation, Oxford.

Leith, J.A. (ed.) (1977) 'Facets of education in the eighteen century', *Studies on Voltaire and the Eighteenth Century*, vol.167, Voltaire Foundation, Oxford.

Locke, J. (1694 edn) *Essay Concerning Human Understanding*, 2nd edn, London.

Locke, J. (1989) *Some Thoughts Concerning Education*, edited by W. John and S. Yoeton, Clarendon Press, Oxford.

McEachern, J.E. (1989) *Bibliography of the Writings of Jean Jacques Rousseau*, vol.2, The Voltaire Foundation, Oxford.

Piau-Gillot, C. (1983) 'La misogynie de J.J. Rousseau', *Studies on Voltaire and the Eighteenth Century*, vol.219, pp.170–82, Voltaire Foundation, Oxford.

Rousseau, J. J. (1974) *Émile*, translated by B. Foxley, Dent, Everyman, London. (First published 1911.)

Rousseau, J-J. (1988) *The Confessions*, Penguin Books, Harmondsworth.

Sonnet, M. (1987) *L'education des filles au temps des lumières*, Les éditions du cerf, Paris.

Wilson, A. M. (1976) '"Treated like invisible children" (Diderot): The Enlightenment and the status of women', in P. Fritz and R. Morton (eds), *Woman in the Eighteenth Century*, A. M. Hakkert, Toronto and Sarasota.

9 Further Reading

9.1 Rousseau texts

Boyd, W. (1956) *Émile for Today*, Heinemann, London (selected extracts from the text, with commentary).

Rousseau, J.J. (1974) *Émile*, translated by Barbara Foxley, Dent, Everyman. (First published 1911)

Rousseau, J.J. (1986) *The Social Contract and Discourses*, translated by G.D.H. Cole, Everyman.

Rousseau, J.J. (1987) *Reveries of a Solitary Walker*, translated by Peter France, Penguin Classics.

Rousseau, J.J. (1988) *The Confessions*, translated by J.M. Cohen, Penguin Classics, Harmondsworth. (Rousseau completed *The Confessions* in 1760 and they were first published in 1781.)

9.2 Biography

Cranston, M. (1983) *Jean-Jacques: The Early Life and Works of Jean-Jacques Rousseau 1712–1754*, Penguin Books, Harmondsworth.

Cranston, M., (1991) *The Noble Savage: Jean-Jacques Rousseau 1754–1762*, Penguin, Books, Harmondsworth.

(Vol.3 of Cranston's biography of Rousseau is forthcoming).

9.3 Critical Studies

Claydon, L.F. (1969) *Rousseau on Education*, Collier-MacMillan, London. (Commentary on *Émile*, with substantial extracts from the text.)

Williams, D. (1968) *Rousseau* in *French Literature and its Background*, vol.3, 'The Eighteenth Century', pp.134–47, Oxford University Press, Oxford.

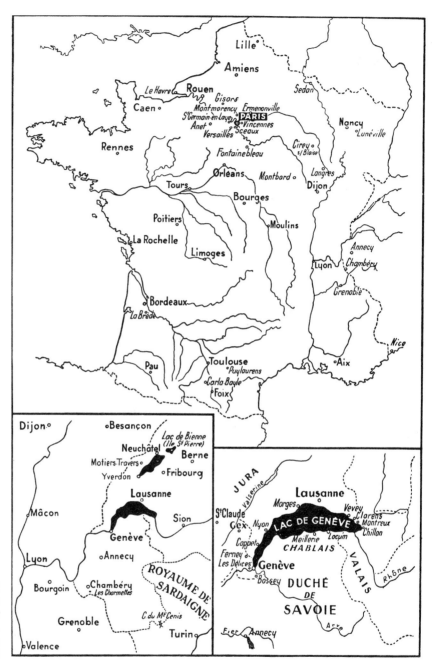

Map 1

Maps showing the location of places visited or lived in by Rousseau. (Collection Littéraire Largarde et Michard)

10   Appendix

10.1   *Chronological outline of Rousseau's life and works*

28 June 1712 Born in Geneva. Mother dies a few days later. His father's sister brings him up.

1722 Father goes into exile.

1722–4 Educated by Pastor Lambercier in Bossey, near Geneva.

1725–8 Apprenticeship with Abel Ducommun, engraver.

1728 Leaves Geneva. First meeting with Madame de Warens at Annecy. Becomes a Catholic convert in Turin.

1728–31 Wandering and a variety of jobs (mainly music tuition) in Italy, Switzerland and France.

1731–40 Lives mainly in or near Chambéry, protected by Madame de Warens who becomes his mistress in 1733. Idyllic months at Les Charmettes, an estate just outside Chambéry, in 1735–6.

1738 Break with Mme de Warens.

1740–1 Tutor in Lyons.

1742 Settles in Paris. Unsuccessful presentation of a new system of musical notation to the Academy of Science.

1744–51 Makes a living as secretary to an Ambassador to Venice, tutor and musician, protected by the Dupin family. Collaborates on the *Encyclopédie* and associates with Diderot, Condillac and other men of letters.

1745 Beginning of liaison with Thérèse Le Vasseur. Performance of his opera, *The Gallant Muses.*

1749 'Vision' on the road to Vincennes, where he was to visit Diderot in prison. This was the moment of his 'reform', when he determined to expose (in his essay to be submitted to the Academy of Dijon) the ills brought upon society by the arts and sciences.

1750 Academy of Dijon awards prize for his *Discourse on the Arts and Sciences*, published in 1751.

1752 Successful performance of his opera, *The Village Soothsayer*, at Fontainebleau.

1754 Visits Geneva, returns to the Protestant church.

1755 Publication of the *Discourse on Inequality.*

1756 Moves to the Hermitage, a house on the estate of Mme d'Epinay near Paris.

1757 Love for Madame d'Houdetot, sister-in-law of Mme d'Epinay. Quarrels with Paris friends, whom he suspected of betraying his love for Sophie to her lover. Leaves the Hermitage.

1757–62 Living at Montlouis, near Montmorency, working on a series of major books.

1758	Publication of *Letter to M. d'Alembert on the Theatre*, in which he argues that the introduction of theatre to Geneva would corrupt its citizens' morality. Break with Diderot.
1761	Publication in Paris of *La Nouvelle Héloïse*.
1762	Publication of *Émile* and *The Social Contract*. Leaves France to avoid arrest.
1762–5	Living in the Prussian principality of Neuchâtel. Acquaintance with Earl Marischal Keith.
1763	Renounces Genevan citizenship.
1764	Decides to write *Confessions*; composes preamble.
1765	House in Môtiers stoned. Takes refuge in the Island of Saint-Pierre.
1766	Takes refuge in England. Stays at Chiswick and Wootton, Staffs. Public quarrel with Hume.
1767	Pensioned by George III. Returns to France, using pseudonym. Publishes *Dictionary of Music*.
1768–70	Living in the Dauphiné.
1770	Returns to Paris. Public readings of the *Confessions*. Takes up music copying again in order to earn a living.
1772–6	Composition of the *Dialogues*.
1776–8	Composition of *Reveries of the Solitary Walker*.
	Dies at Ermenonville (2 July 1778).
1794	Remains transferred to the Panthéon in Paris.

The Thought of Mary Wollstonecraft

*Prepared for the Course Team by
Susan Khin Zaw*

Contents

The Thought of Mary Wollstonecraft *(Study week 28)*

Studies/Texts	Radio	TV	AC	Set Books
Studies, II				
Texts, II	-	-	-	-

For this week's work you will need this volume and *Texts*, II. You will also find TV16 very relevant.

The Thought of Mary Wollstonecraft

1 The philosophy of A Vindication of the Rights of Woman

The subject of this study is the English writer and philosopher Mary Wollstonecraft (1759–97). Wollstonecraft (Fig.22) was a challenging figure in her own time and remains so today. She lived at a time when the American and French Revolutions were giving concrete political expression to Enlightenment ideas of the natural equality of man, (see de Jaucourt's article *Natural Equality* in the *Encyclopédie* (*Texts*, I, p.13), and their success appeared to be threatening the whole European social and political order (as you may recall from Catherine the Great's reaction to the Revolution, *Studies*, I, pp.91–3). Wollstonecraft, along with other radical intellectuals in the early days of the French Revolution, enthusiastically embraced and publicly defended a new democratic politics, developed by political radicals – in England, often Dissenters – from Enlightened principles (though the *philosophes* who laid down those principles might have been shocked to see where they eventually led). Wollstonecraft, unlike the French Revolutionaries, went on to urge an even deeper transformation of society, carrying the Revolution further, into the social relations between men and women. Law and the conventional morality of the time subordinated woman to man: Wollstonecraft attacked this as a form of irrational tyranny, closely related, she believed, to the political tyranny she saw in most of the countries of Europe – the tyranny of arbitrary rule by a hereditary ruling class, typically a hereditary monarch supported by a wealthy hereditary aristocracy. These views were proclaimed in the two works which made her reputation: *A Vindication of the Rights of Men* (1790), in which she defended the infant French Revolution against the onslaught of the great orator and statesman Edmund Burke; and *A Vindication of the Rights of Woman* (1792). The latter is the work for which she is best known today, and is the main focus of this study; but we shall need to make brief excursions into other works to elucidate it.

Our study concentrates on Wollstonecraft's most overtly political/philosophical work. However, she was not only a political and philosophical writer – for instance, she also produced two novels: *Mary, a Fiction*, and (unfinished) *The Wrongs of Woman, or Maria*; a travel book, *Letters written during a short residence in Norway, Sweden and Denmark* (all of these available in modern paperback editions); as well as a book of children's stories, *Original stories from real life*, (one edition of which was illustrated by William Blake), a book on female education, a study of the French Revolution, and a great quantity of literary journalism.

As a writer she is difficult to categorize, not only because of the diversity of her output, but also because of the way each work tends to cross conventional genre boundaries. Her novels express her political and philosophical views, her political/philosophical writings draw frequently on her gift for sharp and witty characterization and the telling concrete detail, her travel book is permeated with unrequited love. This makes her always an intriguing but often a difficult writer to read, since her work continually disappoints or baffles expectations formed by familiarity with conventional genres.

Figure 22
Mary Wollstonecraft, painting by John Opie, c. 1797. (National Portrait Gallery, London)

Wollstonecraft[1] was as unconventional in her life as in her writings.[2] She was the eldest daughter, and second child, of six born to an unsuccessful first-generation gentlemen farmer. Her father had inherited enough money from manufacturing forebears to set himself up in this more elevated social position, but gradually lost his inheritance in a succession of farming ventures through a combination of incompetence, extravagance, and drink. Wollstonecraft seems to have been neglected as a child – in some ways an advantage, as she was spared the constrictions of an eighteenth-century lady's education; she was allowed to run wild, mostly in the country, and acquire the most minimal of educations in country day-schools. Like most intellectually ambitious women in the eighteenth century, she was largely self-taught. Parental love and attention were concentrated on the eldest son, who inherited from his grandfather a portion as big as his father's; the girls got nothing. Domestic life was marked by frequent moves, increasing poverty and occasional tension – her father became violent when drunk, her mother was weak and seems to have had little interest in her daughters. Wollstonecraft sought independence early, but at first followed, more or less, the path then marked out for unmarriageable middle-class females. Against the wishes of her parents, she went at the age of nineteen as a companion to an elderly lady in Bath,[3] where she remained till called home to nurse her mother in her final illness. At her mother's death,[4] the family broke up, and after various domestic dramas among family and close friends (throughout her life, Wollstonecraft had a propensity to initiate intense and demanding friendships and rearrange, sometimes disastrously, the lives of those close to her), she started a school with her sisters at Newington Green,[5] then a rural suburb of London. She was fortunate in her choice of location: Newington Green had a famous and widely respected Unitarian Dissenter as its minister, Dr Richard Price, political radical and correspondent of many eminent thinkers of the day, such as the American revolutionary Jefferson, the French philosopher Condorcet, and the English scientist Dr Joseph Priestley, a fellow Dissenter. Wollstonecraft was befriended by the Dissenting community at Newington Green, met Price, and began to come into contact with other London intellectuals, including some women writers. Since Dissenters rejected the established church they were excluded by law from state institutions; the response this tended to evoke from them was political radicalism and the setting up of their own educationally advanced schools and colleges. Enlightened belief in the perfectibility of man was widespread among Unitarians, and with it a deep interest in education. It was Price's Dissenting, rationalist, politically liberal circle that first set the course of Wollstonecraft's intellectual development, and she revered him as a morally exemplary man and minister.

---

[1]   Born in 1759

[2]   The following account is indebted to Tomalin (1974), from which most of the quotations from contemporary sources are taken.

[3]   1778 Moved to Bath.

[4]   1782 Death of mother.

[5]   1784 Moved to Newington Green.

Wollstonecraft's school failed; she was encumbered by debts and other financial responsibilities – she did not shirk the monetary consequences of taking over other people's lives, and received no financial help from her more prosperous elder brother, who violently disapproved of her. After dashing off a book at top speed to raise cash (*Thoughts on the Education of Daughters*, which was published by another radical Dissenter, Joseph Johnson), she opted for another conventionally female occupation: she went as a governess to an aristocratic and wealthy family in Ireland.[6,7] She found the position demeaning, though she managed, perhaps by sheer force of personality, to get her employers to treat her with more than usual consideration. But they could not long tolerate a social inferior who too often behaved as if she were an equal – even though, or perhaps because, the children who were her charges had become very attached to her. (Many years later the eldest daughter described her as 'an enthusiastic female who was my governess from fourteen to fifteen years old, for whom I felt an unbounded admiration because her mind appeared more noble and her understanding more cultivated than any others I had known – from the time she left me my chief objects were to correct those faults she had pointed out and to cultivate my understanding as much as possible' (quoted in Tomalin, 1974, p.50).) After less than a year, Wollstonecraft was dismissed. She returned to London with a poor view of the aristocracy and disgusted with traditionally female occupations, resolving, instead, to try to make her way as a professional writer. To this end she sought the help of her publisher, Johnson, taking with her the manuscript of the novel she had started in Ireland – *Mary, a Fiction*.

Once again, she was fortunate; Joseph Johnson[8] was a successful publisher with genuine radical sympathies who was generous with help in all the forms she most urgently needed: somewhere to live, friendly support both financial and emotional, intellectual stimulation and a social life. He was hospitable to his authors, many of them radicals, and their friends; among those he published were Tom Paine, William Blake, William Godwin, Cowper, Wordsworth and Coleridge. Wollstonecraft habitually dined at his table. Most important of all, he provided her with work; she began to write reviews and translations for his monthly periodical *The Analytical Review.*[9] It was during this period in London that she became involved in the political controversy which formed her thought, and produced the two *Vindications* of which the second is the main concern of this essay. For brevity I shall refer to them as the *Rights of Men* and the *Rights of Woman* respectively. We shall return to the controversy later; here I need only say that the first *Vindication*, the *Rights of Men*, was an answer to Edmund Burke's *Reflections on the Revolution in France*, an attack on the French Revolution,[10] then still in its first year and not yet regarded with

---

[6]   1786 Governess in Ireland.

[7]   1787 Publication of *Thoughts on the Education of Daughters*.

[8]   1787 Return to London; association with Joseph Johnson.

[9]   1788 Publication of *Original Stories from Real life* and *Mary, a Fiction*; Johnson founds *Analytical Review.*

[10]   1789 Storming of Bastille; Price's *Discourse on the love of our country* (see the headnote on the extract from Burke in *Texts*, II, p.251).

any great alarm. (It was in fact largely Burke's *Reflections* which first raised the alarm.) Wollstonecraft's *Rights of Men* attacked Burke, and defended the Revolution as the expression of rational, Enlightened politics; it appeared anonymously barely a month after the publication of Burke's *Reflections*, and was an immediate publishing success.[11] The first, anonymous, edition sold so well that a second edition was brought out under Wollstonecraft's name,[12] and she became famous. However, like all her books, it was written extremely fast; appearing so soon after Burke's, it is clearly more in the nature of an immediate reaction than the result of mature consideration. But the result of mature consideration turned out to be, not a further work on French or English democratic politics, but, two years later, *A Vindication of the Rights of Woman*. This was a best-seller, and established her reputation; her fame spread to both Europe and America.

The *Rights of Woman* was dedicated to an aristocratic Revolutionary, Talleyrand, the bishop of Autun, who had written on education; Wollstonecraft hoped (vainly) to persuade him to advocate the realization of some of her own ideas on female education in post-Revolutionary France, and he returned the compliment by calling on her when he came to England on Revolutionary business. A few months after publication of the *Rights of Woman*, she went alone to Paris to observe the Revolution at first hand; it was by then becoming violent.[13] Her reputation preceded her, and she was taken up by various expatriate sympathizers of the Revolution living in Paris, and befriended by the moderate Girondins; she frequented Mme Roland's salon, and became friendly with Mme Roland herself. Various groups were by now fighting ferociously for control of the Revolution; Wollstonecraft was to see many of her Girondin friends, including Mme Roland, executed, and when war was declared between Britain and France, to live in some danger herself. During these difficult and anxious times[14] she fell in love with a young American businessman, Gilbert Imlay, and had a daughter by him; he was able to offer her some protection through her adoption of his name, as America was friendly to France. During her pregnancy, she completed *An Historical and Moral view of the French Revolution*, published by Johnson in 1794;[15] in this, despite 'the calamitous horrours produced by desperate and enraged factions', Wollstonecraft still concludes that 'Europe ought to be thankful for a change, that, by altering the political systems of the most improved quarter of the globe, must ultimately lead to universal freedom, virtue, and happiness'. (*Works*, vol.6, pp.6, 222).

Wollstonecraft and Imlay lived together for a short time, she was still using his name and apparently expecting the relationship to be lasting;

---

[11]   1790 Publication of Burke's *Reflections* and Wollstonecraft's *Rights of Men*.

[12]   1791 2nd edition of *Rights of Men* published under Wollstonecraft's name.

[13]   1792 *Rights of Woman* published; Wollstonecraft goes to France.

[14]   1793 Execution of Louis XVI; Outbreak of war between Britain and France; Terror in France; Wollstonecraft's association with Imlay.

[15]   1794 Birth of Fanny Imlay in Le Havre. Publication of Wollstonecraft's *French Revolution*.

but he was frequently absent, and soon tired of her. However, for some years he lacked the resolution to break with her unequivocally, and she found it impossible to abandon hope. After two and a half years in France, she returned to England with her baby, and, deeply depressed, took a large dose of laudanum; Imlay's response was to suggest that she go to Scandinavia for him, to make enquiries about a failed business venture.[16] This she did, taking with her her little daughter, now just over a year old, and a nursemaid. The trip is described in her *Letters from Sweden*,[17] an edited version of her letters to Imlay during her travels. These comment as acutely as one would expect from her on the country and the people – she obviously enjoyed the trip, despite her painful emotions with regard to Imlay – and reveal an unexpected gift for sensitive and poetic descriptions of nature; characteristically, the painful emotions are left visible in the published version.

Wollstonecraft's efforts on Imlay's behalf did not revive the relationship, as she had obviously hoped, and after her return to England, another, more serious, suicide attempt followed; she was plucked unconscious from the Thames after jumping off Putney Bridge, her clothes saturated with rain to ensure drowning rather than floating. It was while recovering from this attempt, cared for by friends, that she put together the *Letters from Sweden* for publication – she needed the money – and started working again for *The Analytical Review*; she was determined to support herself and her daughter by her own efforts. Imlay was by now preoccupied with a new mistress, and she began to accept that she had finally lost him.

She was not, at this stage, generally shunned, despite having committed the cardinal offence in the conventional moral code for females by having 'lost her virtue', that is lost her virginity to a man not her husband. Her respectable friends accommodated themselves to her situation by appearing to believe that she and Imlay had been married in France – she was still known as 'Mrs Imlay'. Even those who knew the real story were often more inclined to commiserate than to condemn. Coleridge's friend Thomas Poole, who had long admired her work, wrote in a letter:

> I have heard with pain from my sister Mrs Wolstencraft's story … it is a sublime though melancholy instance of the injustice of Providence, that we seldom see great talents, particularly that class which we peculiarly denominate genius, enjoying an even tenour of human happiness … In their moments of mind … they form plans which would be practicable only if those moments were of continued duration; but in their career they feel like other mortals the sad burdens of mortality, and these being overlooked in their scheme of life, in the form of various passions they enter the fenceless field, making unbounded havoc. What a striking instance of this is Mrs Wolstencraft! What a striking instance is my beloved friend Coleridge! (quoted in Tomalin, 1974, pp.190–1)

The publication of the *Letters from Sweden* created further sympathy for Wollstonecraft; a female admirer wrote, 'the cold awe which the

---

[16] 1795 Wollstonecraft returns to London; attempted suicide; trip to Scandinavia.

[17] 1796 Publication of *Letters from Sweden*.

philosopher has excited, was lost in the tender sympathy called forth by the woman. I saw nothing but the interesting creature of feeling and imagination' (quoted in Tomalin, 1974, p.190). The public image of the stern 'philosophess' began to melt into the much more generally acceptable one of wronged romantic heroine. Wollstonecraft herself, however, had started to move on; she was beginning to re-enter London intellectual life, and started her second novel, *The Wrongs of Woman, or Maria*. This contains an apparent attempt to grapple with her own recent personal experience, in the fate of a romantically-inclined wronged wife who flees from marital oppression into adulterous love; but it also for the first time in her writing gives sustained attention to the much grimmer conditions of life for wronged lower-class women, by including the story of a second, extremely unromantic, lower-class, heroine, who interestingly emerges as the much more impressive character of the two. This novel, however, remained unfinished and was not published in her lifetime.

While Wollstonecraft was thus reconstructing her life, she became better acquainted with the philosopher William Godwin, whom she had met during her earlier period in London. Godwin was by now the acknowledged intellectual leader of the radical cause, which was beginning to suffer from a series of prosecutions of its adherents for treason. The two became lovers; both set a high value on independence, and both professed in principle objections to the institution of marriage, as it was then constituted by law. However, when Wollstonecraft once more became pregnant, they married, it seems with some little hesitation on Godwin's part; though they set up house together, he kept up a separate house in which to work. Curiously, this regularizing marriage seems to have done Wollstonecraft more harm among her acquaintances than her irregular liaison with Imlay; some of her new circle dropped her, presumably because she had now publicly exploded the fiction that she and Imlay had been married (since he was known to be still alive). The marriage was happy, but short; Wollstonecraft died a few days after giving birth to a daughter, Mary Godwin – who would grow up to marry the poet Shelley and write *Frankenstein* and other novels.[18] (Wollstonecraft's elder daughter, Fanny Imlay, committed suicide at the age of 22.)

Godwin was overcome with grief at his wife's death, and intending to honour her memory, published an extremely frank biographical memoir of her. This was a disaster for her reputation; friends wondered at his lack of judgement. The conventional immorality of her sexual conduct discredited her writings; a hostile clergyman saw her death in childbirth as a peculiarly apt Providential punishment of a woman who had sought to escape from the sex's allotted sphere. Political opponents transformed the pathetic romantic heroine into a presumptuous whore. At best, she was seen as well-meaning but misguided, her doctrines dangerous to herself and others. A review in the *European Magazine*, April 1798, commented:

> The Lady ... appears to have possessed good qualities ... but with an overweening conceit of herself, much obstinacy and self-will and a disposition to run counter to established practices and opinions.

---

[18]   1797 Marriage to Godwin and death.

> The latter part of her life was blemished with actions which must consign her to posterity as one whose example if followed would be attended by the most pernicious consequence to society, a philosophical wanton, breaking down the bars intended to restrain licentiousness. A female unrestrained by the obligations of religion, [Godwin was an atheist] is soon ripe for licentious indecorums. Such was the catastrophe of a female philosopher of the new order; such the events of her life; and such the apology of her conduct. It will be read with disgust by every female who has any pretensions to delicacy ... (Nixon, 1971, p.252)

Even the more moderate public reactions thought her views too unconventional to be accepted; a review thought to be written by one of her friends and admirers, the Dissenter Anna Barbauld, one of Price's circle, says:

> Mrs Godwin was not only possessed of great genius ... but had also an undaunted and masculine spirit ... Her sentiments however in some respects are too much at variance with those which have generally been adopted. We are not afraid to express our opinion that the doctrines upon which she has principally insisted are unfriendly to human happiness, and if practically followed might injure the sex they are intended to vindicate and protect. (quoted in Nixon, 1971, p.252)

Such reactions produced an almost total eclipse of her reputation which ensured that her works remained unread by the 'repectable' for almost two hundred years.

2   *Wollstonecraft's project*

What were these views which seemed so dangerous to Wollstonecraft's contemporaries? She was addressing the problems of her time: can they still be of interest to us now? Is the *Rights of Woman*, in particular, of interest to anyone who is neither a feminist nor interested in eighteenth-century social history? Before we consider these questions, please do the following short exercise; don't spend more than ten minutes on it.

EXERCISE   I have suggested that there is a strong connection between Wollstonecraft's 'Enlightened' democratic politics and the *Rights of Woman*. What would you expect this connection to be? (Suggestion if you are stuck: Look at the articles on *Natural Equality* and *Woman* (i) (*Woman: Natural Law*) from the *Encyclopédie, Texts* I, (pp.13–14, 16–18) and consider Wollstonecraft's life up to the time of writing of *Rights of Woman*.)

DISCUSSION   The answer that leaps to mind is something like this: 'Enlightened' politics claimed to ground the right to liberty, and therewith claims to other political rights, in human nature; this gave previously disenfranchised and powerless classes a claim to liberty and political rights simply on the basis of their humanity; women were a conspicuously disenfranchised and powerless class in the eighteenth century; they too could embrace Enlightened political ideals and similarly claim liberty and political rights on the basis of their humanity. Wollstonecraft would have experienced some of the economic and social constraints on women at first hand in her struggles for economic and social independence, and encountered in the Enlightened politics of Price's circle an intellectual framework which enabled her to see these as infringements of her basic human rights. What more natural than that she should put the two together, and, having 'vindicated' the rights of men by defending democratic politics in the first *Vindication*, go on in the second to contrast the actual legal and social position of women with their rights according to Enlightened, democratic principles, and demand equal treatment of women in accordance with natural *human* equality?

There are signs that Wollstonecraft did think she was making a progression very much like this in moving from one work to the other. But the result is not quite what one would expect, as we shall see.

EXERCISE   Read the chapter headings of the *Rights of Woman* (Extract 1 – *Texts*, II, p.239), noting the amount of space devoted to each topic. What do they suggest the work is about? Does it seem to 'vindicate' women's rights in the way just suggested? Is there anything in it you find surprising in a work claiming to champion the rights of woman?

DISCUSSION   The chapter headings suggest a preoccupation more with the character of woman than with her rights, and indeed with the character attributed to her by others as much as with the character she actually has. There is not much sign of the kind of 'vindication' of women's legal or civil rights suggested by the *Encyclopédie* article; rights are mentioned only in the first chapter – one of the shortest. The only other chapter which looks as if it might have something to do with this is Chapter IX, 'Of the pernicious effects which arise from the unnatural distinctions established in society', and it, too, is one of the shorter chapters. By far the longest chapter in the book is V, 'Animadversions on some of the writers who have rendered woman objects of pity, bordering on contempt', and the discussion of 'The prevailing opinion of a sexual character' spreads over two chapters. There are signs, too, that the female character as it actually is, is not very highly regarded: woman is, apparently, in a state of degradation, and a revolution is called for not in female rights but in female manners.

In fact, the *Rights of Woman* is a discussion not of female civil and political rights, but of eighteenth-century conceptions of the female character, of the relation between the sexes and between sexuality, morality and politics, and of moral education. Why? The reason can be found in the *Encyclopédie* article on *Woman (Natural Law)*, *Texts*, I, p.16. You may have noticed that there, de Jaucourt finds *theoretical* natural equality between the sexes perfectly compatible with *actual* legal inequality: 'We do not deny that in a relationship involving two people it is necessary that the legislative rights of one or other partner should be given precedence; and since it is normally the case that men are more capable than women of effectively managing private business matters, it is very prudent to establish as a general rule that the man's opinion should prevail'. Why is it assumed that men are 'normally ... more capable than women of managing private business matters'? The answer is: because of the different 'character' attributed to the two sexes. Wollstonecraft wanted to change the prevailing relation between the sexes. But the Enlightened conception of natural human equality was of no help to her unless she could break down 'the prevailing opinion of a sexual character' – and that, precisely, is her object in the first six chapters of the *Rights of Woman*. She devotes a lot of space to it because, in her view, the whole of conventional eighteenth-century morality, and therewith the whole existing social and political order, was permeated and corrupted by sexual notions, which were in fact the product or expression of male sexual appetites. Not even Enlightened (but male!) *philosophes* were immune from this malign influence – as the *Encyclopédie* articles on *Woman* bear witness; see especially *Woman* (ii) (*Texts*, I, p.16), in which 'the prevailing opinion of a sexual character' and Enlightened scientific ideas about female physiology and psychology mutually reinforce each other. The ramifications of the idea of a sexual dichotomy extended much further into eighteenth-century thought and culture than just the social relation between the two human sexes, as you will see in TV16; but for the moment, I want to concentrate on just one strand in this tangled web.

EXERCISE   Please now read the second *Encyclopédie* article on *Woman* – *Woman (Morality)*, *Texts*, I, p.17: Is there anything in it which sounds familiar?

DISCUSSION   You may have picked out all sorts of things, but what I want to highlight is that *reason* is assigned to men and *sentiment* to women. (Compare the modern version: men are logical, women emotional.) This is the crucial difference for an understanding of Wollstonecraft's thought.

The idea of sexual difference extended into morality: different moral codes were thought appropriate for men and women – as you will have seen from Rousseau's *Émile*; and in fact the character of Sophie in *Émile* remains very close to conventional eighteenth-century notions of the ideal female character, despite all Rousseau's revolutionary zeal in other departments. Wollstonecraft wanted to replace this gendered morality with a new, human, gender-neutral morality which could be directly grounded in *human*, not male or female, nature and in a concomitant natural equality between human beings regardless of sex. We have seen that in order to do this, she had to break down 'the prevailing opinion of a sexual character'. But a major difficulty for her in this regard was that, at least as far as existing men and women were concerned, she thought this prevailing opinion (in particular, the assignment of reason to men and feeling to women) was, by and large, *true*; that is to say, contemporary women fitted the descriptions provided by the prevailing opinion. This is 'the state of degradation to which woman is reduced by various causes'

(Chapter IV of the *Rights of Woman*). But Wollstonecraft thought actual women were like this *not* because it was part of female nature, but because they were made to be so by the corrupt and tyrannical societies in which they lived: the character manifested by actual women was an artificial, not a natural, character. The first six chapters of the *Rights of Woman* are taken up with arguing that this prevailing character is morally highly objectionable, and that it is artificially produced: the conventionally 'virtuous' and ideally 'feminine' woman is a degraded human being, but she has been made so by man and not by nature. This supposedly admirable but really degraded creature has been designed by man principally to be an alluring and docile sexual object. The remaining chapters suggest what true female virtue might be and how it might be achieved.

Explaining all this took Wollstonecraft deep into questions of moral psychology: into the relation between reason, feeling, and morality, and between sexual appetite, love, and tyranny. These are issues of perennial interest, regardless of one's attitude to feminism; and in my view, what Wollstonecraft has to say about them is often right and always interesting. Unfortunately this is not always easily seen, because though she is an impressive analytical thinker, she is too often a terrible writer: she is simply not good at making herself understood – quite common among philosophers. (Late in her life she acknowledged that she needed lessons in grammar – one of the results of the deficient education then thought adequate for females.) Extracting her meaning from her text is often a long and laborious task. We are therefore going to study her by means of extracts (the *Rights of Woman* is in any case a long book). However, bear in mind that Wollstonecraft's thought is much richer than can be encompassed in the space available for the extracts; and be warned that the extracts have been selected, and abridged, for clarity – that is, passages not immediately relevant to the issue being discussed have been omitted, so as to bring out lines of thought by no means so evident in the original. This process obviously risks giving different kinds of false impression; so bear in mind also that the extracts do not necessarily give an accurate impression of Wollstonecraft's style of presentation, and that, more seriously, as they stand, they represent a particular interpretation of her thought. Ideally, the interpretation you are offered in the extracts should be checked against the complete texts before it receives full assent. If what you learn of her here interests you enough to send you back to the complete texts, to see if your view of them coincides with mine, I should be delighted. The extracts have been taken from the excellent Todd and Butler (1989) Pickering edition of her complete works; but for ordinary purposes the Penguin paperback edition of the *Rights of Woman* is perfectly adequate. For the purposes of this course, however, there is no need at all to go outside the extracts. Still, one of my objects in this study has been to make the complete texts easier to read and understand.

We turn now to a reading of Wollstonecraft. The object of what follows is to extract from her text the core philosophical views which inform her thought. Wollstonecraft is not highly rated as a moral philosopher – indeed, she is not rated at all – but this seems to me a mistake. It is, however, largely her own doing; in the *Rights of Woman* she seems to regard her moral philosophy as both so obvious and so self-evidently true that she scarcely bothers to state it, let alone argue for it; her eye is instead always on her political, social and educational objectives, that is to say on the practical application of her moral philosophy. Nevertheless, she *has* a moral philosophy sufficiently original and interesting to make one wish she had devoted more energy to developing it and more care to expounding it. For her negligent exposition and stylistic idiosyncrasies have combined with misconceived readings to render this moral philosophy almost invisible. My aim in this study is to restore it to view.

3 Wollstonecraft's moral philosophy

The argument of the *Rights of Woman* is rooted in Enlightened political ideas, and that is where our efforts to understand it must start.

EXERCISE

Bearing in mind our earlier discussion of the *Encyclopédie* articles on *Natural Equality* and *Woman*, please read now Extract 2, from the *Rights of Woman* Chapter I, 'The rights and involved duties of mankind considered' (*Texts*, II, p.240). In this passage, Wollstonecraft states the three fundamental principles which form the bases of her argument throughout the work (one principle on each for reason, virtue and knowledge).

1 Can you see any logical connection between these principles, and natural equality and the female character as defined in the *Encyclopédie*?

2 Do you think what Wollstonecraft says about reason, virtue and knowledge is true?

DISCUSSION

1 Is there a logical connection with the *Encyclopédie* definitions of natural equality and the female character? I think there is a possible connection *via* the first principle, whose point seems to be to distinguish humans from animals, that is, to say what *human nature* essentially consists in. If human rights are grounded in natural equality, and natural equality springs from our common human nature, and our common human nature is constituted by the possession of reason, then to deny women reason is to deny them both humanity and natural equality. Conversely, if to be human is to have reason, admitting women are human entails granting them reason, natural equality and human rights. If, further, the acquisition of virtue depends on the exercise of reason, then women can become virtuous only to the extent that their reason is allowed to develop; similarly, if human nature is perfected by the acquisition of knowledge, and if the acquisition of knowledge depends on the exercise of reason, then women can perfect themselves only by perfecting their reason. This is, in fact, Wollstonecraft's argument in the *Rights of Woman* in a nutshell.

2 However, arguments are not very helpful in nutshells – as I hope you discovered when you came to consider whether what Wollstonecraft says about reason, virtue and knowledge is true. You may, like her, have thought that the first and second principles at least are self-evidently true; but I hope that, more cautiously, you felt you had to suspend judgement until you discovered what all these claims *meant*. I find the third principle pretty mysterious; and this I

think should warn us against assuming too readily that we know what the others mean, since Wollstonecraft seems to think of them as interconnected ('from the exercise of reason, knowledge and virtue naturally flow'). For instance: if we assume that 'knowledge' means, say, scientific knowledge, then it seems uncontroversial that it naturally flows from the exercise of reason; but from the third principle, it looks as if this is *not* what Wollstonecraft has in mind by 'knowledge' – for the third principle says knowledge is acquired by struggling with the passions: hardly a description of scientific method. We are not in fact in a position to decide whether what Wollstonecraft says here is true until we know what she means by it – and the rest of the *Rights of Woman* is, in a sense, an explanation of this. This is not to say that Wollstonecraft methodically undertakes a series of explicit, formal definitions of her key terms: far from it. Rather, informal definitions emerge in the course of her discussions of accounts of the female character and related subjects. Nor do these discussions follow the direct, logical path one would expect from a modern academic philosopher: again, far from it. There are two reasons for this. First, she was *not* a philosopher of the modern academic variety: academic disciplines had not yet split up into the distinct departments we are familiar with today. In claiming to be a philosopher, she was, rather, claiming to be a *philosophe*; and this means that she favours different types of argument from those usually favoured by modern academic philosophers.

EXERCISE   Please now re-read the *Encyclopédie* article on *philosophe* (Text, I, p.9), and summarize in a sentence or two the main characteristics of the *philosophe*.

DISCUSSION   Notice that the *philosophe*, unlike the modern academic philosopher, operates like an empirical scientist, basing his arguments on observation and knowledge of facts rather than on pure logic and abstract theories. Notice also that he is defined as someone who lives in a certain way, as much as someone who thinks in a certain way; and because of this, as someone who must necessarily study social relations.

The other reason for Wollstonecraft's rather rambling and diffuse style of argument is this. Her main object is always to expose and dismantle the complex and ramifying assemblages of ideas spreading out from the idea of sexual difference; and what holds the assemblages together is, precisely, *not* logic, but such things as analogy, metaphor, and the historical association of ideas. TV16 explores some of these assemblages, so I will say no more about them now; but Wollstonecraft's discussion follows, and takes on the shape of, the target she has in her sights. As she says in Extract 2, 'Such deeply rooted prejudices have clouded reason, and such spurious qualities have assumed the name of virtue, that it is necessary to pursue the course of reason as it has been perplexed in error, by various adventitious circumstances, comparing the simple axiom with the casual deviations' (*Texts*, II, p.240). I think what this (characteristically ill-constructed) sentence means is that she is going to describe the various erroneous views as their convoluted nature demands, showing what is wrong with them from time to time by comparing them with the three simple principles laid down in Extract 2; and that in fact is what she does. In the course of these comparisons, the meanings of the key terms in her three principles gradually emerge, piecemeal – and the simple principles become rather less simple as they do. Understanding Wollstonecraft's thought is understanding these meanings; and the next exercise is suggested as a method of building up this understanding. It is also a way of checking up on what I say. You can continue it through all the readings, and into your own reading of the complete texts, should you decide to undertake this.

GENERAL EXERCISE   As you read any passage from Wollstonecraft, look out for anything new that you learn about reason, virtue or knowledge. (By 'new', I mean 'anything different from what you have learnt about these from previous Wollstonecraft readings'.) Look out also for anything you learn about feeling. Note down what you have learnt as you go along under four separate headings (i.e., reason, virtue, knowledge, feeling). This should gradually build up a picture of what Wollstonecraft's principles mean and how she intends them to be applied (I don't in fact think you can separate these two). When you have completed the readings, look through your notes and see if they can be put together into a coherent view of morality. I am going to start you off with what I would put down from the first three paragraphs *only* of the next reading, Extract 3, to give you some guidance on how to proceed; but you may well have different thoughts of your own about these paragraphs. You should not assume that they are wrong just because they are different from mine.

EXERCISE   First, read right through Extracts 3 and 4 (from Chapters II and III, 'The prevailing opinion of a sexual character discussed' and 'The same subject continued', respectively) of the *Rights of Woman*, to get an overall picture of what is being said. Then go through them again, making notes as described under 'General Exercise' above. *Warning*: DON'T assume that every time you see the words 'reason', 'virtue', 'knowledge', or 'feeling', you have found something that should go down on your lists – think before you write. Remember that the object of the exercise is to reach a better understanding of the three principles from Extract 2, that is of the following passage:

> In what does man's pre-eminence over the brute creation consist? The answer is as clear as that a half is less than a whole; in Reason.
>
> What acquirement exalts one being above another? Virtue; we spontaneously reply.
>
> For what purpose were the passions implanted? That man by struggling with them might attain a degree of knowledge denied to the brutes; whispers Experience.
>
> Consequently the perfection of our nature and capability of happiness, must be estimated by the degree of reason, virtue and knowledge, that distinguish the individual, and direct the laws

which bind society: and that from the exercise of reason, knowledge and virtue naturally flow, is equally undeniable, if mankind be viewed collectively.

DISCUSSION   My sample notes (below) refer to the first three paragraphs *only* of Extract 3.

Reason: Apparently nothing new on reason; unless soul = reason?

Virtue: ? Obviously some connection between having a soul and being virtuous, but what? See under reason?

Knowledge: *Lack* of knowledge is said to produce vice; so it looks as if knowledge is supposed to produce virtue – but how?

Feeling: Nothing on this in the first three paragraphs.

Notice that these brief preliminary notes already suggest further questions about Wollstonecraft's meaning, whose answers one would try to find in the rest of the text(s).

Now complete the General Exercise on Extracts 3 and 4, if you haven't already done so, and try to update these notes of your own views as you read each Wollstonecraft text. Do this as well as the other exercises I set, which are designed to bring out my own readings of them; compare your views with mine as you go along. My own views on Extracts 3 and 4, with regard to the General Exercise, are summarized below.

I said that the most mysterious of Wollstonecraft's three principles was the third: Man was given the passions so that by struggling with them he could acquire knowledge denied to brutes. Wollstonecraft's formulation invites two groups of questions. First, she seems to believe in a Divine Creator. ('*For what purpose* were these passions *implanted*'?) Does this religious belief affect her moral beliefs? Can her arguments for them only be accepted by fellow-believers? Second, what sort of knowledge does she have in mind, and how does it relate to virtue/morality? Extracts 3 and 4 have done something, but not a great deal, to answer these questions. It is now clear that she does believe in God. But the extent to which her arguments depend on this belief is not clear. As for knowledge, it now looks as if the relevant knowledge might be 'knowledge of the human heart' (p.243a), and this is got by 'comparing what has been observed with the results of experience generalized by speculation' (p.242–3). But the meaning of this, in turn, is not at all clear; and how on earth can this new method of acquiring knowledge fit together with the struggle with the passions which the third principle says is the way we acquire knowledge? Well, the struggle with the passions is certainly something we *experience*; could it perhaps be that the struggle with the passions is the experience whose results have to be 'generalized by speculation', whatever that means? This would fit with the knowledge we need for morality being knowledge of the human heart, but the picture is still very unclear. We also have, as yet, learnt very little about the role, if any, of feeling in morality. The references to 'the heart' in connection with what is needed for virtue (e.g. in addition to 'knowledge of the human heart', p.243a, see also 'such an exercise of the understanding as is best calculated to strengthen the body and form the heart', p.242a) suggest that feelings come in somewhere; but the account of love, and the ideal female character sketched in Extract 4, seem to indicate that Wollstonecraft does not rate feeling very high on the moral scale. Is the role of feeling, perhaps, just to be an obstacle to morality, which has to be 'struggled with' in order to achieve virtue?

EXERCISE   Read Extracts 5 and 6, from sections v and iv respectively of Chapter V, 'Animadversions on some of the writers who have rendered women objects of pity, bordering on contempt', of the *Rights of Woman* (*Texts*, II, pp.249–50). What answers do they suggest to the questions about God, knowledge and feeling?

DISCUSSION   Extract 5 tells us that though Wollstonecraft uses religious arguments, she insists that religion must be founded on reason. What does she mean by this? We get some idea from Extract 6. The central religious argument for morality is that things ought to be a particular way because that is how God wills or means or intends them to be. In Extract 6, God is identified with justice; and in fact in Wollstonecraft's arguments, God usually functions as a compendium of fundamental moral values such as justice, benevolence and wisdom. It is these, rather than a view of God derived from, say, scriptural authority, that determine what purposes can be assigned (*rationally* assigned, Wollstonecraft would say) to God. Attributing to God only what is consistent with our own moral ideals is, for Wollstonecraft, what it is for religion to be founded on reason. (God *must* be like this, because God is by definition good, and the ideals sum up what it means to be good.) This means that it is belief in the moral ideals, rather than belief in any particular religious doctrines, that carries the weight of the argument. Because of this, it is often (though not always) possible for unbelievers to extract the core of Wollstonecraft's religious arguments and rewrite them without reference to God. Alternatively, Wollstonecraft also claims in Extract 6 that there is a utilitarian justification for acquiring virtue – 'That the plan of life which enables us to carry some knowledge and virtue into another world, is the one best calculated to ensure content in this, cannot be denied'; virtue is worth acquiring, in her view, *both* because that is what God wants for us, *and* because it is the surest path to a happy life (indeed, it sometimes seems God wants us to be virtuous *because*, being benevolent, he wants us to be happy!) As yet, though, we do not know the basis of this claim.

What about knowledge and feeling? Extracts 5 and 6 seem to confirm what has been said so far, but add little to it. The understanding, that is, reason, is said to 'train up' the heart, or feelings, as the person matures, but we still don't know exactly how; and virtue does seem to be a matter of following reason instead of feeling.

At this point we need to go outside the *Rights of Woman* to understand it properly. For in fact Wollstonecraft's view of reason and feeling is more complex than it often appears to be in the *Rights of Woman*. With regard to these, it is often helpful to turn to its predecessor, the *Rights of Men*, and Wollstonecraft's controversy with Burke; because the way she saw this controversy determined the way questions about the rights of woman presented themselves to her.

EXERCISE   Please now read the extract from Burke's *Reflections*, Extract 7; be sure to read the headnote on it first. How would you describe what Burke is trying to do in the extract?

DISCUSSION   Burke *feels* very differently from Price about the events to which they both refer, and believes Price's feelings are the result of a corruption of 'moral taste': 'This *"leading in triumph"*, a thing in its best form unmanly and irreligious, which fills our Preacher with such unhallowed transports, must shock, I believe, the moral taste of every well-born mind.' Price's revolutionary politics have 'tempered and hardened his breast' in preparation for the 'desperate strokes' (such as those perpetrated on the King and Queen of France), and 'stopped up the avenues to his heart' – otherwise he would feel about the 'triumph' as Burke, and all right-thinking people, do. Burke, in fact, regards *feeling*, not reason, as the basis of moral judgement (we have met similar ideas in Hume), and is trying to arouse in his readers the feelings about the 'triumph' which will make their moral judgement of it coincide with his rather than Price's.

You will remember that Wollstonecraft defended Price against Burke in her first *Vindication*, the *Vindication of the Rights of Men*.

EXERCISE   Read Extracts 8 and 9, from Wollstonecraft's *Rights of Men*; Extract 8 gives her comment on this passage of Burke. What is her objection to Burke? What is at issue between them? And what now appears to be her view of the relation between reason and feeling?

DISCUSSION   In Extract 8, Wollstonecraft doubts the sincerity of Burke's feelings, and accuses him of, so to speak, *artificially* conjuring up feelings in his readers – as poets do in the theatre: he is 'moving the heart with a mechanical spring', and thereby 'clouding the understanding', in order to trick his reader into a false moral judgement. In Extract 9, we learn more about these 'mechanical' feelings: we find that Wollstonecraft distinguishes between two different kinds of feeling. On the one hand there are the 'mechanical instinctive sensations', or passions, (which she calls hope, fear, love and hate), which we have in common with animals, and which she thinks of as barely distinguishable from physical/physiological excitation. (There is a modern psycho-physiological term which is very close to this idea of feeling as physical excitation or sensation: arousal of the autonomic nervous system.) On the other hand there are 'the emotions that reason deepens' which have an intellectual/rational component, and which are specifically human, learned *achievements*. It is to the former

Figure 23
'Be calm my child, remember
that you must do all the good
you can the present day'.
(Published by permission of
the British Library Board)

Illustration by William Blake to Chapter X of
Wollstonecraft's Original Stories from Real Life,
with Conversations Calculated to Regulate the
Affections and Form the Mind to Truth and
Goodness *(1788). The virtuous governess*
Mrs Mason has just told her two pupils, Caroline
and Mary, the story of the ruined house in the
picture: it was brought to ruin by its owner's scatter-
brained delays in carrying out good intentions, and
his indulgence in excessive grief and remorse at his
own failings. Because of his delays and self-
absorption a friend and benefactor who had saved
him from ruin, and whom he could in his turn
have saved, died destitute in a debtor's prison, as a
result of which his friend's daughter lost her reason
and was confined to a lunatic asylum by a vicious
husband. The little girls are understandably upset
by this sad tale; hence 'Be calm my child…'. Notice
the calming effect of the long vertical of Mrs
Mason's figure; notice too that the two girls seem to
be clinging to her for support – cf. Extract 5 (Texts,
II p.249) 'The business of education … is only to
conduct the shooting tendrils to a proper pole.'

kind of feeling that reason is opposed: virtue (or vice), of which only humans are capable, is produced by reason 'turning these passions (feelings as basic motivating sensation) to good or evil'. When the passions are turned to good, they become the 'feelings of humanity', that is *moral* feelings. Burke is someone of great *sensibility*: a key eighteenth-century word, which spans the physiological and the psychological. This means that feelings of the first, mechanical, sort are very easily aroused in him, and, says Wollstonecraft, mistaken by him for feelings of the second sort – moral feelings. Moral feelings, far from being opposed to reason, are its children.

What is it for reason to 'turn the passions to good'? How does it do this? The answer emerges most clearly in yet another of Wollstonecraft's works: her children's book. This is by no means a frivolous production, as its full title reveals: *Original stories from Real Life, with Conversations Calculated to Regulate the Affections and Form the Mind to Truth and Goodness.* This appeared in 1788, two years before the first *Vindication*, and immediately after her experience as a governess; it is in fact a parents' 'do-it-yourself' kit for 'forming the heart' of children by the application of reason, and thus training them up to virtue. It was illustrated by William Blake.

EXERCISE   Please now read Extract 10, the first and part of the second of the *Original Stories*; the first story is complete. You need to know that Caroline and Mary are 12 and 14 respectively, and have been neglected by their parents and badly brought up, mostly by servants. Their mother has just died, and their father has placed them in the care of the virtuous Mrs Mason, who is to correct their faults. (One is irresistibly reminded of a gardener training a young shoot.) Then answer the following questions:

1   Why does Wollstonecraft say when she does that the children's hearts 'now first felt the emotion of humanity'?

2   Can you work out from what Mrs Mason says the meaning of Wollstonecraft's claim that the function of reason is to 'generalize matters of fact', and to 'compare what has been individually observed with the results of experience generalized by speculation'? Does Mrs Mason herself do either of these two things?

3   Why does Mrs Mason say to the girls, 'You have acted like rational creatures'?

4   Can you now say what Wollstonecraft's definition of virtue might be?

5   What is the knowledge that we gain from struggling with the passions?

6   Given the relation between virtue and the passions, can you guess why it might be claimed that virtue makes happy?

Figure 24
'Look what a fine morning it is. Insects, birds and animals are all enjoying existence'. (Published by permission of the British Library Board)

Blake's illustration to the end of Chapter I of Original Stories *(Texts, II, p.258). The little girls have started to become 'rational creatures': so Blake has drawn them standing erect, no longer needing to lean on Mrs Mason. The picture illustrates Mrs Mason's enthusiastic response to the goodness of nature, and the goodness of God shown in nature, and to my eye all three figures seem on the point of ascending into heaven; their postures recall those in religious paintings – Mrs Mason reminds one of the figures of the Virgin Mary drawing her cloak of charity over her petitioners, the two girls of saints portrayed in postures of devotion or ecstasy. Their ecstasy consists in the dawn of 'feelings of humanity', replacing 'mechanical instinctive sensations'. Blake is trying to portray, not mere pleasure in a nice day, but an emotion with a moral component – the girls and Mrs Mason have been made happy by seeing what is good and doing it. Hence the reminiscences of religious art.*

DISCUSSION 1 Two reasons (a) Because this is the first time the children have acted 'from disinterested love' (see the final paragraph of Extract 10, *Texts*, II, p.258). They had wanted to save the previous mother and her nestlings at least partly from selfish motives – they wanted them as pets; but in saving the second nestful, Caroline acts unselfishly, purely for the sake of the birds, even sacrificing her own interest to do so (when she gives the boy her own money.) (b) Because the emotion which prompts the saving of the second nest is one that has arisen as a result of the reasonings put to them by Mrs Mason; contrast their attitude to creatures at the beginning of the story, before she has got to work on them.

2 Mrs Mason 'generalizes matters of fact' when, from the facts of how conveniently various creatures relate to their environment and to each other, she draws the conclusion that every example of this is an instance of the same thing – God's tender loving care to all. She 'compares what has been individually observed with the results of experience generalized by speculation' when, for the benefit of the children, she compares the way she behaves towards animals of different kinds in different circumstances, with the two general principles of behaviour (avoid hurting anything, and give as much pleasure as you can) which she worked out from speculating about God's relation to the world (tender loving care), and from the way they world is (the convenient arrangement of creatures).

3 They have changed their behaviour towards animals as a result of reasoning; they have managed to act on 'emotions which reason has deepened', as a result of knowledge of rational principle (Don't hurt anything, maximize pleasure in others). It is *not* that they make a logical deduction about what to do from the rational principles construed as universal laws; rather, the rational emotion, the disinterested love for all creatures, which they are now capable of feeling, *is* the rational principle written in their hearts, so to speak.

4 One is virtuous when one acts habitually from feelings of humanity rather than mechanical instinctive sensations; this is what it is to act from reason rather than feeling. The girls recoil from killing the wounded bird (and, perhaps, Mrs Mason averts her eyes) from mechanical instinctive sensations; Mrs Mason treads on the bird's head from feelings of humanity.

5 I'm not too sure about this, but I think it includes knowledge of how human beings are and ought to be (as described in 1–4 above) – 'knowledge of the heart' – and *self*-knowledge – knowledge of what I have to do to my own heart in order to become a better person.

6 I think there are two reasons. First (as we see from what Mrs Mason says about the pleasure of being like God), Wollstonecraft believes that virtuous behaviour just is, or can come to be, psychologically rewarding: becoming virtuous is becoming the kind of person who takes pleasure in virtue, in behaving rightly. Second, *failing* to gain control of the passions is a sure way of *not* being happy: another of the *Original Stories* is about a spoiled child who is always at the mercy of her desires (i.e. of her passions) because they have always been indulged, and is therefore always discontented.

Figure 25
'Indeed we are very happy!'
(Published by permission of
the British Library Board)

Blake's illustration to Chapter VIII of Original
Stories. *In this chapter Mrs Mason and the girls*
are overtaken by a storm while out walking, and
take shelter with an old crippled sailor and his
family, who have been saved from destitution by
Mrs Mason's charity; they now make a living by
supplying her with fish – hence his exclamation,
'Indeed, we are very happy!'. The girls have been
staring and laughing at deformed people, in
particular an old woman of excellent character who
has behaved well to them. They hear from the
crippled sailor how he has known many hardships,
finally being shipwrecked in a storm far worse than
the one that has just frightened them; nevertheless he
kept up his courage and hopefulness, and became
crippled through trying to save others from drowning
in the shipwreck. This checks Caroline's propensity to
laugh at his awkward gait. Note how the two girls
mould themselves to Mrs Mason, and how their
group of three gives an impression of unity, harmony
and tranquillity, while there is a hint of darker
things – perhaps reflecting the sailor's hardships – in
his family group.

We have now arrived at what I hope seems to you fair and plausible interpretation of Wollstonecraft's three principles. It remains to ask how she applies them to the condition of women. Please now re-read Extract 3, and read Extracts 11 and 12 from the *Rights of Woman*, Chapter IV and VIII respectively; in these she diagnoses what is wrong with the relation between the sexes. Then read Extract 13, where, as well, she offers a remarkable redefinition of the conventional female virtue of modesty, which I think displays her as a moralist of great subtlety and a startling ability to transcend the cultural limits of her time. It is difficult to appraise her diagnosis of what is wrong, as the world she is criticizing has now vanished; but we can compare what she says with contemporary literature, for example Laclos, Rousseau, many of the poetry texts. It seems to me we recognize there much of what she describes.

4   *References*

Nixon, E. (1971) *Mary Wollstonecraft, Her Life and Times*, T.M. Dent & Son Ltd, London.

Tomalin, C. (1974) *The Life and Death of Mary Wollstonecraft*, Weidenfeld and Nicolson, London.

Wollstonecraft, M. (1989) *Works*, edited by J. Todd and M. Butler, William Pickering, London.

Diderot's Salon of 1765

Prepared for the Course Team by
Linda Walsh

Contents

Diderot's Salon of 1765 (Study week 29)

Studies/Texts	Radio	TV	AC	Set Books
Studies, II	-	TV15	AC2018/R(blue)	
Texts, II				
Illustration Book				

Diderot's Salon of 1765

1 Introduction

1.1 Why study a Diderot Salon?

Diderot was, by his own admission, mercurial. He referred to himself and his work as a 'pack of contradictions', and in a highly critical response to a portrait of him painted by Louis-Michel Van Loo and exhibited in 1767 (when he was 54 years old; see Fig.26) he spoke proudly of his volatile temperament and of the difficulty artists experienced in discovering the 'true' Diderot:

Figure 26
Louis-Michel Van Loo, Denis Diderot, 1767, oil on canvas, 81 cm. × 63 cm. (Musée du Louvre, Paris. Photo: Photographie Giraudon)

> In any one day my face might reveal a hundred different expressions, depending on what moved me. I was serene, sad, dreamy, tender, violent, passionate, exhilarated ... I had a large forehead, sparkling eyes, quite large features, the head of a true ancient orator and a good-heartedness which bordered on stupidity and on the rustic simplicity of the old days. (Bukdahl, Delon and Lorenceau, 1990, vol.xvi, p.82; my translation)

He found van Loo's portrait too 'pretty', 'dainty' and 'effeminate'. Diderot was not a systematic thinker; nor was he a practitioner of compromise or moderation in his writing. He thrived on extremes, between which his arguments would swing like a pendulum, leaving the reader to deduce the final resting place or solution to his debates – or to confront the absence of any clear conclusion. When we read his art criticism, published as a series of *Salons* ('Salon' was the name given to biennial exhibitions at the Louvre in Paris but also formed the title of many of the critical accounts of those exhibitions), it is difficult to identify any consistent thinking on such matters as the purpose of art; the proper choice of subjects for painting; the proper manner of executing such subjects. However, his art criticism acts as a crucible in which are merged the diverse elements of debate and controversy current in the art world of eighteenth-century France.

In order to explore these debates and Diderot's position within them, I shall focus particularly on sensibility – the cult of feeling in art, literature, morals and society discussed in the Introduction to Part E (pp.125–30 above). You will find it useful to look over the section of this Introduction entitled *Feeling* before embarking on the main sections of this study. Review in particular the discussion of the meanings of the word 'sensibility'. Nature, another theme central to this part of the course, will also occupy us. The significance of the term 'nature' in the eighteenth century is also discussed in the Introduction to Part E.

I shall organize the discussion as follows:

An Introduction to the French Royal Academy of Painting and Sculpture and its Exhibitions – Here, we'll look at contemporary values and practices in the art world in order to establish a context for Diderot's views.

Sensibility in Diderot's art criticism: the foundations of taste – This section will examine the respective roles of sensibility and reason in Diderot's critical method. Did he veer towards reasoned objectivity or pure emotionalism in his judgements on paintings? (As you have already seen,

Hume's essay *Of the Standard of Taste*, Part B, dealt with very closely related issues.)

Sensibility, art and morality – This section will examine whether Diderot's participation in the cult of sensibility encouraged him to blur the distinctions between art and morality. Did he succeed in setting virtuous emotion apart from feelings of other kinds in his criticism?

Art and reality – Here we will see how Diderot perceived the relationship between art and the reality or nature it seeks to represent. Is the real, observable world sufficient inspiration for all artists?

Nature, feeling and genre – In this section we'll ask: Did Diderot uphold or challenge the traditional hierarchy of genres? How was his attitude towards the latter influenced by his views on the relationship between art, feeling and nature?

Sensibility in the work of the artist – Here we'll seek to discover which is, in Diderot's view, more important in an artist: reason (judgement), feeling (sensibility) or skill?

In examining the roles of feeling and nature in the work of critics and artists, it is hoped that this study will help you to forge links with the other texts in the course which deal with these key concepts.

You are asked to study extracts from *one* of Diderot's *Salons*. (He wrote nine in all.) Obviously, much of the richness and complexity of thought will have been lost in this process of selection. There is sufficient, however, to open up the key issues outlined above. Before we proceed to Diderot's text and to an examination of the paintings he discusses, a few historical details on the French Academy of Painting and Sculpture and on the exhibitions it organized in eighteenth-century Paris will give you a context in which to locate Diderot's text.

2   An Introduction to the French Royal Academy of Painting and Sculpture and its Exhibitions

2.1   Status and hierarchy in the Royal Academy of France in the eighteenth century

The Royal Academy of Painting and Sculpture was founded in France in 1648 by Colbert, a minister of Louis XIV. It was a vehicle for governmental control of artistic activity. Status and hierarchy were embedded in every aspect of its organization.

2.1.1   Artistic rank

The normal route for promotion was as follows. *Élèves* (pupils/apprentices) could become *agréés* (pupils who had shown particular promise and who were given the responsibility of executing a particular work for the Academy: they were 'on probation') and then *académiciens* (artists who were accepted – or *reçus* – for full membership on the strength of such a reception piece). In 1765 Vernet and Baudouin (the artists responsible for the works in the *Illustration Book*, Pls 162–8, 183–5 and Col. Pl.30) were fully fledged academicians. Greuze (Col. Pl.31, Pls 169–70, 172–3) was still, at that point, an *agréé*, as he had not yet submitted a reception piece.

Chardin, whose works are represented in Pl.187 and Col. Pls23, 25–9, was a *Conseiller* (senior academician) and treasurer. Above him were the assistant professors, professors (the professor in charge of the life class would change monthly), assistant *recteurs, recteurs* (directors) and, finally, the holders of high office – *Chanceliers* (Chancellors) like Carle Van Loo (Pls 157–8, 188–90) who was Director in charge of the Academy and Director of the Royal School for Aided Pupils (or *L'École Royale des Élèves Protégés*) in 1765. Boucher (Col. Pl.24 and Pls 177–82) was a *recteur* and had been appointed first painter to the king, a post bestowed on him by the *Directeur des Bâtiments* (Director of Public Buildings). There were about 50 officers in addition to the 50 or so ordinary academicians and 40 or so agréés. The higher one's status, the greater the possibilities of court patronage: the Academy had a monopoly of royal commissions. Artists' works were listed in exhibition catalogues in order of their makers' ranks.

2.1.2 Hierarchy of genres

The hierarchy of genres codified at the end of the seventeenth-century by the theoretician André Félibien continued to hold sway in the eighteenth. I am using the word *genre* in its broadest sense here. In French the word *genre* means 'kind, sort, type'. When paintings were classified according to genre, they were classified according to their subject matter and function. (*Style* labels, such as the rococo, can cut across different genres or subjects. The pastel colours and intricacy of form typical of the rococo style could be found, for example, in history paintings, domestic scenes and portraits.)

When artists were accepted into the Academy, they were accepted as practitioners of a particular genre or genres. Each genre would bring with it a set of expectations and conventions which were highly influential in the creative process. (You have already encountered the idea of genre. See *Studies*, I, pp.xiv, 5–6.) History painters, for example, were expected to conceive a scene of grandeur which would remove the viewer from everyday reality and to display a mastery of drawing skills, facial expressions, classical conventions and learning which would refine, enhance and dramatize the elements of their compositions.

History painting was at the highest point of the prevailing hierarchy. This genre could include scenes from the Bible, ancient mythology or history, allegorical subjects and, increasingly throughout the eighteenth-century, scenes from more recent national or European history (see Pls 131, 171, 175, 176, 177, 188). The history painter would deploy all his knowledge of literature and history in such scenes, in order to create a morally and intellectually uplifting vision: 'the actions of the heroes of humanity, at moments of moral or historical significance, which might be exemplars for the common run of men' (Conisbee, 1981, p.14). Emulation of Poussin, a seventeenth-century history painter, was common. History painters often aspired to the idealized representations of figures and subjects characteristic of this master.

Portraiture was next in the hierarchy. This was perhaps the most lucrative of all the genres, as a large, wealthy middle class grew in eighteenth-century France and enlarged a flourishing market. (The history painter had a much more restricted market: large-scale compositions could be housed only by those with mansions of a sufficient size or in public and ecclesiastical buildings.) One expectation of this genre was that it would allow its patron to express his or her status through art; but from the early 1740s onwards portraiture increasingly emphasized another function: its capacity for intimate, psychological penetration. Reviews of the Salons demonstrate this dual interest. They comment on costume (as an indication of wealth and rank) but also on the gestures, expressions, character and occupations of the sitters. Critics and officials anxious to steer artists towards the history genre deplored the increasing popularity of portraiture. The government intervened and regulated the prices of portraits (according to their size) so that they would become slightly less lucrative and there would be less incentive for artists to abandon the history genre.

Lower than portraiture in the hierarchy was genre painting. I am now using the word genre in its narrower sense of a painting depicting scenes from 'everyday life'. (Thus we can speak of the history genre, the portraiture genre and the genre genre.) Genre paintings depicted everyday actions in familiar settings, both indoors and out. (See Pls 134, 184, 185.) Sometimes there is an apparent conflation of two different genres (types) of painting, as an individual portrait is combined with an everyday action or scene. (The title, in such cases, may tell us on which genre the emphasis lies, as in Chardin's *The Scullery Maid*, – Col. Pl.25 – where the central figure is not given any specific identity: the emphasis is on her actions and environment.)

Genre painting enjoyed increasing popularity and sales throughout the century. Dutch and Flemish masters such as Teniers (1582–1649) were admired for their naturalistic scenes of everyday life, made available to a wider audience through the medium of engraving. The French engraver Le Bas engraved many of the works of David Teniers the Younger, whose works included religious subjects, landscapes, interiors with peasants and many versions of *The Alchemist* (see Pl.133). The paintings of Teniers fetched fantastic prices until the end of the century. At a sale in 1768 his *Good Old Man Distributing Bread to the Poor* was sold for 7,200 livres (1 livre = 20 sous; the price of a large loaf of bread being 8–15 sous), while a Titian portrait went for less than half the price. Another painting, *Prodigal Child*, fetched 30,000 livres. History paintings may have enjoyed a higher status but it was often the lower genres which thrived in the market place.

Next came landscape. The most prolific and renowned landscape artist exhibiting at the 1765 Salon was Vernet. (See Pls 162–8 and Col. Pl.30.) He submitted both topographical and imaginative landscapes. The latter included idealized studies of the Roman Campagna. This genre had a lower status because it was felt that it did not call upon the higher intellectual and aesthetic insights of the history painter, nor did it give prominence to that 'highest' test of artistic ability – the human figure. In the seventeenth century Claude Lorrain (known as Claude) and Poussin had popularized a 'higher' strain of landscape resonant with historical, poetic or classical references. (See Pl.132.) This strain of landscape art preserved a higher status than other forms of landscape in the eighteenth century because of its greater *transformation* of nature (through the use of colour, light and composition) and because of its classical and literary allusions, which extended a painting's appeal beyond the purely visual to the intellectual. Although many landscape artists of the eighteenth century borrowed extensively from Claude's visual vocabulary and conventions (e.g. in the use of tonal gradations to suggest depth; in the use of trees as framing devices etc.), a higher status would be conferred on their work only if they made explicit reference to the subject matter of the higher genres (e.g. mythological figures).

Landscape artists found that their works were in great demand from private collectors, despite their low official status. Vernet also received a royal commission to make a visual record of the major ports of France in the mid-century, as he had acquired a reputation for making accurate studies from nature. (He had made topographical studies of the Bay of Naples.) It was really only in the second half of the eighteenth century that studying landscapes from nature became more widely practised. Not until the second half of the nineteenth century did it become the dominant practice. In this context, it could be said that Diderot's praise of Vernet's fidelity to nature helped to change the expectations and conventions associated with the landscape genre and to encourage its movement away from the copying of other works, studio models and perspective boxes and artificial lighting: the genre should encompass a closer observation of nature or the external world.

Again, officials were concerned by the increasing popularity of this 'low' genre. The *Salon de Correspondance* exhibitions set up by Pahin de la Blancherie as an alternative to the Government-controlled Salons included a Vernet exhibition in 1783, in an attempt to encourage genres other than history. It was suppressed by d'Angivillier, then *Directeur des Bâtiments*.

Still-life painting was regarded as the lowest genre, requiring the least transformation or enhancement of nature in the raw within a narrow range of traditional subjects. (See Broadcast Notes to TV15.) The still-life artist was regarded as closer in status to an artisan or craftsman than to a fine artist. (Compare Reynolds in *Texts*, I, p.209.) Nevertheless, the career of Chardin (see biographical note in *Texts*, II, pp.292–3) demonstrates that an artist could be received into the Academy on the basis of such works. (See Col. Pls 23, 25–9 and Pl.187 and TV15.) But perhaps the key to Chardin's success was the fact that he provided a subtler transformation of nature than other artists working within this genre. As TV15 shows, he extended and refined the conventions of the genre in which he was working.

2.1.3 Hierarchy of artistic skills

Students were normally allocated to a master in whose workshop they learned the practical skills of painting (e.g. mixing colours and preparing canvases), sculpting or engraving. Academy classes, however, concentrated almost exclusively on drawing and principally upon the human figure. Drawing or draughtsmanship[1] was regarded as the most important aspect of art and the theory behind it as the core concern of artists. Although students received some lectures on colour, drawing remained the priority. The battle between colour and drawing had gained impetus in the seventeenth century in France when *Poussinistes* (followers of Poussin) had come into conflict with supporters of the style of Rubens –

---

[1] Most preparatory drawings were executed with brush, charcoal, chalk or pen/quill and ink as the lead pencil was not in general use before the end of the eighteenth century. See *The Primacy of Drawing*, exhibition catalogue by Deanna Petherbridge, The South Bank Centre, 1991.

Rubénistes or champions of colour. *Poussinistes* believed that drawing, line or form conferred a kind of intellectual appeal on painting, independent of its subject matter, which far outweighed the primarily visual and emotional appeal of colour. Collectors and patrons of art continued to be divided on this subject throughout the eighteenth century, but the Academy asserted a marked allegiance to Poussin.

Pl.131 offers an example of the kind of nobility or grandeur of line which was so highly esteemed in the work of Poussin and which was regarded as an inheritance of the antique. Raphael and Le Sueur were also admired for their draughtsmanship. Nevertheless, some academicians continued to celebrate the powers of colour in the work of artists like Rubens, Rembrandt, Veronese, and Titian. Colour *could* achieve official recognition if allied with grandeur of purpose or subject, and a greater degree of eclecticism crept into the instruction of artists from the mid-century onwards.

The Academy held a monopoly of life-drawing classes (which were, at times, forbidden in the studios of individual artists) and centralized control in the way in which drawing should be taught, that is by close observation of replicas of ancient statues and in accordance with the principle that artists should make a judicious selection of the forms and elements with which nature provided them. Students would spend many hours studying statues such as those in Pls 135–8. Anatomical details, poses, expressions, gestures were carefully noted in an attempt to study the ways in which ancient sculptors had selected from and transformed nature. Now look at the *Encyclopédie* plates illustrating the article on *Drawing* (Pls 139–43). The classical idea that beauty arose from the harmonious relationship of parts to the whole still held sway in the eighteenth-century and reinforced the importance of the study of mathematical proportion.

The normal education in drawing proceeded thus: (1) copying of drawings or engravings of anatomical details such as heads and limbs, eyes, noses, mouths etc (Pls 144–8); (2) copying academic drawings executed by professors; (3) drawing casts from antiquity in the Academy's collection; (4) the study of live models (Pls 149–52). Most models were male and their profession was highly respected: when 'off duty' they were entitled to wear a sword and the king's livery. Pls 149–56 show the conventional range of poses adopted by models in typical figure studies or *académies*. Traditional accessories for such studies included rope, staff, box and cushion. Note, then, how late artists came to living 'nature': and even then, nature was carefully posed. Both Diderot and Chardin lament this fact in the *Salon of 1765*. Cochin's *Drawing Academy* (Pl.159) summarizes, from left to right, the stages of such an education. Pl.160 emphasizes the controlled, artificial lighting in which artists learned to draw.

Formulae and convention also dominated the depiction of human emotions. The study of physiognomy (the way in which the face mirrors the 'passions of the soul') was heavily influenced by the schemata or codified visual formulae of Charles Le Brun in his *Treatise on the Passions* (1698). (See Pl.161.) The Academy succeeded in perpetuating such conventions by organizing, after 1759, competitions in the rendering of facial expression – one of the rare occasions, it seems, on which female models were used.

Geometry, perspective and anatomy were also taught at the Academy, and there were lectures on past masters and on various aesthetic issues. Like its British counterpart, the French Academy wished to establish its liberal (as opposed to mechanical/trade) status by expounding a body of theory. Gifted students (e.g. those who won scholarships to the French Academy in Rome) aspiring to the higher genres also received instruction in history, literature and geography.

You may find it surprising that, in such a highly structured context, there was animated debate in eighteenth-century France about the role of *feeling* in art.

EXERCISE Please turn to the Art History cassette AC2018/R (Side 2, Section 2) which accompanies this Study. You will need your *Illustration Book* and Cassette Notes. The exercises on the cassette are designed to allow you to explore specific paintings in greater detail in order to exemplify the broader points made above and to prepare you for Diderot's text.

2.2 The Royal Academy and its exhibitions

From 1667 onwards biennial exhibitions were held by the Academy. During the wars of the early part of the eighteenth century they were sometimes suspended and then, in the second quarter of the century, they were sometimes annual. The exhibitions were all held in one of the royal palaces, the Louvre, which the court had left to occupy Versailles. From 1725 the *Salon Carré* (square hall or saloon) was used, and the exhibition itself became known as the Salon. From 1746 the walls were hung with green cloth as a background to the pictures. Extra space was available in a room alongside and large sculptures were often exhibited outdoors.

The exhibitions usually lasted about 20 days and between 1746 and 1791 they opened on 25 August, the King's feast day, *la Saint-Louis*. Members of the Academy organized the exhibitions but they were always under the strict supervision of the *Directeur des Bâtiments*, the government official in charge of public buildings and cultural events. The Treasury picked up part of the bill for the exhibitions, that is payments for fitments, guards on duty and, from 1763 onwards, the picture-hanger (*tapissier*). The latter was chosen by the Academy and between 1761 and 1773 Chardin, a painter of still lifes, portraits and genre subjects, filled the post. Artists chosen for this position were often well established and acceptable to the court. They knew that any portrait of the king must occupy a central position; that large religious paintings should be well lit; that inferior works should be relegated to the staircases and that paintings should generally be arranged three or four high on the walls (see Figs 27–30). Sculptures were usually arranged haphazardly. Chardin fulfilled his role more conscientiously than many picture-hangers and remained in attendance during the exhibition so that he could answer his artist colleagues' queries.

Only members of the Academy could exhibit their work at the Salons, although a few non-members were sometimes allowed to exhibit in the doorway. Many of those who exhibited had been admitted to the Academy very recently, so that their names may not always appear in the

Figure 27   *Saint-Aubin, The Salon* of 1765, General View, *watercolour. (Louvre, Cabinet des dessins. Photo: Cliché des Musées Nationaux)*

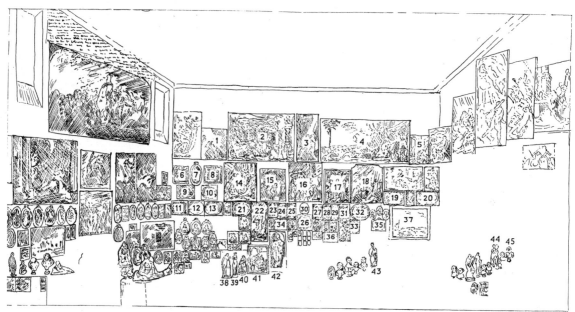

1 *bis*. 1. Lépicié, Baptême de Jésus-Christ. 2. Challe, Hector et Pâris. 3. Brenet, Baptême de Jésus-Christ. 4. Hallé, Hippomène et Atalante. 5. Lépicié, Saint Crépin et Saint Crépinien.

6–13. Chardin. 14. Vien, Marc-Aurèle. 15. Carle Van Loo, Suzanne (*inscription*: Mr. Michel Van Loo pour 5000). 16. Carle Van Loo, Auguste. 17. Carle Van Loo, Les Grâces (*inscription*: dé-rose-myrte). 18. Hallé, Trajan. 19–20. Vernet.

21. La Grenée, La Bonté et la Générosité. 22. Boucher, Pastorale. 23–

Loo, Portrait de Carle Van Loo. 31. Boucher, Pastorale. 32. La Grenée, La Justice et la Clémence. 33. Boucher, Jupiter et Calisto. 34. Boucher, Angélique et Médor. 35. La Grenée, Diane et Endymion. 36. Vernet (*inscription*: Mr Vernet). 37. Vernet, Le port de Dieppe.

38–42. Falconet. La Douce Mélancolie, l'Amitié, l'Hiver, Apelle et Campaspe, Saint Ambroise. 43. D'Huez, Saint Augustin. 44. Pajou, Bacchante avec l'enfant Bacchus (*inscription*: satyreau, tambourin). 45. Pajou, Le Maréchal de Clermont-Tonnerre.

Figure 28   *Key to Fig. 27. (From Seznec and Adhemar, 1979, vol. II)*

Figure 29
Saint-Aubin, The Salon of
1765, Left-hand side,
*watercolour. (Louvre, Cabinet
des dessins. Photo: Cliché des
Musées Nationaux)*

catalogues. The right to exhibit was a great privilege and the only honourable way available of displaying one's work. The Academy of Saint Luke[2] and other institutions sometimes organized exhibitions but these lacked the status of the Royal Academy, and the annual exhibitions held at the *place Dauphine* were looked down upon as a kind of artisans' fair at which artists might rub shoulders with sign-painters.

Four hundred and twenty-six works (229 of which were paintings, the rest consisting mainly of sculptures and engravings) were exhibited at the 1765 Salon. This represented a sharp increase on the number of exhibits in previous years. Originally artists could submit as many works as they wished. In 1748 a commission was set up to vet works and make a

---

[2] Traditionally, the patron saint of artists.

Figure 30
*Key to Fig.29. (From Seznec
and Adhemar, 1979, vol.II)*

2 bis. 1. Lépicié, Guillaume le Conquérant (*inscription copiant le livret*). 2. Lépicié. Baptême de Jésus-Christ. 3. Challe, Hector et Pâris.

4. Fragonard, Corésus et Callirhoé. 5. Amand, Mercure et Argus. 6. Deshays, Saint Paul. 7. Deshays, Saint Jérôme. 8–15. Chardin (*au-dessous des Chardin et au-dessus des portraits, inscriptions*: M. Bretin—M. le Roi—M. Carpentier—M. Romieu). 16. Vien, Marc-Aurèle. 17. La Grenée, La Bonté et la Générosité.

18. Roslin, Un père arrivant à sa terre. 19. De Machy, Inaugura-

tion de Sainte-Geneviève. 20. Casanova, Une marche d'armée.

21. Vassé, La Comédie. 22. Bridan, Saint Barthélemy. 23. Pajou, Pendule. 24–27. Challe, Bustes de Floncel et de Mlle La Cour, L'Eau et Le Feu. 28. Caffieri, Triton. 29–31, *inscriptions*: Francisque, Deshays, Vénus. 32. Falconet, La Douce Mélancolie. 33. Falconet, L'Amitié.

34. Gravure (*inscription*: Carle Van Loo). 35. Cochin, Frontispice de l'*Encyclopédie* (*inscription copiant le livret*).

final selection, but very few works were rejected and those of Academy officials did not have to undergo this formality.

The public visiting these exhibitions grew steadily throughout the reign of Louis XV. Some 8,000 catalogues were sold in 1755 but this figure increased to 20,000 in 1793.[3] In the 1760s there would be

---

[3] The reception piece of Jacques-Louis David, *Andromache mourning Hector*, was exhibited at the Salon of 1793 and probably accounted at least in part for the large crowds that year.

approximately 800 visitors a day. Many of these would go on to visit the private studios of famous artists like Boucher and Greuze, who preferred to exhibit their works independently. Entry to the Salons was free and the public represented a broad social mix, from *grands seigneurs* (who often exploited the snob value of visiting on days when the exhibitions were not open to the general public) to lackeys. Perhaps the most important visiting class was the *bougeoisie*,[4] who were often prepared to enlist the services of a guide (i.e. someone who had read the catalogue assiduously), closely followed by wits and intellectuals of the day.

Let's now examine, against this background, Diderot's judgements on art in the *Salon of 1765*.

3 Sensibility in Diderot's art criticism: the foundations of taste

As you read the extracts from the *Salon of 1765*, you will discover that there is nothing overtly systematic about Diderot's critical method: private jokes with Grimm, to whom the *Salon* is addressed,[5] cries of despair, digressions and insults are an important part of his critical repertoire.

EXERCISE   Please read the introductory preface to the *Salon of 1765* extracts in *Texts*, II, p.269 and Diderot's own opening remarks (pp.269–70). As you read the latter, try to make a list of the characteristics which he identifies in his own critical method.

DISCUSSION   The list might go something like this:

1   His criticism offers more than a 'distracted superficial glance'.

2   He can distinguish 'precious morsels' from 'mediocre works'.

3   He considers the 'motives' behind his likes and dislikes.

4   He allows paintings and their effects to 'enter his soul'.

5   He takes into account the opinions of lay people (the 'old man' and the 'child'; 'ordinary people') as well as those of the learned ('the man of letters').

6   He had studied and learned to apply the technical vocabulary of art (e.g. 'drawing a fine line').

7   He is aware of the difficulties faced by artists, ('how long, painful and difficult') but merciless when asked to comment on the merits of their work ('and if I happen to wound the artist').

8   He 'describes the pictures' he judges as he is aware that most of his readers, living abroad (see *Texts*, II, p.269), will not be able to view the paintings in person.

---

[4]   I refer here to all wealthy commoners living off earned or unearned income.

[5]   It was in order to oblige Grimm that Diderot undertook his work on the *Salons*: they were destined for Grimm's journal, the *Literary Correspondence*. See *Texts*, II, p.269 on the readership of this journal.

9   His criticism will be like 'light emerging from the smoke'. Enlightenment in action?

Admittedly, this list represents *Diderot*'s view of what he has to offer. In this section of the study you can form your own assessment of Diderot's critical method. You will also form a picture of the foundations of Diderot's taste: that is of the principles implicitly guiding his aesthetic preferences. (Bear in mind that there is a distinction to be made between taste and criticism: the latter involves explanatory and/or persuasive treatment of the aesthetic preferences which constitute taste.) Did Diderot's allegiance to the cult of sensibility outlined in the 'Introduction to Part E' (above, pp.125–30) allow emotional responses to guide his preferences when looking at paintings, or did reason and objectivity play an important part?

3.1   *The role of feeling in Diderot's judgements on art*

Most of the critical accounts of the Salons written before Diderot's were sober, unemotional, uncontroversial (in that they upheld the canons of taste laid down by the Academy), factual and superficial. We do not have space here to present a history of these accounts;[6] but one critic, La Font de Saint Yenne (who is considered by some scholars to be the first true art critic in France, although some bestow this honour on Diderot) openly condemns their lack of discrimination:

> They are nearly all a mass of exaggerated, unadulterated praise, the most lethal poison for artists, as it will undoubtedly retard their progress by making them blind to their defects. (La Font de Saint Yenne, 1970, p.7)

Such accounts consisted almost entirely of conventional praise – commonplaces such as 'this artist has worthily sustained his high reputation'; 'this work is of a noble composition'; 'the artist presents all we have come to expect from him'. They were published either in periodicals (of which the most famous were the *Mercure de France* (*French Mercury*), financed by the aristocracy, and the *Année Littéraire* (*Literary Year*)) or under separate cover, as pamphlets. Most journals appeared monthly or bi-monthly and, as they were quite expensive, had a restricted readership. It was common practice for authors to lift commentaries, unacknowledged, from one another's work.

There was an alternative strain of criticism. Many pamphleteers (or *brochuriers* as they were called in France) were known for their propensity for sarcasm and satire. Libellous, witty accounts of the Salons, bursting with disrespect, became more common from the 1760s onwards. Unlike the *Mercure de France* and other journals such as the *Année littéraire*, they were not afraid to insult the academy and its aristocratic hinterland.

---

[6]   See Zmijewska (1970) who states that there were approximately one hundred review periodical titles in circulation in eighteenth-century France. More recent research has discovered 1,267 French-language periodical titles (covering a range of subjects) in circulation throughout the world in the period 1600–1789 (see Sgard, 1992).

Most criticism, then, resorted to extremes of politeness or sarcasm. In neither tradition was there a sense of the critic's personal engagement with the works he scrutinized. There were, however, a few precedents for what has come to be called 'la critique sensible' (i.e. criticism involving feeling or sentiment). La Font de Saint Yenne, Lacombe, Mathon de la Cour, Baillet de Saint Jullien and Laugier were among the critics who indicated the emotional impact of the paintings they viewed. Thus Lacombe summarized the impression made on him by the Salon of 1753:

> Here I fly by a friend, of such a keen likeness that he seems to call me, smile at me, speak to me; there a touching scene moves me; further on lovers make their intoxicated passion enter my heart; joy, grief, pleasure, admiration – in fact all the feelings which exist – seize me one by one. There, Sir, are the effects produced by a first view of the Salon on a sensitive soul. (*Le Salon*, p.8; my translation)

For a handful of critics, then, it was quite legitimate to consider the impact of a painting on the emotions.

The theoretician Abbé du Bos had provided the impetus for such views earlier in the century with the publication of his *Reflexions on Poetry and Painting* (1719), in which he stated:

> Now, feeling is a better guide to whether a work moves us and makes the desired impression on us than all the dissertations composed by critics to explain its merits and to work out its perfections and defects ... Reason should therefore not intervene in the judgement we make on a poem or a picture except to justify the decision that feeling has already decreed.[7] (quoted in Brookner, 1972, p.49)

EXERCISE   Please read the following entries on artists and look at the relevant illustrations:

Vernet (*Texts*, II, pp.279–81) Col. Pl.30, Pls 162–8
Greuze (*Texts*, II, pp.283–7, 290–1) Col. Pl.31, Pls 169–70, 173
Loutherbourg (*Texts*, II, pp.287–8)
Le Prince (*Texts*, II, pp.288–9) Pl.174
L' Épicié (*Texts*, II, pp.289–90) Pl.175
Amand (*Texts*, II, p.290) Pl.176

As you read, make notes on the following questions:

1   How important is feeling or emotion in Diderot's responses to paintings? (this question assumes, of course, that we can take Diderot's words as an accurate reflection of what he actually *felt* – a rather large assumption!)

2   Does he appear to make any effort towards objectivity in the judgements he offers? (Can you detect any consistent or technical principles guiding his opinions, or does he surrender to a total anarchy of feeling?)

---

[7]   It must be emphasized, however, that this relatively early statement of allegiance to the cult of feeling was much more tentative and moderate than the outright wallowing in emotion which took place later in the century.

DISCUSSION *1 The importance of feeling*

These extracts demonstrate the importance attached by Diderot to a painting's ability to arouse emotion. They also show how he used his own emotional responses as a measure of the merit of works of art: if a painting failed to move him, it was dismissed as mediocre. He expresses his personal involvement in Vernet's art ('... and I hope that they will succeed' – p.280; '... and try not to feel the grief of her husband ...' – p.281; '... this touching scene ...; p.281): he empathizes with the characters and becomes caught up in their drama. The shipwreck scenes are brought alive by his dramatic use of the present tense ('I can see some floating'). Emotional involvement is taken to extremes in his commentary on Greuze's *Young Girl Crying Over her Dead Bird*. The picture is described as 'perhaps the most interesting in the salon'. (In the eighteenth century the French 'intéressant' and its English equivalent, 'interesting' carried overtones of 'engaging the emotions'.) Diderot's imagination is stimulated so that he creates a drama which further intensifies his emotional response. This response is sentimental and, to the modern reader, slightly ridiculous.[8] Diderot's biographer, Arthur Wilson, identifies the motives behind Diderot's admiration of the wilting heroines of Greuze:

> Another equally plain fact is that when he looked at these pictures he felt the way middle-aged men are likely to feel when they see a provocative young starlet in a movie. (Wilson, 1972, p. 538)

The plain fact is, however, that Diderot does not admit to such feelings. He responds to the charm and sorrow of the scene with *some* self-mockery ('... aren't you laughing ...' – p.284) but with a great deal of pride. He claims to be one of the few to understand both the symbolism behind the painting and its true subject: the corruption of innocence. (Most critics saw it as a probable reference to a famous poem by Catullus, 'Lugete, O Veneres Cupidinesque', on the theme of a young girl's first encounter with mortality, rather than as a lesson in corrupted innocence.)[9]

Proud to be one of the few who have 'felt the horror' of scenes like Loutherbourg's *A Storm Breaking at Sunset*, Diderot saw his own heart as a reliable barometer of aesthetic merit (i.e. of the value or quality of a work of art): he was moved for good reason. He saw himself as particularly blessed in this way, as a keen heart or soul is an essential instrument of taste. The art of Le Prince 'goes straight to the soul' (p.288), to which it delivers a 'delicious sensation', a sure sign that it cannot be bad. Diderot is categorical:

---

[8] On the sexual overtones of Diderot's response see below, p.260.

[9] Greuze's art fused the influence of Teniers (see above, p.246) and other naturalistic Dutch and Flemish artists with that of Murillo (1617–82), the Spanish master, whose art combined emotionalism with sensuality, and Guido Reni, known for his sentimental depictions of the heads of female saints. (See Pl.171.) Murillo's works fetched high prices in the eighteenth century and were extensively engraved. Guido Reni's paintings were also in great demand: the duc d'Orléans owned fifteen of his works. It is thought that many of Greuze's female figures show the influence of quietism, a religious movement fostered in the seventeenth century – a religion of 'pure love' or amorous self-abandonment and mystical visions. (See Brookner, 1972, pp.10–14, 42.)

Painting is the art of getting to the soul by way of the eyes. (*Texts*, II, p.289)

That is, no amount of technical merit or *visual* effect ('the vigour of your colouring, the magic of your chiaroscuro') will impress him if his soul is not moved. L'Épicié's art is described as a missed opportunity: he *could* have inspired veneration and enthusiasm. Amand's art inspires a 'deadly chill' and fails to break Diderot's heart. The acid test of a good painting, it would seem, is its capacity to feed and arouse the emotions, particularly those of Diderot.

How does all this tally with the Diderot you met in the *Encyclopédie*, with the cynic of *Adore*? In the realm of art, Diderot's eulogy of feeling and imagination seems to undermine some of the moral and philosophical beliefs he states elsewhere. L'Épicié's art is criticized for its lack of emotive power: it does not reach out to the hearts of a congregation and inspire veneration in them. In a highly controversial passage (which, remember, would not be published in France) he suggests that religion would quickly be seen as 'metaphysical balderdash' were it not for the visual images and symbolism which sustain it. However, when he goes on to describe religious ceremonies and the spectacles they provide, he positively enthuses over the emotion generated by such occasions and thinks it ironic that many religious officials ('purveyors of lies') are wary of the very images and ceremonies which help to swell their ranks. Emotion, it seems, is enjoyed here by Diderot *for its own sake* – even if it serves religion! There is conflict here between Diderot the *philosophe* and sceptic, and Diderot the commentator on art. (Are some of the ambiguities in *Consecrated Bread* in the *Encyclopédie* more understandable in the light of the more purely aesthetic criteria outlined in the *Salon of 1765*? – see *Studies*, I, p.37.)

2   *Any effort towards objectivity?*

The passages which you have just read could be said to offer some evidence that Diderot's taste and critical method were not completely anarchic: there were *some* rules and principles behind his outpourings of feeling, even if these were not always stated explicitly. The Vernet entry refers to 'variety of characters, actions and expressions'; to an effective use of light or mist ('how the feeble pale light of the moon contrasts ...'); to 'fine nuances' of colour and, above all, to naturalism; ('... has been cut out and transposed onto the artist's easel') or truth to nature. The fine drawing skills of Greuze (e.g. in the hand of the young girl crying over her dead bird) are admired. Note also, however, the minor criticisms of scale and colour (the relative sizes of the head and hand; the 'rather purplish colour tone') in the latter painting: these are not sufficiently true to life. Also, Diderot asserts his professionalism by providing reasoned explanations of his responses – hardly the procedure of one surrendering uncritically to emotional impulses?

Generally speaking, Diderot is quick to praise works in which a harmonized visual effect is achieved by the right choice and distribution of colour, light, figures and objects. He is also quick to praise those which reflect a close observation of nature ('natural and true-to-life actions' – p.280). 'Truth to Nature' and 'a harmonious relationship of parts to the whole' were highly respected aesthetic criteria from antiquity onwards. (Cf. *Studies*, I, pp.229–32, on Shaftesbury.) Perhaps, then, Diderot did attempt to provide consistent standards of taste, and although the reader *infers* these standards from specific statements on paintings, rather than seeking an explicit credo, there is perhaps pattern rather than anarchy in his judgements. Equally, it could be argued that his emphasis on the emotive qualities of art does not blind him to its technical aspects. On the contrary, he was aware that colour, light and shade (chiaroscuro), drawing, handling of paint, facial expression and composition could help to enhance or destroy the emotional impact of a painting or its appeal to the senses (e.g. the inexpressive and poorly coloured Joseph fails to arouse the interest of the spectator – p.290; the position, character and clothing in Le Prince's *Russian Pastoral* contribute to the painting's charm and simplicity).

Diderot was constantly anxious to stress that his reliance on his own emotions as instruments of taste did not mean that he had fallen into the abyss of anarchic subjectivism. Like Hume, whose arguments you have encountered in *Of the Standard of Taste*, he believed that there was a standard on which the judgements of the discerning would converge. (See *Studies*, I, p.243.) In his *Essay on Painting*, his first major theoretical work on painting, written between the *Salons* of 1765 and 1767, Diderot said:

> If taste really is a matter of caprice, if there is no rule of beauty, what is the origin of these delicious emotions which arise so suddenly, so involuntarily, so tumultuously in the depths of our souls, which grip or release them, and which force tears of joy, grief or admiration from our eyes at the sight of a great physical phenomenon or on hearing the account of a great moral feat? *Apage Sophista!*[10] You will never persuade my heart that it is wrong to tremble or my entrails that they should not be stirred. (Assézat and Tourneux, 1875–7, X, p.517, my translation)

In other words, Diderot wants to have his cake and eat it. He wants to use his personal emotional responses as indicators of aesthetic merit *and* claim that these responses are attuned to an objectively defined standard of taste, within the grasp of a small elite of sensitive beings. Like many of his contemporaries, he was an eager participant in the swelling cult of sensibility. Also like them, he lived and wrote at a time when there were strict attempts to control and centralize taste through the Academies, and to protect the classical canon and a reasoned and learned approach to art.

Perhaps we should allow a hearing of a statement by Diderot which sheds further light on the matter. In the following passage from the *Essay on Painting* he discusses the role of sensibility (a capacity for keen emotional responses) in taste:

> Just as we see men practise justice, benevolence and virtue through well-grounded interest, the spirit and love of order, without

---

[10] 'Begone, sophist!' The sophists were a school of Ancient Greek philosophers. In later ages the term 'sophist' acquired pejorative connotations and denoted a thinker whose reasoning was clever and subtle but often misleading.

experiencing their voluptuous delights, taste may exist without sensibility and sensibility without taste. When sensibility is extreme it becomes undiscerning: it is moved by everything, indiscriminately. One man will state coolly: 'that is beautiful!' Another will be moved, in raptures, intoxicated … He will stammer incoherently; he will fail to find any expressions which adequately render the state of his soul … Reason sometimes rectifies the rapid judgements of sensibility. (Assézat and Tourneux, 1875–7, X, p.519)

Diderot could not decide whether he was a rational *philosophe* or a Romantic ruled by his heart, and tried to compromise by assuring us that *his* emotional responses to art were rationally justifiable: they were a condition, rather than the essence, of aesthetic judgement, and reliable indicators of merit because they were grounded in extensive empirical knowledge.

If you feel undecided about the relative strengths or weaknesses of Diderot's critical method, take heart from the fact that there have been many scholarly quarrels on this subject. The most famous of these disagreements took place in the 1960s between Virgil Topazio and Gita May (see Topazio, 1963, pp.3–11 and May, 1963, pp.11–21). Topazio saw Diderot as an emotional, subjective critic unsympathetic to the unique vision and technical expertise of artists:

> To appeal to Diderot, a painting had to arouse his emotions. If it did not, it was summarily dismissed, regardless of artistic merit. (Topazio, 1963, p.5)

Diderot, argues Topazio, was too inclined to judge a painting in accordance with the narrow framework of his own emotions and experience. He cites the example of a moonlight painting by Vernet, the colours of which were originally felt to be wrong by Diderot:

> Fortunately for Vernet, Diderot happened to look out the window one night and to his amazement saw the exact duplicate of the canvas. (Topazio, 1963, p.10)

Diderot, mortified, apologized for his previous 'blasphemy' of nature.

Gita May, on the other hand, views Diderot's art criticism as an 'experimental laboratory' in which 'broad investigations in aesthetics and ethics' take place: it would be wrong to expect anything systematic or fixed of them. May also argues that Diderot *was* skilled in analysis of the technical aspects of painting and that his contradictions were nothing more than the perfectly respectable changes of view of the empiricist responding to the changing evidence before him. (For it can be argued that the empiricist who claims to base arguments on experience *can* argue only on the basis of his *own* experience.)

What do you think? Let's turn to another area of confusion in the thought of Diderot and of his contemporaries.

4 Sensibility, art and morality

One of May's points is that Diderot found it difficult to disentangle ethical (about morality) and aesthetic (about art) arguments because his experience as a *philosophe* had made a concern for public morality a part of his nature. Tensions can occur in his art criticism as a result. For example, we've already seen how Diderot praised Greuze to the skies for his moral preaching but found deficiencies in his drawing and colouring. The general impression, however, is of an effusive welcoming of the emotion generated by Greuze's art. This, I think, is because a certain *kind* of emotion is generated: emotion of a moral kind, which indicates both a capacity for and a sensitivity towards virtue. There is a profound 'sadness' (p.285) in *Young Girl Crying over her Dead Bird*, which breeds compassion (emotion of a moral kind) in the viewer contemplating the girl's plight. *The Well-beloved Mother*, an elevated, didactic, pictorial equivalent to the bourgeois drama, inspires moral feelings associated with domesticity ('domestic peace').[11] Feelings of this nature were perfectly in accord with the relationship between virtue and a feeling heart established in the thriving cult of sensibility in the mid-century. (See 'Introduction to Part E', above, pp.125–30.) Those who can experience the emotions of compassion and love generated by such paintings are more likely to be virtuous in all their thoughts and actions. Diderot is proud to possess such a 'soul' (p.287) himself.

How does all of this square, however, with the sensual (erotic?) response to *Madame Greuze* (p.285) and *The Kiss* (pp.290–1)? Or with the sexual overtones of his response to the *Young Girl Crying over her Dead Bird?* Greuze's 'virtuous' heroines often exude a sensuality through their pose, gestures, expressions and dress, which, for the twentieth-century viewer, sits ill-at-ease with moralism. They often have at least one breast bare as they gaze at the viewer from their 'didactic' setting. If Diderot (or, indeed anyone) unleashes his emotions and places faith in the power of sensibility or the heart, will the result *always* accord with virtue? Is there anything intrinsically moral in the emotion generated by Vernet's shipwrecks and storms?

EXERCISE   Please read now the commentaries on Boucher's 1765 exhibits (pp.273–6 and Col. Pl. 24, Pls 177–82). Boucher was a practitioner of the *rococo*[12] style of art. This style was very popular during the reign of Louis XV, was a playful successor to the baroque and was succeeded later in the century by the more severe neo-classical style. Used widely in the decorative arts (wall and ceiling decoration, porcelain, furniture, clocks etc.), it was typified by asymmetry, florid S-curves and C-scrolls and by naturalistic motifs derived from rocks, shells and plants. Associated with a frivolous aristocracy, it gained a reputation for immorality and an avoidance of realism. Idyllic, pastoral preoccupations, sensuous flesh tones and pastel colours were also typical. As you read Diderot's comments on Boucher, try to identify the reasons for his dissatisfaction with this artist.

---

[11]   This painting shows the family of a wealthy financier, Jean-Joseph de Laborde and was commissioned by his mother-in-law, Madame de Nettine, who is in the centre of the painting. The Marquis returns from hunting to his (unconvincingly humble) abode and expresses delight at the sight of his happy wife and six children. The Rousseauesque ideal of the 'natural' mother breast-feeding and caring for her own children is forcefully expressed.

[12]   This term did not come into general use until the 1830s, and long retained a pejorative implication when applied to eighteenth-century art.

DISCUSSION   Diderot's opening remarks on Boucher seem to fall into two categories of dissatisfaction:

1   His work is immoral ('corruption of morals'; 'decency, innocence' etc. are unknown to him).

2   It is an insult to nature (his grass is unrealistic; he has 'not for one instant seen nature').

Leaving aside the lack of realism or truth to nature for a moment, the moral prudishness of Diderot comes through strongly in the professed aversion to 'breasts and buttocks' explicitly and provocatively depicted. Boucher's works are totally alien to the severity and dignity of a 'bas-relief'. (Keep your notes or thoughts on the realism issue to hand, as we'll return to this later.)

Could this be the same Diderot who swoons over the charms of Madame Greuze or celebrates the joys of sexual pleasure in the *Encyclopédie* article *Enjoyment*? There is a genuine tension here between an anarchic unleashing of feeling, which leads Diderot to appreciate emotional and sensuous experiences of *all* kinds (including the sensual, the horrifying and the melancholic), and a purer, nobler brand of *moral* sensibility. Is it really possible to isolate and cultivate the latter in human nature, without unleashing the 'darker' or more selfish emotions? Is compassion to be regarded as a separate entity, functioning independently of all other feelings? Is the association of emotion with morality in the eighteenth-century cult of sensibility inherently unstable? Look back at the 'Introduction to Part E', above, pp.125–30.

EXERCISE   Read quickly through Diderot's comments on Baudouin's art (pp.281–3) and look at the relevant illustrations (Pls 183–5). Is there any evidence here of virtuous feeling, in the paintings or in Diderot's responses?

DISCUSSION   Diderot seems to succumb here to the 'continual debaucheries' of the 'old men, stick in hand, backs bent …' whom he satirizes. He contrasts Baudouin's indecencies with Greuze's virtue and talent and wants to 'reformulate' one of Baudouin's subjects so that virtue rather than vice is portrayed and fruitful pity aroused. He is quickly distracted, however, by a 'smutty' project, in which he advises Baudouin on how to add spice to his compositions. Further evidence that his submission to feeling and instinct did not always have a virtuous outcome?

Diderot was not alone in trying to forge stronger links between art and morality. The idea that the *good*, the *beautiful* and the *true* were intrinsically connected had antecedents in antiquity and was frequently reiterated by European aesthetic theorists of the late seventeenth and early eighteenth centuries. (You've already met this linking of moral and aesthetic issues in Hume's *Of the Standard of Taste*, Part B.) Aware of his role as a mentor to public taste in the *Salons*, Diderot used his allegiance to *virtuous* feelings (those inspired by some of Greuze's paintings) to strengthen the role of art as a school of morals. On a personal level, however, his enjoyment of a much broader range of feelings emerges. In *Enjoyment* he legitimized sexual pleasure in the name of Nature. Nature offers many more feelings than those arising from the innocence of young love (*Young girl crying over her dead bird*) or domesticity (*the Well-beloved Mother*).

Unfortunately, Diderot's moralism often blinded him to many of the qualities in Boucher's art admired by critics today. In 1761 he described Boucher's art, as 'an agreeable vice'. Later (in the *Salon of 1767*) however he went so far as to say that Boucher's name would not live on. Obsessed with the lack of virtue and realism in Boucher's art he failed to celebrate its mastery of linear rhythm, skilful juxtaposition of textures and use of high-keyed colours.

It is possible that Diderot saw Boucher as a particularly dangerous enemy of the moral seriousness of art because of his influence at court (as first painter to the King and a protégé of Mme de Pompadour) and in the Academy (as a teacher). It is also true that Diderot was attracted *in theory* to the contemporary wave of anti-rococo criticism even if he did not consistently respect it in practice. This wave of criticism occurred from the mid-century onwards. One critic, La Font de Saint Yenne, published his *Reflections on some of the causes of the present state of painting in France* in 1747. He criticized the vogue for decorative painting (e.g. erotic mythological scenes designed to complement rich, white and gold rococo interior decoration) encouraged by wealthy patrons such as Mme de Pompadour. His review of the 1747 Salon stated that history painters (and Boucher's mythologies were a lower branch of the history genre) should nourish the moral understanding of the public by 'presenting to our eyes the great deeds and virtues of famous men', and he saw women as the main culprits behind the growing taste for 'trivial trinkets' of contemporary art: artists should be less eager to please them.

Competitions were organized by successive *Directeurs des Bâtiments* in order to stimulate and reform history painting, and artists were encouraged increasingly to travel to Rome and immerse themselves in classicizing influences. The second half of the century witnessed a revival of elevated, classical art exemplified in the work of David. (See Pl. 186 – *The Oath of the Horatii*.) David's art succeeded in combining the morally and intellectually uplifting subject matter of classical and Renaissance art with a more naturalistic method of depiction. There is none of the sumptuous artifice which had crept into many history paintings of the earlier part of the century. Settings, costumes and accessories are rendered with greater attention to detail and accuracy and his sober, economical backgrounds contrast with the swirling 'clutter' of a Boucher.

Diderot frequently expressed support for attempts to restore ancient severity and dignity to the history genre. He admired the seventeenth-century works of Poussin, and if you compare Poussin's *Dance to the Music of Time* (Pl.131) with Boucher's *Jupiter Transformed into Diana* (Pl.177), you can see that the former uses classical allusion, a formal composition and antique, statuesque figures to comment upon the way in which all human pleasure and wealth falls victim to the passage of time (the *vanitas* theme), while the latter uses colour, light and intricacy of design to enhance the sensual appeal of his work. The different functions of these images dictate different treatments of classical elements. (These paintings are discussed at greater length on your cassette.)

From 1767 onwards, Diderot was pleased to note the increasing influence of Poussin and the bas reliefs of antiquity on history painting. It could be argued, however, that he judged Boucher's art by inappropriate criteria: his works were decorative rather than public-spirited in nature and were designed to complement the rich rococo interior decoration of royal and aristocratic homes. (Boucher also designed theatre backdrops, porcelain and tapestries.) Not only did his allegiance to nature and feeling create tensions within Diderot: what he perceived as the social and moral mission of art could, at times, blind him to its other functions. Contemporary pressures such as the anti-rococo movement informed – or rather entangled – the conflicting strands of his own critical viewpoint.

5   Art and reality

Quite apart from the *moral* defects of Boucher's art, Diderot detected its lack of realism or truth to nature. Look back at the notes you made earlier on the Boucher article. His highly artificial rococo visions are 'the dream of a fool'. His landscapes appear, from a distance, like a 'square bed of parsley'. Boucher is accused of copying and repeating figures from previous paintings ('turned and turned again'), without consulting nature (in the form of a human model) in his *Jupiter Transformed*.

Boucher is accused of stylistic laxity in many ways. His compositions are cluttered and disorganized ('insupportable hubbub') – although the 'sober and simple' pastoral scene described on pp.275–6 is a refreshing exception. There appears to be no link, claims Diderot, through visual form or association of ideas, between the diverse elements within a Boucher painting ('a cushion, my friend ...'). There is no unity of style and content: if *Jupiter Transformed* is meant to be a sensual work on the theme of seduction, Boucher should have chosen different colours and flesh tones, drawn hands more accurately, avoided frivolous distractions, stripped his nudes of their cosmetics. But it is, above all, the defective or lack of observation of nature ('you will not find one taking part in some real-life activity ...') which infuriates Diderot.

EXERCISE   Please read the entries on Chardin (*Texts*, II, pp.277–9); the last paragraph of the article on Bachelier also concerns Chardin. Look at the reproductions of the works discussed (Pl. 187 and Col. Pls 23, 25, 26, 27). Describe Chardin's response to the real, observable world as discussed by Diderot.

DISCUSSION   Chardin's art is associated with the 'search for truth'. His works are a faithful and accurate representation of the observable world: they are 'nature itself'. Objects which appear loosely sketched when viewed close up are 'true to nature' from a distance. However, Chardin is not a servile copyist of nature. Diderot constantly refers to the 'harmony' of his paintings, achieved through a careful choice and arrangement of light, colour and shape. ('The light of the sun ... incompatible colours'.) There is 'much technique' in his art, for example in the careful balancing and opposition of colours in *Third picture of refreshments.* Chardin's 'truth to nature', then, was based on a careful rearrangement and juxtaposition of natural elements. This point is explored in greater detail in TV15. (Cf. Reynolds's *Discourses, Texts,* I, p.219, in which he states that beauty 'does not consist in taking what lies immediately before you' and Johnson on the 'interpreter of nature' – *Studies,* I, p.166.)

EXERCISE   Please re-read now Diderot's comments on Boucher's *Angélique et Médor* and his *Four Pastorals.* Is nature (in the sense of the real, observable world) the only guide recommended to Boucher?

DISCUSSION   You've probably noticed that anatomical details ('no feet, no hands, no truth') and landscape details ('parsley on the trees') are criticized for their lack of truth to nature. There's more to it, however, than that. They are praised or criticized also on the basis of their fidelity to literary or poetic traditions – to nature mediated by culture. *Angélique et Médor* falls short of Quinault's vision ('How much more beautiful ...'). The pastoral scenes are praised for their matching up to the standards set by Fontenelle, if not those of Theocritus. Diderot measures these paintings against a strong imaginative conception generated by literature. You have already encountered in the study on eighteenth-century poetry the traditional association of the pastoral with an idyllic innocence. Similar traditions existed in the art world. This is an *idealized* conception of the natural world which has little to do with everyday reality.

Diderot speaks harshly, throughout the *Salon of 1765,* of history painters whose powers of mind or imagination are below standard. When his impatience becomes extreme, he resorts to re-thinking the subject (the chosen moment of action, characters, activities, groupings, expressions and poses of figures, site, accessories) on the artist's behalf. As a literary man he felt well-qualified to make pronouncements on matters of 'invention' or conceptualization, and he increasingly used his art criticism as a vehicle for his own creative skills as a writer. Pastoral and mythological scenes, as well as 'higher' branches of the history genre (biblical and historical scenes) often qualified for such treatment by Diderot: they were, after all, supposed to enlarge on or enhance reality through the uplifting or (in the case of the pastoral) 'rosy' use of the imagination – to reflect nature idealized or made beautiful.

EXERCISE   Reconsider Diderot's responses to Boucher, Chardin and Greuze and say whether you think his assessments of their works reflect the traditional views of the status of various genres. (Re-read the entries on these artists in the *Salon of 1765* and above, pp.256–64 if you need to refresh your memory.)

DISCUSSION It seems to me that Diderot's judgements are largely untouched by contemporary prejudices regarding the hierarchy of genres. Greuze's appeals to sensibility or feeling (particularly that of a moral kind) win Diderot over ('Here is your painter and mine') despite the relatively lowly genre within which he is working. Boucher's 'higher' art fails to impress because it does not move or convince Diderot. Chardin's stylistic harmony or technique and the quiet emotions ('what repose!') he inspires, more than compensate for the fact that he is dealing with 'inanimate objects', 'less interesting', intrinsically, than the human figure. He does not require the 'verve' or 'genius' of a history painter, but his technical mastery may be celebrated in its own right. (See also p.277 on Chardin's *Scullery-Maid*.)

It was common for critics to praise Chardin's 'truth to nature' and the 'magic' of his technique. His art was popular with critics and collectors and he received commissions for the royal châteaux of Bellevue and Choisy, for large decorative paintings displaying attributes of the visual arts and music, which he executed in the 1760s. The account of the 1765 Salon in the *Mercure de France* contained the statement that 'perfection in the art [of painting] places every genre above distinctions of rank' and that, in the case of artists like Chardin, the status currently attached to different genres was wrong. Most critics, however, praised his 'industriousness' and 'perfect imitation of nature' while upholding the relative inferiority of the genre within which he was working. In such a context, Diderot's attitude was challenging: Chardin's genre may be the 'easiest to master', but it could achieve its own form of greatness. Close observation of the natural world (in the case of Chardin) and emotive energy (in the case of Greuze and Vernet) could release an artist's work from the constraints of traditional critical criteria.

6   Sensibility in the work of the artist

We've already seen that Diderot was reluctant to surrender taste to a full-blooded anarchy of feeling. His views on the creative process were equally cautious. Neither he nor his contemporaries were yet ready for the full flowering of the Romantic movement. It was common to repeat Horace's dictum that the poet who wants to move others must first be moved himself by his subject. (Compare the views of C.P.E. Bach in *Studies*, I, pp.184–5.) However, this was only a small part of the story. We've already seen the rigorous routine of theory, formula and tradition to which artists were subjected (above, pp.247–9). Diderot's own views on the imitation of nature, a theme of central concern to his contemporaries, combined a respect for the ancients' ability to construct an idealized, refined view of Nature with an emphasis on close empirical study of the observable world. The function or genre of a work affected the emphasis he placed on these elements. (Compare Gill Perry's discussion of Reynolds's shifting response to the antique and to an exact likeness in portraiture in *Studies*, I, pp.253–63.) We know that Diderot read Leonardo da Vinci's *Trattato della Pittura* (*Treatise on Painting*), which emphasized the importance of close observation of nature *and* a judicious selection from nature in the interests of avoiding the monstrous.

It is hardly surprising that such aesthetic priorities gave rise to an emphasis on study, experimentation and careful judgement or reasoning (all sound Enlightenment qualities) in the work of artists. Many contemporary theorists shared Diderot's view that *at some stage* artists must become imaginatively and emotionally involved with their subject ('enthusiasm' was a word often used to describe this kind of creative fervour),[13] but there was something quite calculated and controlled about this process as they described it. Roger de Piles (1708) recommended that artists should study themselves in a mirror or use skilled models in order to render effectively physiognomic expression (in which character or the feelings of the heart are expressed in facial features) in their paintings: they should prepare their work through careful reasoning and through the *control* of the imagination common in actors. Theorists rarely specified any sequential relationship between rational thought and flights of enthusiasm in the creative process but agreed that both elements were necessary.

EXERCISE   Please read Diderot's commentary on the art of Carle van Loo (*Texts*, II, pp.271–3) and look at the relevant illustrations (Pls 188–90). Which qualities and faculties does he feel are important to the artist?

DISCUSSION   The most striking ideas on this subject, in my view, are those expressed in the first paragraph of the commentary on the *Sketches for the Chapel of Saint Gregory*. Van Loo is described as a 'brute', uneducated and melancholy,[14] an untameable bird very different from the 'chaffinches' or superficial wits of the contemporary social and artistic world. (Cf. his association of great art with crime at the beginning of the Greuze entry, p.283.) Diderot seems to imply that the great artist submits to uncontrolled ('wild' and 'untameable') emotion or inspiration. He frequently responded in a positive manner to sketches, which he saw as a less finished and controlled but more direct expression of the artist's mood or feeling. (See his commentary on *The Well-beloved Mother*, *Texts*, II, p.287.) He therefore challenged implicitly the traditional respect accorded to highly finished paintings. To Diderot, the sketch was analogous to poetry, powerful in its use of the inexplicit. Here we encounter a marked vein of pre-romanticism.

True to his propensity for contradiction, however, he did not advocate such values in a whole-hearted way. His commentary on *The Graces* decries van Loo's inadequate powers of imagination and conceptualization. He did not succeed in equalling the beauties of the subject extracted by ancient poets. (And Diderot is anxious to prove that his own mind and imagination *are* equal to this task.) At first it seems that Diderot

---

[13]   The word 'enthusiasm' often assumed a more pejorative meaning when used to denote religious fervour. See Gibbon in *Texts*, I, p.296 and the reference to 'Fanatical credulity' in *Studies*, I, p.318. See also *Studies*, I, p.x.

[14]   On the positive, fashionable connotations of 'melancholy' in eighteenth-century English verse see *Texts*, II, p.101.

is advocating a poetic abandonment to the feelings and visions latent in the subject. Very quickly, however, he resorts to common-sense argument as he criticizes van Loo for his inappropriate attempts to preserve decency in the scene ('those little scraps of material ...'). The artist's handling of paint is inappropriate for the figures of the Graces; the cloud 'doesn't make sense'. It is not only the artist's imagination which is deficient but also his morality, his ability to learn from the ancients and his ability to construct a coherent composition which makes internal 'sense'. Van Loo, according to Diderot, has committed basic errors of *judgement*, a faculty indispensable (however implicitly or intuitively) to artists. (Cf. the early views of Reynolds on genius, of which *intellectual* labour was an important component. See *Studies*, I, p.266.)

In his discussion of *Chaste Susanna*, Diderot praises the choice of colours, the facial expression of Susanna, the drawing, the unified effect, the harmony of light and shade. Drapes, and the actions and expressions of the old men are, however, less successful. Van Loo has failed to produce the full emotional intensity and interest inherent in his subject. Diderot speaks as if paintings are susceptible of an internal *logic* (harmonious relationship of parts) which must be intuitively grasped by artists. He does not object to the possibility that Susanna has been painted from a carefully posed model. Reasoned calculation of the effect of a painting is quite legitimate in his view. Reason and common sense are an important part of an artist's armoury.

You may recall how, in the commentary on Vernet (p.280), Diderot described his vivid dramas, as the result of a combination of 'verve' and 'judgement'. Vernet was described as wielding a thunderbolt as powerful as Jupiter's: yet, at the same time, he was 'harmonious' and 'wise'. Artists like L'Épicié, who lack imagination, and paint in a routine manner, attract Diderot's scorn. But those who submit to 'enthusiasm' must not allow this to lead them into errors of judgement, such as the 'slack and yellow bosom' of Mme Greuze (p.286). Chardin's technique achieves wondrous effects despite the lack of 'verve' in his paintings: this is less important, implies Diderot, in the lower genres.

Diderot embodies the aspect of Enlightenment thought which sought to assess the claims of reason and feeling. Nature, it seems, demands both for its effective representation in art and for a full appreciation of all the experiences it offers. In a work entitled *The Paradox of the Actor* (1773) Diderot tried to identify the essence of great acting. He concluded that the great actor, like the great artist, must experience emotional excitement but must control this in order to give an effective performance:

> Calmness must temper the delirium of enthusiasm. (Diderot, 1964, p.309; my translation)

In another work, *d'Alembert's Dream* (1769), he put forward the thesis that great artists are those who learn to control their unusually keen emotional sensitivity:

> Now the superior man who has unfortunately been born with this kind of disposition will constantly strive to suppress it, dominate it, master its impulses.... Then he will keep his self-possession amid the

greatest dangers and judge coolly but sanely ... by forty-five he will be a great king, statesman, politician, artist and especially a great actor, philosopher, poet, musician, doctor, in fact be master of himself and everything around him ... (Diderot, 1964, p.357)

For Diderot, extraordinary talent in any sphere arose from the power to control a special gift of sensibility – the quality he so proudly detected in himself.

7 References

Assézat, J. and Tourneux, M. (eds) (1875–7) *Ouevres complètes de Diderot*, vol.X, Garnir Fréres, Paris.

Brookner, A. (1972) *Greuze*, Elek, London.

Bukdahl, E.M., Delon and Lorenceau, A. (eds) (1990) *Oeuvres complètes de Diderot*, vol. xvi, Hermann, Paris. (The full works are edited by Dieckmann *et al.* and are listed below in 8.1.)

Conisbee, P. (1981) *Painting in Eighteenth-Century France*, Phaidon, Oxford.

Diderot, D. (1964) 'Le Rêve de d'Alembert' in *Oeuvres philosophiques*, Garnier, Paris.

Diderot, D. (1968) 'Le Paradoxe sur le comédien', in *Oeuvres esthétiques*, Garnier, Paris.

La Font de Saint Yenne (1970) *Sentiments sur quelques ouvrages de peinture, sculpture et gravure écrits à un particular en province*, or *Some Thoughts on Works of Painting, Sculpture and Engraving, written to a Person in the Provinces*, Slatkine reprint in the 1754 edn. Geneva.

Lacombe, J. *Le Salon*, Fonds Deloynes V Item 55, Bibliothèque Nationale, Paris.

May, G. (1963) 'In defense of Diderot's art criticism', *French Review*, vol.37, pp.11–21.

Piles, R. de (1708) *Cours de peinture par principes* or *Lessons on the Principles of Painting*, Paris.

Seznec, J. and Adhemar, J. (1979) *Diderot: Salons*, vol.II, Clarendon Press, Oxford.

Sgard, J. (ed.) (1992) *Dictionnaire des Journaux 1600–1709*, Universitas, Paris.

Topazio, V. (1963) 'Diderot's limitations as an art critic', *French Review*, vol.37, pp.3–11.

Wilson, A. (1972) *Diderot*, Oxford University Press, New York.

Zmijewska, H. (1970) 'La Critique des Salons en France avant Diderot', *Gazette des Beaux-arts*, July-August.

8 Further reading

8.1 Texts

For those who read French:

Diderot, D. (1759–81) *Salons*. Complete French text with illustrations, vols.I–IV, Oxford, Clarendon Press, 1960. (Text established and introduced by Jean Seznec and Jean Adhémar. *The Salon of 1765* is in Vol.II (1st edn. 1960; 2nd edn. 1975).)

Dieckmann, H., Mauzi, R., and Varloot, J. (1984) *Oeuvres complètes de Diderot*, vol.XIV, Hermann, Paris. (This edition contains excellent editorial information on Diderot's text and on the paintings he discusses.)

8.2 General works

Brookner, A. (1972) *Greuze*, Elek, London (good on sensibility).

Conisbee, P. (1981) *Painting in Eighteenth-century France*, Phaidon, Oxford, (excellent historical introduction, to which the historical survey in the present study is largely indebted).

Conisbee, P. (1986) *Chardin*, Phaidon, Oxford.

Crow, T.E. (1985) *Painters and Public Life in Eighteenth-Century Paris*, Yale University Press, New Haven and London, (good on the official status of art, artists and exhibitions.)

Levey, M. (1966) *Rococo to Revolution*, Thames and Hudson, London.

Laclos – Dangerous Acquaintances

Prepared for the Course Team by Angus Calder

Contents

Laclos – Dangerous Acquaintances *(Study weeks 30–31)*

Studies/Texts	Radio	TV	AC	Set Books
Studies, II	Radio 7	TV16		*Dangerous Acquaintances*
Texts, II	Radio 8			

For this fortnight's work you will neeed this *Studies* volume and *Texts*, II as well as the set novel edited by Richard Aldington.

Laclos – Dangerous Acquaintances

1   Introduction

Best sellers commonly perish like gnats in autumn. Some survive longer, only to die after two or three generations of readers have used them. Macpherson's *Ossian* is a salient example from the eighteenth century. Laclos's novel *Les Liaisons Dangereuses* shows, however, that a title can make its way back to general acclaim after two centuries.

EXERCISE   You should by now have read, or be reading, the novel. Please now read, or re-read, Aldington's Introduction, and note what he says about its first reception.

DISCUSSION   When the novel appeared in Paris in 1783, a first printing of 2000 copies sold out immediately. The print run was promptly repeated. The first English translation (*Dangerous Connections*) appeared in 1784, a little later than the first German version. 'Pirated' editions, from which Laclos received no profit, appeared in spate in France. Laclos authorized an edition published in London, but in French, in 1796. The title *Dangerous Acquaintances* emerged with a second English translation in 1797. The book limped into Spanish in 1818. But its status was due to decline steeply.

In France, it was relegated to the level of pornography. In Britain, there was a precocious but furtive revival only in 1898 when that archetypal poet of the 'decadent' Nineties, Ernest Dowson ('I have been faithful to thee, Cynara, in my fashion') had his new translation privately printed. The first new version in German for exactly 100 years followed in 1899, the first-ever translation into Italian in 1914. Meanwhile, two biographies published in France in 1905 did something to detach Laclos from his monstrous fictional protagonist, Valmont. Richard Aldington's still-standard translation into English, in 1924, confirmed Laclos's significance in the history of the European novel.

But, if interest in France was vivid in the years after the Second World War (where existentialist philosophy and the feminism of Simone de Beauvoir made their impact, and where, in 1959, a modernized version of the story was filmed) it was not until 1968 that the novel, in P.W.K. Stone's translation, became available in Britain as a 'Penguin Classic', and not till the late 1980s that the success of Christopher Hampton's stage adaptation in London and New York, and of Stephen Frears's film based on Hampton's script, confirmed the novel's 'great' stature here.

What this pattern of transmission over two hundred years demonstrates is not merely that, for some reason, late twentieth-century audiences felt an affinity with Laclos's text impossible for most readers of earlier generations – but also the existence of that huge intervening gap which calls into question our capacity to relate to the text at all. There is no continuous history of response. In 1917, the dominant English critic

Figure 31
Portrait of Laclos.
(Musée d'Art Local et
d'Histoire, Amiens. Photo:
Giraudon)

of the day, Professor George Saintsbury, explained his exclusion of *Dangerous Acquaintances* from his *History of the French Novel* on the grounds that he was 'unable to find any redeeming features in it'.

A similar problem, as Susan Khin Zaw has shown, exists in the case of Mary Wollstonecraft. With a text marginalized and excluded over such a long period, we may have to jettison our usual confidence that we know 'how to read'; we may have to explore new ways of reading. If we relate too easily to the matter presented by these two writers, aren't we 're-writing' their texts to suit our own generation? (A colleague reports on an audience's reaction to Hampton's play, how it 'colluded with, and egged on the atrocious behaviour on the stage. Stout-booted feminists in the audience were manifestly taking pleasure in the debauching of a sister'.) But trying to read Wollstonecraft and Laclos on 'their own terms' involves an effort of historical imagination.

They have more in common, we find, than the fact that both were controversial in their own time and thereafter anathematized, misunderstood and neglected. Both were preoccupied with the problem of how to weight feeling as against reason. Neither could produce an easy solution: in Laclos's novel the issue is exposed but in no way resolved. Both were profoundly concerned with an issue which Rousseau's *Émile* had 'resolved' at the cost of glibness and effectual inhumanity: what sort of 'human nature' did women possess, what were their valid roles and legitimate scope, and how should they be educated – or *educate themselves* – for life?

Thinking about Laclos's posthumous reputation, one might superficially, though usefully, jump to conclusions like these: (a) Laclos's frank presentation of sexuality was relatively acceptable in the 1780s, and for a time thereafter, when 'Enlightened' tolerance and suspicion of priestly codes of behaviour made for freedom of thought. But (b) by the mid-nineteenth century the classic 'bourgeois' values which we can perceive as evolving in the paintings of Chardin dominated over most of Europe: these elevated the domestic role of woman as wife and mother, and made Laclos's novel too terrifying to be read. The revival of his 'serious' reputation (c) in the couple of decades before the First World War relates to new stirrings of 'free' thought and the political expression of feminism. Aldington was an important writer on the fringe of the tendency known as 'Bloomsbury', where ideas of 'free love' were carried out more-or-less openly. And (d) it is not surprising that the Penguin translation should arrive in a decade, the 1960s, where, partly thanks to the invention of the 'pill', 'free love' became a much more widely acceptable idea; nor (e) that the final triumph of Laclos in Anglo-Saxon culture – as dramatized – should coincide with the 'realism', or cynicism, of the 'Yuppie' decade, the 'Thatcher years'.

Such observations in fact help to explain not what the book is or says but why it was published and found an audience. So far from advocating 'love', let alone 'free love', Laclos's novel is in effect deeply sceptical about the value of 'love', very alert to its extreme dangers. So far from presenting an arena of hedonistic, carefree sexuality, Laclos brings before us characters who are locked claustrophobically into social conventions which make the open expression of intent and emotion impossible and necessitate one-to-one clandestine interviews and obsessive letter writing. Hampton's excellent adaptations for stage and film work very well, but can only do so at the cost of violating – or inverting – the very nature of Laclos's novel. It is crucial in *Dangerous Acquaintances* that there is no direct meeting between Madame de Merteuil and Valmont until, very near its end, he bursts in on her treacherous twosome with Danceny. To tell the story as drama, Hampton has to transfer their plotting from correspondence to conversation. Whereas, if they were often together, the novel could not exist.

Such an 'epistolary novel' can hardly be written in the late twentieth century. To say that a modern Valmont would use fax machines and a portable telephone is to show at once that there can be *no* modern Valmont. Just as his activities reflect the scope, and lack of scope, of an *ancien régime* aristocrat, so his methods, even his personality, depend on letter writing. This is not perhaps a wholly 'lost art', but since the invention of the telephone, people haven't used letters of absolute necessity for intimate correspondence. We may find in Valmont or Merteuil dilemmas and impulses which relate to those which we believe to be our own (note that the novel forcefully confronts us with the problem of how well we can truly 'know ourselves'). But we cannot agree, as Aldington does in his introduction, with the notion that they are eternal 'types' of something innate in human psychology. They belong in that foreign country, the 1780s.

Why did the book scandalize some people then? Not because of explicit descriptions of the sexual act. *Dangerous Acquaintances* is rarely if ever at all titillating. The act of human coupling is usually referred to by the curt verb 'avoir', 'to have'. An experienced adult will find Valmont's account of his sexual assault on a minor, Cécile, in Letter XCVI (pp.260–5) graphic enough. But an 'innocent' young person would not be able to understand it and could not possibly be corrupted by it. In one of the funnier passages in a novel which can, for a reader in the right mood, be very mirthful indeed, Valmont tells Merteuil how he is teaching Cécile the technical terms related to their lovemaking. 'Nothing could be more amusing than the ingeniousness with which she already uses the little she knows of this speech! She does not imagine that anyone can speak otherwise' (Letter CX, p.306). But a convent girl reading the book would receive no hint as to what words were employed or what they denoted. Much lewder books – some of them mentioned in *Dangerous Acquaintances* itself – were available to French readers in the 1780s: *Le Sopha*, by Crébillon, for instance. Turnell (1950) noted this and concluded that fine ladies must have got cross with Laclos because he 'let the cat out of the bag' – revealed aristocratic sexual behaviour realistically in all its nastiness' (p.52).

Aldington offers a rather more complex explanation (pp.6, 7). Because it was supposed that Laclos had based his novel on real people, 'keys' to the novel were circulated in conversation. It upset people who were held to be models for Merteuil and Valmont: the dignity of a class wasn't at stake, only the reputations of individuals within it.

Nevertheless, Aldington himself pushes us to suppose that the book was a 'political' gesture. It is very tempting to see Laclos, subsequently a Jacobin, then a Napoleonic general, as a closet revolutionary, demonstrating with rage in his novel that it was decadence within the ruling class which made Revolution inevitable. But we know and can deduce little about Laclos's deeper feelings from the remaining biographical evidence. We do know that some members of the aristocracy read work by Enlightened *philosophes* and some came out in support of revolution – notably the King's cousin, the Duc d'Orléans, to whom Laclos became secretary in 1788. As Lord Byron, born in that year, would exemplify, it was perfectly possible to combine promiscuous aristocratic sexuality with support for liberal revolution.

We may take more seriously Aldington's point (p.6) that 'All the women were angry with the creator of Mme. de Merteuil'. The novel, read superficially, might seem to imply that all women are either cheats or dupes – and, beyond that, presents, in the Marquise, a figure as 'wicked' as any in literature. Surely it wasn't the novel's erotic subject matter which caused immediate scandal and, in the nineteenth century, drove it underground? It was, more likely, its seriousness; Laclos's uncompromising refusal to balance Merteuil's evil with virtue strong enough to counter it, and his subversion of the idea of 'love' both in its earthly and divine aspects. Not only the evil Merteuil but also the good natured Madame de Rosemonde see the 'feminine' propensity for self-sacrificial love as dangerous to women. But if women cannot fulfil themselves in love, what other sphere remains in which they can find significance?

The major poet Baudelaire, who made notes on *Dangerous Acquaintances* in the 1850s, regarded it as a moral work 'as lofty as the most elevated, as profound as the most profound'. The vices of Merteuil and Valmont, the follies of their dupes, are sternly punished (though the rehabilitation of the womanizing Prévan shows that society at large will go on as before). Laclos provides no answer to the questions he raises, but they are very serious questions, seriously raised, and are characteristic concerns of his period. They are dramatized for us through invented characters (it is quite immaterial whether Laclos had real-life 'models' for them in mind). Though the 'story' is mostly presented to us by Merteuil and Valmont, neither represents the author's viewpoint, and we are invited to assess their opinions objectively, along with those of other invented personages. We are also invited to consider how conventions, determining the ways in which we write, may modify and distort the expression of fact and feeling.

2   An epistolary novel about letter writing

By the time when Laclos came to use it, the form of the 'epistolary novel'[1] was well established. In 1739, a middle-aged London printer, Samuel Richardson (1689–1761) agreed to a proposal by two booksellers that he should compile a volume of model letters for unskilled writers. He duly did so, but was further inspired to develop a story which he had heard into a novel told through a series of letters: *Pamela* (1740). He followed up its vast success with *Clarissa* (1747–9) – a work well known to both Valmont and Madame de Tourvel – in which the heroine is tragically seduced by a charming aristocrat, Lovelace. This stimulated the use of the epistolary form throughout Europe.

The novel in letters permitted a richer exploration of individual psychology than was then possible through the use of alternative conventions. The succinct, quick-fire narrative of Voltaire's tales, seen in *Candide*,

---

[1]   From 'epistle', a letter.

is no more fitted than present-day 'comic strip' to the exploration of motive and passion in depth. The 'comic-epic-in prose', as Fielding called his *Tom Jones* (1749) – a book which Laclos greatly admired for its skill in construction – depended on the convention of an 'outside' narrator, knowing about his characters but not, so to speak, 'inside them'. The fictitious autobiography, as developed by Daniel Defoe (*Robinson Crusoe*, 1719; *Moll Flanders*, 1722) did indeed permit 'self exploration' by the narrators, much as we find in Equiano's *Life* of himself: but stories are developed 'in hindsight', and the narrator's own self-analysis cannot be contested. What the epistolary form permitted was the illumination of the psychology of people in the midst of unresolved crisis, and the presentation of several different views of the crisis in question. It had some of the immediacy of drama.

But on the stage, characters are supposed to be delivering their thoughts and feelings more or less spontaneously. This cannot, as a rule, be the case with letters. To revert to Hampton's play and film script based on *Dangerous Acquaintances*: while they can convey the calculating, artificial behaviour and speech of Merteuil and Valmont, they necessarily omit the dimension – letterwriting – in which they carefully, *in absentia*, present themselves to each other. A whole layer of potential deviousness and of sophistication in artifice is therefore stripped away.

EXERCISE   Please read, or re-read letters II and IV in Laclos's novel (pp.67–71), then read the following extract from Hampton's film script. Consider, first, what the latter 'leaves out', and, secondly, in what ways it may simplify the Merteuil–Valmont relationship.

MERTEUIL: And he'd get back from honeymoon to find himself the laughing stock of Paris.

VALMONT: Well …

MERTEUIL: Yes. Love and revenge: two of your favourites.

(*Silence*. Valmont considers for a moment. Finally, he shakes his head.)

VALMONT: No, I can't.

MERTEUIL: What?

VALMONT: Really, I can't.

MERTEUIL: Why not?

VALMONT: It's too easy. It is. She's seen nothing, she knows nothing, she's bound to be curious, she'd be on her back before you'd unwrapped the first bunch of flowers. Any one of a dozen men could manage it. I have my reputation to think of.

(Merteuil frowns, displeased. Valmont moves over to sit next to her.)

VALMONT: I can see I'm going to have to tell you everything.

MERTEUIL: Of course you are.

VALMONT: Yes. Well. My aunt is not on her own just now. She has a young friend staying with her.

(At this point Valmont's voice becomes 'voice over', he says 'Madame de Tourvel' and we have cut to a shot of Tourvel and Rosemonde together in the garden of the latter's château.) (Hampton, 1989, pp.5–6)

DISCUSSION The most notable feature of the text which is wholly 'left out' is the easy, witty, bantering tone with which Merteuil and Valmont address each other in these first letters. In the novel, each professes affection for the other, each speaks lightly of alternative attractions. 'You see that love does not blind me', writes Merteuil, referring to her 'reigning Chevalier'. 'I must have this woman, to save myself from the ridiculous position of being in love with her,' retorts Valmont. Whereas the film gives their relationship a 'heavy' aspect. ('Merteuil frowns, displeased. Valmont moves over to sit next to her.') In the novel, the pair are accomplished ironists, urbane wits, whose manners of writing are very similar and whose attitudes are equally cynical: in the film, Valmont is at once established as being at some disadvantage – *he* moves over, *he* says 'I can see I'm going to have to tell you everything'. This pre-empts answers to questions about their relationship which are in suspense throughout Laclos's novel and are never clearly resolved.

A further point. In the novel, Valmont tells Merteuil and us that he finds Tourvel alluring. But he does not describe her physical charms. He does not need to, since Merteuil has seen her. (Merteuil, on the other hand, needs must describe Cécile to him: she does so rather in the manner of a race-horse owner offering a filly for sale.) What is left unclear is whether it is her physical loveliness (Rosemonde calls her 'Beauty') or the challenge of her moral uprightness which chiefly compels Valmont towards her. The film, showing us an actress playing Tourvel in an idyllic setting, again pre-empts heterosexual judgement, this time in a more complex way: a male member of the audience might not find the actress especially beautiful, or even sensuous, but whether or not that is the case, his first response to Tourvel is as a physical rather than moral phenomenon.

Merteuil, we must assume, is teased by the question we've asked as much as we are. Does Tourvel represent to Valmont, as he himself protests right to the end, primarily a 'challenge' to be overcome as he advances his 'career' as the most notorious libertine of the day? Is she, rather more weightily, a representative of the 'enemy' – the virtues which stand against the materialism and cynicism which he shares with Merteuil? Or is he 'really' allured uncontrollably by her physique and personality?

We'll return to this matter. Meanwhile, I ask you to remember the extent to which Laclos emphasizes to us that we are reading *letters*. In letters certain conventions apply (the simplest being those which compel us to address enemies as 'dear' and to profess ourselves 'faithful' or 'true' or 'sincere' towards people to whom we are lying).

The choice of style is always available to us, if we have skill enough to exercise it (but even the least skilful writer addresses loved one and bank manager differently).

EXERCISE Please now read, or re-read on to the end of the novel, thinking about the implications of 'epistolary style'.

DISCUSSION In Letter CL (pp.389–90) Danceny goes on at length about his sense of deprivation because Merteuil has declared that their correspondence must cease. Danceny insists that letters from the loved one – talismanic even if unopened, even if unread – provide the direct expression of feeling, put lovers directly in touch with each other's inner selves … 'A letter is the soul's portrait'. Through letter writing, the solitary lover can pass on each emotion in turn – 'joy … involuntary sadness'. The deliciously absurd Danceny almost implies that the sharing of feelings through letters makes meeting redundant. The highly artificial business of putting pen to paper becomes in his imagination as 'natural' as the singing of shepherds is supposed to be in pastoral tradition.

These characteristic absurdities would be merely amusing had we not just read Letter CXLIX (pp.386–88). In Madame de Volange's factual-seeming account of the death of her friend Madame de Tourvel, it is clear that a final letter from Valmont effectually kills her. Ironically, Danceny's blatherings contain an element of truth – letters may not be natural outpourings of spontaneous feeling, but they are powerful things: so powerful that they can kill Tourvel and (as we shall soon see) utterly ruin Merteuil. *Dangerous Acquaintances* is not just a 'novel-in-letters' – it is a novel about letter-writers writing letters.

Letter XLVIII (pp.151–2) is so significant and striking that its composition is included in the Hampton–Frears film. It's the one which Valmont composes to Tourvel, 'from the bed and almost in the arms of a girl, interrupted even for a complete infidelity …', using Émilie's naked body as his desk (p.150). As he triumphantly tells Merteuil, it provides 'an exact description of my situation and my conduct'.

Yet it reads as a wholly 'conventional' outpouring of love towards Tourvel.

This is indeed a 'restless night'. Valmont, in truth, 'can scarcely preserve sufficient control' over himself. And so on. Laclos/Valmont's subversion of the conventional language of love is consummated (so to speak) when 'the very table upon which I write to you, which for the first time is devoted to that use, becomes for me the sacred altar of love …' The satire here should lead us to question every expression of feeling in the novel: by demonstrating how language can be simultaneously truthful and mendacious, Laclos points to the instability and imprecision which are latent in all uses of language, and the fact that we write and read within conventions, designed to bring language under control and make it intelligible, which are inherently limiting and artificial.

With Letter CXVII (p.321), even in translation (since Aldington is skilful in differentiating epistolary styles) we can see how different from Cécile's previously artless expression is the conventional language dictated to her by Valmont. But, having taken this point, what do we make of the previous letter from Danceny? He is well on the way to being seduced by Merteuil (or, as he will flatter himself, seducing her).

EXERCISE   Do we take Danceny's expressions (pp.320–1) at face value? If not, is it necessary to accuse him of insincerity?

DISCUSSION   Obviously, knowing more than Cécile, we are inclined to snigger over Danceny's exalted enthusiasm. But I think that what we smirk over is not a deception of Cécile, but Danceny's failure to understand himself: he deceives himself, idealistically, in believing that 'friendship' alone draws him to Merteuil.

With cleverer and more experienced letter-writers it is more difficult to see where the borderline between calculation and self deception might lie. This applies even to Madame de Rosemonde: what part do her affection for Valmont, and fears concerning him, play in her letters to Tourvel? With Merteuil and Valmont, deliberate deception of others is often declared. But to what extent are they deliberately deceiving each other? And do they, despite their attempts to cultivate an invulnerable cynicism, truly deceive themselves?

EXERCISE Look at the very important Letter CXLI (pp.371–4), in which Merteuil herself asks Valmont, 'Tell me the truth: are you deluding yourself or are you trying to deceive me?' How do we interpret her own motives at this point? Is she 'really' in 'love' with Valmont, determined to wrest him from Tourvel? Or is her motivation in writing this different? If so, what can it be? Finally how does the tone of this letter compare to that of Letter II (pp.67–8), her first in the novel?

DISCUSSION Taking the last point first, there is still a strong element of elegant, self-possessed banter, of dry wit depending for its effect on Valmont's sharing her own sense of irony. ('He who abstains from it today is considered romantic; and I do not think that is the fault I blame you for.')

But there does seem to be an element also of genuine fury. Over what? From the fourth paragraph we might deduce two somewhat contradictory motives. First, she is jealous of Tourvel – 'You left me "for this great event" '. Secondly, that she is outraged by what we would now call Valmont's 'male chauvinism' – 'like a Sultan, you are never a woman's lover or friend, but always her tyrant or her slave'.

There follows her apparently playful 'story'. Rather than pursue her anger, she teases him with the prospect that he will lose his reputation as the cynical libertine *par excellence*, and offers him a weapon which she correctly prophesies will be lethal to his affair with Tourvel, the appalling letter of which the refrain is 'it is not my fault'. Then she returns to business as usual. Whether, by this stage in the novel, one finds her witty 'condolences' to Valmont on the loss of his 'posterity' (through Cécile's miscarriage), funny or shocking may depend on one's own mood.

In any case, Merteuil's letter is immediately, astonishingly, effective. Valmont 'gets the message' and acts immediately. But what are *his* motives? It is clear that he expected Tourvel to reply almost at once. Why is he so impatient for her reply? Is it because he wants to show it to Merteuil and claim his long-anticipated copulation with her? That is what he suggests to Merteuil. Or does he (perhaps sub-consciously) want to put Merteuil decisively down? She taunts him with the superiority of her 'system' to his: very well, he will show her that contrary to her supposition, Tourvel will not break with him entirely.

The element of *rivalry* in the Merteuil–Valmont relationship is obvious. Is it, furthermore, the case that Merteuil really hates Valmont and is, from Letter II onward, plotting to destroy him? This has been argued. Perhaps, Patrick Byrne (1989, pp.77ff) suggests, Merteuil only picked him, after her humiliation by Gercourt, because she could dominate him and manipulate him, not only as an instrument through which to retaliate against Gercourt, but as a man to be humiliated in his turn. Valmont deludedly believes that her promise, in Letter XX (pp.96–7), to 'sleep' with him (as we, strangely, say) after he has accomplished his mission proves that she loves him, whereas she proposes it merely as an incentive for him to hasten his affair with La Présidente and get on with debauching Cécile. Meanwhile, she cynically betrays what she knows of Valmont to Madame de Volanges.

I myself rule this interpretation out. Would the woman Byrne imagines be so foolish as to put into Valmont's hands the long autobiographical Letter LXXXI (pp.220–9), which Danceny (Letters CLXVIII and CLXIX, pp.414–8) will eventually single out as the means of wholly destroying her reputation? But other readers may find it illuminating, as I did, to consider Byrne's interpretation. It helps one to dispose of the rather sentimental notion that Merteuil exposes Valmont to Danceny only because she loves him and is insanely unbalanced by her jealousy of Tourvel.

What is at issue between them is power. To aid them in the quest for power, both have, we must assume, 'good looks' and abundant charm. They are also the best-read people in the novel, the wittiest, and the best letter-writers. Through letters, they advertise their powers to each other, and through letters they manipulate those other people whom they consider to be mere automata, creatures of 'Nature', of carnal instinct (Cécile) and of convention (Volanges and Danceny).

The letter as social convention is, to repeat an earlier point, a subject within the novel in its own right. Letters hover between 'direct self-expression' and 'complete literary artifice', and we are perpetually tantalized, reading and re-reading this enigmatic book, to decide which extreme we are closest to.

3   Love and marriage – 'reason' and passion

The major figures of the European Enlightenment were unimpressed by the elevation of sexual passion to transcendent value. The ideas that man and woman could find eternal happiness in each other's arms and constant company, or that the lover's yearnings might be compared to those of the soul towards God, were at odds with the drive towards demystification present in the dry, ironical scepticism characteristic of the period.

Even the genial English novelist Henry Fielding, while presenting a case for True Love against the 'arranged marriage' in his ever-popular *Tom Jones* (1749), couldn't resist poking fun at his young people and their amorous raptures: his hero, while good-hearted, is very far from monogamous. Mozart's operas contain poignant and delicious expressions of love – but these are presented either on the level of fantasy and folk-tale (*Seraglio, The Magic Flute*) or in a quasi-realistic context where every character, however heartfelt his or her outpourings at any one moment, is apparently capable of intriguing against, and betraying, each or all of the others (*The Marriage of Figaro, Così Fan Tutte, Don Giovanni*). While the paintings of Boucher and Fragonard radiate no more than titillating carnality, the bourgeois morality of Chardin shies away from passionate abandonment. And so on.

The era produced epic figures of promiscuous sexual adventure. Besides the Great Tsarina, Catherine, there was Giovanni Jacopo Casanova (1725–98), still a by-word today. The horrors of VD did not deter the interminably randy James Boswell, nor his much more wholesome compatriot Robert Burns. The latter's best work explores real tenderness, as well as frank lust. But though Burns, loyal to his Jean in his fashion, can be seen, like Mozart, as anticipating the 'Romantic' movement, neither was actually 'Romantic' in attitude. They shared in the level-headed view of sexuality characteristic of the *philosophes*.

Like Gibbon, Hume eschewed the tribulations of marriage. Diderot wrote to his friend and lover Sophie Volland that what he liked in a brothel was that you could be yourself there. 'You find all sorts of things in these ladies of easy virtue that you would not hope to find in a respectable woman, quite apart from the great advantage of being yourself with them, not vain about your good qualities or ashamed of your bad ones.' Voltaire was deeply shocked by the death of his long-term mistress Madame de Châtelet in 1745 – then sensibly had his niece Mme Denis combine the functions, at Ferney, of housekeeper and bedfellow. From the frontier country of North America – acclaimed by French thinkers as the house of noble Red Indian savages and of austere republican virtue – the voice of the esteemed scientist, journalist and, eventually, statesman Benjamin Franklin had produced perhaps the most direct statement (outside Laclos) of Enlightened Man's rational attitude to sex, in a letter of 'Advice to a Young Man' published in 1745. For Franklin, the Pennsylvanian, and his commercially minded American readers, the *appearance* of virtue was an important business asset. And marriage, Franklin averred, was the most likely basis for 'solid Happiness'. But if you don't fancy marriage, yet 'persist in thinking a commerce with the sex inevitable', the best idea is to go for 'old women'. First, they knew more about the world. Having, secondly, 'ceased to be handsome' they strove to 'maintain their influence over men' by being 'tender' and 'amiable'. There was, third, no risk of children. Fourthly, being experienced, they could conduct 'an intrigue' discreetly without hazard to a man's reputation. And, fifth:

> In every Animal that walks upright, the deficiency of the fluids that fill the muscles appears first in the highest part. The face first grows dark and wrinkled, then the neck, then the Breast and Arms, the lower Parts continuing to the last as plump as ever; so that covering all above with the Basket, and regarding only what is below the Girdle, it is impossible of two Women to know an old one from a young one. And as in the Dark all Cats are grey, the Pleasure of Corporal Enjoyment with an old Women is at least equal and frequently superior; every Knack being by practice capable of Improvement. Better to make an old woman happy than to debauch a virgin. (Franklin, 1940, pp.226–8)

Attempts to debauch virgins had sustained the plots of *Pamela* and *Clarissa* by Samuel Richardson, Laclos's predecessor in the epistolary novel. *Clarissa* is the archetype of the 'novel of sentiment'. From about 1750, a new current in European sensibility begins to flow: readers like to shudder and weep over the sad fates of others, or brood on the melancholy of unrequitable 'love'. Tearful heroes appear, like Henry Mackenzie's *Man of Feeling* (1771): in one later edition of exactly 200 pages, 47 instances of tears ('Chokings, etc., not counted') are listed in a tongue-in-cheek index. The noble struggles with passion of Rousseau's protagonists in *La Nouvelle Heloïse* (1761) prepared readers for the tragic fate of the hero of Goethe's *Sorrows of Young Werther* (1774) – another epistolary novel. Werther blows his brains out, hopelessly in love with a virtuous married woman. His last letter to her reads in part:

> I want to be buried, Lotte, in the clothes I have on. You have touched them and made them sacred ... My soul floats over the coffin. Please let no one go through my pockets. The pale pink bow that you wore at your breast when I saw you for the first time with your children – kiss them a thousand times and tell them the fate of their unfortunate friend. The darlings – they are tumbling all around me. Ah, how I attached myself to you from the first moment and could not let go. This bow is to be buried with me. You gave it to me on my birthday. (Hutter, 1962, p.126)

Yet the same Goethe, in one of his 'Roman Elegies' of the late 1780s perhaps remembered Valmont as he wrote of his mistress:

> Often too in her arms I've lain composing a poem,
> Gently with fingering hand count the hexameter's beat
> Out on her back. (Hamburger, 1958, pp.228–9)

The cult of Sentiment in which he had himself participated threatened that happy equipoise between carnality and reason which Goethe's poem displays. In the great plays from the previous century still seen on French and British stages, the dangers of Passion were starkly dramatized. Shakespeare's *Othello* murders out of sexual jealousy, Ophelia goes mad with love. In the claustrophobic world of Jean Racine's 'classical' seventeenth-century French tragedies, the Goddess Venus has her teeth sunk in her hapless prey, 'love' drives men and women inexorably towards death. Yet the Enlightenment stood in reaction against excesses of sexual passion as it did against religious fanaticism. When the subtle Hume said that reason was and should be the slave of the passions, he was not thinking of Racine's tragic *Phaedra*: he distinguished between socially useful passions and those that were destructive.

It was not only Franklin's commercial bourgeoisie who regarded marriage as essentially a business arrangement. Aristocratic men sought wives with useful material possessions – land or cash – which became theirs with marriage. Women, offering such material gains or the charm of their young bodies, sought to advance their rank in society. The marriage arranged between Cécile de Volanges and the Comte de Gercourt, for whom the prize is the girl's virginity, was in no way a perverted one – according to eighteenth-century convention. The notion that young persons should be free to marry for 'love' was, in the 1780s, still extraordinary outside literary circles. In the debates about marriage during the French Revolution, one way-out deputy actually demanded that parental consent be abolished *after the age of 21*. In 1806, young Joseph Droz of the French Academy (1773–1850), in a manual about how to be happy, argued that while husbands should still exert authority, they should win the love of their wives, and treat them sexually in the same way as they treated their mistresses. But the idea that love should *follow from* marriage – that love was a duty owed by women to their husbands – persisted long after Droz's *Essai sur l'art d'être heureux* (*Essay on the art of being happy*).

EXERCISE   Briefly assess where each of the main characters in Laclos's novel stands in relation to the marriage market and to sexual opportunity.

DISCUSSION   My summaries go like this:

Valmont. Has no need to marry until he wishes to perpetuate his aristocratic 'line'. Meanwhile, can please himself with peasant girls and prostitutes, and gain reputation by 'conquering' other men's wives.

Merteuil. Has profited from a brief marriage to a much older man. While maintaining the front of a respectable widow, she can attain 'Corporal Enjoyment' (as Franklin called it) with men, if she proceeds discreetly.

Danceny. Is too poor to rate highly in the marriage market: Cécile would be a catch for him indeed.

Cécile. Ruins her own value on the marriage market when she succumbs to Valmont – or so she thinks? Granted her physical charms, and her family's affluence, a real-life Cécile could surely have escaped the convent.

Tourvel. Nor need La Présidente have died, ostentatiously ruined, in a convent, though her case is more desperate than Cécile's. She has appeared to be dutifully loyal to her husband. Both her childlessness and the prolonged absence from him which she seems to accept without demur suggest that there is little or no basis of sexual attraction in their marital relationship. Tourvel, exhibiting Passion in its Racinian, tragic mode, riding it into the jaws of death like Werther, exemplifies the awesome frightening power of Sentiment unbridled. Yet one might conclude that she is probably 'sex starved', and thus extremely vulnerable to such a charming seducer as Valmont.

EXERCISE   Please re-read the following letters, noting briefly in your own words what definitions and views of 'love' are expressed by the writers, or conveyed through the incidents involved. LI (p.157), LII (p.159), LXXII (p.196), LXXXI (from 'Ah, keep your advice', p.222 to 'weapons against love', p.227), LXXXIII (p.231), XCVI (p.260), CV (p.290), CXXIV (p.332), CXXVI (p.343).

DISCUSSION   'Love', or *'amour'*, like 'passion', is a word which then, as now, might stand for an emotion of the most mundane or whimsical kind. 'I love prawns' ... 'I have a passion for pasta'. Merteuil tells Valmont in letter XX (p.97) 'I am passionately fond of the child; it is real passion'. (*'Je raffole de cet enfant: c'est une vraie passion'*, is the French original). What do we understand from this? That she is bisexual and capable of lesbian attraction to Cécile (quite likely)? That she is 'head over heels' in love? Certainly not. More generally, 'Love' applies to the *act* of 'having' another person as well as to the emotion which people may feel for persons they *can't* 'have', or *shouldn't* 'have'. We can 'make love' with previous strangers in one-night stands or 'die for love' like Tourvel or Werther. As Laclos's letter writers use the word, 'love' is fraught with all its habitual instability.

1   In LI, Merteuil accepts that Cécile's 'love' for Danceny has reality: the girl is obsessed with him. The emotion is an 'involuntary sentiment' – it cannot be easily opposed by reason or willpower – yet as Merteuil drily observes, as soon as one ceases to oppose it, it ceases to be involuntary.

2   In LII, Valmont represents himself as being in the grip of 'unalterable' love. This 'love' is contrasted with the mere 'intrigue' and 'intoxication of the senses' characteristic of amorous adventure in French high society: ... 'Surrounded with seductive but contemptible objects, my soul was reached by none of them.' His love therefore has a quasi-religious status, transcending carnality, attached to the quasi-divine virtues of Tourvel herself.

     Yet this loftiest of emotions is tangled in paradox. We may recognize a well-attested psychological truth – that men and women can be desperately possessive of, 'in love with', people whose indifference tortures them. But Valmont accuses Tourvel, here and elsewhere, of *deliberately* torturing him. Though her soul is 'virtuous and gentle', she perversely maintains a 'prohibition' which is both unjust and harsh'. She goes in for 'cruel persiflage'.

     Valmont's expression, is, of course, highly conventional. He exploits a tradition rooted in the 'courtly love' and Petrarchan conventions of the Middle Ages and Renaissance in which men lament the cruelty of their nevertheless-perfect loved ones (see any number of European sonnets, *c.*1500–1600.) Yet he also exploits, we assume, Tourvel's genuine 'good nature'. Because she is indeed a 'gentle' person, the accusation of cruelty will hurt her.

3   In LXII, Danceny is on the face of it, artless. The word 'love', repeated incessantly, seems to stand in an uncomplicated way for 'total devotion each to the other, excluding all other objects of desire, and even of thought'.

4   Merteuil (on p.222) distances herself contemptuously from the view of love espoused by Danceny. Monogamous devotion is equated with superstition: the expression of love in letters is the height of folly, since the possession of letters conveys power to the recipients. By her own account, Merteuil studied from girlhood to control her involuntary emotions. She approached 'love' in its carnal aspect, with curiosity and without sentiment. ('My head alone was in a ferment; I did not desire to enjoy. I wanted to know.') Her first night in bed with her husband was for her 'simply an opportunity for experience', yet she experienced pleasure – which she carefully disguised from him. In an extraordinary passage (on p.225) she indicates that she carried on 'experimenting' with lower-class men on her husband's country estate, and 'made certain that love which they tell us is the cause of our pleasures, is at most only the pretext for them'. This last sentence can be construed in more than one way. It might imply that the exalted emotion 'love' is merely the 'pretext', hypocritically deployed, for the pleasures of lust. Or it may suggest that the delights of deceiving a husband and of exercising power, through control of sexual favours, over other men, are the real joy – love, or lust, is only their occasion.

5   By Letter LXXXIII Valmont has made progress with Mme de Tourvel, who has offered him 'friendship'. This allows him more scope for verbal ingenuity. 'Friendship', surely, by its very nature, must listen to 'love'. There's another paradox here: it is precisely Tourvel's *virtue*, he says, which makes her so *seductive* to Valmont.

6   In Letter XCVI, Valmont, for Merteuil's benefit, writes about Tourvel as an actress in a tragedy – drawn into the utmost peril by her love, struggling in a way he calls 'touching' between love and virtue. This is his excuse for prolonging his seduction: the emotions which yield pleasure in the theatre are even more 'interesting' in reality.

    Like Merteuil, he attributes definite existence, real force, to Cécile's 'love' for Danceny 'She had to combat love, and love supported by modesty or shame, fortified above all by the annoyance I had given, which was considerable …' But his male power triumphs: 'We did not separate until we were satisfied with each other.'

    Valmont has done all he needs to revenge himself on Gercourt. Yet he carries on 'having' Cécile presumably because of the physical 'satisfaction' this brings. However, as sharply as Merteuil, he separates this from the grand emotion 'love', at which he sneers. And the exercise of *power* – of 'imprescriptible' male 'rights' – over Cécile is a source of pleasure in itself.

7   In Merteuil's mocking Letter CV to Cécile, she conflates two kinds of 'love', the sentimental and the physical. 'You only cherish the pains of love not its pleasures!' Anguish at separation is an inevitable part of spiritual or sentimental 'love' – but the word also applies to the purely carnal pleasure which Cécile has had with Valmont. In the course of the letter (designed to ensure that the girl will marry Gercourt and so clinch Merteuil's revenge), she insinuates that clandestine sexual pleasure with Danceny, rather than idealistic marriage, should be Cécile's aim.

8   In Letter CXXIV, Tourvel – apparently convinced that Valmont is turning from her towards a life of Christian sanctity, wallows in condemnation of love. 'Dangerous poison … disastrous passion, which leaves no choice between shame and misery …'. She has rationalized her acceptance of Valmont's painful visit on the grounds that he will then tell her she is 'nothing to him'.

9   Madame de Rosemonde, Tourvel's confidante, takes her letter at face value. Her reply, Letter CXXVI, offers common-sense consolation: the pain 'will disappear of itself' – and even if it remains will be easier to endure than remorse. 'Love' is an 'alarming illness', incurable except through natural lapse or 'complete lack of hope'. Yet Rosemonde herself confesses to 'loving' Valmont 'to a point of weakness': the same word applies to strong family affection and to the 'disease' which kills Racine's Phaedra. The first usage involves an inevitable tribute to Valmont's charm and admirable qualities: the latter a catastrophic intervention by the Gods, by destiny, like a sudden fatal illness.

Throughout all these letters we are conscious, on re-reading, of structural irony. Merteuil and Valmont employ local verbal irony with witty malice to all and sundry, not sparing each other, but structural irony (we also talk of 'tragic irony') is implicit in the shape of the story. Valmont does in the end, in a sense, 'die for love' of Tourvel, as his flowery language has threatened he might. Rosemonde's diagnosis of love as a killer disease is all too apt for Tourvel, and common sense will prove impotent against it.

So – 'love' is powerful. We infer that it is powerful primarily because it is rooted in animal appetite, but it is dangerous only when it goes beyond 'satisfaction' of that, and involves obsession with a single object. Appetite may (or, more likely, may not) be accommodated within the bonds of marriage. 'Love' appears to be wholly uncontainable within these bonds, unless by rather weird coincidence.

We could stack up opposites like this:

reason   appetite
willpower   'Love'
marriage   passion

But the antitheses prove false. Appetite may be reasonable – like Voltaire's for his niece – or utterly irrational, like Boswell's reckless adventures with VD-prone prostitutes. Love may inspire mighty feats of will power, though in its origins it is involuntary. 'Reason' itself may become a passion: Merteuil's desire to prove her detachment from emotion is a source of fatal pride. Finally, can marriage be a 'reasonable' institution when its conventional forms guarantee adultery, frustration, or both at once? In or out of matrimony, 'love' may strike and bring danger and damage.

Especially – let us not take this for granted – to women. When Laclos's follower Byron had his sad Julia write to his *Don Juan*:

Man's love is of his life a thing apart,
'Tis woman's whole existence – (Canto I, 1820, st. 194)

he might have been recalling Rosemonde's warning about men to Tourvel in Letter CXXX (p.350):

Do not think, my dear child, that their love is like ours. They feel indeed the same ecstasy; they often put more vehement emotion into it; but they do not know that anxious eagerness, that delicate solicitude, which in us produce those tender and continuous attentions whose sole end is always the beloved person. Man enjoys the happiness he feels, woman the happiness she gives.

Men wrote both the passages just quoted, of course. But that Laclos and Byron should give such words to invented women points to something which Susan Khin Zaw has discussed in relation to Mary Wollstonecraft. In the 1780s – and in the 1820s – women were identified with *feeling* as against male *reason*, and even a brilliant free-thinking woman like Wollstonecraft could not get round this conventional distinction. 'Love' in its grand sense – exalted, ecstatic, tragic – is admirable: on the stage. In practice, even unremitting affection in 'real-life' contexts has its forlorn aspect – men are not expected to respond in kind: they are 'attentive' only till they have had their way, whether their objective is dynastic (marriage, a dowry, an heir to land and title) or purely amatory – a 'conquest'.

In the very important Letter XX (pp.96–8) where Merteuil almost casually tells Valmont that as soon as he has 'had' Tourvel and can show her letters to prove it, he can 'have' her own body again, she concludes: '*si vous n'avez pas cette femme, les autres rougiront de vous avoir eu*' ('If you do not have this woman ... others will blush at having had you').

Yet is Merteuil's conventional reduction of sexual experience to the verb 'have' the index to its true status in her life? For Valmont, casually taking a whore or a Vicomtesse to bed as chance arises, 'having' straightforward satisfaction of desire ('I'll have that peach') may be all there is to it. But Merteuil, according to Hemmings (1987), is defying a double standard when she 'has' men. Her aristocratic society accepts male promiscuity, officially frowns on female laxness. Merteuil, alone among women in Laclos's novel, 'refuses to accept this social embargo on the free indulgence of the instincts.' She is 'an ardent sensualist who privately repudiates the rules imposed by a hypocritical society' (Hemmings, 1987, pp.12–13). She says she thinks Prévan physically attractive (Letter LXXIV, p.198). 'I want to have him and I will have him' (Letter LXXXI, p.229). In the end, her desire for victory leaves her little time with him (Letter LXXXV, pp.243–4). But she gets more from her 'Chevalier' (Letter XI, pp.82–5) and from Danceny. She reserves (Letter CLII, p.392) to herself the right to conduct sexual adventures when and how she pleases – this, she tells Valmont, is why she never remarried. Can she not be seen, therefore, as a feminist heroine, asserting the equality of women by usurping 'imprescriptible rights' accorded by society only to men?

Yes, you might retort, but only in so far as she triumphs (up to a point) by denying the 'feminine' virtues of loyalty, tenderness, caring – she behaves 'like a man'.

4   Conquest and glory

Let us now consider the eighteenth-century obsession with 'glory', most notably achieved on the battlefield, most recently available for French men in the War of American Independence (1776–83).

Laclos himself did not see action on a battlefield till he was 60. Nevertheless, he was for most of his life a capable army officer. He specialized in artillery. He was credited with a series of experiments which led to the replacement of the solid cannon ball with the explosive shell. His work required the practical application of mathematics – and it is possible to argue that there is a mathematical spirit at work on his novel, where symmetry controls variety, so that both Cécile and Tourvel write 24 letters while both are seduced by Valmont as they try to be faithful to someone else. Furthermore, the 'tactics' and 'strategy' of the novelist are sensible subjects for our discussion, as, with what I have called 'structural irony', he marshals his characters toward suitable fates.

Two of these characters, Merteuil and Valmont, are likewise preoccupied with tactics and strategy. They pursue 'careers', aim at glory.

EXERCISE   Please now re-read Valmont's Letter IV pp.69–71, and Merteuil's Letter X (down to 'valour and skill', pp.81–2). Are the military metaphors which are employed merely facetious or decorative?

DISCUSSION Valmont's diagnosis – '*To conquer* is our fate, and fate must be obeyed; perhaps we shall meet again at the end of our *career*' – might seem to be as frivolous as his comparison of Merteuil and himself to evangelists for the 'faith'. But when he identifies Tourvel's virtue as the 'enemy' which he is attacking, compares her to a 'prize' won by conquest and alludes to the 'honour' he will gain, he opens up a vein of imagery which will be exploited throughout the novel. Merteuil, in Letter X, is, as usual, drier, more evidently 'in earnest' than Valmont. Here, violence is rather mockingly evoked. 'Weapons … force … attack … violence … defence … defeat'. Merteuil sees Valmont and herself, in their 'careers', as soldiers in a battle. Note, also, her evocation of 'ancient tournaments'.

Chivalric ideals ran deep in the French aristocracy. More than their harder-headed commercially-minded British counterparts, they lived consciously within the remnants of a tradition in which the role of a nobleman was to fight for his king. The triumphs of Louis XIV on the battlefields of the late seventeenth century had given medieval notions of chivalry some renewed life.

But the people we meet in Laclos's novel have no function, civil or military. Their wealth leaves them free to devote themselves to trivial social intercourse. Valmont's obvious talents have no worthwhile outlet.

We know from Volanges (Letter XXXII pp.117–9) that he is an idol and oracle for younger men. His reputation is that of the most successful amorist of his day. Yet what is it based on? We are told (Letter XLVII pp.149–51) of a skirmish, which leaves him 'master of the battlefield', with a drunken Dutchman – the prize is a courtesan. In Letter LXXI (pp.192–6) he tells Merteuil: 'I do not waste my time …' His proof? That he bedded the Vicomtesse de M … in her château where both her husband and her regular lover were sleeping, and escaped ingeniously from the crisis arising when he discovered her door to be locked. His request: that Merteuil should publicize this episode of bedroom farce. Note that his desire that Merteuil should humiliate Prévan must be motivated by the wish to relegate a threatening rival. Can we believe the story he tells her about Prévan's talk over supper in Letter LXX, (p.190)? Might he not be inventing it to spur her on?

It is important, I think, to see that his plan to conquer Tourvel involves an attempt to *raise himself above* the general level of amatory intrigue. She is pious, adores God. She belongs to the *noblesse de robe*, the class of professional people elevated by their useful work rather than by titles based on ancient military exploits. She is morally and socially outside the world of Prévan and the Vicomtesse de M … And Valmont's aim is supremely ambitious: he works to supplant God in her consciousness.

Ironically, though he dies, he can be said to have succeeded in his strategy. In Letter VI (p.75) he writes to Merteuil:

> I shall even dare to ravish her from the God she adores … Far be it from me to wish to destroy the prejudices which torture her! They will add to my happiness *and my fame* … I shall indeed be the God she has preferred.

Having deceived her with his apparent act of secret charity, he exults (Letter XXIII, p.105) 'What God did she dare to invoke? Is there any sufficiently powerful against love? In vain does she now seek outside aid; it is I who control her fate.' In Letter XCVI (p.261), his assurance of Victory over God is undiminished. 'Fervent prayers, humble supplications,

all that mortals in their fear offer to the divinity. I receive from her ...'
Tourvel's piety itself helps to undermine her resistance. 'The God who
created him must cherish his work', she exclaims to Rosemonde. 'He did
not create that charming being, to make him only a castaway' (Letter
CXXIV, p.333). By Letter CXXVIII (p.347), Valmont has gained his end.
'He alone shall be my judge', Tourvel writes. 'As I shall only have lived for
him, my memory will rest with him: and if he is forced to recognize that I
loved him, I shall be sufficiently justified.' Taken literally, this means that
Valmont has indeed supplanted God, who judges humankind and
'justifies' his chosen ones. 'I love him with idolatry and even then much
less than he deserves ...' (Letter CXXXII, p.354).

In the light of this remarkable 'conquest', Valmont's military metaphors take on surprising weight. In Letter CXXV (pp.335–43) he tells
Merteuil, 'it was a complete victory, achieved by a hard campaign and
decided by expert manoeuvres ... Judge me then as you would Frederic
or Turenne [the 'Great' Prussian King, the great French general]'
(pp.335–41). Later, he exults over Tourvel's flight to a convent – 'if she
persists in so praiseworthy a resolution I shall add to all the obligations I
already owe her that of the celebrity which will follow this adventure'
(Letter CXLIV, p.376).

While Valmont succeeds in his strategy, Merteuil fails deplorably in
hers. She kills Valmont whom she perhaps loves, she drives Danceny,
whom she tries to corrupt, into the arms of the Church and likewise
Cécile, whom she has corrupted. Consummate actress though she has
made herself, she is eventually exposed to shame in, of all places, the
theatre. What destroys her, we can argue, is her quest for 'glory', and the
way in which it does so casts ironic light on the limitations of Valmont's
'victory'.

EXERCISE   Please now re-read the whole of Letter LXXXI (pp.220–9). What are the
objects of Merteuil's campaign, her 'career'? What do we learn of her
relationship with Valmont?

DISCUSSION   She and Valmont, sharing a choice of career, are rivals. She argues that
she is his superior – 'What then have you done that I have not surpassed
a thousand times? – ... You fought without risk ... For you men, defeats
are simply so many victories the less.' Woman 'is at the mercy of her
enemy and is without resource if he is without generosity'. So – 'since I
was born to avenge my sex and to dominate yours, I must have created
methods unknown to anybody but myself'.

As we read her account of how she consciously trained herself for
her 'career', we may willingly concede that she is an unparalleled 'strat-
egist', planning a long campaign of almost impossible difficulty. Why
then does she break, writing thus to Valmont, her firm principle of action
– 'never writing'? She concludes, 'I must conquer or perish ...' Yet she
hands to Valmont the weapon with which, posthumously, he will destroy
her.

She can appreciate the true magnitude of Valmont's aim: to supplant God, because they share an 'enlightened' conception that God is
merely a bugaboo created by humankind out of superstitious fear. But if

God does not exist, 'destiny' does. Hers is to dominate the male sex. Because she is a woman, her triumph depends on maintaining the appearance of virtue. She can easily spread Valmont's 'fame' by gossip. But he is the only audience for her own exploits. If she does not tell him the truth about her strategy, of which she is so proud, *no one will know.* Tourvel imagines that Valmont is her sole judge: in the case of Merteuil this is literally true.

But why set her story down in a letter? One might guess that this is because face-to-face communication is problematic. As Philip Thody (1970) suggests, if Valmont and Merteuil were to meet they would have to confront a critical choice: either to bed or not to bed. As it is, Valmont breaks a promise to call on her (Letters XLVII, p.149 and LI, p.157) and she fails to respond to his suggestion that they should meet at La Maréchale's (Letters LXVI, p.186). In relations between the sexes, where special preference is involved, pure rationality is barely possible . To concede that she either 'loves' or does not 'love' Valmont especially would be to destroy his value to her as the 'looking glass' in which she can behold her own achievements, set out in measured and reasoning prose. In the end, when she decides on 'war' against *him*, she throws her whole campaign against men in general away by a rash attack on the one particular man who has it in his power to ruin her.

5 The rights of women

A well-established reading (or defence?) of Laclos's novel holds that its thrust is feminist. Cécile's part in the story demonstrates the dangers of educating young girls in convents and denying them both experience and useful knowledge. The novel shows how the convention of arranged marriages encourages promiscuity. It further presents, in Merteuil, a woman with remarkable qualities whose intellectual power and athletic sexuality are misdirected into a secret campaign of vengeance against the male sex by the 'double standard' in sexual morality.

Perhaps all this seems self-evident. Yes, that's how we now read the novel, and readers in the 1780s would probably have taken in the points set out above, even if they would have summarized them differently.

But as Susan Khin Zaw has warned you, the terms of debate over the position of women, whether in relation to their role in society, or to their status as moral and philosophical subjects were, in the days of Laclos and Wollstonecraft, such that present-day feminist thinkers are baffled in the attempt to find clear-cut heroines, let alone heroes.

EXERCISE Please now read in your *Texts,* II, p.297, the extracts from Laclos's *Discourse on the Education of Women.* Granted that Laclos is *concerned* about the role of women in society, how is he disposed to *change* it?

DISCUSSION His opening implies male condescension and invokes a stereotyped idea that women are inquisitive, 'curious', as men aren't : bad news. But isn't it good news that he at least assumes that women, once aroused, can change their own fates? 'You must realize that there is no escape from slavery except by means of a great revolution.'

This, in 1783, was potent rhetoric indeed. Through 'revolution', Britain's North American colonies had just thrown off the yoke of Whitehall. 'Slaves' had often been known to revolt in the Caribbean, and 'revolution', eventually led by slaves, would shortly sweep the French out of St Domingue (Haiti). To compare women with slaves was to activate on their behalf all the humanitarian feelings now strong on behalf of brutally treated black plantation workers: sentiment mobilized in France, for instance, by the Abbé Raynal's *Histoire des Deux Indes*, a best seller. (See the article on *Slave Trade* from the *Encyclopédie*, and Voltaire's *Candide*, *Texts*, I.)

The extract from Chapter I, defining 'woman,' however, emphasizes their distinctiveness from all males whether white or black. Though Laclos's novel (Letter CX, p.306) has a reference to the practice of contraception, Laclos assumes that 'pleasure' for women necessarily entails motherhood.

The extract from Chapter VIII, imagining a 'perfectly happy' woman, is still more limiting. Laclos's contention that he portrays woman in a 'state of nature' shows his allegiance to the thought of the contentious Jean-Jacques Rousseau. Living 'without ambition and without fear' as an ideal mother, married to a 'man who is never dull', this ideal woman is implicitly subordinate, even if in the 'state of nature' her man, too, is 'without ambition'.

But what follows in the remaining extracts marks an advance on Rousseau. The latter, in his *Nouvelle Héloïse*, had made marriage seem potentially a much nobler state than society had allowed it to be. But in *Émile*, as Linda Walsh has pointed out to you, he exposes his view that women should have nothing to do with 'matters of morality and all that concerns the understanding'. They should stick to their own sphere – serving, tailoring, child-rearing. That's natural!

Laclos, on the contrary, believes that a woman of rank and fortune is under obligation – 'more … than most to cultivate her reason, her heart and her mind.' She needs to read 'history' (a term which in the eighteenth century embraced what we would now call 'geography' and 'social science'). Laclos would give women Émile's education, not Sophie's. Women should learn to speak the same language as men about interesting subjects. They should, like men, have training in the Greek and Roman classics. Their education should be wary of novels: but Richardson's *Clarissa*, carefully explained, can be of great use, since it shows how a simple step against her parents' wishes plunges the heroine into disaster. Laclos's 'revolution' amounts to no more than *mental* emancipation. Social and economic emancipation are not thought of.

However, since Merteuil's wide reading has helped to make her a more efficient enemy of men and subverter of social convention, it could be argued that the novelist Laclos had admitted the existence of a problem which the essayist, Laclos, glosses over. A woman educated to live on equal *intellectual* terms with men might surely strive to match them in other ways.

While contraception can provide the safeguard for a 'career' of childless 'pleasure', developed intelligence gives the means of intrigue and manipulation, comparable to the activities of men in politics, in business and (Merteuil herself thinks) in war. Her defeat is implicit in her situation: she has to adopt, outwardly, the conventionally approved role of virtuous widow, and once that cover is broken her 'career' is finished. Yet the cold, impressive vehemence with which he has her pursue it suggests that Laclos sensed, what he could not, perhaps have explained or expressed in the terms available to him (as to Wollstonecraft) – the potentially explosive effect of female 'revolution' on all existing social institutions.

6 Les Liaisons Dangereuses *and morality*

It is hard (for me) to re-read this novel without feeling more and more affection for its characters. All seem equally victims of 'fate'. To know all, conventional wisdom has it, is to forgive all. (Milos Forman's brilliant film, *Valmont*, 1991, suggests to me that its director feels the same way. He adapts Laclos very freely. At the end, Cécile gets married, carrying Valmont's child.) We don't 'know all' about these fictitious creatures, who have no existence beyond what Laclos gives them in their letters, which are enigmatic and hide as well as display. But the propensity of readers inclined to defend Laclos against the charge of 'immorality' was from the outset to throw blame away from his characters, on to society: as in the early notice in the Jesuit *Journal de Littérature des Sciences et des Arts* which referred to the novel as 'a new novel giving the most frightful and the most truthful picture of the corruption of our morals' (Hemmings, 1987, p.10).

Laclos's claim to have shown only 'every-day truth' is a moral claim, such as has been made for many controversial novels in the 'realist' tradition since his day. 'This is reality', the novelist argues. 'You don't like it? Then change it.'

However, more needs to be said (in this as in other cases). The specific situation which Laclos presents is now very remote from us. We can hardly conceive of a society in which rich people conducted elaborate intrigues in front of, and in collusion with, the servants who were almost omnipresent in their mansions (Forman's film is especially sharp about this), a world in which rigid Catholic prudery coexisted with constant exuberant sexual scandal. Our own moral predilections and principles are, therefore, in a way, irrelevant.

But the issues *about* morality which Laclos exposes are still with us. It is, or can be, 'immoral' to give way to 'passion', strong feeling – yet it may be equally immoral to stifle it, as one might argue that Valmont, tragically, does. Is a woman 'morally' justified in refusing to accept the tender, caring role conventionally assigned to her and in striving mannishly for power? Contrariwise, are not the conventions which bind her to virtuous caring in themselves deeply 'immoral' because they violate her freedom?

Now that Godlessness is widespread and widely respectable, this aspect of Valmont and Merteuil is not enough in itself to make them damnable, as it was for pious Victorians. We might even regard them with a measure of sympathy: as intelligent persons trapped in a stupid society, justified in attacking its conventions, though not in their deliberate cruelty.

But attempts to read the book as comedy (like Mozart's and Da Ponte's *almost* equally 'cynical' *Figaro*) founder with the pathos of Tourvel's awakening to ecstasy in Valmont's arms and her appalling end soon after. The unanswered question which her fate poses is perhaps unanswerable: how does one weigh the human 'right' to happiness against the ties of family and social convention? Rousseau, as you've seen, can't really answer that. Granted that Tourvel has not been granted the happiness of that woman contentedly in love with her husband in Rousseau's 'state of nature', how far should she go against the admittedly evil conventions of society? (This is just what Catherine the Great asks in documents 19–20, *Texts*, I, pp.74–5.) Can we act 'morally' outside the conventions of 'society' which (as Hume would insist) provides the element in which morality exists, in which it is created? Burns, impressed by Enlightened philosophy, applauds the idea of 'social union' in principle. In practice, the society in which he lives seats him in the stool of repentance in church for fornication and hounds him for his libertarian principles: meanwhile he has his beloved children to feed. He submerges his principles, works for the state as exciseman. Is *that* 'immoral'? Or would participation in political 'revolution', more violent than Laclos imagined for women, have expressed his 'morality' better?

Woman, Laclos recognizes, is an autonomous agent, intellectually and morally. So it is up to her to decide to be either a slave or free. But free agents still face 'moral' choices, balancing 'reason' against 'feeling' and balancing the claims of 'nature', which demands (say) sexual satisfaction, against those of societies seeking to impose restraint.

7 References

Byrne, P.W. (1989) *Les Liaisons Dangereuses: A Study of Motive and Moral*, University of Glasgow French and German Publications, Glasgow.

Franklin, B. (1940) *The Autobiography*, edited by C. Van Doren, Pocket Books, New York.

Hamburger, M. (trans.) (1958) *Great Writings of Goethe*, edited by S. Spender, New American Library, New York.

Hampton, C. (1989) *Dangerous Liaisons*, Faber, London.

Hemmings, F.W.J. (1987) *Culture and Society in France 1789–1848*, Leicester University Press, Leicester.

Hutter, C. (trans.) (1962) *Goethe's Sorrows of Young Werther*, New American Library, New York. (Original published in 1774.)

Thody, P. (1970) *Laclos: Les Liaisons Dangereuses*, Edward Arnold, London.

Turnell, M. (1950) *The Novel in France*, Hamish Hamilton, London.

8 Further reading

Davies, S. (1987) *Les Liaisons Dangereuses*, Grant and Cutler, London.

Laclos, de. C. (1981, edn. 2 Volumes) *Les Liaisons Dangereuses*, edited by R. Pomeau, Imprimerie Nationale, Paris.

Michael, C.V. (1982) *Choderlos de Laclos: The Man, His Works and his Critics*, Garland, New York.

Poisson, G. (1985) *Choderlos de Laclos*, Grasset, Paris.

Vailland, R. (ed.) (1953) *Laclos par lui-même*, Éditions du Seuil, Paris.

Conclusion

Linda Walsh

You might find it useful, at this point, to pause to consider ways in which the Part E texts and studies relate to earlier parts of the course.

1   Nature

If we look first at the use of the term nature, we can detect instances in which Part E texts continue the Enlightenment tradition of viewing nature as governed by a system of universal laws detectable by those who cultivate the human faculty most highly valued in the Enlightenment – reason. These 'laws' of nature systematize physical imperatives regulating humankind and the universe (e.g. Newton's explanation of gravity; Rousseau's theories on digestion and the production of human milk) but are also often extended to nature in the sense of 'everything observable in human beings, in themselves, their environment and their spheres of activity'. Thus, art, literature, morality, economics, society, politics and psychology are all fair game in eighteenth-century pronouncements about nature. Despite the many differences between Johnson and Rousseau, both were equally comfortable with moving from the particular to the general and with making broad statements sanctioned by nature. Thus, while Johnson, in his evaluation of Shakespeare, admired in literature '… just representations of general nature' (Johnson set text, p.420), Rousseau was happy to condemn the entire meat-eating population of the world by reference to the same authority:

> The indifference of children towards meat is one proof that the taste for meat is unnatural; their preference is for vegetable foods, such as milk, pastry, fruit etc. Beware of changing this natural taste and making children flesh-eaters, if not for their health's sake, for the sake of their character; for how can one explain away the fact that great meat-eaters are usually fiercer and more cruel than other men … (Rousseau, 1974, p.118)

It could be argued that Part E texts corroborate Lessing's statement, 'Nature, you do not lie!' (*Nathan the Wise*, Act I.5) in their continuing allegiance to Nature as a source of truth and authority. Nevertheless, we have to be constantly alert to the fact (to which the *Introduction* to this Part briefly alludes) that eighteenth-century statements about Nature could refer to 'laws of nature' (some derived from more empirical study than others) *or* to nature in the sense of 'everything that is', regardless of any conformity with any neat set of rules governing beauty, virtue or science: *there is a constant interplay of the ideal and the real.* We have encountered this in earlier parts of the course. A suitably deferential attitude towards an idealised and neatly regulated conception of nature is evident in Reynolds's statement:

> Deformity is not nature, but an accidental deviation from her accustomed practice. (Reynolds, *Texts*, I, p.218)

Contrast this with the less deferential response to the *reality* of nature, warts and all, in the following:

> ... nor has nature guarded, with the requisite accuracy, against all disorder or confusion. The irregularity is never, perhaps, so great as to destroy any species; but is often sufficient to involve the individuals in ruin and misery. (Hume, *Texts*, II, p.49)

The Lisbon earthquake in *Candide* is further testimony to such 'ruin and misery'. Nature can only be a source of truth and authority in her ideal, carefully regulated state.

Any deference towards nature disappears when its fragile balance is disturbed and reality subverts the ideal. The Marquise de Merteuil, in defiance of the dictates of nature, constructs a social identity through 'profound meditations' (*Dangerous Acquaintances*, p.223). Suppressing all natural feeling, she is guided by principle and subterfuge:

> Encouraged by this first success, I tried to govern the different expressions of my face in the same way. Did I experience some grief, I studied to show an air of serenity, even one of joy; I carried my zeal so far as to cause myself voluntary pain and to seek for an expression of pleasure at the same time. (*Dangerous Acquaintances*, p.223)

This is precisely the kind of betrayal of nature feared by Rousseau:

> We should be ourselves at all times, instead of struggling against nature; such vain attempts exhaust our strength and prevent the right use of life. (Rousseau, 1974, p.316)

Nature can remain a source of truth and authority only if protected from excessive, 'unnatural' human intervention.

Alongside the belief that 'Nature' stands for the ultimate expression of human reason there arises a growing conviction, in Part E texts, that nature must be protected from any extreme form of human manipulation or corruption. In many of the texts you have studied, this awareness results in a plea for 'the simple life':

> Yes! let the rich deride, the proud disdain,
> These simple blessings of the lowly train;
> To me more dear, congenial to my heart,
> One native charm than all the gloss of art;
> Spontaneous joys, where nature has its play,
> The soul adopts and owns their firstborn sway.
> (*Texts*, II, Goldsmith, *The Deserted Village*, ll.251–6.)

Rousseau's aversion to city life in *Émile* and the *Reveries* and Diderot's aversion to excessive artifice in art further exemplify this trend. To Diderot, aesthetic merit is closely related to firsthand observation of nature:

> Take a paint brush which you have just dipped in light, water, mists; the different phenomena of which your head is full, and which only ask to escape from there and fly to the canvas. (Diderot, *Texts*, II, p.288)

To Rousseau, simple nature is to be trusted more than human intervention in the field of medicine:

> Live according to nature; be patient, get rid of the doctors; you will
> not escape death, but you will only die once, while the doctors make
> you die daily through your diseased imagination ... (Rousseau,
> 1974, p.46)

There is a marked contrast here with the elements of scientific progress
outlined in TV1, 'The *Encyclopédie*'.

2 Feeling

If we turn to the second of our major themes, feeling, we can see how
Part E texts devote to this subject a degree of attention which is unprecedented in the rest of the course. This is not to say that feeling is unimportant in the other texts you have studied. In an earlier study (*Studies*, I,
p.187) we met the view that the 'fluidity of human emotions' seems to
have been 'the discovery' of musicians in the second half of the eighteenth century and the early part of the nineteenth. In the legal writings
of Beccaria the ideal of moral sensibility is alive and well:

> What man of any sensibility can keep from shuddering when he sees
> thousands of poor wretches driven by a misery either intended or
> tolerated by the laws ... (Beccaria, *Texts*, I, p.97)

This kind of moral feeling can be related to the ideal of Humanity (or
benevolence) regarded as a key element of Enlightenment thought,
although there is no *necessary* connection between the two: there is no
obvious emotion behind John Howard's plea for better conditions in pri-
sons or behind Catherine the Great's statement that 'we must do one
another all the good we can, and no evil' (*Texts*, I, p.73). A concern for
the welfare of others *could* be the product of reasoning.

In Part E there is an emphasis on the role and significance of feeling in art and life. Diderot exclaims:

> Where did you get the idea that it was permissible to show me a
> scene like that without breaking my heart? (Diderot, *Texts*, II, p.290)

The village priest in Goldsmith's *The Deserted Village* personifies the moral
and social advantages of natural compassion:

> But in his duty prompt at every call,
> He watched and wept, he prayed and felt, for all. (*Texts*, II, p.139)

Even the cynical Valmont is forced to acknowledge the force of moral
feeling:

> I must admit my weakness; my eyes filled with tears and I felt an
> involuntary but delicious emotion. I was astonished at the pleasure
> there is in doing good. (*Dangerous Acquaintances*, p.100)

As in the case of Nature, however, Part E texts are alert to the dangers
inherent in an *abuse*, masquerade or perversion of feeling. What, for
example, are we to make of the following statement by the manipulative
Valmont in *Dangerous Acquaintances*?

> I have misunderstood your heart, it is not made for love; mine,
> which you constantly depreciate, is alone sensitive, yours does not
> even feel pity. (Valmont to Mme. Tourvel, Letter XXIV, *Dangerous
> Acquaintances*, p.107)

We are also invited in this novel to examine the powers and claims of uncontrolled sensation and selfish passion alongside those of more honourable moral feelings.

This close attention to feeling and to its ethical strengths and weaknesses introduces an element of tension into the claims made on behalf of reason and science in Enlightenment thought: to what extent, if at all, should feeling supersede reason in human relationships and in the search for knowledge? The study of Mary Wollstonecraft (above) indicates the need to look beyond the traditional *opposition* of reason and feeling and towards their potential compatibility: there is a certain *kind* of feeling which is consistent with the idea of being a 'rational creature'. However, it could be argued that in *Dangerous Acquaintances* the moral feeling experienced by Mme de Tourvel is dwarfed by the perverted feelings and reasoning of Mme de Mertueil and Valmont. Whatever you own interpretation of these texts, it is clear that the nature and status of reason must be re-assessed in the light of this closer attention to feeling. Mme de Mertueil is an accomplished empirical reasoner who would have no difficulty in consenting to the following statement by James Lind:

> I shall propose nothing dictated merely from theory; but shall confirm all by experience and facts, the surest and most unerring guides. (Lind, *Texts*, I, p.372)

3   Society

Turning now to the theme of Society, it becomes apparent that the humanitarian critique of social and political conventions evident in the writing of Beccaria, Voltaire and the contributors to the *Encyclopédie* is evident in most of our Part E texts. Recourse to the concept of nature does sometimes encourage a conservative outlook, as in the following pronouncement by Rousseau:

> The early part of education is the most important, and belongs incontestably to the province of the females. If the Author of nature had designed it for the males, he would doubtless have furnished them with milk, for the nourishment of their children. (Rousseau, *Texts*, II, p.172)

Generally, however, there is evidence of a significant dissatisfaction with the status quo.

Goldsmith's questioning of the values held by the rich in the extract from *The Deserted Village* quoted above is matched by Rousseau's constant diatribes against wealth and luxury in *Émile* and in other texts mentioned in TV14. Rousseau's relatively militant social criticism is unambiguous in statements such as: 'The many will always be sacrificed to the few, the common weal to private interest ...' (Rousseau, 1974, p.198). In the writings of Rousseau and Wollstonecraft a concern with the distribution of political power and privilege is linked with issues of gender. Rousseau takes a somewhat rosy view of the life of the lower classes as he denounces the lifestyle of the rich, particularly that of rich women:

> The lower classes are seldom dull, their life is full of activity; if there is little variety in their amusements they do not recur frequently; many days of labour teach them to enjoy their short holidays ... The chief curse of the rich is dullness; in the midst of

costly amusements, among so many men striving to give them pleasure, they are devoured and slain by dullness ... women more especially, who do not know how to work or play, are a prey to tedium under the name of the vapours; with them it takes the shape of a dreadful disease which robs them of their reason and even of their life. (Rousseau, 1974, p.316)

Is this the fate suffered by some of the principal characters of *Dangerous Acquaintances*?

Mary Wollstonecraft underlines the unsatisfactory relationship between the weak and the strong in her discussion of gender relationships. In her comment that women resemble soldiers in their 'blind obedience' (*Texts*, II, p.241) to authority and in their lack of 'depth of understanding' (*Texts*, II, p.243) she might be seen to adhere to the Enlightenment ideal of independent thought. Women are, she says, their own worst enemy:

> And I am persuaded that in pursuit of knowledge women would never be insulted by sensible men, and rarely by men of any description, if they did not by mock modesty remind them that they were women: actuated by the same spirit as the Portuguese ladies, who would think their charms insulted, if, when left alone with a man, he did not, at least, attempt to be grossly familiar with their persons. Men are not always men in the company of women, nor would women always remember that they are women, if they were allowed to acquire more understanding. (Wollstonecraft, *Texts*, II, p.263, fn.52)

This passage implies the possibility of an ungendered form of intellectual enquiry. It is rather, perhaps, in the suggested union of reason and feeling discussed above, that a more feminine emphasis is added to the Enlightenment ideals of reason and knowledge.

For Wollstonecraft, the issue of women's roles and status is bound up with broader considerations of political liberty and popular representation:

> ... as sound politics diffuse liberty, mankind, including woman, will become more wise and virtuous. (Wollstonecraft, *Texts*, II, p.247)

The texts in Part E address such issues in a determined and, at times, impassioned manner. You may feel that, although there is obviously continuity with some of the thinking evident in texts from other parts of the course, there is a different 'centre of gravity' in the texts of Part E. The emphasis on feeling and the increasing references to 'pure', 'simple' or 'primitive' nature may account, in part, for this. In the General Introduction to the Course the Enlightenment was said to be characterized by 'light, clarity and order', a 'critique of despotism', 'dispassionate empirical enquiry', a 'coolly sceptical temper' and a 'restrained and disciplined approach'. The degree of conformity of Part E texts to this list of values will be determined, to some extent, by the extracts selected from our texts and by the questions we ask about them. It would be useful, nevertheless, to ponder the shifting concerns and priorities of eighteenth-century texts and to consider the reasons for any changes you identify. Here is a possible starting point, offered by Laclos:

> ... it is here that one sees different nations, and often the same nation, in turn elevated by enlightenment and virtue, or degraded

by brutishness and vice, according to the stimulus which they get from religion, government, laws and customs. (Laclos, *Texts*, II, p.299)

4 *References*

Laclos, C. (1984) *Les Liaisons Dangereuses* (*Dangerous Acquaintances*), translated by R. Aldington, Ark Paperbacks, Routledge, London.

Rousseau, J. J. (1974) *Émile*, translated by B. Foxley, Dent, Everyman, London. (This is the same modern translation to which you are referred in parts of the Rousseau study. It should be more accessible (through a library) than the eighteenth-century translation by Kenrick if you decide to follow up references to parts of the *Émile* text not included in *Texts*, II.)

General Conclusion

Robert Wilkinson

You have now studied a good number of important texts from the period of the European Enlightenment; and here, at the end of the course, taking a look back at them, it is of interest to reflect on this body of works to see whether a general sense has emerged of what this period was like. Was there a tightly unified movement which one can call 'the Enlightenment', or did it vary significantly from decade to decade and from country to country? Did it manifest itself very differently in different areas of thought and art, or is there a feature or set of features common to all the works in the course which mark them out uniquely as products of the Enlightenment? When did it begin to change into something new? And what was it that changed which makes us want to say that it did become something new?

One feature of our period which marks it off from other major epochs of European cultural history is that the term by which we standardly refer to it, the Enlightenment, is a term coined and discussed during the period itself. The Enlightenment was, so to speak, self-conscious to an unusual degree. A fruitful way of approaching the questions raised in the last paragraph is to take some ideas about the nature of enlightenment which were put forward by one of the greatest thinkers of the period itself, the German philosopher Immanuel Kant (1724–1804), and see how well they fit the material we have studied. Kant's essay, *Beantwortung der Frage: Was ist Aufklärung? (1784, An Answer to the Question: 'What is Enlightenment?'*), the last text in our course, was published in a prestigious monthly journal, the *Berlinische Monatsschrift (Berlin Monthly)*, in response to the question having been raised in an earlier issue. The question as to what the term 'enlightenment' might mean was a subject of debate even then.

Please read Kant's essay now, in conjunction with the following comments.

Kant announces his answer to the question, 'What is enlightenment?' in the opening sentence of his essay: 'Enlightenment is man's emergence from his self-incurred immaturity,' ('*der Ausgang des Menschen aus seiner selbstverschuldeten Unmündigkeit*') and 'immaturity' is defined as 'the inability to use one's understanding without the guidance of another'. The enlightened person, then, is one who makes up his or her own mind about the questions posed by existence. Such a person is to be contrasted with those who rely on various authorities to supply ready-made answers to these questions. It is clear that Kant regards this latter attitude as mental laziness or even cowardice. Kant would dismiss as not only unenlightened but also a backslider anyone who defended a belief by saying 'I believe this because the church/the government/the monarch (or any other source of authority) tells me I should believe it'. However difficult a task it may be, we have an obligation to examine the evidence for ourselves, and make up our own minds. This is what lies behind Kant's injunction 'Sapere aude' (Dare to know), one of the most quoted of remarks about the character of the Enlightenment.

This is a fairly stern injunction, with widespread implications for our conduct in many areas of life, as will become clear below. Kant was perfectly aware of this, and yet he is entirely firm in advocating it as a desirable universal mode of conduct. This firmness becomes understandable if we take account of some other beliefs which he held, beliefs which, when put together, constitute a very useful paradigm of 'enlightenment' as it was understood in Kant's time.

The first of these beliefs is Kant's *rationalism*, that is, his belief that the power of human reason unaided is sufficient to allow us to arrive at the truth in any area of investigation. Kant has many ways of putting this point, but nowhere more approachably than in another short essay he contributed to the *Berlinische Monatsschrift, Was heisst: Sich im Denken orientiren?* [sic] (1786, *What is Orientation in Thinking?*):

> Friends of the human race and of all that it holds most sacred! Accept whatever seems more credible to you after careful and honest examination, whether it is a matter of fact or of rational arguments; but do not deny reason that prerogative which makes it the greatest good on earth, namely its right to be the ultimate touchstone of truth. (quoted in Reiss, 1991, p.249; translated by H.B. Nisbet)

It will be clear that Kant must believe this if his injunction to us to think for ourselves is not to be pointless: it would be idle to recommend that we use our understanding were our native mental capacities too feeble to get at the truth.

Secondly, Kant makes an important claim about human nature. He maintains that human beings have a built-in inclination, impulse or drive to think freely: it is *natural* to us to inquire, to pursue the truth, to follow wherever the line of inquiry leads. He thinks that this impulse is deep within the human psyche: it is neither transient nor superficial, but remains with us permanently. It may be frustrated by various institutions but it cannot be eradicated. As he puts it, it is 'the germ on which nature has lavished most care' (*Texts*, II, p.309).

Thirdly, he believes that we are in an important sense *free* to develop this impulse to the pursuit of truth: hence his comment in the initial definition of enlightenment that the immaturity from which the enlightened have emerged is '*self*-incurred.' To claim otherwise he would have regarded as self-deception. Moreover, Kant believed not only that we are free to develop this natural gift, but that it is morally obligatory for us to do so. He makes this point in one of his important philosophical works, *Grundlegung zur Metaphysik der Sitten* (1785, *Fundamental Principles of the Metaphysic of Morals*), where he makes it clear that in his view, a rational being must will 'that all his powers should be developed, since they serve him, and are given him, for all sorts of possible ends' (Paton, 1966, p.86).

Fourthly and finally, Kant believes that the unhindered exercise of the human impulse to rational inquiry will result in *progress*. He believes that we will not go round in circles or continue in benighted superstition: we will acquire more true beliefs and ever more powerful theories. As he puts it: 'Men will of their own accord gradually work their way out of barbarism so long as artificial measures are not adopted to keep them in' (*Texts*, II, p.308). He speaks with contempt of institutions which no-one is allowed publicly to question. A ban on such free debate 'would virtually nullify a phase in man's upward progress' (*Texts*, II, p.308), an 'upward progress' whose occurrence he takes for granted. This belief indicates a certain optimism – though in a non-Leibnizian sense – in Kant's outlook.

Putting these ideas together, the following position emerges: human beings are endowed with reason, and this capacity unaided is sufficient to allow us to penetrate to the truth. Further, we have an impulse and an obligation to pursue rational inquiry, the free and public conduct of which results in progress or the advance of knowledge. The enlightened person is at the forefront of this endeavour, refusing to accept any belief solely on authority, weighing the evidence in the light of reason and furthering progress by engaging in public debate on all significant issues.

It is pertinent to ask at this point whether, in Kant's view, it is easy or difficult to bring about the enlightenment of human beings. He gives his answer in a note to his essay, *What is Orientation in Thinking?*, which is worth quoting at length. In it, he not only answers the question just raised, but also clarifies his definition of 'enlightenment': it consists not in having extensive learning or specialist knowledge but in having a particular attitude to the evidence at hand:

> *To think for oneself* means to look within oneself (i.e. in one's own reason) for the supreme touchstone of truth; and the maxim of thinking for oneself at all times is *enlightenment*. Now this requires less effort than is imagined by those who equate enlightenment with *knowledge*, for enlightenment consists rather in a negative principle in the use of one's cognitive powers, and those who are exceedingly rich in knowledge are often least enlightened in their use of it. To employ one's own reason means simply to ask oneself, whenever one is urged to accept something, whether one finds it possible to transform the reason for accepting it, or the rule which follows from what is accepted, into a universal principle governing the use of one's reason. Everyone can apply this test to himself; and when it is carried out, superstition and zealotry will be seen to vanish immediately, even if the individual in question does not have nearly enough knowledge to refute them on objective grounds. For he is merely employing the maxim of the *self-preservation* of reason. It is consequently very easy to lay the basis of enlightenment in *individual subjects* by means of education; one must merely begin at an early stage to accustom young minds to this reflection. To enlighten an *era*, however, is a very protracted process; for there are numerous external obstacles which either preclude that mode of education or make it more difficult to implement. (Reiss, 1991, p.249)

In other words, it is not difficult to instil enlightened attitudes into the young by means of a suitable education, and make these attitudes habitual; it is much harder to spread enlightenment in all the generations alive in an 'era' where 'numerous external obstacles' present themselves.

What Kant is referring to by means of his last phrase is spelled out fully in our present text. The injunction to think for oneself rather than follow authority may be welcome to some, but it is not calculated to appeal to those elements of society which constitute the authorities the enlightened may or may not bow to, as their reason dictates. It would not in general be welcome to the holders of political power, who require order and obedience – to sustain their hold on power (think of Catherine the Great's reactions at the time of the French Revolution); nor would it have appealed to most churches, which require belief in their authoritative custodianship of religious truth. Kant was aware of this, and goes to great lengths in this essay to make it clear that he is not advocating any form of civil disobedience or contract-breaking which would threaten the social order. He stresses that the way to change public structures is not to ignore one's obligations to them, but to engage in public, rational debate and so arrive at a consensus for change. Whether in practice, however, the citizens of Europe in our period both accepted Kant's recommendations for the conduct of our mental life, and remained good citizens and good parishioners, is another question, and is a point one can reflect on in connection with most of the figures in this course.

Ten years after the publication of his essay *What is Enlightenment?* Kant himself was to have direct experience of the type of conflict described here. In 1793 he issued his work *Die Religion innerhalb der Grenzen der blossen Vernunft* (*Religion Within The Limits of Reason Alone*). The book is an essay on religious belief from the point of view of Kant's complex and refined rationalism, setting strict limits as to those beliefs defensible by means of unaided reason. It was generally and wrongly interpreted as an anti-Christian work and the King, Frederick Wilhelm II (Frederick the Great's conservative successor, 1744–97, acceded 1786) objected to it. He threatened Kant with 'disagreeable measures', and the latter, though he did not retract his opinions, was forced to give the King his word to write no more on the subject of religion. Only after the King's death did Kant feel released from this promise, and gave details of this conflict in the introduction to his last work *Der Streit der Fakultäten* (1798, *The Quarrel of the Faculties*).

Kant's essay *What is Enlightenment?* concentrates in a few pages a number of notions and beliefs important in our period: rationalism; a certain sort of optimism and belief in progress; our freedom, impulse and obligation to inquire. His ideas are a useful starting point when gathering one's thoughts at the end of this course, and they raise a number of questions: how many of the figures on this course would recognize in this essay a statement of their intellectual credo or ideals? One can see how these ideas can be applied by philosophers, historians and scientists, but how would they be applied by a musician or a painter or an architect? Is there any link between these ideas and adherence to classical models? How can they be applied, and were they applied, in works of literature? Again, how would they have been regarded by the monarchs and churches of the time? Now these are complicated questions, and they cannot be dealt with exhaustively here. However, it is possible to indicate, by means of examples drawn from our course, just how qualified the answers are likely to be, and from these qualifications we can draw one final lesson. Let us look briefly at three figures from the course with Kant's ideas in mind.

First, Frederick the Great. In some ways, Frederick appears as a model of enlightenment: for example, his rational, utilitarian attitude to the relationship between the ruler and society; his reforms of the judicial system of his country which made Prussia a model of fairness by the standards of the day; his standpoint on religious toleration, which was equally unusual and forward looking. Again, the educational aims for the Noble Academy, that is the production of independent-minded young officers and administrators, look very similar to what Kant is recommending. Desiring to show his own excellent taste, Frederick invited Voltaire to Prussia, gave him rooms in the palaces in both Potsdam and Berlin, made him a Court Chamberlain and gave him a sizeable salary. Having secured for himself the foremost of French writers as mentor, the King sent Voltaire his efforts at French composition for scrutiny. Yet, as we have seen, Frederick had another side to his nature, both in matters of taste and in politics. While admiring Voltaire's writings and philosophy, the King regarded him personally as a sort of malicious monkey and not to be trusted: fit to correct the King's alexandrines, but to be kept away from the serious affairs of state. Again, this author of alexandrines, this man of sensibility who wept over Racine's verses, was the same man who created one of the largest standing armies in Europe, its discipline a byword for brutality, and whose foreign policy exemplifies *realpolitik* at its most ruthless.

Rousseau, by contrast, has regularly been presented as a man who made a dent in the ideals of the Enlightenment: the thinker who advocated the importance of feeling; who proposed a return to nature and describes in beautiful prose the joys of solitary contemplation on an island home far from the corruptions of the major cities and their wicked, desiccated inhabitants. Yet if one considers the assumptions underlying many of Rousseau's works and puts to one side knowledge of his deeply neurotic personality, what emerges is not so very different from what was being said by the *philosophes*. For example, he says that society is corrupt and must be changed; we have departed from the paths of right behaviour, but these paths can be discovered empirically by looking into the hearts of uncorrupted persons, children or noble savages. Once the right paths have been discovered, we can change the social order so as to reflect them, and what we discover will be true for all human beings everywhere and at all times, since uncorrupted human nature is always the same. There is no suggestion in what Rousseau says that what might be a good form of life for a European might be wrong for a Chinese or an Indian, or vice versa. Relativism of this kind is absent from Rousseau's thought, as it is from that of the *philosophes*. There is no suggestion that the educational nostrums of *Émile* are suitable only for local or temporary application.

It is not necessary, however, to use figures so clearly paradoxical as Frederick or Rousseau to make the same points. Diderot must seem initially to be a paradigm of the ideals of the Enlightenment: how could it be otherwise with one of the prime movers of the *Encyclopédie*, an enterprise built on the assumptions of rationalism, optimism and the possibility of progress? Yet, when one turns to aesthetic matters, Diderot turns out to be more complicated than might be expected. There is no slavish adherence to classical models, no adulation of rules. Instead, faced with a sketch of the Chapel of St Gregory by Carle Van Loo, which he admires, and trying to explain what he likes about the picture, Diderot writes this:

> Distrust those people who have their pockets full of good cheer and scatter it about at every opportunity. They haven't got the demon. They are not sad, sombre, melancholy and dumb. They are never awkward or stupid. The chaffinch, the lark, the linnet, the canary chatter and chirrup throughout the livelong day. When the sun goes down, they tuck their head under their wing, and off they go

to sleep. It's then that the genius takes his lamp and lights it, and then that the solitary bird, wild and untameable, brown and sad of plumage, opens his throat and begins to sing making the woodland resound and melodiously breaking the silence and darkness of the night. (*Texts*, II, p.273)

This is an expression of praise for artistic genius, and what a genius does is to go beyond models, rules, and imitation to create something new and unpredictable which moves or stirs or disturbs us. Faced with the works of art which pleased him, Diderot found that he could not account for their success by reference to previous models or their copying, and, in common with other thinkers of the time – he is joined in this view by Pope, Hume, Reynolds and many more – has to have recourse to the notion of genius. On this point, Kant, in other ways like Diderot an exemplary rationalist, agrees entirely. In his major work on aesthetics, the *Kritik der Urteilskraft* (1790, *Critique of Judgement*), Kant argues that one can draw a distinction between works of art which are alive, which effortlessly engage our attention and are a delight to contemplate, and those which are dull, boring and lifeless. The latter may be produced so as to accord perfectly with received taste and artistic practice, and therefore correctness is clearly not enough for artistic success. What is needed is genius, an innate talent, inexplicable to those blessed with it, whose productions elude all explanations in terms of rules yet which reward contemplation and stimulate valuable thought seemingly without end (cf. *Critique of Judgement*, sections 46–50).

Examples such as the above could be multiplied, and they suggest a general reflection as follows: in order to give structure and order to the course, the Course Team have often referred to analyses and definitions (like Kant's) of what the term 'the Enlightenment' might mean, or whether a given figure is 'enlightened' in such and such a respect. To repeat, this is essential if the material is to be ordered in a digestible way. There is a danger inherent in such a method, however, which the above brief examples are meant to indicate, and which has been referred to at various points in the course. The danger is that one can be blinded, by the tendency to sum up, docket and pigeon-hole, to the rich complexity of these figures and their times. They can easily come to seem two-dimensional, mere instantiations of tendencies identified and tidied up by historians of ideas, rather than what they were, human beings doing their best to make sense of the complex, messy circumstances in which they found themselves, and inventing solutions as well as they could to the difficulties which faced them. They were individuals like us, with beliefs and practices which shifted over time as they changed and their circumstances changed, beliefs (etc.) which were about as clear, consistent, orderly and worked out as beliefs generally are.

The Course Team has tried to make these people and their works come alive, and we hope very much that you have found more than a little to enjoy in this course.

References

Paton, H. J. (trans.) (1966) *The Moral Law*, Hutchinson, London.

Reiss, H. (ed.) (1991) *Kant: Political Writings*, 2nd edn, Cambridge University Press, Cambridge.

Index